Princess in Paradise

Princess in Paradise

by *Alexandra K. Schmeckebier*

with a preface and epilogue by
Laurence E. Schmeckebier

PHOENIX PUBLISHING
Canaan, New Hampshire

Schmeckebier, Alexandra K.
  Princess in paradise.

  1. Schmeckebier, Alexandra K.   2. United States—
Biography.   3. Kluge family.   I. Schmeckebier,
Laurence Eli, 1906-   II. Title.
CT275.S34456A36   973.9'092'2   [B]   81-12099
ISBN 0-914016-80-6   AACR2

Printed in the United States of America

Contents

ACKNOWLEDGMENTS

Of our many friends who have collaborated in this enterprise I should like to acknowledge with sincere gratitude the work of A. L. Morris for his superb design and layout of the book, Adrian A. Paradis, Frank Kirk, Katharine Putnam Beal, and Basil Milovsoroff for their editorial counsel, and Violet Orthwein Marrow and Thaïs Holzer Keuls for their assistance in solving the many problems of content and historical data. It was the devoted help and encouragement of Thaïs, in particular, which became major factors in both Alexandra's original writing of what we then called "The Englewood Saga" and the subsequent assembly of the material for publication. Among Alexandra's life-long friends who provided valuable background material and information about their life at Dwight School and Vassar College were Deborah Elton Allen, Anna North Coit, Averell Ross duPont, Sarah Dodge, Nancy Gaines Jaeger, and Elizabeth Earhart Kennedy.

L. E. S.

Preface

ALEXANDRA was a remarkable person, and her career is an equally remarkable story.

The background itself is unique, involving a gracious Russian mother of noble lineage and a genial though somewhat Bismarckian father from the German Rhineland. Alexandra's uncle Igor had once traced the de Moravsky line back to the twelfth century, and the legend persists that a Moravsky had been one of the wives of Ivan the Terrible, an idea that used to frighten the daylights out of us whenever it was told.

There were four children, of whom Alexandra was the oldest. She and Thaïs were born in New York, but the two boys, Emile and Serge, were born and reared in Englewood, New Jersey, where they lived a happy and adventurous life through the opulent 1920s, somewhat isolated in a formidable stone house on the hill known as Greystone.

Under these circumstances, "Sa" (the American nickname for Sasha, which the Russians usually call those named Alexandra) enjoyed certain advantages which determined much of her career. As a youngster she was taken several times to Moscow to see the indulgent grandparents before World War I. This was followed by prolonged visits to relatives in Germany in 1922-23 and again in 1926 which, with the presence of French and German tutors and nannies, gave her a natural facility in languages which she always used.

Formal education began in Englewood's Dwight School, from which she graduated in 1926. Then it was Vassar College, class of 1930, presumably for a major in economics but much more involved in French and Russian literature, music, and the drama. An undergraduate romance prompted her cautious father to send her with her sister, Thaïs, to Europe and the University of Munich to study music and literature—and "keep her out of trouble."

In the summer of 1930, after an exciting year of travel, study, and the incredibly rich cultural resources of Munich and elsewhere in Germany—and "more trouble" when she met a young doctoral student in art and philosophy and Thaïs met her future husband, a German student in economics—the girls returned to Englewood and the reality of the depression. After a year's secretarial training at Katharine Gibbs, Sa took a job with Alfred A. Knopf's publishing house, first as a foreign reader and then as Knopf's personal secretary.

Alexandra was blessed with certain unique characteristics, no single one of which could be isolated by special definition, but all an integral part of the personality and character that was typically hers. She was endowed with a brilliant mind which never showed up in the usual form of academic honors but in the sheer perfection of performance and the personal satisfaction of its successful achievement. Tall, lithe, and incredibly versatile, she was a born athlete, one of those who could reach up into the air of a tennis or basketball court and the ball would somehow be there. She loved the outdoors and was always an ardent summer camper. Her father had been one of the original backers of the rugged and beautiful Camp Mudjekeewis on Maine's Lake Kezar near Fryeburg, which she and Thaïs had attended for many years, followed by their children in the next generation.

She was therefore a genuine artist in the classical sense, but the idea of an "artist's way of life" was never talked about; one just did it. It was a continuous process: from the homemade children's costumes for Halloween to the teenagers' party dresses, the usual knitting and quilting projects, and wedding dresses of our three daughters with their precious heirloom Russian laces.

Home was of her own making, from the interior itself to the surrounding flower garden; the placement of the trees and shrubs; and, in the case of our retirement home in Lyme, the placement of her husband's sculpture along the entrance road and around the pond.

She was a superb hostess, and every party or reception was a work of art, from the planning of the guest list, to the menus (usually Russian in some form or other), the table setting, and the cooking itself. We in the family all had our assigned jobs to do, but hers was the artistic concept, the design, and its execution. In the end, one had the impression that the entire affair just happened by itself.

There was always an incredible loyalty to the family. It may have been the diverse combination of Russian and German backgrounds and the strong religious faith of the Russian tradition which dominated the home in Englewood. Alexandra and Thaïs, Emile and Serge were the closest of friends as well as sisters and brothers. So it was with her children, whose unswerving love and devotion was one of her greatest joys. In her particular way this attitude seemed to carry over into the various circles of friends she cherished throughout her lifetime. They were not large in number, but the friendships were deep, direct, and lasting.

She was a good student and a thoroughly independent one in the old Vassar tradition where distinction was a matter of personal performance rather than of political doctrine. The year in Munich was concentrated largely on German literature and music. At the University of Wisconsin, the year Xenia, our first daughter, was born, she carried a full program in Russian, American history, nineteenth-century German literature, and Goethe (under the great A. R. Hohlfeld). Then in Minnesota there were further studies in pioneer history with T. C. Blegen. Finally it was at Syracuse in 1965 that she took a master's degree in library science with honors (Beta Mu Phi). Her thesis on the newly acquired Cloud Wampler Collection of Prints was published by Syracuse University under that title and was so thoroughly done that it could easily serve as a reference handbook on the history of printmaking.

Though not a consistent performer, Alexandra loved music, not only Beethoven (the sonatas and the quartets), but Wagner (*Tristan und Isolde* and *Parsifal*), Mozart (*Figaro*), Schubert (*Tod und das Mädchen*), Tchaikovsky (the *Pathétique*), and Russian folk songs and liturgical music. She was an avid reader, and though the subject matter was endlessly varied, there was a persistent pattern of favorites that reveal something of her character and ideas.

In the early years these included Tolstoy, whose family home was located only a few miles from the Moravsky-Konshin estate near Moscow. She loved Goethe's *Faust,* not just the romantic search for love and knowledge expressed in Part One, but the Olympian vistas suggested in Part Two. Then it was Pearl Buck's *The Good Earth* and Sigrid Undset's *Kristin Lavrandsdatter,* Rolvaag's *Giants in the Earth,* and the writings of Conrad Richter. By way of contrast she was fascinated by the gaudy glamour of Scott Fitzgerald. She often described the varied and colorful characters who breezed through Alfred Knopf's office in those years when she served as his secretary: Henry L. Mencken, George Jean Nathan, Willa Cather, and Thomas Mann. It was not that she was overwhelmed by a distinguished presence. She just understood them by nature.

Alexandra always had a special literary flair which was both critical and creative. She has volumes of diaries which she faithfully kept from her early teens. Her letters to friends and family had the verve and vivacious spirit of direct conversation. That spirit was full of love and a genuinely romantic sensitivity, but it also reflected the courage and earthy realism of the pioneer.

In good Russian tradition inherited from her mother and consistently maintained at home, Alexandra loved to tell the stories that were handed down by the family as well as about the colorful and extraordinary life she had lived. She assembled volumes of diaries, scrapbooks, and memorabilia that had been accumulated over three generations from Russia, Germany, and Englewood, always with the idea that someday she would write the family history "for our children." It was not until the period of recovery after her first operation in 1977 that she managed, with characteristic verve and concentration, to set it all down in manuscript form before she died just one year ago. This we now present as a tribute to an extraordinary lady. Though she is not the Princess in this story, the nobility of her mother's character seems to persist in the process of the telling.

Laurence E. Schmeckebier

Lyme, New Hampshire
March 10, 1981

Princess in Paradise

An Old
Russian
Folk Tale

*L*ONG AGO *there lived an old king Vladimir who ruled a vast kingdom and lived in a beautiful palace with many rooms and servants. He had two beautiful and desirable daughters. The older, Princess Vasilisa, was active and aggressive, whereas the younger, Princess Marina, was more reserved, deeply religious, and filled with great love and compassion for her people. Since one son was a priest and the other a soldier, the king had carefully trained his daughters to become rulers of the land.*

Now it came to pass that Vasilisa fell in love with a handsome young huntsman and ran off to marry him without even consulting her father. The old king banished them from the kingdom forever.

Not long afterwards Princess Marina fell in love with a young musician but she knew her father would never consent to their marriage. So she went to the parish priest to ask his advice.

"Honor they father but to thine own heart be true," was his solemn reply. "Have faith, pray, and God will speak to you."

Marina had faith, prayed, and waited but God never spoke to her. The poor musician pleaded and begged but to no avail. Years passed, there were other suitors but no love. Then one day a gorgeously dressed merchant prince from a foreign land appeared, showered the king with many presents, and told of his father's rich kingdom. The king was overjoyed when he asked for Marina's hand.

Marina was not sure she loved him and was reluctant to leave her father's magnificent palace, but the dream of a beautiful kingdom beyond her father's

1

realm, and her father's wishes, were convincing. Still God did not speak to her and she doubted the truth of the priest's advice. So they were married and began life in the foreign land which she thought would surely be paradise. They too had four children who in their early youth also enjoyed the pleasures of a beautiful palace. Here they enjoyed many years of happiness and prosperity. Their two daughters in turn fell in love, each being betrothed to a royal prince.

Then came tragedy. A plague of locusts destroyed the crops and impoverished the kingdom. Marina dutifully took care of the prince until he died, a sad and disheartened old man. Then she retired peacefully to a convent, and lived a quiet life of service to the poor.

There God spoke to her.

I

Our Englewood

*"They too had four children who in
their early youth also enjoyed the
pleasures of a beautiful palace."*

Ty, Emile, and Sa at Englewood, 1920.

Halcyon Days

NGLEWOOD was home, the place where we grew up and where the life of four children unfolded, but it was also a complex vision. It does not mean the geographic spot on the map—a little New Jersey town across the Hudson River from New York City. Nor is it just the massive and mysterious stone house on top of the hill with the formal name of Greystone. Nobody ever spoke of going *home* to Greystone. It was Englewood which meant to us our little enclosed world, our special way of life. Many years later when things had changed, anybody reminiscing would say, "Remember at Englewood when . . .?" rather than, "At Greystone. . . ."

Seen from the outside, it was a formidable closed box; one would have to penetrate the walls to discover what was going on inside, to learn who actually lived there, and gradually to unravel the secrets. As when a mythical box is opened, the tales about Englewood come tumbling out, not in any particular sequence, but one linked to another, building a picture, revealing personalities, explaining what made life there something special. Right from the beginning the characters were somehow unique and had distinctive points of view. They did things differently, often being misunderstood by outsiders and interpreted as being slightly peculiar.

In America after the turn of the century it was not unusual for some families to live in rather palatial homes, preferably in the country, well attended by a large household staff and enjoying all the fashionable

5

The main entrance to Greystone, 1922.

amenities of life—horses, tennis, swimming, boating, and extravagant entertainment. The children were turned over to the care of nurses and governesses, then sent away to private schools. Moving from one establishment to another according to the seasons, with the entire entourage—whether to the south for the winter, to the seashore in summer or, as some chose, to the woods for the "simple camping life"—was part of the normal routine. Going "abroad," whether it meant a fashionable trip on the luxurious ocean liners or the "Grand Tour" of Europe, was nothing unusual.

Englewood, New Jersey, could hardly be called a suburb during the 1900s. In 1912 when the Kluges moved there it was definitely rural. There were still winding unpaved roads, open meadows and hills, and large stretches of woodland. Families lived on estates and the inhabitants kept very much to themselves. The homes concealed behind walls or hidden among big old trees did not disclose their tennis courts, swimming pools, or stables.

Englewood, reached by a ferryboat crossing the Hudson River from upper New York City, was just over the top of the scenic Palisades Cliffs, an impressive, unspoiled natural phenomenon. The single main street, Palisade Avenue, ran straight downhill to the village, passing

Princess in Paradise

lovely tree-shaded Victorian **houses** on either side. At the lower end of Palisade Avenue the village itself was laid out on four levels, with the streets crossing it at right angles. On the highest, in a nicely landscaped open space, lay the high school and elementary schools. Next came the level with the important business establishments—the bank, the moving-picture theater on one side and opposite it Bergendahl's Ice Cream Parlor, an important village gathering place for adults as well as the young. On the third street where the shops of necessities—butcher, baker, grocer, and drygood stores—were lined up, ran the trolley line which connected the farther reaches of Englewood and eventually, after an hour's ride, ended at Fort Lee and the ferry to New York. At the very bottom, the boundary of the settled part of the town, were the Erie Railroad tracks and the station, from which a small group of businessmen commuted daily to their offices in the big city. The South Hills section, where Greystone was located, was three miles uphill and south from the center of the village, quite isolated, with the country club, atop another hill in the midst of the golf course, the only visible building.

To Olga and Emile with the dream of raising their family in the country and leading a life of privacy on an estate, Greystone, with its properly impressive house and extensive grounds, must have looked like their Old World ideal. The inside afforded a generous and almost perfect arrangement of rooms and living quarters. The practical conveniences, such as large kitchen and pantry, central heating, and work spaces, were amply provided for and quite up to date. The surrounding property offered endless possibilities for the expansion of gardens and the addition of buildings. Since they were both familiar with living on the large, isolated estates of Russia, there seemed nothing particularly new in adapting to this "American way of life" of the period.

The house, built by an English architect around 1900 in Palladian-Old English style, of heavy limestone blocks, with its basic square shape and a feeling of being further enclosed by surrounding verandas, could look very forbidding. The bright red tile roof was a cheering touch and was visible from far away. The four tall chimneys gave something of a lift to the horizontal boxlike appearance. The windows of the third-floor rooms were set in dormers behind little balconies in the slope of that red tile roof.

The main entrance, not very prominent architecturally, was on one side under a porte cochère, reached by a winding gravel driveway. Just beyond it one discovered an extended ivy-covered wing, almost an independent section, which housed the kitchen and service rooms with the help's quarters upstairs. From the service entrance and "back porch" the driveway led past a grove of fruit trees to the two-story carriage house-garage-stable building, built of the same massive gray stones and also with a red tile roof.

A handsome feature of this building was the central arched gable with wide double doors that opened out from the hayloft, into which the hay and feed for the horses were periodically hoisted by rope and pulley, to be distributed from there into assorted bins, then sent by chutes down into the stables. On either side of the main garage entrance a wing came forward to enclose a courtyard. The wing on one side contained a complete and independent two-story home for the caretaker, or head gardener, and his family. On the other side was a two-room apartment for the chauffeur or the "riding master," as the case might be. Directly above this, reached by a narrow ladder that went straight up the wall, was a tiny room for the stableboy, partitioned off from the hayloft and looking down precipitously upon the box stalls of the horses.

Behind the stable building, along the service road, one found a line of kennels and storage sheds for the garden and farm equipment. Concealed among the wilder growing trees a bit farther on was an enclosed area known as the "deer park." It may have been started by the former English owners, then further developed by Olga for some romantic nostalgic idea. In any case, it was inhabited by a dozen or so deer. It provided a pleasant stroll from the house for Olga and children and guests to visit the deer and feed them and at the same time to look over the dogs and horses. The deer themselves could not have been too happy, because more than once they tried to jump over the fence, resulting in broken legs and other injuries requiring the attention of a veterinarian, as well as personal care and worry that outweighed the aesthetic pleasure they provided. Their area was soon occupied by cows and a goat.

Farther back in the woods stood an eerie Gothic weather-beaten barn from whose tower pigeons emerged, and on the ground floor were spaces for farm animals. The permanent resident was Jim, the big, brown workhorse, needed for plowing and for mowing the lawns. The cows and goat lasted only as long as the children needed their fresh milk. Their spaces were next occupied by a litter of pigs, to be fattened and eventually to furnish hams and sausages. Emile soon conceived the fantastic idea that if the pigs had little ones they would

Princess in Paradise

provide our own delightful little suckling pigs, often the special feature for festive dining occasions, so he was soon adding more pigs for breeding purposes. On another side of the barn was the chickenhouse, filled sometimes in spring with a new supply of chicks to admire, and always a source of excitement in collecting the eggs or hunting for them in the hayloft above.

One of the first projects of expansion was the plowing up of a goodly section of lawn to create a "kitchen garden," hidden from the house by an arbor of rambler roses. Besides supplying a fine crop of assorted vegetables and the "ordinary" flowers, there were rows of gooseberries, raspberries, and currants. After a few years a greenhouse took its place beside the garden, and this became the source of exotic, fragrant, and colorful potted plants, which filled the house with blooms through all seasons. The solid building attached to the greenhouse, needed as a furnace and workroom, was designed with a root cellar for winter storage of the fruits, potatoes, and other vegetables collected on the place. An upper story became the living quarters for the German gardener, whose whole life was centered on the care and production of his famous vegetables and flowers. The little square structure appeared to be a watchtower against human and animal intruders—which indeed it was.

Anyone passing along the road beside this property and trying to peer through the screen of shrubs and trees would have seen no sign of life and hardly would have guessed that the place was inhabited. Perhaps a closer approach would draw forth the fierce barking of a chained watchdog. At night barely a light was to be seen glimmering from the top of the hill through the deeply recessed windows. Even those living in the house or the other buildings, at such distances apart, could scarcely be aware of any activity in another corner of the property.

Nevertheless there was a certain amount of regular going and coming within the grounds. Every morning the chauffeur-driven car leaving early to take Mr. Kluge to his factory in West New York, New Jersey, was gone until evening. This left those at home with virtually no outside communication. Any urgent errands must depend on the horse-drawn buggy, or sleighs in winter. Sometimes one had to resort to going by bicycle or on foot to the village three miles away. Fortunately, the house had a telephone at that time, so one was not entirely cut off from the outside world.

Inside the house communication was carried out by a system of bells

Our Englewood

The living room at Greystone.

and speaking tubes. Every room had its button to be pressed for service. Each call registered on a black box in the pantry where a little white disk dropped down with such designations as "Parlor," "Living Room," "Chamber 1," or "Chamber 2," and would bring the properly authorized person running. There were a few places such as the upstairs hall and the living room, where one could connect directly with a person in the kitchen by talking into a tube through a brass opening in the wall, while the person at the other end put his ear to the tube opening and tried hard to understand the message that was being shouted into it from above.

It was a great innovation and relief when a private interhouse telephone system was installed. That meant that by pressing the correct button on a small wall switchboard one could connect with instruments in different parts of the house and even with the outside buildings, talking into a regular telephone and listening through a receiver. It was a great luxury, a modern convenience, to be able to call the garage directly and say "Bring the car around now!" or to the stable with "Please have the horses saddled in half an hour," or to talk to the cook in the kitchen or receive a message from the faraway greenhouse.

Princess in Paradise

Many of the regular necessities of living were conveniently taken care of by a system of deliveries from the outside. The postman walked up the hill twice a day to deliver and call for the mail. Every morning the milkman with his horse and wagon plodded up the front drive to deliver from dripping boxes of melting ice the racks of quart bottles with the milk needed for the day. One forgets, after it became common for the milkman to drive a motor truck, the advantages of the horse-drawn wagon and the mutual devotion of the driver and his animal. A horse learned the daily route and all the stops along one street, so that while the milkman would jump out and carry a delivery to one house, the horse would either wait patiently or slowly plod on to meet his master at the next stop.

The iceman drove to the back door in his truck, loading many hundred-pound blocks from his back through a special outside opening into the twelve-foot, built-in wooden icebox. Later an electric refrigerator took over, but the additional "cold room" built into the cellar was still used. The garbage removal truck came and went at regular intervals down the back road, well screened by a high hedge. The coal supply for the furnace was delivered by a procession of trucks which dumped the noisy black gravel down chutes through a window into the basement, leaving a day's worth of cleanup—inside as well as outside.

The management of the outside staff was well ordered and inconspicuous. The riding master was the authority in the stables and was responsible for the care and grooming of the horses as well as for their daily exercise schedule. The little stableboy prepared their food and kept the leather saddles and harnesses polished. The "outdoor dogs"—two Russian wolfhounds, a Scotch collie and the German shepherd trained as a watchdog—were fed, loved, and cared for by the same young handyman whose duty it was to feed the "house dogs"—our pet tame German shepherd and the children's white toy poodle. The chauffeur obviously had to find time between his driving and waiting periods to keep the cars shiny and in working order.

The classification of the gardeners was a delicate matter. One who had studied horticulture considered himself of professional status, raised his special flowers scientifically, and supervised the trimming of the trees and shrubs. The old German, who just naturally understood how things grew and to whom every superb example of vegetable was like a child of his own, prided himself in showing off his results. He was also the affectionate and understanding master of Jim, the big farm-

Our Englewood

horse. They spent a lot of time together mowing the lawns, Jim pulling the double mowers and rollers with the suspended metal seat on which we children were always begging for a ride.

The inside housekeeping was much larger, diversified, and complicated by a mélange of nationalities and temperaments of both sexes. Managing the whole establishment and staff was twenty-five-year-old Olga de Moravsky Kluge in her fourth year of marriage and living in this foreign country, her only training being the experience of her own childhood home. In the tradition of the justly famous women who managed large estates in Russia, she was expected to take care of the books, handle the personalities and troubles of those working for her, watch over the daily life of her children, plan for all the supplies and necessities of the house and its inhabitants, and make the decisions in any crisis.

According to the customs of the time, the duties of the household staff were specific and stratified. Each employee had special training and a special area of work, and failure or encroachment on another's province could be quite a touchy affair. In the kitchen Anna, the Austrian cook, was queen, holding sway over the hotel-sized gas range, supervising what went into the mixing bowls and pots, and reigning as prima donna at the pastry table. But it was Rosa, a young Bohemian scullery maid, who prepared the vegetables, tidied up, scrubbed the pots, and jumped to assist the cook at her beck and call. The English butler, later replaced by a Japanese, had a parlor maid as assistant. He never stepped into the kitchen but confined himself to his working area in the pantry, then presided in all his dignity in the dining and living rooms.

Upstairs, Olga Lopatina was Mami's personal maid and really her confidante, since the two had grown up from childhood on the Romadanovo estate in Russia. A young, inexperienced "chambermaid" was usually required to do such things as make beds and clean. Pauline, the "upstairs maid" who was with us for twenty years, gradually assumed the role of housekeeper. Always with a bunch of keys rattling at her waist, she was in charge of the linen closet and of the other household supplies, which were kept in locked storage. All the sheets, pillowcases, and towels had to be counted when they came back from the laundry, then sorted and put into proper piles. There was a separate closet for the good tablecloths and fine napkins, each always counted, tied with identifying colored ribbons, and sorted by size and quality. Downstairs every cabinet for silver, china, and glassware had its own key, which added to the volume of the housekeeper's bunch and caused panic and frustration when mislaid or needed in a hurry. In the basement the wine cellar, constructed like a vault against the cool, thick stone foundation of the house, also had its separate key and private access. Inside it was subdivided into closets according to types of wine, all carefully stacked, listed, and counted.

In the basement too was the so-called handyman's closet, really a toolroom and repair shop, a place to store and keep in order the myriad assorted things needed for everyday practical maintenance of the house, from electric wiring and plumbing parts to furniture —repairing and luggage-patching equipment. Josef, a young German from Bavaria, who also fed the dogs and stoked the furnace, might at some time also have been called a footman or doorman, since he was generally on duty to carry baggage and packages and do the less dignified chores of polishing the brass and sweeping the porches.

There was additional daytime help in the form of a laundress who kept busy over a row of tubs in a light, airy laundry, where the special feature was an enormous built-in clothes dryer, in and out of which rolled heavy metal racks with tiers of drying rods. Another visitor who came for a stretch of days was a seamstress, who worked in an upstairs sewing room. Her assignment was partly to repair clothes and linens and do alterations for everyone, but chiefly to sew the new clothes, especially for the children but often for the adults too.

This whole crew of more than a dozen household help had to be fed regularly three meals a day. This meant a separate marketing list and planning for their menus. They ate at a big table in a pleasant servants' dining room opening onto the back porch, decorated with potted plants, and containing a treat which even we in front did not have—a large standing wind-up gramophone with a lily-shaped horn. All would be fine if everyone ate at the same time, but often the handyman or the gardener would turn up late, or the chauffeur had to eat at odd hours. These separate meals had to be prepared and served by the cook and the kitchen maid in addition to those they had to prepare for the front dining room. When the schedule seemed to turn chaotic, one could hardly blame the high-strung cook for an exhibition of temperament.

The children's department in the house was practically a world unto itself, occupying most of the third floor except for the billiard room under the eaves of the wing. The principal division was in the two big rooms called the Day Nursery and the Night Nursery. Most of our memories start at the time when there were three of us together. Little brother Serge came along years later. First there were the two little girls, Alexandra (soon changed from Shouritchka or Sasha to Sa) and Thaïs (who became "Ty"), and then there was baby brother Emile. We grew up a tightly knit, devoted band holding our own in the continuous battle against those grown-ups. At the beginning Emile had his own English nanny, and we girls had the German governesses. They had complete charge of us, from instruction and speaking German all day, to teaching us music, supervising our recreation, brushing our hair, and putting us to bed—plus the privilege of spanking us with a hairbrush when they deemed it necessary.

Emile was a blond, blue-eyed, roly-poly baby who wore Russian-style suits with cross-stitch trimming, handmade by his nurse, and was paraded in his pram with the two sisters escorting. At some point when he was about three his docile nature rebelled. It happened on a certain memorable day: when told to hurry up, this little cherub stood still in his tracks, then shifted one foot ahead an inch at a time. To our loud delight and the impatient threats of the nurse he deliberately carried on this performance for some time while his sisters cheered, "Hey, Mule, you stubborn mule! Hurry up, Mule!" From then on the nickname stuck. It was also our triumphant secret discovery that under this placid good nature there was something tough and stubborn and that we could use him when needed to back up our mutual rebellion.

The Day Nursery, where the baby and nurse had an alcove, was really the playroom. All our toys, books, games, and dollhouses were stored in cases around the walls. In the center at a big round table we had our lessons, and there we ate all our meals, which were served to children and governesses together. The Night Nursery, or dormitory, was carefully organized. The three beds were well separated, and each had between it and the next a substantial bureau and wall closet plus a small table and chair. We slept, napped, and dressed there together. Even with all the sharp-eyed supervision it was impossible to control the after-dark whispering or the giggling during nap time and the invention of deviltries and tricks against each other or those watchful "ogres." Sometimes this combination of three got to be so uncontrollable and frustrating that Fräulein would actually put on her hat and go downstairs to announce that she was giving up.

The names we attached to our parents, Mami and Papi (German spelling!), stuck to them as personalities all their lives, either because people who heard us thought it was cute or because each name somehow denoted a special character. Very few friends were intimate enough to call our mother Olga. Among the Russians when they arrived later, she was naturally Olga Alexandrovna. But Mami was picked up by young and old alike—our school friends, fashionable ladies from the city, and dignified businessmen. It was not exactly because she was the motherly type, but there was about her an aura of graciousness, gentle leadership, and personal interest that caused people to regard her with both warmth and respect.

Papi was likewise not responsive to the American custom of intimacy and first names, but that title represented his distinctive character. With his formidable figure, he was six feet four inches tall, with an average weight of 350 pounds, he was the impressive autocratic head of the whole establishment. He terrified us children by his discipline, yet often revealed to us and others a lively sense of humor, great generosity, and tenderness, and he was always ready for a good time.

Blue-eyed and blond and bald as far back as I can remember, his attraction was further complicated by a livid purple birthmark on the left side of his face, from the temple around the eye to the cheekbone. We of course never noticed it, but in later years I was always intrigued to observe how the shock of his first appearance to a stranger would have the peculiar psychological effect of drawing that person close in sympathy and understanding, all of which became an integral part of Papi's fascination for other people.

Finally, there was Papi's booming voice and positive accent— very German, to be sure—but he always spoke a perfect and articulate English, laced on occasion with appropriate phrases in French, Italian, Spanish, and of course Russian. Thus it was that customers, business associates, and friends of all ages—and especially his young lady friends and bridge partners—were impressed and attracted to him and adopted the name Papi. Even our lady school principal, who so often heard us whisper the name in terror when it came to report cards or special privileges, would say, "You'd better go get permission from Papi."

Childhood Memories

The moods and events of Englewood changed over the years, as did we along with them, but as children we were brought up in a carefree and isolated world. We were not supposed to be aware of troubles; nor was there much sharing in, or understanding of, the personal lives of

Our Englewood

our parents. If there were crises "downstairs" or with the personnel out on the grounds, we were not aware of them. Friction or unhappiness called for inner discipline and self-control. News of the war in Europe and of the tragic events in Russia was kept from us, and we were unaware that Mami was deeply upset after learning of her mother's death and the brutal extinction of most of her family. Likewise we had no idea that our parents sometimes—when we were not present —laughed over some of the things we said or our clownish antics, or that they ever took our side in arguments with the governesses.

Our days were full and happy. With three of us together there never was a feeling of being shut in or lonely without companions. We had our play yard in a corner of the garden. There was the sandbox and gymnastic equipment, with swings, trapeze, rings, parallel bars, and a balance beam. Beside it we had our own wall tent, with screened windows and door and inside our play furniture; and nearby was a huge old apple tree with branches too inviting to resist climbing. Between our combined imaginations and the stories that were read to us, we could keep busy day after day for weeks acting out one fantasy after another. A wheelbarrow and an old blanket had us in a covered wagon pioneering out west. The closed black buggy standing in the garage, which had purple curtains one could pull down over the windows, became a Pullman car for a long trip to California. There were always the circus acrobatics and new tricks to work on. In the woods behind the old barn were a brook and some big fallen trees, which became drawbridges to a castle or Robin Hood's hiding places or oceangoing steamships. During several seasons we played Indians —each of us was a whole tribe and had our separate camps, naturally at war with one another. Our tepees were the hollow spaces under the branches of the great clumps of lilac bushes, where one could hide or defend oneself. There we each horded such treasures as we could capture—cookies, berries, and sunflower seeds from the garden; boxes of beads, bugs, or jewels; and our own improvised utensils. The gardener made us real bows and arrows, which we used with limited effectiveness against the dogs or each other.

One time a fantasy became unbelievably real. One day in the woods across the road we discovered a complete, full-scale Russian village —log houses with thatched roofs lined up along a dirt road, at the end of which stood a wooden church with porch and steeple; in front of it was the village well. A moving-picture company had erected it, and we were allowed to watch them all day long—the exciting action of horses

Princess in Paradise

and wagons, costumed people, and the director with his crew shouting instructions from various angles. When it was over and we went to inspect at close range, there was great disillusionment. Every house was just a flimsy facade; the church was propped with braces from behind; and the well also was a dud. We played there until it all vanished one day on a truck. But our imaginations had been kindled. Interestingly enough, each of us at various stages in school had written compositions with descriptions of life in a Russian village. Coupled with the stories we always heard from Mami, we transferred ourselves very vividly into a different world.

Our daily routine was strictly maintained, but there was nothing painful about that. For the whole morning we were confined to the lesson table on the third floor. There, facing one or another governess, sometimes English, most often German, we received our original instruction in reading, writing, arithmetic, and languages; and this continued in much the same way, at our different levels, until we were ready for school. With books all around us and our own marvelous discoveries in *The Book of Knowledge,* with the freedom to ask questions and go off into discussions on geography and history, in looking back one cannot help but feel that through this personal instruction one covered a broad field of information and that the basic disciplines were deeply instilled in us.

One of the happiest parts of the day was our lunch alone with Mami. Without restraint we could chatter or giggle or complain and thus reveal to her much of what was going on. It was also a little private time for lessons in manners, morals, and religion. She, for her part, would entertain us with stories of her past, descriptions of her homes in Russia, the family, and her adventures—they were such lively tales that we continually begged for more. If she began a story about a trip here or there—Italy, Germany, or Switzerland—it broadened into a graphic travelogue, sometimes with postcards and photographs, showing the towns, characterizing the different people, describing the famous sights including the great masterpieces and the names of the most renowned artists.

Our afternoon session was the one we faced with less relish—the riding lessons. The horses provided especially for us two little girls were stocky tan ponies, Tip-Top and Top-Notch by name. Actually, they were a breed called Swedish horses, and although short were full grown and much stronger and less docile than any English ponies. The pony's back seemed awfully broad when I sat in a saddle, and the

Our Englewood

ground seemed very far below. When we progressed from just riding around in a circle to being taken out on the roads, the riding master was always on his horse beside one of us, and the ponies were kept on a tight lead rein. Many times they shied or bolted, and we flew off, only to be picked up, put back in the saddle, and told to carry on, ride home, and start over again the next day. When these two spirited ponies were harnessed to the pony carriage, even the two governesses could not manage them. A man had to do the driving.

The thing that terrified us was the Sunday ritual—the family ride—when we all proceeded together in a cavalcade, Mami beautiful and dignified in her romantic long sidesaddle skirt, Papi, even for his size, sitting militarily straight on his white Irish hunter. We were supposed to show that we could manage our horses alone. It was not until much later when we each acquired a regular, well-trained riding horse of our own that we discovered that riding could be a pleasure, going off into the woods and along dirt roads, enjoying the independence and the solitude as well as the exercise.

Every afternoon Mami had tea served under the big apple tree near our play yard, and we could either join her or continue with our wilder games. If Olga Lopatina was with her and they were sewing, it was a chance for us to learn embroidery and practice fancy stitches for the gifts we were supposed to make for Christmas.

A much more pressing obligation was to go on the daily "inspection tour," either by ourselves or with Mami. From one end of the place to the other we were supposed to check on the happenings of the day and be able to give a full report to Papi that night: one had to visit the horses and give them sugar; the dogs had to be let out for a run; one listened to the gardener and saw how the vegetables were coming along; one must report if any animals were sick, if the hay or coal had been delivered, and anything else that might have been going on. Woe betide us if we missed something that was discovered later!

At the end of the day we had our little evening session with Papi, at which we appeared all clean and dressed up for inspection. We then retired to our third floor for supper, followed by games and story hour; and our parents, either by themselves or with guests, dined formally at the big candlelit table in the dining room. It was more than a few years before we were put to the test and allowed to join them, and then suddenly we had to overcome the training instilled in us: "Children should be seen but not heard!"—and learn to carry on a conversation with adults.

Princess in Paradise

🌿 Our Grandmother and the Christening

A very special event in the summer of 1913 was the visit of Mami's mother from Moscow who came for an extended stay to have a look at the life of her daughter in America and to enjoy the new house in the country. Her arrival followed soon upon another exciting family event—the birth on May 6 of Emile Kluge, Jr. A celebration for the two as well as the showing off of the new home was planned as a festive christening party late in the fall.

Madame la Général de Moravsky arrived with her personal maid, the mother of her own daughter's childhood companion, Olga; and the customary amount of baggage—wardrobe trunks, steamer trunks, hat trunks, shoe trunks, suitcases, and her jewel case. She was settled into the best guestroom on the second floor with the prettiest view, and everyone did everything possible to make her happy on this, her first inspection trip to this reputedly wild new country. She passed her days horseback riding with Mami, walking about the grounds, or reading fairy tales to her two little granddaughters in Russian or French. The family also tried to show her the attractions of New York City where they had a small and distinguished group of Russian friends, the Russian ambassador, Mr. Bakhmetieff, and his wife; Alexander Smirnov, the Metropolitan opera singer, and his wife, Thaisa; the sculptor Paul Troubetskoy; and Alliette de Carrière, a young friend from Russia, who I remember as my beautiful young godmother, now is married to an American industrialist, a Mr. Taylor.

Emile's christening was to be an elaborate affair, with engraved invitations for December sixth, nineteen hundred and thirteen at three o'clock in the afternoon in Englewood. The religious ceremony was to come first, followed by a reception and dinner. Men arrived in white tie and tails, ladies in gorgeous gowns with trains, and Olga appeared in her Russian court dress. The archbishop from the Russian Cathedral came out from New York with two priests and a deacon.

The christening proper was to take place in the gold damask-walled parlor. In the center of the room on a linen-covered table stood the baptismal tub festooned with lace and flowers. In the ritual of the Russian church the baby is supposed to be completely immersed three times. Everything was in readiness, the guests standing in a circle, the two little sisters in the front row. With chanting and swinging of incense, the priests proceeded with the blessing of the waters in the font. Then, as everyone waited anxiously for the appearance of the

Our Englewood

Mami's parents, General Alexander
de Moravsky and Elizabeth, Moscow ca. 1885.

baby swathed in lace-trimmed blanket and sheets in the arms of his
godmother, in burst Miss Lord, the imposing white-uniformed English nurse.

"Wait!" she commanded as she stepped up to the tub.

"Miss Lord—wha—what is this?" Mami asked, obviously horrified.

Ignoring the question, the nurse dropped her wooden bathtub
thermometer into the font to check the temperature of the water and
make certain it was safe for her charge. She leaned down, squinted one
eye expertly, then stood erect.

"It is all right," she announced in her crisp professional manner as
she stepped to the rear of the crowd.

Mami's and Grandmother's red faces betrayed their embarrassment.

"I'm—I'm terribly sorry," Mami stammered to the priests assembled before her. "Would you mind repeating the ceremony?"

There was nothing to do but apologize to the clergy and have them
repeat the ceremony for the blessing of the waters. Finally the baby was
presented, and the service proceeded through all the various lengthy
steps, ending up with parading the lace-smothered wet little bundle
among the guests to be admired. After that everyone could relax and

Princess in Paradise

celebrate at the reception. Later on followed the gala dinner, catered by Delmonico's of New York, with the seven-course menu and list of special wines printed in French. An electric fountain, smilax bedecked, sparkled in the center of the table, and a string trio played behind a bank of palms.

We were too young to know our Russian grandmother, Elizabeth Konshin de Moravsky, very well, but her pictures show her as being quite diminutive, with a dignified bearing and a whimsical little smile. What impressed us most was her collection of jewels—neck pieces of emeralds and rubies in sparkling diamond and gold settings along with similar rings, bracelets, and earrings, which we were allowed to fondle when they were spread out before us. Her most famous and most treasured piece was a necklace of oriental pearls, allegedly equalled in quality only by those in the collection of the Empress. This was one long string—365 for the days of the year—of perfectly matched half-inch pearls. She brought it along and wore it for this special occasion. On entering the United States, Emile had to post a large bond with the U.S. Customs Bureau to guarantee that those pearls would not be sold over here. Apparently already sensing unrest and trouble abroad, Emile tried to persuade her to leave the pearls here. Olga, who was supposed to inherit them, was reticent about pressing to keep them at the time. They also urged her to remain in this country with them, but she never felt quite at home and wanted to return to her family. She was a firm little person, and she prevailed. She departed and the pearls went back with her; no one could have guessed then that this was to be a final parting.

In 1917, amid the bloody Red Revolution in Russia when everyone was fleeing for their lives and the big houses were being ransacked, Elizabeth de Moravsky was trying to reach Kiev in the south. She refused to carry her jewelry along with her. With the help of a young nephew she buried the pearls and other jewels in the garden of the Moscow house. Neither of them ever returned. The next inhabitants were the Bolsheviks who, after looting and vandalizing the building, converted it into a hospital. After another war ended in 1945 all traces of old buildings in that area completely disappeared, and new ones have since sprung up. The famous pearl necklace remains just a picture and a family legend.

Our Englewood

Summer and Winter Paradise

N EUROPE yachting, like horses or hunting, was one of the customary sports of gentlemen. Papi was no sailor, but he liked boats and he belonged to several fashionable yacht clubs, like Larchmont and the Columbia on the Hudson River. There was a succession of yachts. The first one was the *Mustang,* a small cabin motorboat with a rounded forward deck, rope railings, and manned by a crew of one—someone who knew the mechanics. There were no overnight accommodations or cooking facilities, so obviously there was no room for children and governesses. It was kept anchored at the Larchmont Yacht Club and used for small weekend excursions. The few times we children were taken along—to start getting used to the water!—we had fun playing on the beach. But even though we were equipped with water wings, when it came to going into the water from the boat, down a straight ladder into that enormous expanse of water, we were terrified. Emile was a tiny baby, and Mami handed him naked and screaming over the railing into Papi's arms. What one realizes only later is that Olga and Emile were still a young married couple—at least they were young to me—and they were away from everybody else and having fun with their children. When we had picnics on the beach, they laughed and clowned around and went barefoot in the sand and took pictures as other young couples did.

22

❧ The "Joyeuse"

The *Joyeuse,* which they acquired about 1915, was quite a different enterprise. It was a graceful, sleek, speedy yacht, one hundred feet long with a crew of eight and cabin accommodations for the whole family. The boat became our winter home in Florida.

The dining room and main salon were two separate glass-enclosed rooms on the main deck. A large afterdeck under an awning with lots of wicker furniture was really the living center when the weather was right. Below, the cabins were small and narrow with sloping walls, built-in bunks, and bureaus; the light would come in through small portholes across which the water would splash.

The trip south had to be started before Christmas. Somehow the memories of Christmas are that it was usually miserable. Since the yacht had a deep draft (and the Inland Waterway was not yet developed), they had to make the stormiest run of about twenty-four hours in the open ocean around Cape Fear from Beaufort, North Carolina. There was no Christmas celebration—no tree, no food, everyone sick, and the furniture and dishes pitching and sliding. Finally reaching the calm port of Charleston or Savannah and being enveloped suddenly by sunshine and warm southern air was something of a compensation. There was only one Christmas worth remembering. Because of the bad weather ahead we were held up in the pathetic little port of Morehead City and tied up at a shantylike wharf where there was a factory for canning terrapin soup. One of the sailors went ashore to find a Christmas tree. He came back out of the nearby woods hauling a magnificent fresh pine and a real holly tree full of shiny red berries.

Whether the boat was under way or whether we were settled, the children's routine of morning lessons was carried on just as regularly as at home. Of our two German governesses Fräulein Blum's role was more that of a nurse, caring for our clothes and personal needs; the more severe one, Fräulein Schmiedinger, was the schoolteacher in charge of the books and instruction. When the boat was anchored at Palm Beach or Miami we seldom went ashore, and our activities were entirely with these two ladies. If we went to play at the beach, we were covered practically from head to toe with long black bathing suits. One

Our Englewood

Dinner party on the after-deck of "Joyeuse" with Ella and Albert Upman, 1915.

of the Fräuleins undertook to teach us swimming at a hotel pool. With water wings blown up and a strap around the waist attached to a length of rope, we were supposed to go through the motions of breast stroke as the Fräulein, holding on to this rope like a leash, marched around and around the deck of the pool in her long skirts and wide straw hat, loudly counting out the strokes (in German, of course).

Sometimes we were treated to a ride in one of the popular basket carriages, pedalled from behind by a little black boy, riding thus luxuriously along the beautiful promenade of tall arching royal palms which led from the Royal Poinciana Hotel to the Breakers Hotel on the ocean side. We were hardly aware of what went on by way of the family's social life, either ashore or on board. We heard about parties at the magnificent Flagler mansion, about dancing outdoors at the Coconut Grove, and something about gambling at Bradley's Casino. Sometimes there were formal evening parties aboard the *Joyeuse,* and during the day many guests came and went by launch. At other times they would go off with a group of friends on a chartered boat for deep-sea fishing and come back proudly exhibiting their huge catches of tarpon and sailfish, retelling their stories for many days.

Princess in Paradise

and the Bahamas and to visit their friends the Upmanns in Cuba. Meanwhile, we children were parked with the governesses for a month in a little cottage right on Miami Beach. It was a delightful, free, simple life, with us sleeping and eating on a screened porch and being busy all day on the beach with turtles, shells, and sand castles.

As was the custom, we were not necessarily kept informed about family troubles nor even such disagreeable news as that of the world war. We realized that business and social activities were very restricted, and so for a few winters there were no Florida trips. We rather enjoyed the winter at home with the snow and the sleighing and our own fun right in Englewood. Later we learned that the *Joyeuse* had been sold in 1917 to the Coast Guard because she was such a sleek, fast cruiser. Not until after the war were our Florida visits resumed. When in 1920 the *Pioneer* was introduced, a much larger, houseboat-type yacht, times were different, we were older, and a new set of adventures was involved, as will be told in a later chapter.

Greenwood Lake

Partly because of troubles caused by the war in Europe, we shifted from spending our summers in Englewood to moving the whole family to a "camp" at Greenwood Lake, New Jersey. One of the reasons was the difficulty of keeping adequate help to man the Englewood house. Another which we could not understand was that apparently there was a growing feeling of enmity and suspicion in this little community against the "foreigners" or "aliens" who lived up on the hill, and then there had been threats of violence. More of this later, but for now the immediate result was that our first summer at Greenwood Lake extended into late October. Although it was an adventure that we thoroughly enjoyed, it meant that we were again taken away and kept isolated among ourselves, just as we always had been up till now.

Greenwood Lake, about ten miles long, lies on the northern border of New Jersey, half of it in New York State and half in New Jersey. Surrounded by low green pine-covered hills, it looks very much like the many lakes of Maine, New Hampshire, and the Adirondacks. The few houses and camps with their boathouses and docks were concealed amid the trees close to the water. There was only one public road on the western side of the lake, far up the hill and out of sight; a small railroad line ran along the eastern shore, ending halfway up the lake at the only town, Sterling Forest, where the mail arrived and where there were a few stores. Also at Sterling Forest was the main pier of the two-decker lake steamer that slowly made its daily rounds to the few resorts at the northern end.

Pine Island was where we settled down for the whole summer. It really was an island, about one mile long, with no connection whatsoever to the nearest shore about a quarter of a mile away. It looked thoroughly wild, it was covered with tall trees, and the shore was lined with huge gray boulders. The family had leased it from Colonel Abercrombie of the sporting goods house, Abercrombie & Fitch, in New York City. His four children had grown up there but were now old enough to be independent. However, the buildings and the organization of the kind of life led there were characteristically his. It was patterned after the typical nineteenth-century Adirondack camps, those rustic hideaways of the fashionable and sporty city dwellers for whom of course Colonel Abercrombie was the complete outfitter, from clothes to furniture to hunting and fishing equipment. Those "camps" varied from the fifty-room chalet of the Vanderbilts at Raquette Lake to the kind with comfortable lodges, substantial little cabins clustered about, and hidden tennis courts, bowling alleys, and billiard rooms, to the simple cottages built of rough-hewn logs with a porch across the front and one big all-purpose room with fireplace. Whichever it was, the idea was to get away to the "simple life."

On our island the rustic buildings were all clustered at the northern end astride a rocky crest with a view up the ten-mile lake. The central feature was a real log cabin, the owner's home, with a screened front porch and on the inside one large high space divided by Japanese folding screens into a big living room with two bedrooms. Behind the cobblestone fireplace in the middle was a bathroom and storage room. Grouped around the log cabin were four tents, one for each pair of children, or for boys and girls or guests. They were quite substantial affairs of canvas set on wood frames and platforms with cloth screen windows and door. Inside they were prettily decorated, each in a different color scheme, with chintz curtains, iron cots and bedspreads, and packing box furniture. On the improvised washstands were sets of lovely flowered china water pitchers and basins, soap dishes, waste jars, and odd old-fashioned things. There was no electricity at the beginning; everyone used kerosene or candle lamps.

The lodge, the general meeting place, was a long one-story clapboard building with an open porch along its entire length, made

Princess in Paradise

inviting with rocking chairs and wicker furniture. The inside plan was again a central living room with fieldstone fireplace, comfortable lounging furniture around and housing a precious old grand piano, and at the corners four built-in bedrooms. These were mainly for guests, but one was reserved for the petite and delicate French lady who was the governess at the time.

Next to the lodge was the so-called dining tent, really a wood-framed pavilion, screened on three sides, with drop curtains for bad weather. Attached to it was a wooden kitchen shed with large range, zinc sink, and shelves around for all the dishes and supplies. A bit farther back in the trees was the two-story icehouse, with two separate cold rooms at ground level. The big blocks of ice were stored in the gable above. They were cut from the lake in winter and hauled up onto land and packed with sawdust, which preserved them for most of the summer. From the main buildings a winding path led down to the water, the boathouse with a gameroom above, and the swimming dock. Beyond this encampment the island was entirely wild, with tall pine trees, mossy boulders, and banks of wild rhododendron and laurel bushes, which were usually still in bloom when we arrived. A trail led along each side of the island to the farther uninhabited point, where there was a secret little meeting grove of our own.

There were hardly enough hours in our days for all our climbing, exploring, and hiding. Here was the ideal place for acting out Tarzan and the Swiss Family Robinson, and certainly for playing Indians. We had also discovered spy stories and codes, so were constantly writing mysterious notes to each other and depositing or picking them up in special hollow stumps. The poor French governess had to keep us together for lessons each morning, and we each still had to put in that piano practice time. However, there was no delay answering the whistle for the afternoon swim. In Florida we had basically learned to swim with water wings in a pool. Here we developed our own strokes and jumps and competed among ourselves. On the Fourth of July and Labor Day we went up the lake to the yacht club to watch the competitions in real swimming, diving, and canoeing, so we could see how they were correctly done—and we were great imitators.

Besides our rowboat, canoes, and slow-chugging work launch, we had a power speedboat named *Alexandra*. That was used for the five-mile run to Sterling Forest where the mail and guests came by train. The slower boat carried supplies and the lower echelon of passengers from the nearer mainland about a mile away where our cars were

Our Englewood

parked at the home of our friends the Jack Looschens. There things were unloaded, and everything—trunks, equipment, food, children—had to be transferred to the boat no matter what hour we arrived, often in the dark, and sometimes requiring more than one round trip. Since we moved up here completely for the summer and the amount of baggage grew enormous, Uncle Jack devised a homemade square barge to be towed by the motorboat. One time it hit a rock or just somehow sprung a leak, so that it filled up with water before it reached the dock. There were plenty of problems with wet grocery boxes and duffel bags, but the greatest damage was to our French governess, whose trunk was soaked through and her entire wardrobe ruined by the red dye from some garment running over everything else, especially her best white flannel suit. The excited chatter about that went on for most of the summer.

Right from the beginning Greenwood Lake seemed to be more sociable than anything we had known before. Everybody had motorboats and took friends out for spins by daylight or moonlight, stopping for visits on the way. At night we could hear music floating over the water from Awosting, the gaily illuminated restaurant and dance terrace just across from us. One of the inherited Pine Island traditions was the Fourth of July clambake. It was a perfect setting, with permanent U-shaped wooden tables for about a hundred people in a shaded grove and off at one side the barbecue pit. Everyone came, young and old, and everybody helped. Our "foreign" parents soon learned how these things were managed. Starting the day before, fires were built to heat the stones in the pit, and on the day itself our men friends arrived early to see to the roasting of the chickens—I cannot imagine how many! Later on, seaweed was thrown onto the hot stones for the steaming of barrels of clams. Crates of restaurant china had to be unpacked along with stacks of mugs to hold all the beer from the kegs standing around.

Japanese paper lanterns and red, white, and blue bunting had been strung between the trees. One year there was a sudden downpour, and the colors from the bunting dripped all over people and tables. Everyone ran screeching for refuge on the porches, so the next year a rustic, open pavilion for dancing was erected. All day long we watched from the sidelines the many comings and goings and the buildup of excitement, till finally everyone settled down to the feast. There was continuous dancing to the music of a black jazz band—Deacon Doubleday's—from Paterson, and after dark there were of course fantastic fireworks, also managed by the faithful group of men friends.

Princess in Paradise

Our feuding with the governesses never ended. As we changed from happy docile babies to more independent individuals our main object became to harass those female dictators into utter frustration. It was then that Mami hit upon one of her cleverest ideas. She asked us how we would like to have a "camp counselor," and she produced for us Lucy Abercrombie, the second daughter of Colonel Abercrombie, who had grown up on this island. She was first of all an *American* and she was *young*. She did things along with us, like playing tennis and exploring. She loved nature and she introduced us to the books of Ernest Thompson Seton, among them *Two Little Savages,* and the dog stories of Albert Payson Terhune. She taught us how to build fires in the woods and to blaze a trail, and she knew many good secret hiding places where we could picnic away from the grown-ups. Best of all, she went swimming with us instead of sitting on the dock in ruffles and with a parasol. Lucy knew how to do the swan dive, jackknife, and flips. We admired everything about her, and we would do anything she told us to do. She stuck with us for three happy summers. One year she brought along her twelve-year-old brother, David. We looked on him with awe because he knew all about motorboats and could run them by himself. When his friends came around, they seemed to us so marvelously independent and grown up. This was the first time we had really seen other children, American children, of nearly our own age.

Part of the excitement of moving for the summer to Greenwood Lake was the process of getting there. Somehow everything was collected and packed for us. It was another strenuous job for Mami, who had to manage not only the staffing and opening of the place but the food supply, which was stocked by the week and delivered in the factory truck. On the day of the move all six of us were packed into the beige Cunningham touring car, Mami and Papi wrapped in dusters, veils, and cap in the back seat; we children on the two jump seats; the governess in front; and the picnic trunk strapped onto the rack in back. Sometimes the isinglass windows were fastened all around us, but usually just the canvas top was up, and sometimes we rode entirely in the open. Jake, our beloved black chauffeur, very proud of himself in beige uniform to match the car, with his huge grin and big shiny goggles, stood by to receive directions, then saluted and we were off. It was more than a fifty-mile trip, slowed up by the winding roads and having to go through numerous small towns. It took nearly a whole day, with a stop for the picnic lunch on the way. But Jake was proud of

Our Englewood

being a smart driver and loved the sleek car, and we raced along the dusty roads well beyond the speed limit of thirty or thirty-five miles per hour. He kept his eye on the rearview mirror, and we all were supposed to be on constant lookout—but sometimes there would come the surprise of a long sharp whistle, the screeching stop at the side of the road, and there would appear a state trooper on a motorcycle beside us. A uniform and a cross-looking policeman had us all terrified and embarrassed, but after a few such experiences Jake became confident, and we all learned to sigh and take it patiently as part of the adventure. The beige Cunningham and Papi soon became well known to most of the small-town New Jersey police, and he somehow, with a discreet gratuity, knew how to make friends with them. Then through some political contact he acquired the badge of an Honorary Police Inspector, which he always wore inside his coat. It gave him such pleasure to flash it at the surprised "officer," get a salute, and be told to drive on. Jake too enjoyed this part of the fun.

As we drove north in New Jersey we passed through little towns whose names later became famous—Hackensack, Paterson, Pompton Lakes, the home of Albert Payson Terhune and his dogs. Another was West Milford, which scared us because we had heard tales of the dangerous arms and ammunition factories there and the frequent explosions. In fact, one night from our windows on the hilltop at Englewood we had seen the western sky lit up with an orange glow and could hear the rumblings of one of those big explosions, which lasted most of the night. To us the people on the street of that little town looked suspicious, and we were sure those rows of mysterious low sheds would blow up as we tore by. For variety a different route took us through Sterling Forest and the wild Hewitt copper mining country, then past Tuxedo Park where we would all be herded into the famous Henry's Inn at Suffern for a rather formal luncheon stop.

While there may have been troubles in Englewood owing to America's entry into the war and a lack of domestic help, we led a peaceful, sufficiently well tended existence on Pine Island. As we continued going there until 1923 and as prosperity returned, we again had a large mixed ménage. Papi stayed in Englewood and came to the lake just for weekends, always with the only car and Jake the chauffeur. Mami ran the establishment on the island, with no telephone and the only available communication by boat to the Looschens' house on the mainland. We usually had a reliable maintenance man who could run the motorboats, keep the pump and generator in working order, and do the general heavy work.

At one point there was a Japanese chef, an Irish maid, the American handyman, plus the usual French governess and the black chauffeur, Jake. They all ate together and paired off for their afternoons or days out. What was brewing and how it came to a head we never knew. We always heard the exciting stories after something had happened. Katy, the Irish maid, was pretty and evidently the object of the attentions of each of the men. One night after dark she came screaming into the main house to get Mami—the Japanese chef and the chauffeur had had a fight over her. Right now the Japanese chef was chasing Jake around the kitchen brandishing the biggest of his personal collection of carving knives and had already knicked him once or twice, so that blood was splashed around the floor and over the kitchen table. Enter Mami to separate the knife wielder from his victim, while Katy ran to the tent in the woods for Mike the Sailor, our husky handyman. With his help the chef was disarmed and hauled off to his bedroom, behind a door that could be barricaded; Jake was patched up by Mami and the governess and then sent to his own tent. Mike was dispatched by boat to the mainland to bring back Uncle Jack Looschen to assist, while Mami kept watch in a rocking chair to see that neither Katy nor Jake tried to get to the door or window of the Japanese chef's room. The solution seems to have been that Uncle Jack packed up the chef and his baggage and took him for the night to his own house, to drive him into town the next morning. One could take no chances on Jake driving his rival, with his package of knives, alone in the same car.

Our wonderful summers at Greenwood Lake continued for several years after Sergey was born and even after we had been sent in alternate years to camps in Maine. Sergey shared swim time with us, paddling about in an ingenious homemade device of wooden slats resembling a fishing crate, which was hung over the side of the dock, where he was both safe and somewhat free. We three now competed with each other, showing off our swimming prowess and our fancy diving tricks. Lux, our favorite German shepherd who was always with us, was right there when it came to swimming, whining and worrying on the dock until he could stand it no longer and jumped in after us, or rather on top of us. Even Papi was so proud of Lux's "rescue" training, hanging deadweight onto his collar and then letting him paddle all the way to shore dragging the victim with him.

Our Englewood

Another thing we had learned at camp was handling a canoe, and we liked to show off in front of the family. One day Papi, the irrepressible sportsman, said, "Alexandra, give me a ride." By the rules we had learned, the heavier person sits in the stern and does the steering. I got into the bow and waited, well aware that Papi knew nothing about steering. Then he, still in his dockside outfit of straw hat and German terrycloth robe, cautiously lowered his corpulent three-hundred-and-fifty-pound figure onto the little stern seat and shoved off. Those watching on shore saw little Alexandra rise slowly into the air till the paddle could no longer reach the water, while the stern gently settled into the water down to the gunwales—and more. Quite calmly the canoe filled and went down, and Papi was left standing in the water, with his straw hat still on and the flowered bathrobe floating in a circle all around him. It was one of those times when Papi could laugh as loudly at himself as all the onlookers who were in hysterics on the shore.

Our end-of-the-season swimming test was to swim across the lake to the big icehouse nearly a mile away. It was a complicated expedition, with someone to man the rowboat escort and watch three children in the water going at different paces, and Lux also swimming along all the way. The climax of my own accomplishment was to turn around and swim all the way back. With everyone as determined and as proud as I, nobody gave a thought to the sun, now near noontime, directly overhead. The more memorable part of the event was that later I became really sick, evidently with something of a sunstroke, and was the object of special attention, being hovered over with icepacks in the parents' log cabin—much to the annoyance of the others, who considered their feats just as important as mine.

During those slightly more grown-up years we took part in the Labor Day swimming meets of the yacht club, never achieving much distinction in our various age groups but being subjected to the discipline of getting in there and sticking it out to the shamefaced end. While there we could watch and admire and sometimes even talk to a few of the other young people from around the lake. There was Eddie Thimmie, a college student, who was a magnificent diver; Duncan McMartin from prep school who was really an outstanding swimmer; and one of the good-looking girls from our neighbors, the Fox family, who in a slinky tank suit usually took the women's prizes. Herbie Looschen, Uncle Jack's nephew, regularly won the race for dinghies and other little boats.

Princess in Paradise

The most important event of Labor Day weekend was after various other classes of motorboat races—the Lake George Handicap, in which any size boat could participate. At the starting gun the whole flotilla of boats took off, each at her top speed; when the fastest one reached the buoy many miles ahead, a signal was fired and every boat turned around and headed home. Times were strictly watched, so that one returned at the same speed at which one went out, and sometimes, by skill or circumstances, a small boat could win. But the perennial winner, first out and fastest back, was usually Uncle Jack Looschen's *Royal Flush.* She was a graceful, long, slim boat that everyone admired, and its owner was loved by everyone.

However, once the Kluge boat did stir up surprise and excitement. That was the *Alexandra,* a shorter, heavier, seagoing powerboat which had been the launch for the *Joyeuse.* She was fast and turned up a beautiful big spray from her bow, and she was kept in fine mechanical shape. As Papi would have it—and one never argued—young Miss Alexandra, age twelve, was to pilot that boat, with of course the experienced mechanic along as the permitted crew of one. We did make it—the fastest one out and the first one back. I must admit I was thrilled and Papi could not have been prouder, especially when I, red-faced and trembling, had to step up in front of all those people for the presentation of a very impressive silver cup.

The Looschens

The Looschens, who became our dear and devoted friends at Greenwood Lake, were a distinct influence in our growing up. More than that, they played an important part in the Americanization of the Kluge family, parents and children. To us they were Uncle Jack and Auntie Tottie and were practically our foster parents. Having no children of their own, they lavished their affection on us, understood problems of which we were quite unaware, and gave us personal attention we were not used to receiving. We noticed that they used words like "folks" and "neighbor." Papi who would only patronize the prestige establishments in New York City, learned from them that they could shop successfully at places like Sears, Roebuck and Bamberger's. They lived in a modest house on a side street in Paterson, and in their conversation they were not trying to be impressive. They were always sincere and admiring friends of both Papi and Mami.

Uncle Jack was tall and wiry, his bald head encircled with a fringe of blond hair, his eyes marked by friendly wrinkles from his permanent smile. He dressed sportily in tennis shoes and white flannels and wore his yachting cap at a jaunty angle. His laugh and his sense of humor were irresistible. Auntie Tottie was a tiny, plumpish homebody, teetering in high heels on her birdlike feet or rocking in an armchair with short legs dangling. She too had a ringing laugh and unfailing good humor and just exuded affection.

In Paterson, Uncle Jack owned and ran his family business, the Paterson Piano Case Company. It was originally a cabinetmaking factory, and he knew and loved fine woods and finishes, as well as being a knowledgeable craftsman himself. From full-time production of piano cases and Victrola cabinets he went on to manufacturing radio cabinets until troubles and competition drove that business into decline. Then he developed and patented an ingenious Simplicity Boat Hoist, using a gear principle, by which a single man could raise or lower his motorboat inside his boathouse. He demonstrated and exhibited at motorboat shows and was successful for many years, gradually making that his entire business. To everyone's surprise after his death his modest, sheltered homebody of a wife carried on the Boat Hoist business herself, not only running the office and production, but visiting and demonstrating at boat shows, meeting all their old friends, and being gayly entertained by them.

At Greenwood Lake his speedboat the *Royal Flush* was admired for the fine craftsmanship and his successful personal design. She had a long shiny mahogany foreward deck over the motor, and in the open cockpit wicker chairs for twelve people. It was a treat for anyone to go for a spin in her because one could comfortably make the ten-mile trip up the lake and back with stops for visits besides. He cared for her as affectionately and meticulously as he did everything else—his house and garden, the lawns, the car, and his prize collection of giant dahlias.

The Looschens' house was one of four built close together along the shore, the families all longtime friends and neighbors, and they became that to us also. There were the Foxes with four attractive daughters, all good swimmers; Gerald Stalter, Papi's attorney and a sporty widower; and Iva McMartin, a stunning blonde Canadian mining heiress with a wild and independent young son, Duncan. All the houses were of the rustic summer cottage type, with sapling-supported front porches filled with hammocks and wicker furniture, the cooking done on wood or kerosene stoves, and their boathouses lined up next to each other. The gayest of all were the Looschens, theirs the gather-

Princess in Paradise

ing place for neighbors and family, known for their good cheer and hospitality.

The Looschens took upon themselves the broadening of our education. It was they who insisted on taking us to the circus in New York. We were quite young the first time, and they obviously had great fun watching three wide-eyed children going through this new experience. It was the Ringling Brothers-Barnum & Bailey "Greatest Show on Earth" in Madison Square Garden, with three rings and two stages going in continuous performances, plus the clowns and animals and the amazing introductory parade. Uncle Jack had been a circus addict since his boyhood and had always watched the setting up of the great tent in the country. He knew every act, every clown, and every other performer by name. His favorite acrobat was Lillian Leitzel, who did one hundred turns hanging by her teeth.

Our family went en masse, parents, friends, governess, and children and occupied an entire box, but Uncle Jack would tolerate no restraint, no snobbishness on this occasion. He insisted that we be allowed to have popcorn and lemonade and cotton candy; and afterward we must join the crowds to see the animals close up. When we got home we were exhausted, confused, and speechless. Then the enthusiasm and the memories began to pop up the next day, and for weeks thereafter we were talking and acting out the wonders we had seen at the circus.

A few years later he introduced us to another American tradition —the same Ringling Brothers Circus in a tent, set up in a field somewhere in New Jersey. That was even more exciting with the dusty outdoor parade, the animals in wagons, and the entirely different atmosphere of the same gigantic performance done in a tent about three blocks long. It then became a yearly event that the Looschens should have their fun by making it *our day* at the circus. To us it was of course a much greater treat than if our parents had taken us.

We owed another big adventure to the Looschens. After much persuasion and insisting that it was for our educational good, they took us on our first trip to Atlantic City—just the two of them and we three. We had rooms at the Traymore Hotel, high up in a tower, and saw the strange world of big hotels with romantic names such as Hadden Hall and Marlborough-Blenheim. We strolled on the boardwalk, rode in wheeled carriages, observed the crowds, and wandered into shops. When we wanted saltwater taffy or buttered popcorn, they bought it for us. We had our pictures taken sitting in crazy buggies or on

Our Englewood

motorcycles. Being free from discipline and constant reminders about good behavior made us feel we had entered a different life. We chattered to them without restraint and they laughed with us. They let us do almost anything we wished, and we adored them.

Like the circus, a summer trip to the amusement park at Coney Island became another annual treat. It meant a whole day's expedition from New Jersey by ferry, then way out to Long Island. The family insisted on luncheon being their part and took us all to some fancy hotel or the yacht club, but after that we were free and, under the Looschens' guidance, encouraged to try everything—and often they were right along with us—the steeplechase, the huge slides, the merry-go-rounds, the roller coasters and the flying machines. We could scream and laugh and jump all we wanted, and we sensed that our enthusiasm made the day more successful in their eyes. We could eat popcorn and ice-cream cones as we walked around, things never allowed at home.

Whenever the family went away on trips, of long or short duration, the Looschens came to stay with us at Englewood. They managed the house, and they managed us. We could hardly wait till our parents had gone out the door. The rejoicing must have seemed almost hysterical. We dressed up in Mami's long clothes and staggered around in her high-heeled slippers, drowned Emile in Papi's opera cape and top hat. We put on wildly exaggerated opera performances and at bedtime carried on with circus acrobatics, bouncing up and down and across our three beds—yet they always managed to calm us down. As the time drew near for the family's return, we became fearful, tried hard to be on our best behavior, and begged them to give a good report. They always did. At least what we heard them say was, "Oh, they behaved like angel children!" and our binding tie to Uncle Jack and Auntie Tottie for many years was that smiling understanding—"You are our angel children!"

The War Years, 1914-1920

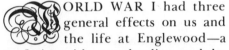ORLD WAR I had three general effects on us and the life at Englewood—a servantless house, trouble and confusion with our schooling, and the social life involving the family's military friends. Although actual United States involvement in the European war lasted only from April 1917 to November 1918, which itself seemed extremely long, repercussions had been felt since 1914. Political sides were taken with violence, and prejudice grew to an almost hysterical pitch, leading up to such well-known incidents as changing "Sauerkraut" to "Liberty Cabbage" and forbidding the playing of Beethoven and Wagner or suppressing the publication of all German-language newspapers. These occurred not only on the eastern seaboard but with even more fervor in the old German communities like Milwaukee; Chicago; St. Louis; Stuebenville, Ohio; and Fredericksburg, Texas.

Trouble in Paradise

With the outbreak of war in Europe, many of the foreign working people fled or were summoned back for service to their homelands. My vivid recollection of the summer of 1914 is that suddenly there was a big emotional crisis among the household help in Englewood. After all, we had quite an international gathering. There was Anna the Austrian cook, Rosa her Bohemian kitchen maid, the English butler,

37

the Irish parlor maid, and the German houseboy. Upstairs we had the German housekeeper Pauline and our governesses, Emile's English nurse, and Olga the Russian maid. Outside there were the English riding master, the German gardener, and a Belgian chauffeur. They all ate together every day. Within a week their political arguments became so heated and personal that some refused to speak to each other, and then nearly all packed up and departed. For a time American domestics replaced them until there came the economic boom with factories enlarging production and the new movement of women going into jobs they had never tackled before.

At home in Englewood there were abrupt changes. Some things were given up, like the yacht and a few horses, but still the formal style of life was expected to be carried on as usual. What impressed us children the most was not having one less governess but being allowed for the first time to go into the pantry and the kitchen, with a chance to help a bit. There was emphasis on the strict economy of electricity, and at table we were made aware of the rationing of butter, sugar, and flour, but dinner parties continued, and the silver had to be polished. So we were enlisted as for a game to do some of the chores such as setting the table, putting away linens, and having a silver-polishing bee.

To us it was great fun, and evidently Papi thought so too. From that time on it struck him as quite cute to have one of his little girls serve the cocktails and the other pass the hors d'oeuvres. My privileged sphere became the wine cellar, which was entrusted to me with a bunch of keys and the combination to the safety vault door. Gradually I learned how the collection was arranged, with different racks for the champagnes, the red or the white wines, a separate closet for the liqueurs, and behind another locked door the whiskeys and rums. Ty, the artistic one, liked setting the table with decorative variations of the pretty placemats and the good china and glassware. Along with us, Emile had already learned the different names of the flowers in the garden, so we picked and arranged them.

At that time two of Papi's brothers were living with us on extended visits—Adolf, his oldest, and Karl, the youngest. That meant not only making our beds but also helping take care of the other rooms. In spite of all these various ups and downs, it somehow never went so far that Mami had to go into the kitchen to cook. Nor were we ever allowed near the stove even for fun. We could find our way around quite nicely in the complex refrigerator system, and we learned to balance trays

Princess in Paradise

and serve at the table. However difficult it was, the house at Englewood was kept going with a minimum amount of help.

Until then we had lived our lives in our private third-floor realm. For the first five or six years our schooling progressed systematically through the personal tutoring by the governesses and their day-long attention to us—instruction on the piano, singing German and French songs, memorizing poetry, learning sewing, reading and being read to, looking at books and pictures. However, this also meant that we never played with other children, nor did we know what they were like. It did not bother us then, since we knew nothing else and we always entertained ourselves happily.

A change came when we two girls began going to the Dwight School and Emile to a private kindergarten. I was six going on seven and started in the third grade; Ty began in the second grade. We were bashful and scared, and looked decidedly odd with probably a mysterious reputation, so we made hardly any friends. At the desk next to me sat a blonde pigtailed girl with rather formidable New England features, Ruth Keeler by name, and just curious enough to talk to me. We formed a friendship that lasted through adulthood. Ty acquired one good friend, Marjorie Gubelman, with curly dark hair and a big smile—also a lasting friendship. Nevertheless, though we were now part of a school we felt very different and alone. Everyone else seemed to live nearby and walked or rode bicycles. We were driven up in an open pony carriage and called for the same way as soon as school was out. Our hair was done in two long braids, and along with Emile we three were dressed alike in sailor uniforms with high-buttoned shoes. We carried "school bags," which apparently nobody else did, bringing our lunch sandwiches in them and eating alone at our desks while most other students went home. I remember well that from somebody else eating in school we discovered the intriguing smell of peanut butter, something entirely new and strange to us. We found out the name and begged at home to be allowed to have the same thing. It certainly was an unknown oddity and in that European household was considered ordinary and unrefined.

The academic side of school seems to have gone very well. I received praise from my third-grade teacher, and Ty easily picked up French, rattling off the names of objects in a complicated, colorful farm picture. The principal was an impressive little white-haired Scotch lady, Miss Creighton, who dressed in high-necked satin dresses of gray or

Our Englewood

black and presided at a desk in the central hall of that old Victorian building where she kept her eyes and ears on everybody.

We were as unaware of troubles at school as we were at home. Life was regulated for us, and we followed it. Outside of our own misdemeanors, unpleasantnesses and crises were kept from us. Changes in our routine and variations in the household personnel were the big adventures, so we just accepted the announcement that the household was being moved to Pine Island at Greenwood Lake for the summer. Our schedule of lessons and recreation would keep right on.

But something had gone wrong. When we returned to Englewood late in the fall of 1917 we did not go back to our private school. No explanation was given to us, but we found out later that Miss Creighton, either for our own good or under community pressure, let it be known to our parents that we would not be welcomed back in the fall. It seems our parents were enemy aliens. We had a German name and we spoke German, so it was considered dangerous to have us around. The solution was that we were sent to Englewood Public School.

If we had looked and felt odd in a private school, we were certainly miserably out of place in the public school. With the United States now in the war prejudices had become really violent and unreasonable. Besides, from the viewpoint of the public school way down in the village, anyone living in that big house up on the hill was regarded with suspicion—adding to this was the appearance of three strange children, all dressed alike in uniforms, darting into their classrooms to avoid the playground, terrified of being alone in the coatroom, and scared of everyone around them. Once a big girl came up to me and asked bluntly what my religion was. I dutifully stammered out "Russian Orthodox"—which drew a sneer and left me wishing I could drop through the floor.

The weirdest sight of all was our daily arrival and departure. It looked to us as if the whole school population had stopped their playing and was lined up on the porch which ran the length of the building to shout taunts and jeers at us as we came up the curved driveway. Our vehicle was a somber-looking, closed black Landau —the kind one sees in Amish country—with purple plush interior, purple curtains over the windows, and ornate side lanterns. On the open seat in front sat Karsten, our elderly German gardener, with a little black cap and big drooping mustache, his long whip proudly prodding his favorite horse, Jim, already old and rather decrepit-

Princess in Paradise

looking. Karsten, in all his dignity, never flinched; he probably could
not understand the taunts in English, but we got the full force of all the
heckling, though not quite grasping the meanings. "Hey, here come
the Kaiser's children!" "Look at the Kaiser with his whiskers." "Hello,
Heinies! What's your spy-father up to now?"

Since we lived more than three miles away and there was no second
car, we continued to be driven back and forth in the buggy, winter and
spring. On the long slow ride we kept busy inside playing in our usual
fantasy world. The purple silk curtains always pulled down over the
windows surely made our conveyance look even more suspicious and
strange.

One time we came home as fast as the buggy would carry us, but
without Emile. He had not showed up after school to join us in the
carriage. There were frantic calls from school, and at home our people
were out searching. Finally at dusk this little five-year-old—whom I
will admit did look funny with his round shaved head—was found in
the excavated basement for a new house where he had been taken by
three big neighbor boys, pelted with stones, and left abandoned, disheveled, and with a bloody cut on his head. If he hated school before
now he was scared to death. He had one friend in his first grade, a little
Japanese boy whose sister was in kindergarten. They were called for
every afternoon by their mother, who walked to school dressed in
native Japanese kimono. They too were different from the rest and
were likewise teased, so there was a bond of mutual sympathy. Once
Emile was taken home by the Japanese family because of the danger-
ously mean taunting on the playground. They called Mami, so she
went to that house, probably till then the only home in Englewood she
ever visited. We never forgot her description of the gracious reception
she was given by that sympathetic and dignified little lady.

No doubt the fact that we did well in school did not endear us to our
classmates. Since the school classes were divided into B and A groups,
we easily skipped half a grade each year. The subjects we covered were
not very different from what we had learned at home. Generally the
new experience was the school assemblies, with choral singing, illustrated talks, and student plays. We also heard for the first time talk
about "moving pictures," something we never went to until years later.
The outstanding excitement, when everybody forgot everything else,
came on November 11, 1918, when the signing of the armistice was
announced.

Our Englewood

Photograph of Mami as President of the Russian-American War Relief Society,
from the official program of the 1915 Bazaar.

Princess in Paradise

⚜️ The Family Widens Its Contacts

Both Papi and Mami came from military backgrounds and had grown up with all the pride and dignity that was accorded that class in Europe. Papi, six foot four inches, had served his military duty in the Body Guard of the king of Saxony, who dressed his selected corps of tall men in high shakos with still taller cock feathers. Papi's bearing was always chin up and straight, with a remarkably light footstep, and his handling of a gun when hunting and his weekly horseback riding were carryovers from that former way of life. Mami's father, a general and a military judge in Kiev, was proud of his position and had received in his home an endless stream of colorfully caparisoned and impressively bewhiskered military personages. In addition, her older brother, Mifody, was already an officer in the army, and Igor, the younger brother, had attended the Imperial Corps des Pages in St. Petersburg. Related to this in her growing up was all the gay social life of balls, court receptions, privileged treatment at the opera, and constant contact with men in an array of uniforms. Consequently with these tastes they both readily felt at home in the social circle of the United States military community.

In 1915 Olga Kluge, now twenty-seven, became president of the Russian-American War Relief Society; and the Russian ambassador, Mr. Bakhmetieff, appointed her chief organizer of a big benefit bazaar. It was held at the Seventy-first Regiment Armory at Park Avenue and Thirty-fourth Street in New York City, lasted a whole week, and took an enormous amount of planning. Among the distinguished patronesses listed in the program were such names as Mrs. John Jacob Astor, Mrs. Cornelius Vanderbilt, Mrs. Ogden Mills, Mrs. Frederick Havermeyer, Mrs. Theodore Roosevelt, Jr., and Princess Paul Troubetzkoy. Olga and her lady friends were all dressed in Russian boyar costumes and presided at "kiosks," substantial wooden buildings typical of Russian village houses, where they sold foods, artworks, handcrafts, dolls, and toys. The open floor in the center was for general dancing in the evenings. Besides, for both afternoons and evenings there was a steady program of Russian dancers and singers, including one exhibition by Irene and Vernon Castle. Husbands shared time at the booths, and children too were enlisted. We were dressed in pretty Russian costumes with *kokoshniki* and veils and watched spellbound when two little girls slightly older than ourselves (the daughters of Mr. Chalif, director of a ballet school) put on a remarkable dance exhibition.

Our Englewood

Papi poses in the Crimean Kiosk at the 1915 Bazaar.

It was a great financial and sentimental success for which Mami received personal commendation from the empress; from that time till her death she was regarded as the leader of the "old" (pre-Revolution) Russian community in New York. Being at the Armory had also brought her into contact with the officers of the National Guard. Thus, they formed some of their most sincere and enjoyable friendships with local Americans and fell in with a highly respected, socially active military circle.

One of their happy adventures, again known to us only through scattered anecdotes, happened in 1915 when they were invited to go along on a private train with the officers and wives of the New York National Guard to attend a convention in San Francisco at the time of the Pan American Exposition. The long trip to the west coast was broken up by stopovers in places like New Orleans and Santa Fe, where of course the group was received and entertained officially. Besides the tales of those parties and the sightseeing there were reminiscences about how they whiled away the long stretches of time on the train and stories about the various personalities, male and female, who later

Princess in Paradise

became very familiar friends. In San Francisco there were balls and tours and shopping. They brought back picture books of the Neoclassic buildings at the fair, set in pools of water and gardens, and as mementos for each of us a large mounted jewel from the famous Tower of Jewels.

Col. John Byrne, our particular friend, was commander of the Ninth Coast Defense Command, and in the summer of 1916 our family accompanied them to watch the maneuvers on Fisher's Island, New York. We were small enough to see the parades from the level of the soldiers' marching legs and were terribly moved by the sight of row on row of those handsome precisely drilled young men in khaki passing in front of us, with flags and bands and shouted commands. The special feature of this encampment was the demonstration of the coast artillery's sensational new nine-inch "disappearing guns." From a high point we overlooked a row of circular concrete emplacements, buzzing with activity, and when the guns were about to be fired they did actually rise up twelve feet or more, fire over the wall out to the sea, and then slowly lowered themselves again to their carriages.

To us it was thrilling, although we did not realize what a privilege it was to be able to watch all the activities and just to be in the midst of so many uniformed men. Colonel Byrne became a patron to us children, or rather he adopted us as sort of mascots of his regiment. He called us his "little regiment" and taught us the basic military drills and commands. Since we three were always dressed alike, it amused guests as well as our parents to see us lined up; and then the colonel, with complete dignity and snappy voice, would put us through our paces: "Column forward march. Attention! Company salute! Right face; left face; about-face; parade dress. Company dismissed!" It was interrupted all too often by the confusion of Emile turning left when he should have turned right, or someone being rebuked for a sloppy salute. We took it very seriously and were most proud when Colonel Byrne presented each of us with a regular official printed award, signed by him and inscribed with our names and stating our rank: I became captain, Thaïs first lieutenant, and Emile second lieutenant. After several years, as we grew longer-legged and more self-conscious, and as Papi took over the drilling and used it just to show off *his* discipline, it lost its fun and became another source of our rebellion. Every evening just when Papi's car was expected to come up the driveway toward the house we had to scurry to line up on the front

Our Englewood

Anna Pavlova and Paul Troubetzkoy, from a photo in the family archives taken by J. R. Reid in 1915.

porch and salute as he approached: "Good evening, Sirrr!" Later over his cocktails we would be drilled and have to give our reports of the day: "Yes, sir. No, sir."

Wartime Problems

Maj. Gen. John F. O'Ryan of New York's Twenty-seventh Division was one of our closest and dearest friends. His family lived in the country, in northern Westchester County, and seldom took part in the military and social affairs in New York City. His wife, Janet, was busy at home with three daughters and one son and frankly disapproved of his National Guard career, feeling that he could earn more money and distinction in his earlier profession as attorney. He had attained military prominence during the United States Expedition into Mexico in 1916 where he served under General Pershing. As the European war drew the United States closer and closer to involvement and the National Guard training was stepped up, he became the general in command of the New York State Guard with its Armory in New York City.

Princess in Paradise

He kept an apartment in town and, being a sociable and most charming Irishman, enjoyed the outside recreational demands of his position. He had a gift for mimicking foreign accents and could hold sway during an entire dinner party telling jokes about Irish, Scotch, or "Tschoiman" characters. Thus, when he had to polish up his French for his coming duty abroad, it was not difficult for him to put on a Parisian accent and bark out orders, acting the part of a French commander.

Long before the military draft and the entry of this country into the war, General O'Ryan had been coming to Greystone and bringing along a coterie of officers in uniform, some with attractive wives, some who were lonely and enjoyed the lively parties or the hospitality of a home. Several longtime women friends of the family brought in the shocking breath of progress. Annette MacDonald, an elegant, cosmopolitan French widow, and Bertha Spain, a sporty bachelor lady from a prominent Toronto family, both learned to drive an automobile, bobbed their hair, and were preparing to go to France to drive ambulances.

If there was any suspicion or need to observe the doings of the military personnel, it was not difficult to follow cars to Englewood. To make the trip from New York City they had to line up and wait for the Hudson River ferry and then sit on the boat for the fifteen-minute ride. On the New Jersey side a single road climbed to the top of the Palisades, and there were only two direct approaches to our house in Englewood. Greystone, that big gloomy house set alone at the top of a hill, hidden by trees and bushes, was a mysterious place in any case. With the anti-German prejudice growing more vicious, plus the suspicion that the Kluges were not American citizens, there naturally were whisperings and questionings, if not from the nearer neighbors, certainly from the tradespeople in the village who had no particular sympathy for the people in that big house. Nationalistic feelings had become intense. Chauffeurs talked, and the frequent visits of cars full of uniformed officers were easily noticed.

Many years later we learned from the then Mayor McKenna of Englewood that he knew all about us and had ordered the chief of police to keep Greystone under constant surveillance. He recalled particularly one night when a party was being held: Did we know that the house was completely surrounded, Secret Service men hidden in the bushes below the dining room windows, local guards along the road, and the chief of police on the alert at headquarters? As he said,

Our Englewood

"You may not have realized it at the time but you had every important general and staff officer in there at one time, and they all were due to be shipped overseas under secret orders within the next few days!"

There was more than one visit by the chief of police. He would come to the front door, be announced by the butler, and Papi would get up from the dinner table to greet him personally: "Oh, do come in, Chief. Won't you sit down? Can I offer you a drink?" Thus, they established an open and friendly understanding. If suspicion lessened about the family itself there were still a number of foreign help who were considered questionable.

On one such evening visit the chief of police said rather apologetically, "Mr. Kluge, I am sorry but I am required to search your place. We have a report that someone up here on the hill is sending out code messages."

"Well, please go ahead, do as you like. I have nothing to hide."

As usual, we children were shooed up to the third floor, from where we could observe any proceedings through the stair banisters.

Men did enter and spread through the house. While the family, insulted but patient, waited downstairs they poked into closets, looked out upstairs windows, checked the porches, questioned the servants in the kitchen, and finally combed through the entire basement—even going so far as to shovel around the coal in the coal cellar. Next they probed through the bushes around the house and moved over to the garage and stable. There the chauffeur had to open up his room, and the gardener, who had a separate apartment for his family, had to stand by while they searched through that. Upstairs his Hungarian wife was already in the bedroom, window open, lights on. And there she stood, with her long black hair hanging down, in the act of brushing it. The secret was discovered! Every night, outlined against the bare light bulb hanging in the center of the room, she stood in front of the open window for the ritual of brushing her hair. As her tresses waved back and forth someone at the bottom of the hill jumped to the conclusion that semaphore signals were being sent to enemy spies from that Kluge establishment.

🍃 Happier Recollections

The E. H. Kluge Weaving Company in West New York, New Jersey, which since 1900 had been manufacturing intricately woven labels,

due to its imported German looms, acquired several government contracts. Around every sailor's uniform hat there was a band of black
taffeta bearing the name of his ship in large gold letters. The production of these had to be increased and speeded up, and only one or two
factories were able to produce them. Papi had seen the designs of his
labels grow from simple ribbons with a one-color decoration into the
much more complicated ones for the exclusive stores and businesses.
Furthermore, he was an eager and knowledgeable experimenter, as
well as an enthusiastic salesman. As the U.S. Army was being developed and as the National Guard of each state was putting into
uniform its own division, he observed the traditional regimental markings among his military friends and thought that each soldier, like each
sailor, should have his own divisional identification. Some of the National Guard units already had their regional nicknames or slogans,
such as the Yankee Division, the Rainbow Division, the Keystone State
Division, but many were new and had no fixed symbol. The result was
that he designed shoulder patches or armbands for every division and
specialist corps, such as the artillery, the engineers, the medical, and
for those which had no heraldic symbol he dreamed up a new one. One
of the most ingenious of these was for New York's Twenty-seventh
Division. The letters "N.Y.D." appeared in red on a black background
in which, between the branches of the letters, were worked the seven
stars forming the constellation Orion—in honor of the commander,
General O'Ryan! He was given the army contracts, which meant a
tremendous boom in his business. At home all of us were busy learning
the names of the regiments, collecting the labels and pasting up albums, or sewing them together as pillow covers.

Our childhood visions of the war, from the snatches of stories that
we picked up, were of the life in the trenches, bombardments by the
heavy artillery and the destroyed villages, the mud through which
those Red Cross ambulances drove the wounded, and the exploits of
the new heroes in the air. We were not aware of the Revolution in
Russia nor of the cruelties of the Bolsheviks. Mami showed no visible
signs of mourning; neither did she talk openly about her worries over
her two brothers fighting with the army nor about the rest of her
relatives. Through her Russian maid, Olga, whose mother was still
with the Konshin-de Moravsky household in Moscow, she received the
last news about her ninety-three-year-old grandfather being hidden in
the attic while her aged aunts scrubbed floors and waited on commissars. She must have suffered terribly over the murders of the imperial

1917 pastel portrait by M. Ganz of Mami in kokoshnik and boyar court dress.

Princess in Paradise

family; even we were upset by their pictures, which did appear in our
papers.

In looking back at World War I, especially in light of World War II, I realize that we never did learn the intimate thoughts of our mother and father. Both were newcomers to this country, and both held fast to their ties and habits of their homelands, although from the time they first met English was the language they spoke together. Then suddenly their fatherlands faced each other as enemies. With their own patriotic feelings and highly emotional attitude of the times, they could not help being involved nor avoid the difficult situations of conflicting sympathies. Strangely enough, in World War II it was the same opposing lineup, Germans against Russians, and again the struggle between pride and sympathy for their native people. But this time they had deeply and sincerely become Americans, and their two sons were serving in the American armed forces.

Before World War I there was freedom of international travel, no passports required, and citizenship regulations had not yet been established. Then, because of the war, they had to apply for citizenship papers. After all the formalities and being installed as full-fledged United States citizens, it was with the greatest pride and emotion that they drove together down to the village of Englewood and were able to vote for the first time. One lesson they duly impressed on each of us was the privilege of belonging to this *democracy*.

When General O'Ryan returned from overseas, both young and old shared the same happiness and excitement. We all went into New York City to watch the Twenty-seventh Division's welcome-home parade up Fifth Avenue. From a balcony of the St. Regis Hotel we saw the showers of confetti, the mayor in his open car, then the general and all our officer friends riding horseback in front of the rows and rows of marching doughboys that passed for hours through the thunderous cheering of the crowds on the street. The distinction of the Twenty-seventh Division was that it had been the initial force that broke through the so-called Hindenburg line in the north of France, leading to the final victory of the Allies.

General O'Ryan was close to us for many years, and when he came to dinner we sat spellbound while listening to him telling his experiences. Our mental pictures of the war grew much more vivid. He had a close rapport with his men; knew their varied backgrounds, and could repeat any number of personal incidents, both humorous and tragic, in their regional accents. The most fascinating stories were those of the great personalities with whom he came in contact—Field Marshal Earl Haig in Britain, Marshal Foch in France, and General Pershing in the field—sometimes intimate, sometimes tense situations—and always with that delightful mimicry.

He enlivened many a party at Englewood, on the boat and at Greenwood Lake. His birthday on August 21, the same day as that of Uncle Jack Looschen, was always the occasion for the second-biggest celebration of the summer at Greenwood Lake. We observed that those two could make our severe Papi laugh at their stories and take a great deal of personal joshing and learn to laugh at himself as well. It was through them that Papi acquired the title of "Admiral" (on the boat or at the lake he always wore yachting caps), and that became the name he was called by close friends and strangers alike. If someone asked for his specific title, "Admiral of what?"—General O'Ryan explained: "Admiral of the Swiss Navy." Mami, who was Olga to very few close friends and preferred to be Mami to most people, was always "Lady Olga" to the general.

II

Family Background

*"Marina was not sure she loved him
and was reluctant to leave her
father's magnificent palace."*

Ballroom in the "Palazzo Konshin," Moscow, 1907.

4

The "Gebrüder Kluge"

 HE E. H. KLUGE WEAVING Company, founded by Emile in New York in 1902, prospered for twenty-seven years, growing in international reputation, artistic quality, and modern innovations. It actually brought to the United States an unknown business and pioneered a new idea that developed right along with the general expansion of business in America during the first quarter of this century. It began with the skilled weaving of fancy ribbons and dressmaker trimmings and then introduced the woven label as a badge of quality on wearing apparel. "Be proud of your product" was the first slogan, followed by "If it's worth labeling at all it's worth labeling well," which meant advertising one's product by emphasizing the name or trademark on quantity goods such as household linens, underwear, and clothing. At first the original appeal was to the elite, with its emphasis on high quality and exclusivity, which only later was expanded to the mass market.

Throughout the history of the business, the labels did not sell themselves. It was the label manufacturer who exhibited and promoted the elaborate satin designs that only his skilled foreign craftsmen and imported looms could produce. It was he who convinced the shoe manufacturers that they could sew in a colorful and

56 durable identification. He also, as combined designer and entre-
preneur, invented the striking trademarks and symbols like the Trident
of Munsingwear or the Jantzen Diving Girl that helped sell their
products by the millions. And in America's growing business, if an idea
and design proved to be successful for one, others soon followed along.
It required persistent salesmanship to help a customer decide, or
ingenuity to figure out how to solve his problem or to develop new
ideas as to how and where more of these labels could be used.

From the beginning Emile Kluge was the personality behind all this.
His head was full of all the necessary technical and weaving knowledge,
his eyes and fingers sharp in measuring the quality of thread and color
effects. With his natural good taste, imagination, and ever widening
experience he was teaming with new ideas and new designs; and as a
salesman his exuberance, professional confidence, and worldly charm
made him unsurpassable.

Family History

As far as we know, the Kluge family can be traced back about two
hundred years to the Kingdom of Saxony in what is now East Germany. Friedrich Wilhelm Kluge (1798-1881) is the first great-great-
grandfather whose name is remembered. Born in Hohenstein, a small
village not far from Chemnitz, he married Christine Förster
(1799-1869); and their son Karl Friedrich Kluge (1828-85) later
moved to Chemnitz, apparently as an experienced weaver, a trade he
had learned in his family. Chemnitz (now Karl Marx Stadt), a city
slightly west of Dresden and forty miles southeast of Leipzig, had
become a famous textile center, especially of cotton weaving after the
Thirty Years' War. The three were important industrial cities, with
Dresden the capital of the illustrious, independent Electorate, then
Kingdom of Saxony, ruled by an ancient line of princes with their own
court, and not dissolved until 1918.

Karl Friedrich moved to Bielefeld in western Saxony, another textile center, known for silk as well as cotton manufacture, and there in
1861 he married Elisabeth Wiedemayer (1836-1904) and joined her
father's weaving business. After their six children were born, which
brings us to Emile (born 1867), they moved to Krefeld, known as the
Silk City, where Karl Friedrich ran his own weaving business. Each of
the five sons was involved as soon as he was old enough to be appren-
ticed to the trade. Emile often recalled how, since there was no central

factory, he used to accompany his father on his rounds to the homes of his weavers, where they inspected and picked up the piecework, done on handlooms set up in the family kitchen or parlor, in which the wife and all the children probably participated. The accounting, receiving, and delivering of orders was all done from their own home under the supervision of the mother.

Thus, his mother Elisabeth and each of the children took part in all aspects of the business before they settled on any one for which they showed a special talent. When power looms became common toward the end of the nineteenth century, a central factory was built in Krefeld. There they added to the already successful production of broadloom fabrics in cotton and silk, the Jacquard looms from France which enabled them to weave designs directly into the material. Soon Germany developed its own looms, which became so well known for their precision and quality that they were the ones imported for the business in the United States. The weavers likewise had such a reputation for skill and high work standards that they were needed right along with the looms.

By the time the father, Karl Friedrich, died in 1885, each one of the five boys had become involved in the family business, and the expanded factory became known as the Gebrüder Kluge, with their mother remaining as director until her death in 1904. A remarkable and important idea in the education of the sons had been to send each one to another country at an early age, to learn the language and the ways, to meet the people, and to promote their business. Adolf, the eldest, had gone to America; Albert, the next, to Berlin; Otto to Austria; and Karl to Sweden. Thus, each one either brought home a wife or stayed to establish himself in that country. Emile, the youngest, remained with the factory, and since the family was still connected with Chemnitz, he was called to complete his military service for the king of Saxony.

Thus it was that the tall blond, blue-eyed, powerfully built, though somewhat gangling youth of eighteen was chosen for the elite corps, the personal Body Guard of the beloved King Karl August. He sought out only the tallest young men, all over six feet, then outfitted them with spectacular uniforms—red jacket, sleek white pants, knee-high shiny patent-leather boots, and a tremendous shako topped by waving cockfeathers.

For an eighteen-year-old youth life at the court of the king of Saxony was indeed an eye-opening experience, with an elaborate social life and all the prestige and privileges customarily granted to handsome young officers. They also received athletic training in riding, hunting, and other sports; polishing of manners and social graces; and they had access to all the music, opera, theater, and balls, both ceremonial and private. The king himself provided an unusual aspect of education in that he was democratic, down to earth, and sometimes shockingly human. Countless stories are told of how he was personally interested in the "common people," how he listened to their petitions, even spoke in the broad Saxon dialect, and in what astonishing situations he would turn up, as he loved to wander incognito in the parks or markets, often sitting down beside a stranger and starting a personal conversation before revealing himself. The whole attitude in the court, though formal and elaborate in dress, was friendly and relaxed.

❧ Emile in America

It was in September 1887, just after his twentieth birthday, that Emile landed in New York City to make his way in the United States. It was a momentous event, which in later years he loved to celebrate, and the beginning of an independent career. It was this experience through which he grew, prospered financially, and also developed into the unique character of his later life. Not only was he impressed by the adventure of being in a strange new world with endless possibilities —new needs and new customers—but he was well fortified with a substantial letter of credit and introductions to top social and banking personalities, so that his position was established from the very beginning.

He was not to be under brother Adolf's wing, who had started a small factory in downtown New York, but who still had his best work done back in Krefeld. Emile was to work independently and travel far and wide around the United States to enlist more business for the Gebrüder Kluge. What he was selling was first the fancy Jacquard designed ornamental silk ribbons, then he developed a new "French style" Christmas ribbon in red or green silk with a holly-leaf pattern woven in. But the tall stories that Emile used to tell for many years were not so much about business as about travels and finances.

One tries to recapture a picture of life in the United States in the 1880s and 1890s—the aspect of various cities, the mode of travel, the customs of business and social life. Many were the stories we heard, and Papi used to hold audiences spellbound with his vivid descriptions of places and exciting situations. By the time we were old enough to listen we, like most children, used to groan and close our ears when we heard the beginning: "Forty years ago when I was in St. Louis, . . ." Probably outsiders remember better than we. His imagination and storytelling ability were fantastic, and of course as teenagers we began to suspect that much could be pure fabrication. As tiny tots we did listen wide-eyed to tales of how he had to face a grizzly bear in Alaska, or the dangers of boar hunting in Poland, bandits holding up his train in the West, the Charros and bullfights in Mexico. And always coupled with his tall tales of the wild America were those we liked to hear best, the fantastic descriptions of old Russia, the beautiful ladies and elegant living, adventures on riverboats, and wild gypsy parties.

Thus, for twenty years he traveled the length and breadth of the United States and Mexico, a handsome, prosperous, and charming young bachelor. While this traveling was essentially for business, his greatest pleasure was in meeting personally the heads of each firm, being entertained by them, and reciprocating in lavish fashion. He established a chain of friendships in every city with which even we of the younger generation became acquainted, and he developed his own method of personal selling that was the envy of his business rivals and successors. His remarkable memory made every city come alive; we were familiar with the names of all the "best hotels" in Chicago, Portland, San Francisco, Rochester, Havana; we could visualize the balls and events he attended such as the Veiled Prophet Ball at St. Louis, the Mardi Gras at New Orleans, or the Gasparilla Parade in Tampa; we never forgot the names of his "big-account" families and their children—the Buschs, the Jantzens, the Oehlrichs, the Hickeys—as well as the leading stores in every big city.

Travel by train across the continent before the turn of the century was an uncertain adventure in itself. Each stretch was run by a different company, so one had to change trains frequently. The purchase of tickets could be almost a black-market affair in trying to get the best bargains. One bought and pieced together long streams of elaborately printed paper on which one had to sign his name. When one could pick up a bargain of a partially used ticket with someone's signature on it, one had to practice signing that name in order to pass the ticket off under the inspection of the conductor. If he were caught, there was either a fine or he had to get off at the next stop. Then there was the matter of money—in the West only silver and gold pieces were considered good—so one traveled with his pouch of gold and a bag of silver

Family Background

coins and was either obviously weighted down with jangling pockets or forced to guard with his life the satchels and bags he toted along in great numbers. There were engine breakdowns in the mountains, holdups in the plains by bandits and Indians. Sometimes fierce weather or mechanical problems meant long layovers in small towns where gambling and gossip filled the hours.

The picture seems to be of strictly a man's world—cigar-smoking, cardplaying, mustached gentlemen in the observation car, the heavy oak and plush draped decor of the Pullman cars, where smiling porters set up tables for cards and drinks. In the restrained elegance of the gaslighted dining car one passed long hours at white-decked tables over eight-course meals, either making new friends or suspiciously avoiding the dandies who would like to inveigle one into a "game."

Jewelry was something men showed off, either decorously or crudely—diamond stick pins, gold watches on heavy chains, large flashy rings—and of course the canes, which one learned to use with a special flair. In one's luggage, one carried along the proper attire for anything that might be expected on a gentleman's visit—riding or hunting clothing, yachting flannels and hat, full-dress evening clothes; also there was a hatbox for the various hats; a case for the shoes; and bags for all the suits, shirts, and ties. Emile was a sportman, an impressive figure who could shoot as well as the best. He was at home on a horse, loved the water with the boats and yacht clubs, and was always ready to participate in any entertainment his hosts might offer.

Travel in Europe

Besides his crisscrossing the United States on trains, a great part of his traveling was by steamship to Europe, and then far and wide to all parts of the continent. The famous Atlantic crossings of those days were likewise dominated by the tastes and activities of the men; although ladies were sometimes present, they spent much of their time belowdeck, indisposed in their cabins. On board the luxuries were patterned after the fine hotels—heavy flowered carpets, velvet draperies, massive dark furniture, crystal chandeliers, brass beds, and marble-topped walnut washstands.

The social life for the fifteen days or so was opulent but decorous. One waited several days before becoming acquainted with the neighbor in the deck chair or proposing a game of cards. The important personages sat at the captain's table, and one scanned the passenger list to check on one's prominent company. Between eating and dressing one maintained a busy schedule for each day. And there was plenty of service—there was a large choice of buttons to press in one's cabin as well as in the lounges.

In Europe, Emile's travel pattern was much the same—ostensibly for business but necessarily coupled with an active social life. His brothers who lived in the various capitals had their families and their connections, and this meant a round of formal calls and festivities. Then there were the races and the perennial summer "cures" at fashionable resorts like Kreuznach, Bad Kissingen, or Baden-Baden. But Emile was the only one who traveled to Russia where he had friends in the Crimea, the Gregory Ushkovs near Yalta. They introduced him to others in Moscow, who recommended him further in St. Petersburg. Thus he was early aware of the Konshin family, who owned the largest textile factories in Russia. It was on one of those Volga riverboat trips that he met Feodor Chaliapin, a dramatic young singer of about the same age, not known abroad until 1901, as tall, vigorous, and as much of a bon vivant as Emile; they formed a lasting friendship, bound by the memories of their bachelor escapades in the operas and night spots of Russia.

Emile Meets Albert Lear

New York City was still a comparatively small, charming, and intimate town. When Emile started the first factory of his own, it was as far uptown as one could go—Fourteenth Street. The ladies swished the dust of Fifth Avenue as they walked with their long trains and enormous hats. Friends recognized each other and bowed. On Sundays the elite paraded on the avenue in their carriages, and the young men rode by on their own horses. Emile belonged to the Richmond Hunt Club on Staten Island and kept his horse there. Lunch was a long, leisurely affair with a nap in the big leather chair in one's regular spot in the exclusive Union Club. For dinner one spent the evening at Luchow's or the Brevoort or Delmonico's restaurants where the innkeeper was host and personally knew all of his guests and their tastes. If a young man went to the theater, he might send a bouquet to the leading lady and invite her out for midnight supper at the Lambs Club where the actors and actresses gathered. The Metropolitan Opera also had its stars, to whom a string of admiring men would attach themselves, who would be the focus of elaborate entertaining, as well as gossip—Nellie Melba,

Family Background

Tettrazzini, Geraldine Farrar. There was a distinct social circle—and those who were in "belonged"!

Emile's permanent home became the Holland House, a residential hotel in downtown New York, where he maintained a rather plush Edwardian apartment complete with housekeeper and to which he returned between his many travels. There he was also known as quite a lavish host and dashing man about town.

It was at the Holland House that an incident took place which led to a lifelong relationship. Downstairs in the lobby the little bellboys were always lined up, with their pillbox caps tipped jauntily, a strap under the chin, their short, tight-fitting brown jackets sparkling with brass buttons, small tray in hand, waiting to jump into service to page someone in the dining room, fetch a cigar for a gentleman, or struggle upstairs with the luggage.

Emile noticed one little fellow as particularly alert and willing. One day he asked him, "Why are you always smiling?"

"Because, sir, I notice that if I smile I get bigger tips."

"And what do you do with the tips?"

"Oh, I take them right home to my mother."

"Where do you live?"

"In Hoboken, New Jersey."

"Could I meet your mother someday?"

So it was arranged that one evening Mr. Kluge accompanied Albert home across the Hudson River on the ferry and drove up in a taxi in front of a little frame workingman's house in a rundown neighborhood. He entered the clean, modestly furnished living room with his usual cane and bowler hat in hand and was met by a tiny dignified invalid lady in an armchair and lineup of eight boys and girls standing at attention, all neatly dressed, ranging from about sixteen down to Albert, age eight, all brown-eyed and grinning with the same big open smile—a most appealing sight.

The story came out that Mrs. Lear was a widow but had valiantly kept her family together, and each one of the children went out daily on jobs and brought home their pay, caring for her, the house, and each other in a well-disciplined routine. Their brightness and cheer so impressed Mr. Kluge that at the end of his visit he asked Mrs. Lear if she would allow him to take Albert and give him an education and bring him up in the weaving trade. From then on, just before the turn of the century, Albert Lear became Emile's adjunct. He managed to go to school, to trail along on technical business and social calls, as well as

Princess in Paradise

learning to act as inspector at the factory. From an errand boy he developed into a personal valet and gentleman's secretary. When the E. H. Kluge Weaving Company was formally established in 1902, he went into the factory and learned every technical and clerical aspect of the business.

For ten years up to Emile's marriage Albert Lear was confidant, traveling companion, and domestic manager. For both it was a bit difficult to adjust to the new regime, with a lady of the house in charge, but his cheerfulness and adaptability soon established him in an invaluable and confidential position. As the factory grew and business expanded Albert grew with it. His phenomenal memory could produce verbal reports of all the technical details for every order and each of the hundreds of looms. He knew the customers personally, attended to the social ramifications of the sales end, and was office manager and troubleshooter at the same time. He went along on every trip across the United States, back and forth to Europe, and around Russia. He could take care of the tickets and baggage, pay the bills, type up the reports, and remember the formalities such as sending bouquets or candies to the ladies. He was of course in Moscow for the Moravsky wedding, which meant that he also went along on the wedding trip. It took Olga a bit by surprise always to find Albert around in their hotel rooms, to have him select the color of Emile's pajamas first, then hunt in her lingerie to find something that was trimmed with ribbons to match.

By the time of his wedding in 1909, after twenty years as a bachelor around New York City, Emile had his own apartment and his own ménage. Olga was brought to the Apthorp apartment at Broadway and Seventy-seventh Street to find it completely decorated in best Victorian tradition—gold brocade and plush in the living rooms, the bedroom with heavy red velvet portieres and a canopied bed, the wallpaper with huge red roses, full sets of the finest Dresden china and Viennese crystal—all monogrammed "E.H.K." And there presiding were Marya Coleman, the housekeeper of long standing and Albert Lear the valet-business manager. It was a man's world!

Not only Albert had joined the family; one sister after another was brought into the business after first being sent to school for secretarial or accounting training. Any of the brothers who needed a job could work in the factory or drive a truck. As they married and had children, Emile Kluge's interest and help continued. This lasted for the twenty-seven-year existence of the Kluge Weaving Company, and though Albert did not have the formal education or the polish to become top

Adolph and Karl in the office of the Artistic Weaving Co. in Pompton Lakes, 1913.

Princess in Paradise

man, he was always the indispensable second in command. Probably the most heartrending blow of the 1929 crash and financial debacle was that Albert Lear, who knew all the innermost secrets and business procedures, was the one who led the action to declare the E. H. Kluge firm bankrupt and ousted his former boss.

Albert was a factotum at Englewood as he was in New York, always dependable in arranging for the family transportation or supervising the supplies and extra help for a large party; he was a devoted friend of everyone in the family. It was he who escorted me, age eighteen, on the five-day train trip across the continent to visit the Jantzens in Portland, then continued on a long western sales trip, which included arranging ahead the dinner party I was to give at the St. Francis Hotel in San Francisco, and flowers in our cabins on the Matson liner to Honolulu.

The Label Business

The brothers Emile and Adolf carried on their branches of the label business quite independently even though they maintained close connections with the Grebrüder Kluge establishment in Krefeld. As they prospered over the years, the growing rivalry between the two increased in bitterness. They both used imported looms and brought over skilled weavers from the parent firm, but while Adolf's Artistic Weaving Company confined itself largely to the routine manufacture of cotton labels, depending on a few large and continuous runs with less emphasis on design and innovations, Emile's operation concentrated on the prestige items, largely silk labels with constantly varying designs and new uses.

There were indeed two separate factories. Adolf had started in a loft factory on West Thirty-first Street and then moved out to Pompton Lakes, New Jersey. Emile's original plant on Fourteenth Street was moved to West New York, New Jersey, so as to be handier to Passaic and Paterson, which were the centers for dyeing and spinning the silk. However, he still maintained his sales office at 33 West Thirty-fourth Street in New York.

Adolf had married Grace Mackay and they lived and raised their family in Montclair, New Jersey. There was no friendship between the sisters-in-law, perhaps a feeling of jealousy or rivalry, and the two families grew up in Englewood and Montclair as complete strangers. Of Adolf's two sons only Albert, the elder, was prepared for the family weaving business, having been sent to the Textile School of the University of Pennsylvania in Philadelphia, and he carried on the Artistic Weaving Company until his death in 1956. Willard followed his mother's inclination toward "society"; became very prosperous on Wall Street; married a lovely debutante, Alice Perry; and had two children, Willard Jr., and Nancy.

Adolf was at times unhappy about the family misunderstanding and frequently came to Englewood for extended visits, enjoying Olga's sympathy and a longed-for congenial home life. He suffered dreadfully from asthma and was ordered to go to the Southwest for the winter. It was on a Pullman near New Orleans that he died during the winter of 1921. His son Albert, who was known to all of us as "Cousin Albert," who was almost the same age as his "Aunt Olga," greatly admired her, carried on his father's business in the same rather prosaic way, not very inventive, with no special gift for salesmanship, his talents lying rather in the handling of tough labor disputes, with a down-to-earth manner of getting along with the union personnel. However, he prospered financially and by the 1920s was a fierce competitor of the business of his uncle Emile.

Emile's firm continued to expand, largely through his enthusiastic energy and perhaps domineering personality. It was his imaginative salesmanship which won and held his customers and was coupled with a feverishly searching mind. According to him, he hardly ever slept. He was constantly figuring out new ideas and techniques: What kind of a glamourous label would appeal to an Armenian rug manufacturer (Gullistan)? Why couldn't Elizabeth Arden's powder puffs carry a woven label band? How could White Satin gin be pursuaded to use something in real satin for a label on its bottles? He was also searching for the answer to their arguments of "We can't afford to take the extra time and expense to put on such a label." Besides the compatible mind of Albert Lear, he collected around him other useful talents. One was Edmund G. Stalter, a patent lawyer, who did the necessary research. Another was Mr. Jordan, a patient and amazingly inventive mechanic.

One of the most famous problems that I remember from endless discussions was that of "cutting and folding." If a firm like Lady Pepperell took not thousands but millions of tiny labels, woven in continuous ribbons, it was an expensive operation to cut them into single pieces, fold under the two raw ends, then handle the little things while operating a power sewing machine. From Emile's head came the idea of the Lily Cup dispenser; then it was up to Mr. Jordan to work it out. Finally he did, producing an experimental model, which was patented, for dispensing the individual labels. One could order his labels to come from the factory cut, the ends steam-pressed under, and in a little metal container with a mechanism and a slot at the bottom, which when attached to the sewing machine placed the label in position to be sewed into the hem. It was a triumph.

Similar thought and persuasion went into the orders of labels for rugs, shoes, hatbands, lingerie, and many other items. The variety of names was fascinating: Abercrombie & Fitch, Cannon, Munsingwear, Pendleton, North Star, Jantzen, Hudson's Bay, Jaeger, Hickey-Freeman, Hart Schaffner & Marx, Thom McAn, Knox Hats, Gossard, Kicker-Knick, DePinna, Bergdorf Goodman, Marshall Field, Jordan Marsh, Stix, Baer & Fuller. Some orders would run on automatically for years and years. Others came only through personal persuasion. When the E. H. Kluge Company went out of business and Cousin Albert expected those customers would flock over to him at Artistic, he discovered that the only way he could get them to sign up was to send Emile on a yearly sales trip across the country to talk to each old customer personally and to guarantee that the former quality would be continued.

In Germany the headquarters of the Kluge family remained in Krefeld, and though the two American firms were separated from the German by United States government order during World War I, the Gebrüder Kluge factory continued to function until its destruction in World War II. Adolf's twin sister, Hermine, married Paul Diebel, and had a son, Willi, who was killed in World War I. After the death of her husband, she held the position of respected eldest member to whom everyone had to pay the first call. The second brother, Albert, a short, rotund, bald little man (whom we all knew as "Ati") was a whiz at finances and carried on through both wars as president of Gebrüder Kluge, even though he spent most of his life in Berlin, where he had been sent in his youth and where he married his north German wife, Erna. Their son, Gert, died of polio during World War I, a terrible blow to Ati's dreams. Thus he brought up their daughter, Rita, almost as a son and business successor. She too was smart at finances and inherited the factory property at the death of her father at the end of World War II. Although Krefeld was an easy target for British and American bombing, the Kluge factory continued to function, reverting to broadloom weaving of fabrics for army uniforms. When it was finally so badly damaged that it was futile to rebuild, Rita sold off machinery, tore down what was left of the buildings, and converted the area into a parking lot, and that was the end of the Gebrüder Kluge enterprise.

As the successor of the eldest brother of the German family, Rita took her family responsibility very seriously. Although after she married she moved from Berlin to Munich, when she heard of the devastating bombings of Krefeld she managed to get right up there and inspect the family burial plot. As she herself told the story, she found a huge hole in the ground, gravestones upturned in confusion, and casket fragments and bones scattered all over. So she collected all the bones she could find in a laundry basket, ordered a new family monument with proper dates for everyone, and brought a minister to reconsecrate a common grave.

Otto, also portly with a full mustache, had been assigned to Austria, where he married Paula, a beautiful, blonde, gracious Viennese lady, the one closest in sympathy and tastes to Olga, after she was introduced from Russia. Otto had twinkling eyes and a light sense of humor and enjoyed the pleasant things of life more than business. He was always ready to travel, but they settled in Krefeld, where they were considered a bit snobbish because of their cultural interests. They had one daughter, Alice, and a son, Gunther, who turned out to be a ne'er-do-well until he joined the army. Years later during World War II, when news reports frequently featured the name of a Nazi general, Gunther von Kluge, Emile often wondered whether this could be that same retarded nephew, but no connection between the two was ever established.

Alice married George Pulfrich who became director or manager of the factory, still run by Ati in Berlin, and a very able, progressive, and likable man he was. Unfortunately, he died rather young, and since none of the other brothers had sons to carry on and Rita was an absentee owner, genuine family concern for the business dwindled and any income became insignificant.

Brother Karl, or Uncle Karl as we knew him, remained a bachelor but was fun loving and affectionate and kind, adored both by his peers and us young ones alike. His youthful stint had been in Sweden and the Scandinavian countries, and he had apparently extracted whatever benefits to the business he could. Thereupon he was called to America to work under Adolf. With the new Artistic Weaving factory way out in the country at Pompton Lakes, forty miles from New York, and Adolf kept busy with his family in Montclair and an office in the city, Karl was assigned to manage the Pompton business. He lived there really isolated, in a tiny company house with a German housekeeper and a big dog, the walls hung thick with trophy heads from the other brothers' hunting expeditions, which along with overflow furniture, were unwelcome in their own homes. He and Frau Weigel spoke German together; the weavers were German; and his thick accent in English never improved. For relief or for sociability he would come to stay with us in Englewood for long stretches at a time, or take his vacation with our family on the yacht in Florida. He, like Adolf, worshiped Olga and basked in her kindness and the warm family life. When he became sick Olga nursed him, and when his illness finally was diagnosed as terminal cancer, she stayed home in Englewood with him while the rest of the family went to Florida for the winter. He died in the Englewood Hospital the year that Sergey was born and that Uncle Igor and Aunt Xenia arrived in this country.

The Saga of Tante Auguste

Tante Auguste, the youngest of the seven Kluge Geschwister, lived long enough (she died at eighty-six in 1959) to survive World War II, to preside over the family, and to make a trip to the United States and for our younger generation to remember her with joy. She and her youngest brother, Emile, had gone through many escapades together and had the same penchant for fun and a devilish sense of humor. She was always pretty and sparkling, although by the time we all got reacquainted in Germany in 1922 after the first war, she had the typical portly German figure with a fascinatingly imposing bust. Nevertheless, she had a sprightly step and bustled with energy, was always ready with a sly joke, and in the jauntiest way cocked a cigarette holder between her lips at all times.

Auguste had married an elegant country gentleman, Friedrich Effertz (Uncle Fritz to us, with beautifully groomed red whiskers), whose mother was Baroness Caroline von Francken, from whom he inherited a seventeenth-century country château, Haus Ingenray, and the large estate surrounding it in Geldernland near the border of Holland not far from Krefeld. Surrounded by a moat, the white house stood at the end of an avenue of walnut trees, behind tall iron gates with a cobblestone entrance courtyard and three wings around it. The showpiece and male sanctum was the Jagdzimmer, where chandelier, chairs, and tables and all bric-a-brac were made out of deer antlers and hooves, and the walls were hung with guns and trophies. There was a dainty Rococo parlor in pinks and golds with the family paintings and portraits, and a high-ceilinged, paneled dining room with tall leaded glass windows. All the rooms were heated by fireplaces, and only in later years had the house been converted from gaslights to electricity. In fact, there was running water only in the kitchen and the single bathroom where it came through a special gas heating contraption over the one bath. All the bedrooms were decorated with handsome washstands and beautiful china bowls and water pitchers.

Life there was truly baronial. The chatelaine presided over the children and the household, which included making the butter and cheeses, preserving all foodstuffs, slaughtering the pigs, making and smoking the sausages, and feeding the retinue in the kitchen. When necessary, she rode out on her horse or in one of the carriages. Like the rest, she also rode a bicycle, and she made quite a picture with her long skirts, shapely figure, and hair piled on top of her head. The gentleman of the manor made his regular rounds to visit his tenant farmers and collect the provisions from them, such as the eggs, the fruit, or the flour from their own mill.

On Saturdays, as routine as the breadbaking in the house, Uncle Fritz dressed in his green hunting jacket and knickers, green hat with *Gemsebart*, took up his gun and went hunting for the Sunday dinner, for whatever it was to be—hare, deer, pheasant, or quail. Chickens or a suckling pig were easily enough ordered to be brought in. The three children, Julius, Margot, and Elsa, my twin cousin (born December 26, 1909), grew up amid all these traditions. Later I took part in it all for three happy months in the fall of 1922.

By the time Fritz Effertz died in 1941, the Nazi regime was in full swing and the war was going well for Germany. Margot's and Elsa's husbands and Julius were too old to serve in the army, and all the families somehow managed to hold themselves aloof from Nazi organizations. When the bombing attacks and the Allies' progress became really fearful, Tante Auguste with Margot and her four children got themselves across Germany to Elsa's estate in East Prussia, where like so many others they managed to eke out an existence. However, as the Russians began to advance victoriously everyone was more terrified of them than of the other Allies or anything else that could happen to them in that chaotic, war-devastated country. Elsa's husband found a moving van and, in near panic, loaded her and their four children, Auguste and Margot's family, a couple of household maids, with some bedding and belongings plus a precious kerosene stove, and sent them off, the women driving, to try to reach the Americans in

Princess in Paradise

southern Germany. As outsiders we forget many of the details we heard, but after the war every family told gruesome tales of their wanderings, the sights of cities flattened to rubble, their struggle to survive and stick together, of their courage and ingenuity. Elsa's van did reach an American refugee camp north of Munich, and they carried on bravely together in those wooden barracks along with thousands of others, crowded, confused, penniless, and with no home to return to.

Finally they managed to reach Haus Ingenray; it was in shambles. Its location was right in the path of the bombers to the industrial cities of the Rhineland and the passage of the Allied troops through Holland. The Nazi defenders had vandalized it first, and trenches had been dug beyond the moat and through the apple orchard. The house had been bombed to bits, but in the old kitchen they hung up what was left of the oriental rugs to keep out the weather, patched part of the roof, and kept the stove going with the scraps of wood that lay all about, and there they managed to exist.

Auguste recognized her needs and figured lots of others would be wanting the same thing, wood, for rebuilding—and she owned forest property—and people wanted to work. So she put friends and family to cutting down trees, with handsaws of course. A stone barn beside the river near the flour mill was fitted out as a sawmill, and the news went out. Soon spirits were lifted and business was booming. Life was on an even keel again—almost. The women worked at knitting and sewing items which they could barter for food. Even by bicycle the children could peddle eggs and produce in town. One of the boys became interested in breeding pigs and carried on a good business even after he was grown up.

Tante Auguste lived to enjoy her second trip to America, quite a different one from her visit to Adolf forty years before. She not only flew the Atlantic but saw more of the country than the traditional Niagara Falls. Wherever she was, whether at Olga's Russian Easter party in New York or visiting us, her young relatives, or taken out on picnics, she was sparkling, joking, smoking, and everyone was captivated. She rebuilt half of Ingenray and got the farm going well again, with her son and one grandson, Bodo, tenaciously carrying on. When she died in 1959 at the age of eighty-six, the three children inherited the estate jointly, and inevitably conflicts ensued. Finally the house was sold, the estate divided into small parcels, and like the factory in Krefeld, this last vestige of the Gebrüder Kluge tradition disappeared into limbo.

Family Background

5

The Russian Family

N MARCH 1909 when Olga Alexandrovna de Moravsky came to take up residence in New York as Mrs. Emile Henry Kluge, she was distinguished from two points of view. To Americans any Russian, and an aristocrat at that, was a decided oddity. If there were any visions of that mysterious, Oriental country beyond the sea and way beyond Europe, they were as wildly fantastic as were the visions the Russians had of that barbaric, uncivilized country of the New World. The new bride was young, blonde, beautiful, vivacious, intelligent, spoke English and four other languages as well, was elegantly dressed, and was obviously independent. She was politely not overimpressed by the affluence of her adopted homeland, and throughout all her years she always managed to impress everybody who met her with a quiet dignity, serenity, and poise in the face of any situation. Her sometimes reserved interest covered a deep and sincere sympathy.

Her other distinction was that she was a quite special addition to the then Russian colony in the United States, as centered around the Russian Orthodox Church of North America. Although there had been waves of immigration from Russia and other Slavic countries since the nineteenth century, these had been from the poor working classes flowing into the heavy industrial sections of the country where, like other ethnic groups, they remained congregated together, continuing to employ their own language and customs. An amazing string of typically ornate Russian churches can still be found carrying on in such centers as Scranton, Hartford, Chicago, Cleveland, Minneapolis, Dubuque, and San Francisco, founded in the early 1900s. In New York the Russian Cathedral, supported by the Imperial Crown of Russia, was also a beautiful building in traditional Russian style with its five cupolas, on East Ninety-seventh Street, the seat not only of an arch-bishop but also of the patriarch of North America—at that time, Patriarch Tikhon.

The congregation was a large one, also made up of the immigrants from about the last twenty years, similarly huddled around one neigh-borhood, with their own doctors, stores, and social activities. Their children of course continued to speak Russian at home, and the educa-tion in the church was carried on in Russian. Of the intelligentsia or the aristocracy there were very few, the Russian ambassador, Bakhmetieff, and his wife being the center of such a group. It was he who appointed Mrs. Kluge in April 1915, to organize a large Russian War Relief Bazaar to be held at the Seventy-first Regiment Armory on Park Avenue and Thirty-fourth Street in New York.

Thus, when Olga Alexandrovna came to this church, she was wel-comed not only with open arms but with deep bows and great respect, as a much-needed leader. She could always count on being let in by a small side door when the floor of the main church was solidly packed for a service and ushered into a private chapel to one side of the altar, or up to the choir balcony where one could literally breathe and even have a chair if needed. After mass she would be escorted by an atten-dant monk to the adjoining residence of Archbishop Platon (who became my godfather) where, after paying her respects, she would be invited to sit next to him for a simple glass of tea or for a special repast, as the case might be, and always to be asked respectfully for her opinions—or her help. Along with her education, her international experience, and her comfortable social position, she naturally took upon herself the inherited traditions of responsibility and caring for others around her.

Thus, her position as one of the early leaders of the single Russian Orthodox Church in New York City and the only link between this cathedral and the state-supported church in the mother country was established long before the great influx of émigrés from the Bolshevik Revolution during the 1920s. After that several other Orthodox churches sprang up, causing emotional divisions and endless political complications. The original cathedral building was seized by the

Family Background

Communist government and closed. The Episcopal Church of the United States with the personal intervention of Bishop Manning, came to the aid of the cathedral congregation and donated to them an abandoned church downtown on Houston Street. The old settlers, their ranks now enlarged by the flood of refugees from the Russian upheaval, continued to support the original Archbishop Platon and this new cathedral (now with no government aid from abroad). They realized the need for a little more organization and better cooperation along American lines, but it was still Olga Alexandrovna to whom they looked for direction and advice.

The Moravsky Ancestors

Olga's youth in Russia and the involved background of the two sides of her Russian family were things she would talk about reticently. Few friends were genuinely understanding enough to be admitted to this part of her life, but her tales as they easily tumbled out amid the family on many an occasion always fascinated us children. Our eager imaginations, coupled with the photographs she had to show and the many treasured objects daily surrounding us, conjured up vivid and indelible pictures in our minds. Unconsciously, we lived and relived those descriptions and anecdotes.

Added to all this was our father's consummate skill as a storyteller and his own admiration of Russia and all things Russian. He would regale his audiences of friends or family with tales of his travels up and down that wonderful country, so little known, so wildly imagined, so different from anything Western European, whose people although puzzling in their contrasting temperaments, he dearly loved.

As was indicated earlier, he had made yearly trips there, first in connection with his family's textile business, then for the sake of adventure and revisiting the friends he acquired. He would rattle off the tongue-twisting names of towns he knew from the Caucasus to St. Petersburg, down the Volga River, and across the central commercial belt from west to east, always remembering minute details of the railroad or other modes of transportation, the hotels where he stopped, and the amusing or hazardous episodes that caused the story to be something exceptional. Partly for his own amusement, I believe, he would have us practice strings of names—Novorossiysk, Vladikavkaz, Kranoyarsk, Kislovodsk, Erzerum, Trebizond, and Astrakhan; then Pskov, Omsk, Tomsk, Minsk, Khabarovsk, and Nizhniy-Novgorod.

Princess in Paradise

Little brother Sergey was still doing this when Wiley Post flew solo around the world in 1933.

Above all was his tremendous admiration and respect for the Russian women. He was well acquainted with Edwardian England and the formalities of its social system, had enjoyed the metropolitan whirl of New York at the turn of the century, and had lived in the midst of the German industrial bourgeoisie. However, he never ceased to extol the Russian women for their outward beauty, their inner strength, their individuality and charm. In many ways he considered them much stronger personalities than the men.

Russian fiction and drama have quite thoroughly depicted Russian country life, and it seems the predominating interest has usually been centered around the women: some are bored, some flirtatious, others naive, still others intelligent and dynamic with tremendous capabilities. Travel accounts of that period also reveal that all was not decadence, superficiality, and shallowness, as so frequently emphasized in later descriptions. Humanitarian concern played a great part and there are many instances where a desire for progress in their country, including keeping abreast of technological advances abroad, brought in new thoughts and improved working conditions which quite refute the reputation of ignorance and isolation.

In physical types they varied from the blonde, blue-eyed descendants of the Scandinavian line of Rurik in the north, to the dark-haired gypsylike characteristics of Tatar ancestry, to the small, plump Oriental types of the south, to the large segment of "Great Russian" Slavs with their characteristic broad-boned faces and fair skins. Temperaments also fluctuated from one type to another—from the energetic, business-oriented Muscovite to the slow, fateful, resigned Slavic peasant mentality, to the sensuous, self-effacing Near Eastern strains.

We ourselves were reminded of it often enough right there in the family. The "Slavic temperament" of calmness and acceptance, come what may, was one of our mother's most valuable examples to all of us, and a bulwark in many a crisis. Even in the bustling modern USSR foreigners are frustrated by the casual *zavtra!* tomorrow), the *mañana* attitude, or the soothing *podozhdite nemhozhko!* (wait a bit!). At other times, placid Olga could also turn into a dynamic spitfire, defiant to any injustice, ready to jump into a fight for a cause, and with a torrent of words defeat and confuse no matter who it was that falsely accused or assumed the mistaken side of an argument. "There's your mother's Tatar blood rising again" was the explanation.

Family Background

Descriptions of the fairy-tale life in St. Petersburg, especially centered around the Imperial Court, always held us in a spell. Both Olga and Emile had attended those big balls at the court. In the grand ballroom of the Winter Palace three thousand guests could gather in one room to dance, then be seated in another for dinner. The Russian women's boyar costume was always of brilliant colors in satin or brocade, a long straight robe with a graceful off-the-shoulder décolleté, trimmed around the hem with fur, usually sable, with long slashed sleeves over a slim white gown embroidered with gold thread and pearls. The high crownlike *kokoshniki,* also embroidered with sparkling, many-colored jewels and river pearls, held a white or silver veil to cover the hair—a vestige from the old-style Oriental concept of women hiding this object of their beauty from public view. And the jewels which adorned their décolletés, ears, and hands were truly of such dazzling splendor and variety that mere description cannot convey their brilliance. Emeralds, topazes, sapphires, and rubies came from the Ural Mountains; pearls and diamonds from the Orient—all sizes and all shapes, collected within families over hundreds of years.

Even with all this imposing display, the visitor was invariably impressed by the friendliness, the bubbling gaiety, the unaffectedness and joie de vivre of those assembled. The oldest women, seated in all their dignified elegance, seemed to be sharing an exuberance with each other and gathering about them a continuous stream of bowing callers who still enjoyed their wit or intelligence.

When one penetrated into the homes one discovered the same sincere interest in others and the most cordial hospitality to strangers. There were, in contrast to the fabled lavish life of some, those who lived in apartments, not in palaces, whose clothes came not from Paris but were made by local seamstresses, yet who were welcomed at the same big gatherings and treated by the distinguished hosts with the same genuine warmth and appreciation. They in turn would invite their rich hostesses to their modest surroundings, treat them with the same natural manners, enjoy conversation over a dignified glass of tea, or gather an interesting group for an evening of music and discussion. Of course at the opera or the ballet, the same circles would meet and mingle again, greeting each other and gathering in groups from which the animated conversations or perhaps gossip would spout endlessly like a fountain.

In the country the women seemed no less remarkable. Living on the family estates of from one hundred to one hundred thousand acres, they led a busy and active life. It fell primarily to the lady of the manor to supervise the huge household of several hundred servants, consisting of whole families, with the men working in their respective capacities, the women in the domestic domain, and the children participating early both as helpers and as playmates. There would be her own family and children in the nursery to watch over with the responsibilities for the tutors and governesses who took charge of the education. There were the linens and the food supplies to control; and in the kitchens were the duties of attending to smoking the meats, preserving fruits and vegetables, making native wines, and deciding numerous things about the vegetable and flower gardens.

Over all this, she was the independent business manager, or else engaged professional assistants. If the husband was away on military duty or not interested in farming, the lady learned about dairying and poultry, even the breeding of stock; she was overseer of the carpenter shops and the buying of new agricultural machinery; and she decided on the timber cutting—in effect, managing the income on which an entire family had to live. All this was assumed as a matter of course, done graciously without undue attention. In addition, she was expected to be mother to all, responsible for village problems, caring for the sick on her property, keeping in touch with the schools and the local church, presiding always calmly at the tea table to which her husband and children and friends could come for relaxation or to tell their troubles, and always being ready to converse with her friends and have time to receive business callers.

Some of these women turned their energies to charitable works or to education. One hears of many who started industrial or craft schools to educate the men on their estates for a trade and to teach the girls lacemaking, carpet weaving, and dressmaking. Others founded local hospitals and organized nursing schools for their young women. One such friend of the family, Mme. Jekouline, who had studied progressive education abroad, brought to Kiev the first liberal coeducational school in Russia and even won the battle to obtain government support, but more about her later.

Foreigners who had traveled widely and visited Russia, some having actually lived among these circumstances, have recorded their observations about this particular type of wealthy landowner and remarked on the considerable feminine influence. There was concern for bettering their country and an inherited sense of responsibility for helping their less fortunate fellow humans. In some cases the phlegmatic

Family Background

Russian peasant could not be brought to respond, but others reacted with appreciation and seized the opportunities to advance. There were many instances in the later, troubled times when those who had been helped refused to turn against the individuals to whom they were deeply devoted.

In any case, the women of Russia were legally independent; they could inherit in their own right; divorce was acknowledged and remarriage was permitted; they were famous for their charm and beauty and regarded with universal respect by their men, among their friends or peers and by those under their authority.

This was the character of Romadanovo, the country estate where the four de Moravsky children—Xenia, Olga, Mifody, and Igor —spent much of their childhood. They called it "Paradise on Earth" and painted such vivid pictures of it that we of the next generation felt almost as though we ourselves had been part of it.

🌿 The Konshin Ancestors

Of Olga's two family lines, both traceable back to the twelfth and thirteenth centuries, the Moravskys were the nobility and the Konshins the wealthy industrialists. Uncle Igor, being the last surviving member of that old family and the one who has remembered and studied the family genealogy, has left the clearest and only available written accounts, and these are best quoted directly. Just to recall the relationships: Igor's father was Gen. Alexander de Moravsky, and his grandfather, Kazimir Morawski, in the early nineteenth century was married to a Sofia Romadanovski, of old but impoverished aristocratic lineage. According to family legend a Romanovski, Helen or Sofia, was one of the wives of Ivan the Terrible in the sixteenth century. This family had once owned the estate known as Romadanovo, which became the beloved home of their childhood.

Igor's mother, Elizabeth Konshin, was a daughter of Nicholas Konshin, who owned the largest textile mills in Russia. When in the 1860s his wife, Olga Dobrinin, sought a country estate on which to raise their family of six children, they bought some large parcels of property near Kaluga from a branch of the Romadanovski family, who because of their hard times in the eighteenth century had been forced to subdivide their lands. It was only by coincidence years later when the daughter Elizabeth married Alexander de Moravsky that they discov-

ered him to be a descendant of that Romadanovski line—and the two
families were united.

   With reference to the family tree, Igor writes:

The MORAWSKI *(my father changed the spelling to russify the name), were originally a Pomeranian family. Of the two branches, the* DERZIKRAI *and the* NAWENG, *we are the Naweng, which in Polish means towel. The old coat of arms is a towel twisted into a rope and tied into a circle. I have checked the coat of arms, which dates from the 12th century, in the Genealogical Department of the N.Y. Public Library.*

My great-grandfather was very much involved in the Polish rebellion of 1831-32, and after it was crushed the family estates were sequestrated. His son, my grandfather Kazimir Morawski, became a schoolteacher in the town of Kametz-Podolsk. There he married Sofia Romadanovski-Alexandrovski, the daughter of a professor of Slavonic Literature at the University of Minsk, who was of old, aristocratic lineage and naturally Russian Orthodox. In accordance with the Russian laws, children of parents one of which was Orthodox, had to be baptized in the Orthodox Church. Thus my father, his brothers and sisters, were so baptized.

My father Alexander de Moravsky (1843-1912) graduated from the Konstantine Artillery School in St. Petersburg in 1864 shortly after the Polish rebellion of 1861-62 and became more Russian than the Russians. After four years of service he went to the Military Legal Academy and from then on his career was in the legal branch of the army. His last position before retirement was that of President of the Military Tribunal of the Kiev Military District.

As to the de Moravsky, *which like the* von *in German, is the attribute of nobility: In days gone by you were ennobled for services to your sovereign or your country, and since the Moravskys were ennobled in the 12th century, a fact attested by the coat of arms dating from that time, nobody knows exactly for what service they received that honor. Formerly on Russian travel passports, which were worded both in Russian and French, the diplomatic language, the* de *was used to indicate a name belonging to the nobility. Since there is no nobility in this country I officially dropped the* de *when I became an American citizen.*

The KONSHIN *family according to legend dates back to the Tatars of the 13th century. When the Golden Horde invaded Muscovy and exacted tribute from the Russian princes, a tax collector by the name of* KONSHA *liked it so well in Moscow that he remained there after the fall of the Golden Horde. The* KONSHA, *later* KONSHIN, *settled in the town of Serpoukhov, acquiring vast tracts of timberland in the provinces of Moscow and Kaluga. It was my great-grandfather, Nicholas Konshin who in the 1850's became interested in expanding the textile industry*

Family Background

and sent his two sons Nicholas (1825-1918), my grandfather, and John (d.1893) to England to study modern industrial methods. Upon their return to Serpoukhov the two took over the family business and in 1877 formally incorporated the Konshin Textile Company, which prospered and became the largest in Russia.

Already in the eighteenth century the Konshin family was known for the manufacture of burlap and burlap bags in some small sheds on their woodlands near Serpoukhov, some eighty miles southwest of Moscow. Around 1790 they began treating the flax which came from the Ukraine. Then began the spinning and weaving of linen, expanding in the early 1800s into cotton fabrics, the cotton for which could be obtained only from Egypt. After the two Konshin sons, Nicholas and John, who had been sent to England to study the industrialization of the textile industry, returned in the 1850s, they inherited the family business while still quite young, improving and enlarging it greatly, with startling financial success.

But the younger brother John was of a different temperament from that of Nicholas. They had disagreements, and he decided to withdraw from the management and live on his share of the income. He and his wife, Alexandra Ivanovna, were regarded as very miserly, claiming to deposit all their earnings in the Bank of England. With no family to spend their money on and living with hardly any outside contacts, they were considered somewhat eccentric, indulging in what seemed like crazily fantastic projects. She would go to Paris and spend thousands of rubles on the most exclusive clothes and jewelry, which would then only hang in her closets for years. Upon her death they found wardrobes full of the most handsome outfits, each one carefully assembled with furs, hats, gloves, and a pair of shoes to go with it. Late in life they were reputed to have spent 2 million rubles in remodeling the house in Moscow, enclosing with glass a large central conservatory, adding a grand ballroom in Empire style, and importing the most exquisite furnishings from France. Upon the death of the two recluses, brother Nicholas found right in the house caches of cash and government bonds and business investments that literally had to be hauled out by the cartful.

Nicholas, the elder brother (1825-1918), was married to Olga Dobrinin, herself from a family of extensive landholdings. They had six children: Nicholas, a singer (m. Emma/Irene); Alexander (d. 1919), a Dukhobor & Tolstoyan (m. Sofia Rimsky-Korsakoff); Serge; Elizabeth

Nicholas was regarded as the head of the family. As an able and energetic manager, he did much to expand the business. His great pride in his success was that he believed it was helping to develop Russia. He built acres of new buildings and improved the machinery with the safety and working conditions of his employees in mind. He was broad-minded and had a humanitarian concern for his people, convinced that education and a higher standard of living would increase their productivity. The working year was arranged seasonally so that they could maintain their farms, which had become their own after the 1861 emancipation of the serfs. They could go home for spring planting and to harvest their crops in the fall, yet be employed in the factories during the winter. He believed that in that way they would be self-sustaining in the case of any depression or other trouble. In the turbulent years of 1904-5 there were no strikes in the Konshin factories. Their sons advanced and prospered; one, for example, developed a huge sugar beet industry. At the time of the revolution when the Communists came around, the sons had no use for them and saw no reason to give up their private property. These more independent peasant workers were the kulaks, or rich peasants, who suffered just as cruelly as the landowners in defending their possessions or being mercilessly stripped of everything they owned.

The Konshin Factories

The character and extent of the Konshin operations are revealed in a 1911 pamphlet, complete with illustrations, which has been preserved among the family papers. The following statistics are quoted directly from an English translation done in 1977 at the Department of Russian Language and Literature at Dartmouth College.*

In 1877 the N. N. Konshin Textile Co. of Serpoukhov was formed. It had four factories under its control—spinning, weaving, printing and dyeing. This marks the beginning of the enterprise's rapid and notable growth. The Company continuously follows progress in the West and is always improving and expanding its factories.

---

* Ruble (1911 value) = 51.5 cents; pood = 36.07 lb. or 16.36 kg.; verst = .66 miles or 1.06 km.

Family Background

The Company presently has a basic capital of 10,000,000 rubles ($5,150,000) and operates four superb, modernly equipped factories: spinning-weaving, new-weaving, cotton printing and dyeing-finishing. The total number of laborers, not counting other employees, is approximately 14,000.

The factories have 62 steam boilers, 55 steam engines, turbogenerators, oil motors and steam pumps, totalling about 10,000 indicated horsepower. There are 115,000 spindles, 4,039 looms, 28 printers, 18 immersing machines and more than 300 various dyeing machines.

At its factories the Company works more than 280,000 Poods of Egyptian, American and Russian cotton yearly, with a worth of 4,500,000 to 5,000,000 rubles. This requires more than 300,000 Poods of varying sizes of yarn, from #2 to #120. Every year more than 2,800,000 pieces of ready goods are turned out and sold, totalling 28,000,000 rubles.

All of the factories are lit with electricity generated by four large electric stations having twelve dynamo machines producing 750 kilowatts. Attached to the factories are large, completely hygienic sleeping quarters for the laborers, a home for foreign workers, individual houses with furnished apartments for employees, a worker village with 350 separate small houses, a commissary with large up-to-date kitchens, several excellent clinics, schools, a tea room with a theater, and a park for strolling and exercise.

In addition, the factories have several branch enterprises such as foundry and brick-making factories, a metal shop, a joinery, a brushing and carriage workshop and sawmill.

In order to provide the Company with timber materials and fuel the Company owns forest areas consisting of about 14,000 Desyatins on which leveling forestry takes place. For timber and fuel transportation the Company has layed its own railroad thirty Versts in length along its own property and has, in addition, a timber wharf on the Oka River near Serpoukhov. Besides wood fuel the Company uses oil residuum in the amount of 800,000 Poods, and coal in the amount of 1,200,000 Poods. Heating costs are more than 1,000,000 rubles a year.

In its factories the Company produces a large variety of articles, from the most fabulous and stylish fabrics, cambrics and satins, which in terms of quality and elegance exceed even those made abroad, to the most ordinary coarse materials for peasant customers.

For the sale of its merchandise the Company has wholesale warehouses in Moscow, Petersburg, Kharkov, Warsaw, Odessa, Kiev, Kishinev, Baku, Riga, Rostov-on-the-Don, Kokand, Tashkent, Samarkand and operates two retail stores, one in Moscow, the other in Serpoukhov. Goods are also sold abroad. The

One of Grandfather Nicholas's great rewards came at the age of ninety-three, when confined to his townhouse in Moscow, with the Bolshevik Revolution boiling all around him, he received a delegation of Soviet commissars who came to demand the government takeover of the Konshin factories. As Igor tells it, gentle, white-whiskered Grandpapa received them standing, leaning on his cane, and listened attentively. Then he explained that he had always believed in progress and wanted whatever was best for his workers and his country, although he did not quite understand these new ideas. It would be best if they dealt directly with the people at Serpoukhov, but he wanted to warn them for their own good to be prepared in case of resistance.

At Serpoukhov the representatives of the Government of the Workers and Peasants called a meeting and read out the official decree. The reaction of their listeners was polite, puzzled, and surprising: they declared themselves perfectly satisfied with their situation as it had always been; their working conditions were nothing to complain about; and as long as "the old man" was still alive they saw no reason for the government to take over the operation of the factories. In fact, the commissars were warned that they would do best to return to Moscow before they got into serious trouble. Actually, the nationalization of the mills did not take place until some eight months after the death of Grandfather Konshin in 1918.

His two sons, Nicholas and Alexander, had already as young men had to assume their roles in the management of the business. Unfortunately, they did not have the same inherited interest in business as their father. Nicholas, the eldest, fancied himself talented enough to become an opera singer. He went to Rome to study, where he met a beautiful and quite gifted student of voice, who happened to be the daughter of an American Baptist minister from Des Moines, Iowa, Emma by name. They were married and she was christened in the Orthodox Church, receiving the name of Irene. Their first son died at the age of eight of scarlet fever, a tragic blow, and their next two sons grew up in Russia but survived to escape to the United States.

At the age of fifty Uncle Nicholas had an unhappy love affair with an eighteen-year-old girl and shot himself. A year later Aunt Irene married a young tutor of her sons and spent all of her time at their

The "Palazzo Konshin" in 1907.

country place. There she dedicated herself to improving the lot of the peasants. She ran a school where the women made laces and embroideries, and sold these in America at fantastic prices. When the peasants of the village began to prosper and the school became successful, she abruptly dropped her activity. She claimed that because it gave her so much happiness it was selfish, and therefore sinful. No accounts have turned up as to her fate during the Revolution, nor of the whereabouts of the two Konshin sons in America.

Uncle Alexander, the second son, also had a relationship with America—but of quite a different kind. He was a devoted follower of the teachings of Leo Tolstoy. He disapproved of anything to do with his father's wealth or carrying on the family business. He went to America to work as a coal miner in the Scranton Valley. Upon his mother's death he was forced to return to Russia to inherit his share of the fortune but as Igor says, "He soon found a way to get rid of his money!" He was a member of the Dukhobor sect, who were persecuted by the government because of their refusal to submit to the draft and their doctrine of "passive resistance." He went back and forth to Canada, purchasing great tracts of land in the central steppelike wheat

Princess in Paradise

country near Winnipeg and gradually helped to transport there many members of the sect. The Dukhobors are still heard from in Canada, again for their pacificism and defiance of authority. They became particularly notorious for their "nudist strikes," appearing naked at public gatherings even in midwinter. They persist in living in independent enclaves, pursuing their own peculiar life-style and resisting any attributes of modern progress.

After Uncle Alexander returned to Russia he built a small house on land belonging to his brother-in-law, Dr. Sergey Fedorov and sister Eugenia, and lived there as a simple peasant. Sofia, the daughter of General Rimsky-Korsakoff, who had been reared in luxury but was also a Tolstoyan, was left penniless when her father died and had become a schoolteacher nearby. Theirs was a childhood love, so the two idealists were married. Thereupon her tastes changed. She declared she had not become a Madame Konshin to continue living as a peasant. So Uncle Alexander had to return to his father's firm, and after Nicholas's suicide he became the head of the whole enterprise.

An even worse blow came at the beginning of the war when he found himself not only in the peaceful manufacture of cotton but also forced to turn out shells to kill his fellowmen. The bloody horrors of the Revolution and the absolute defeat of all his Tolstoyan ideals left him disillusioned and distraught. He died in Odessa in 1919. One wonders if his name is memorialized among the Dukhobors.

His other legacy was an enormous library, which he had collected in his house on the Fedorov estate, of books related to Tolstoy's ideals and the intriguing history of Russian religious dissent. He had made a particular study of the "Old Believers," a conflict which runs through the whole history of the Russian Church. As would be expected with all such "useless" treasures of the intelligentsia, his books vanished without a trace.

Palazzo Konshin

The Moscow home of the Konshin family became known as the Palazzo Konshin after the extensive reconstruction begun by John and his wife Alexandra Ivanovna in the late 1880s. The address —Kalachnyi Pereulok 12—locates it in central Moscow, in an older section known as the White City, one of the nearer concentric circles which grew outward from the Kremlin from the earliest medieval wooden town. This ring of boulevards, still defined, used to be likened

Family Background

to the St. Germain quarter of Paris. In the sixteenth century it was the district of the court artisans, and their workshops and the street names recall their trades: plothnk (carpenter), serebrianykh del master (silversmith) and kalachnyi (pastry cook), pereulok (lane). In the nineteenth century it became a favorite area where the aristocracy built their large houses. Trying to locate the area in modern Moscow proved quite impossible, even through a guide and official maps. After the bombardment and destruction of two wars—the 1917 Revolution and the later Nazi war—the city was almost entirely reduced to rubble. Those big buildings which survived, whether official bureaus or large privately owned apartments, have since been completely taken over by the government and others built up in front and around them, court after court, so that hardly any historic style is evident.

The original four-story house of wood and stucco was a typical Muscovite mansion built as a quadrangle around an open courtyard. When it was transformed into an Italianate palazzo, the plan hardly changed. A white marble Renaissance facade was superimposed, its walls rising directly from the sidewalk, and in front, in Mediterranean manner, a garden completely walled in. The central atrium became a domed glass conservatory the entire height of the house. One entered through a big gate, passing the block-long front court, green with tall trees and thick bushes, formal flowerbeds and fountains, and drove up to an arched porte-cochère. Inside, beside a welcoming Classical fountain, the marble staircase ascended one floor to the galleried foyer with its crystal chandeliers. From there through the columned entrances the series of family living rooms and parlors opened up one after another like a series of boxes. In back, around the court, were the stables, the carriage house, and other service buildings. On the ground floor of the house were the up-to-date heating establishment; the large, well-appointed and well-lighted kitchen, pantries, and storerooms; and the servants' dining room and lounge.

In the Old World tradition the "head of the family" maintained the home which was the center for all his own children and the nucleus for the ever enlarging circle of married children and relatives. As long as their father was alive his three sons and three daughters belonged to *his* household. After the death of his wife, Olga Dobrinin, in 1888, the eldest unmarried daughter presided, and she divided the duties of managing the house with her sisters.

This was exactly the situation even at the time of the Revolution in 1917-18 when, deserted by most of their help, the old aunts were still there, taking care of their ninety-three-year-old father, scrubbing floors and cooking, carrying on in whatever way they could. True to tradition, they turned the grand second-floor rooms into a hospital in which they also did whatever work fell to their lot. And at the very end, when the Revolution turned into bloody chaos, they concealed their aged father in a small attic apartment so that he would not know the worst, while they opened the ground-floor former servants' rooms to the uncouth rabble, serving them the choice wines from their cellars at the large scrubbed oak tables, and cleaning up the debris of food, smashed glassware, and furniture after them. Their father died upstairs in his house, ignorant of these tragic excesses.

Assorted members of the family passed through the house on their way to escape toward the south. Thus it was that Elizabeth de Moravsky, the mother of Olga and Igor, stopped there to bury her famous rope of 365 pearls in a bottle in the garden and to pick up the last few pieces of jewelry and small gold trinkets which would sustain her, and later Igor, during the frightful unexpected happenings that followed. Of the few faithful servants that remained, one was the mother of Olga Lopatina, Olga's personal maid who had accompanied her to America. Being safe as a "worker and peasant," she could venture onto the streets to round up meager supplies of food, and she was able to send letters, without arousing suspicion, to *her* relatives abroad. Her last news told of Grandfather Konshin's death but never mentioned the fate of the aunts.

The family living regularly at the Moscow mansion was basically large and was being increased continually by husbands, more children and cousins, not to mention the requisite nurses, governesses, and tutors to take care of them. One has no idea how many worked behind the scenes to back up all this activity. In any case, stories were told of the dining table set regularly for about twenty-four and often enlarged to twice that. Dinner, the most formal gathering, took place in the middle of the day. The picture is vivid, as so often described, of the big paneled dining room with its enormous laden table, children and governesses held at bay at one end of the room near their places, and a swirling group of tall mustached gentlemen and high-coiffeured ladies in trailing skirts, all standing and waiting. Then the door opens for the entrance of the benign, white-whiskered, very short man with a cane, who strides in while they all bow to greet him. As he is seated at the head of the table there is a general commotion as the youths rush to their seats, the family settles down according to rank, and his eldest

Family Background

Formal parlor of "Palazzo Konshin," 1907.

daughters take their places on either side of him to supervise the details.

The Russians always seemed to be eating many meals during the day, and in English tradition teatime was very important. Later in the evening there was a cold supper. One of the traditions that Olga cherished most and determinedly clung to through her years in Englewood, and finally in the New York apartment, was "midnight tea." The house on the Opera Square in Kiev or the home in Moscow were the dropping-in places late in the evenings after the performances at the opera or theater, or for the young people after their visits to their "intellectual" salons. The upstairs parlor lights twinkled across the snow, and friends knew they were always welcome. The doorman would take their big fur coats and gather them in a room where a stove was kept going especially so that they would be warm when their owners put them on again to venture out into the cold.

Upstairs the long tea table was set. At one end the lady of the house, usually Elizabeth, sat presiding. The samovar steamed away and the

Princess in Paradise

tea glasses sparkled; a beautiful china bowl was part of the setting, into which one poured off any cold tea remaining in a glass before refilling. Across her lap the hostess had a fine linen towel trimmed with lace and embroidery. As guests and family came by to warm themselves and pay their respects, to stand around over the sweets or sit in small groups, of course the conversation sparkled, from the erudite critique of the music to the small family gossip to the latest political news—men and women, young and old participating animatedly with never a care for the late hour.

It is not surprising to hear how out of these groups of acquaintances bonds were formed that later in times of trouble tied them strongly together almost as a family. In Russian fiction one finds it, and in Igor's memoirs it so often occurs: the reunion in some later crisis of plump Countess So-and-So who had in her salon befriended an odd-looking young student with radical opinions; a noble old general whose son, through a distant acquaintance, came to the rescue; or a harried nurse in a front-line hospital recognized as the onetime pigtailed youngster who had accompanied her parents.

Romadanovo

The mansion in Moscow was the family headquarters for life in the city, the setting for the more formal social life of the winter season. Romadanovo, the estate to which they moved for the summers, provided the idyllic atmosphere that children recall of their youth in the country. Grandfather Konshin and his wife, having six children of their own plus numerous nieces and nephews with their progeny, had the feeling inherent in most Russians that the country was the only place to spend the summer, and he created for them all the ideal vacation spot. In the 1860s he bought extensive property from a branch of the Romadanovski family and the estate known as Romadanovo.

It was located some hundred miles south of Moscow on the river Oka, directly across from the old city of Kaluga. The District of Kaluga was rich in history, having been the southern frontier of the original Grand Duchy of Moscow. In the fifteenth century the Russians turned back the Golden Horde of the Tatars in a battle about fifteen miles north of Romadanovo, where the Ugra River meets the Oka. In the sixteenth century the band of Poles supporting Dmitri, the impostor posing as the youngest son of Ivan the Terrible, under the leadership

Family Background

"Romadanovo," the Konshin summer home on the River Oka, ca. 1890.

of the feudal Lord Mnishchek (whose daughter Marina was to become the pretender's bride), was massacred at Kaluga. It was at Maloyarslavets, just thirty miles to the north, where in 1812 the battle was fought that forced Napoleon to retreat along the devastated road to Smolensk instead of going south along the Kaluga Road as he had planned. Serpoukhov, with the Konshin Textile Mills, lay some fifty miles to the northeast on the way toward Moscow. Almost directly east one finds the town of Tula, famous for several hundred years for its copper and brass manufacturing, from which come most of the traditional old samovars. And between Kaluga and Tula lay Yasnaya Polyana, the estate and home of Count Leo Tolstoy. His vivid descriptions in *War and Peace* of the golden meadows and patches of dark forests, as well as the life on these estates, parallel almost exactly the stories that we heard of Romadanovo.

There being no house on the place, the Konshins built a new home. Contrary to the prevailing style on other estates where the neighbors were building white Classic Revival mansions of stone and stucco, they built theirs on the principles of the traditional wooden structures of the churches and peasant houses of northern and central Russia. The walls were made of logs, cut in half, the round side out, the flat surfaces forming the inner walls, notched at the ends so as to hold together without the use of nails, and those ends were mostly decorated with carvings. The spaces between the logs were customarily stuffed with hemp, but at Romadanovo they used varicolored raw silk. The house was star-shaped, surmounted by a wooden tower from which flew the grandfather's flag when he was in residence, and surrounded by open wooden porches. The supports and eaves of these porches were decorated with intricately carved lacelike wood, and from their high ceilings hung huge embroidered linen curtains, which were drawn together against the weather and insects. The house boasted the distinction of having sixty-two rooms, sixty-two exterior corners, and from the tower supposedly a sixty-two-kilometer view.

In the very center of the house, with the other rooms grouped along galleries around it, was the ballroom, three stories high, lighted by skylights in the roof around the tower. It was so large that it was used as an indoor tennis court; and, according to the children, many was the time when a tennis ball went through a skylight and broke a pane of glass. Then if rain came before it could be repaired there was a great scurrying to put pails and pots under the drips and to keep the floor dry. When it came time for the ballroom floor to be waxed, the children would gather to watch the ceremony in fascination. A whole crew of young peasant girls in their brightly embroidered skirts and floating hair ribbons would come in with special heavy felt slippers on their feet. Holding on to each other's shoulders in dance formation, they shuffled around to polish the floor, swinging rhythmically and gaily singing their tempos.

The house was surrounded by more than a thousand acres of woodland, orchards, and park. Its placement at the center of a hill afforded views in nearly every direction. On either side of the main avenue of approach were the so-called English Gardens. Their formally laid out flowerbeds and beautiful sweep of lawns with very few trees opened up a vista to the east down to the river. Across the river the hill town of Kaluga could be seen with the towers of its forty-two churches, the governor's palace surrounded by the public park, an ancient aqueduct, and the old stone bridge.

On the other three sides the house was enclosed by the beautifully kept park with its enormous old trees. Toward the north it sloped in terraces down to the river, where just around a bend were located the bathinghouses and the boat landing. The vista to the south was

Family Background

through a long *allée* of linden trees down to a tall wrought-iron gate in the wall which separated the estate from its village. Beyond were clustered the wooden *izbas*, the homes of the peasants who worked on the estate, and the school and the hospital maintained for them, dominated by the golden cupolas of the little private chapel. Down this avenue each Sunday morning marched a long procession from the main house, the grown-ups walking in their finery with hats and parasols, a large group of somewhat unwilling children of various ages and sizes with their Fräuleins bringing up the rear. The west side of the house was ringed by a screen of tremendous lilac bushes, behind which were hidden the stables, carriage house, service buildings, and the kitchen gardens.

The nostalgia and romance evoked by the description of these lilac bushes were infectious. From Olga's vivid stories and Igor's descriptions we could almost see them—"much taller than a person on horseback," Igor wrote, and in all colors from deepest purples to white—and the fragrance! In the spring it weighed down the air, and at night the perfume was wafted in through the bedroom windows! You could see them outside your windows, luminous in the moonlight. And then came the nightingales. Nobody who has not heard it can imagine what a nightingale's song is like. You heard them in the lilac bushes just outside your house; you walked through the park and listened to them far off in the distance; or you sat on the cool verandas and dreamed away under their spell!" After the lilac season the whole area turned brilliant and fragrant with the acacia blossoms.

To the west beyond the house, gardens and orchards lay the "park," really the cultivated woodland with its bridle paths and arched *allées*. It became wilder and wilder as it stretched away seemingly endlessly into the dark, dark forest of song and legend.

Summer Pastimes

From June to September there was a constant coming and going of families, guests, children, governesses and tutors, and the daily routine was maintained as set by the grandmother long before any of Olga's and Igor's generation could remember. Dinner at half past one was the only time of the day when everyone gathered together, and, as Igor said, "the table seemed small if there were less than forty people seated at it." Breakfast was served from eight-thirty till noon, afternoon tea from five to seven, and a buffet supper from eight-thirty to midnight.

Princess in Paradise

Children and tutors had to carry on some semblance of education, whether it was regular morning classes, a nature walk or French conversation over meals, in addition to practicing at the piano or voice.

Pleasurable pastimes were many, the only complication being accommodation to the varied wishes of all the guests—horseback riding, taking a drive in a carriage, tennis playing, swimming, or boating; and in the evening it was music, amateur theatricals, or charades with costumes, reading aloud, or walking in the moonlight. For the younger generation a tremendous feeling of independence came with the acquisition of bicycles, since they no longer had to defer to their elders for want of a horse or a boat. They could ride off on their own adventures, away from the watchful eyes of parents and tutors.

Some of this thrill came from the bad condition of the roads; some came from scaring the horses of the peasants, both unaccustomed to the sight of these new vehicles, causing the horses to shy and rear and frequently to upset their loaded carts. Igor, who had acquired a pair of large yellow automobile goggles, took particular pleasure in tearing down the roads in a cloud of dust with appropriate yells, throwing the peasant girls into such a panic one would think that Satan himself had appeared.

Igor also vividly recalls learning to swim. Established firmly by Grandmama's tradition, although nobody quite knew why, every boy aged four or five received his first swimming instructions from "Vasily the Floor Shiner." Vasily was a big burly character whose main job was to polish the floors throughout the house. Whatever his theories, Vasily apparently succeeded with numerous cousins, as he took them one by one down to the river, though nobody ever saw him go in the water himself. However, by Vasily's method Igor learned the fastest when one day his brother Mifa took him boating and, upon reaching the middle of the river, grabbed him and threw him overboard, watching him struggle to keep afloat and make it to shore.

One of the most delightful pastimes for family and guests was a picnic. These would take place on the shore of a lake two miles long and a mile wide, situated in the middle of the woods about six miles from the house. From early morning, wagons and carts would depart in the direction of the lake. First went the cook with his staff, carrying along their kitchen utensils and pots. Later the head butler left with his crew of waiters and young girls, followed by the carts transporting folding tables and chairs, the linen cloths and napkins, the china, the glassware, the boxes of silver, and the samovars. Not the least important was "Ivan the Carpenter" with his helpers and equipment. By the same mysteriously unchanged order of things that made Vasily everyone's swimming instructor, Ivan was in charge of the fishing activities.

Around noon the guests would take their places in carriages large and small, or mount their horses, and the group would proceed to the lakeshore where dinner would be served. Usually the afternoon's principal entertainment would be fishing. With the help of Ivan's crew, individual lines were baited and tended, but the catch was safely supplemented by the large community net, expertly dragged and landed by the professionals. By evening hundreds of fish were sent in barrels filled with water back to the house where they were kept in special tanks near the kitchen. The afternoon would otherwise be passed with napping, swimming, boating, or leisurely strolling along the shore. Supper would be served around sunset on the shore of the lake. Then the homeward movement would begin, usually not as well organized as the trip out, with couples, small groups, and children each traveling at their own speeds, and choosing a variety of routes back to the big house, some arriving long after dark, which apparently posed a mystery to the observant youth.

Though the ladies of the family would take their daily rides through the park along the cool quiet bridle paths, in their graceful sidesaddle habits on their dignified horses, the men and young people could indulge in hunting parties. These spirited affairs meant daylong galloping over the golden meadows and rolling hills, jumping hedges and ditches, perhaps purposefully chasing a fox or rabbit or deer, but also for the sheer joy of the great expanse and the excitement of competition between horses and their riders. The dinner stop would be prearranged at some hunting lodge off in the woods, or it might be another one of those beautifully prepared picnics awaiting the group beside a lake.

A good part of the summer was taken up by planned visits of friends from the city or exchanges between the friends of adjoining estates. Naturally these meant the arrival and departure of entire entourages—family, guests, attendants, children, and pets—and the need to provide an abundance of entertainment. Such visits could be for a day or several days, or stretch out into weeks. Since Yasnaya Polyana, the estate of Count Leo Tolstoy lay about forty-five miles to the west, the members of both families of all ages were on close terms and often exchanged such extended visits. When the last surviving

Princess in Paradise

daughter, Countess Alexandra Tolstoy (often assumed to be the prototype for Natasha in *War and Peace*), arrived and settled in New York, it meant to Olga the renewal of a long-past childhood association. In no time at all she was deeply involved with Countess Tolstoy's charitable activities, assisting and protecting defectors from the Soviet regime, and raising funds for what is now the Tolstoy Foundation.

Another event which took place regularly once every summer was a pilgrimage to the monastery Optina Pustyn, which was widely known and revered throughout Russia. Because it was about sixty miles from Kaluga, traveling there was quite an undertaking but was made enjoyable by the group excursion through beautiful forests. According to legend, Optina Pustyn was founded in the sixteenth century by a notorious highway robber who, after a life of amassing riches, repented and distributed all his wealth among the poor. His example led many another such brigand to follow him and turn to a life of charity. Late in the nineteenth century this rather poor establishment—with a log chapel surrounded by dilapidated huts, some built of bark, inhabited by ragged hermits—was presided over by an imposing, long-bearded monk named Ambrose. His fame as a seer or holy man had spread far and wide. Ambrose too was said to have led a profligate life and by his repentance to have influenced many a ne'er-do-well aristocrat to humble himself and serve his fellowmen.

According to some, this monastery is the prototype for the one Dostoyevsky describes in *The Brothers Karamozov* and Ambrose the figure of his *Starets Zosima*. Count Tolstoy often came from Yasnaya Polyana to visit Optina Poustyn and would disappear for long discussions with Starets Ambrose, for whom he apparently had great respect. In fact, on one of Tolstoy's periodic disappearances from home he was discovered sick and being cared for in the hermitage of the monk Ambrose.

The monastery of St. Tikhon, somewhat nearer on the east, was a different kind of attraction. In the fifteenth century the hermit Tikhon, who was canonized in the nineteenth century, took up his abode in the hollow of a huge oak tree. Flowing past and around the tree was a brook, falling into a series of rock pools, and the water from which the saint had drunk was supposed to have miraculous powers. Furthermore, folk legend had it that if one had a toothache, a bite from the bark of the tree would cure it and as the reputation of St. Tikhon spread, pilgrims both wealthy and poor made their way to the shrine, leaving lavish tributes and modest symbols of their miraculous cures.

Family Background

Consequently elaborate chapels sprang up, covering the rustic pools, and these eventually had to be separated into those for men and those for women. In all piety the faithful lined up and disappeared into the mysterious dark caverns. To the boisterous youngsters hanging around and the cynical student visitors, the challenge was to get inside and observe the proceedings. For the poor it was simple enough to dip in a crippled leg, lower an ailing child, or partially submerge a wizened granny in a sling, some undressing, others popping in and out, shaking the water off their rough burlap rags. It was much more fun to watch the dignified patricians in their summer finery, making up their minds whether to disrobe and if so, how much, the fussing and covering up by their attendants, then the emergence with their garments clinging to either bony or corpulent frames. The inside information, known of course to those impish peepers, was that the water was icy cold, never more than eight degrees centigrade, and the reactions of the dippers were something to watch.

One of the stories gleefully repeated was that of a Princess Ourousoff, wife of the governor of Kaluga, who suffered from a chronic rheumatic disease which doctors declared incurable. Being a very pious person, she decided she would be healed by a miracle and made the pilgrimage to St. Tikhon. She took a plunge in the brook, and all her sufferings were ended forever. The cold water was too much for her heart, and they pulled her out of the pool a dead woman.

Russian Wolves

The stories of the "Wolves of Russia" vary with each person's individual memories and associations, and are embellished by the poets, but in the recollection of most Russians they are as much a part of their background as the snowy landscape, the misty winter sunsets, or the ride in the troika. The most popular image that comes to mind is the traditional illustration of the folktales, even in the children's stories, of the poor little peasant cottage, the ominous dark woods in the background, a fierce grimacing wolf approaching a helpless old *babushka,* seizing her chickens or her lamb, and slinking off leaving a pool of blood behind.

Similar and quite in keeping with real life are the accounts of the little isolated and snowbound village, each house enclosed by a wooden fence, where in the depth of winter the peasants had to be on the alert

Princess in Paradise

for the prowling wolves, hungry enough to come close, slinking around whining and waiting for the chance to attack the animals.

Since Romadanovo was used only in the summer, there were no incidents of wolves to tell about, but in winter week-long hunting parties were organized for "camping" and shooting. A group would drive in their sleighs from Moscow down the Kaluga Road, accompanied by the necessary staff and equipment. One of the foresters' lodges on the estate would be opened and readied—heated by big fireplaces or charcoal braziers, food and drink ready, and the fur rugs unrolled on all the rustic "camping" beds.

To the question of whether they had actually heard wolves at night both Olga and Igor could describe their unsolicited presence in remarkable terms. It was something hypnotically terrifying to hear them howl around the lodge at night: first there would be a long wail far off, then an answering howl, then one held one's breath knowing that invariably another would be heard nearer by. It was like waiting for a thunderclap after a lightning flash. Gradually you heard them coming closer, circling around the house, first farther off then slowly nearer and nearer until they were almost under the windows. Usually the watchmen kept fires going outside, and sometimes it took shots to drive the marauders away. By dawn the chorus would die down, and they would silently disappear again into the dark forest interior.

During the day there was hunting and shooting. Some rode horseback and others used sleighs, the foresters helping by driving as much game as possible out of the woods. For adventure at night there was nothing like the moonlight sleighing parties in the troikas dashing at will across the unmarked snowfields. The sleighs were lined with bear rugs, the passengers bundled up to their noses, and cuddled close, a blanket of lynx or fox tucked around them and some heated bricks wrapped up under their feet. Two coachmen sat on the box in front, and a couple of riders on horseback with guns followed alongside to ward off any pursuing wolves. The familiar picture of the troika, the three-horse sleigh with a tall wooden yoke, usually looks as if they are all pulling in different directions. However, the largest horse—the horse in the center—is trained to trot and pulls most of the weight; the two flanking horses are supposed to gallop, their heads being reined to face outward.

Out of these winter adventures, whether sleighing for the excitement of it or the hunting by horseback, have come so many of the literary accounts with which we are now rather familiar—the mishaps and tragedies in a snowstorm, miraculous rescues and strange meetings in forlorn, unexpected little inns or churches.

❧ Autumn at Romadanovo

The summer season at Romadanovo ended officially early in September when all the uncles and aunts returned to the city, but the Moravsky children remained into November. They loved the fall there with the mists and rains, the long walks in the woods, and the anxious waiting for the first snow. They were moved down to their grandfather's apartment with rooms that could be more easily heated by the old faience corner stoves.

In another wing their aunt Eugenia also stayed on, and she particularly appealed to them. She was the last of the Konshin sisters to marry and acted as hostess at Romadanovo. She had spent several years in Paris studying painting, was very vivacious and attractive, and had the reputation of being rather bohemian. She maintained a studio in her apartment in one of the towers and hired not only young peasant girls but also young boys to pose for her—even, it was whispered, in the nude! She usually took the lead in the theatrical performances. Appearing once as Phaedras, she shocked her audience by appearing barefoot, and at some dramatic moment her Greek drapery, made of sheets, parted to reveal only a bathing suit underneath. Her most daring escapade was when she returned from Paris with a bicycle and appeared to ride it in her newest fashionable sports costume —bloomers!—shamefully exposing her ankles and legs. At the age of thirty-two she married Dr. Sergey Fedorov, professor at the Academy of Medicine and one of the leading surgeons in Europe. He later became the private physician and intimate friend to the family of the tsar.

By tradition, the end of the season also meant a local holiday when the grounds of the estate were thrown open to the people of Kaluga and the surrounding countryside. Hundreds of townsfolk would come with their families, bringing their picnic baskets, to stroll through the park and the gardens, admiring its beauty and picking the remaining flowers and produce. At nightfall the big gates would be closed, not to be opened again until the next spring.

The relationship between the owner's family and the villagers of the

Princess in Paradise

estate was always one of mutual devotion, Grandfather Konshin having a truly patriarchal concern and interest in their welfare. The peasants were on the whole quite well-to-do, owning their houses, land, and stock, and raising their own crops. They had a ready market for their dairy products and vegetables in Kaluga. In the winter months they were employed in the family textile factories at Serpoukhov.

The feast of the Holy Virgin, the patron saint of the local church, which fell on September 8, was also the great general wedding day. The church was decorated with autumn flowers and sparkling with candles, with usually a dozen couples lined up before the priest who performed the wedding ceremonies in rapid succession one after the other. Representatives of the landowner's family were expected to attend, and there would have been hurt feelings if they did not stop in to partake of the hospitality at each bride's home after the mass was over.

The young Moravskys who remained behind loved to attend in that capacity and be welcomed as adult guests. The peasants would be dressed in their most colorful clothes, the bride in a richly embroidered *sarafan*, the groom in a new silk blouse. Igor adds:

the influence of the town in those days would be noticeable in only one way. The groom always wore a new pair of shiny rubbers. It was probably the only pair of rubbers that he would buy during his lifetime, and the reason for wearing them was not to protect his boots from dirt and moisture, but simply because it was their idea of beauty. In fact if the day was rainy and dirty, the rubbers would be brought carefully wrapped up and put on only in church.

After the wedding ceremony everyone assembled in the rectory for the old Russian custom of changing the bride's hairdress. While the male guests were generously treated to vodka, the bridesmaids gathered around the bride, seated in a chair before a mirror. They had to recomb her hair from the one braid hanging down her back, the sign of an unmarried girl, to two braids wrapped around her head, the hairdress of a married woman. During this process the bride was supposed to weep, mourning the passing of her freedom, a custom dating back to the time when peasant marriages were arranged by the parents or, in the days of serfdom, by the landowner. Although the bride was happily marrying the man of her choice, the old tradition was carried on and she must pretend to be weeping. Part of the fun was

Family Background

that if she failed to show sufficient suffering, her bridesmaids would pull hard while combing her hair or the young men would step up and pinch her so that she would cry out in pain if not in grief.

Then would follow the round of calls on the families of each of the newly married couples. The members of the landlord's family would be heartily welcomed and seated in the place of honor, in the "Red Corner," traditional in all old Russian homes, where the ikons were grouped on the wall, the colored oil *lampady* hanging before them, below that a table covered with the very best embroidered linen towel, on which stood the crucifix and a vase of dried flowers. Naturally at each stop they had to accept the proffered food and drink, or at least pretend to, or it would be a terrible insult to their hosts.

One story handed down was about a young officer who was known never to take a drink, but General Moravsky saw him one evening staggering along the village street, singing loudly and obviously very drunk. The General wanted to help him and solicitously picked him up in his carriage to take him home. At that the young man straightened up, saluted, revealed no trace of alcohol on his breath and spoke in a perfectly sober manner as Igor quoted him:

It is the truth, your Excellency! I have not had a single drink. I have just been to a neighbor who had a christening in his house. Now if anyone leaves such a christening party cold sober it means that there was not enough food and drink in the house, and the host acquires the reputation of being a piker. So I rubbed my cheeks with red brick dust and pretended that I was drunk while walking through the streets, so as not to embarrass my host.

🌿 Destruction of Romadanovo

When the children returned to the city to spend the winter, there was always that dream to look forward to of the next summer at their beloved Romadanovo. But the summer of 1907 was the last anyone spent there. In the spring of 1908 while the house was being repaired the lightning rod on the top of the central tower had been removed. An unusually early thunderstorm broke out and lightning struck the house. The huge wooden structure burned down to its foundation in less than an hour, long before the firemen from the neighboring city could reach it. It was never rebuilt. Grandfather took the news rather calmly; he felt he was getting too old, and none of his children was in a position to keep up the estate.

Princess in Paradise

Typically, both Olga and her mother refused ever to revisit the place. For them mental pictures should remain unblemished, and both admitted that ever so many times in their dreams they found themselves wandering through the old home, seeing every alcove, every room, every path in the park in vivid detail.

Mami was sentimentally haunted by the idea that the same thing would be repeated in her lifetime. Actually the house in Englewood, after they had moved out in 1930, was destroyed by a fire, and Mami would never join any of us curious enough to drive out there and peek through the thick surrounding fence of bushes and trees that had grown up and concealed the ruins.

Igor did return to Romadanovo six years later. He described the sight as heartbreaking: the auxiliary buildings crumbling and overgrown, the park neglected, the orchards gone wild; nothing was left of the house but the enormous gaping concrete foundation. The fire must have been terrific. Piles of dinner plates were fused together into solid blocks of china. The spot where the ballroom had been was covered with remnants of the colored glass ceiling, melted by the intense heat into fantastic forms and shapes. He picked up one piece which looked like a flying bird with wings outspread and treasured it for many years—the only souvenir of that dream which was to all of them the nearest thing to "Paradise on Earth."

Family Background

6

Olga in Moscow and the Wedding

Y THE TIME Olga Alexandrovna was of so-called marriageable age she was no shy, provincial flower, nor the reticent, insecure second daughter in the family line. Her elder sister Xenia's elopement in the summer of 1903 at the age of sixteen left Olga a fifteen-year-old schoolgirl at home in Kiev. The parents never got over the shock and disappointment of Xenia's departure. Her father, the General, never saw her again. The mother made a few private visits to her, helped her financially in secret, and once took her along with Olga on a trip to the south of France for a summer vacation. The most constant reminder of the tragedy was the promise the mother extracted from her second daughter not to bring this heartbreak again upon the family and not to marry until she became twenty-one. Olga held to this bond faithfully, and with the same feelings years later repeated the story often enough in the hope that her own daughters would respect it in the same way.

General de Moravsky's house in Kiev was a handsome, two-story Classical mansion provided by the government, located on a parklike square opposite the City Opera House. The large garden in back was beautifully cared for summer and winter by the Southwestern Government Railroad, along with the neighboring one belonging to the president of that provincial railroad, and the other official residences around the plaza. There General de Moravsky as president of the

Military Tribunal of the District of Kiev, maintained a prominent position which combined social and official life with the intimate affairs of family and friends; and as was customary with the huge Russian families, all ages and types were constantly thrown together.

As the daughter of both a noble and a military family, Olga was automatically enrolled at birth and was entitled, even expected, to take her place at the Smolny Institute in St. Petersburg, especially since Xenia had not completed her term.

Life at the Smolny Institute

The original Smolny convent was established in the eighteenth century by Empress Elizabeth as an orphanage, for which Bartolomeo Rastrelli designed a towering central three-domed baroque cathedral (completed in 1764), surrounded by a cloister of low buildings, now restored and still standing. Later, Catherine the Great established the Smolny Institute, a seminary for daughters of the aristocracy, modeling it after Madame de Maintenon's academy at St. Cyr.

One of the delightful sidelights of Catherine's patronage of the arts developed from her personal interest in her favored pupils. She commissioned Dmitiri Levitski (1735-1822) to do a continuing series of portraits of the young ladies. They are depicted in various gentle activities, with relaxed and delicate gestures, in lacy costumes and pastel colors, in a Watteau-like atmosphere. They are immediately noticeable and refreshing in a gallery of Russian paintings amid the lineup of customary formal poses and the severe looks of official portraiture.

The name "Smolny" came from *smolny dvor,* meaning tar yard. Here on a curve of the river Neva in the time of Peter the Great tar pits were discovered and developed, tar being a very essential element in the new great shipbuilding activity. Thus, the convent building later erected there received the name Smolny, and the whole part of the city became known as the Smolinsky District.

The building of Catherine's school covered a long period. Begun by Quarenghi in 1805-6, it was not completed until 1835 by Vasili Stasov in characteristic Russian Classical style. Two wings at the ends of a long facade and a central Greek-columned portico surround a landscaped entrance court. Smolny is now a famous patriotic landmark because it was here that Lenin set up his headquarters on his return to Bolshevik

Russia, and it was in its great handsome ceremonial hall that Lenin was elected president of the Council of Commissars on November 7, 1917.

At the Smolny school the girls were subjected to a life of religious discipline, wearing a severe, almost military uniform, living in the cold Classical buildings, and receiving physical along with social training. They were required to keep up with a stiff academic program, not the least of which was fluency in foreign languages, especially French, the language of the court, although equal proficiency was expected in German and English. However, there were diversions and compensations. When the empress or other royal patrons came to visit, the food became extravagant. It was also the occasion to practice the court etiquette they were so earnestly learning.

Wearing their beautiful long gowns and *kokoshniki,* managing their trains as they walked backward and curtsied was terrifying when practiced before such august inspectors. At large functions in the Winter Palace the gay, giggling girls formed a pretty group of ladies-in-waiting standing to one side. From time to time individual ones were selected to attend some of the younger grand duchesses at special occasions, as at the christening of the baby tsarevitch, or to appear at weddings, sit in the royal opera box, or walk in public processions. Those in the finishing class of course began to take part in the glorious court balls, which meant a chance to meet the young men and look over all the handsome, dashingly uniformed officers.

When in January 1904 the war against Japan was officially declared, the country took it rather lightly, convinced that those "Oriental monkeys," as they were called, would quickly be subdued by the famous Russian Far Eastern Fleet. In that summer the birth of the little tsarevitch, heir apparent and the first son after four daughters, gave a bit of a lift to the general spirits. But by the winter of 1904-5 gloom and misgivings dampened the activities in the capital and the provinces alike. Rumors and stories of the tragic defeats reached everyone, and the wounded were pouring in, brought back on the single-track Trans-Siberian Railroad on a grueling four-thousand-mile trip. In every city palaces and public buildings were converted into hospitals or workrooms, and every lady, old and young, worker or patrician, gave of her time to nursing or rolling bandages. In the Winter Palace in St. Petersburg the ballrooms were filled with beds and the dining rooms with tables to make dressings. The empress herself and all the women of the royal family dedicated themselves to serving many wearying hours. The young girls at Smolny, also adapting promptly to the needs

Princess in Paradise

of the times, were given courses in first aid and nursing and were turned out to assume their share of the patriotic duties.

Olga was stationed in a ward, supervised by one of the grand duchesses, especially for Japanese officers who were prisoners of war. At seventeen, although she had seen something of "life on the farms" and had met foreigners in her travels abroad, this was a soul-deepening education for her that lasted throughout her life. Blood, nursing, and compassion were natural to her, but the revelation that these strange, enemy human beings suffered, were courageous, considerate, even most gentlemanly opened her mind to an understanding quite new in her restrained, aristocratic upbringing. Her nursing training always remained valuable to her, but her talent for soothing and sympathizing with any suffering creature, man or animal, was a quality that radiated from her and touched almost everybody. Later on her stories were less about the hardships and much more about "her" Japanese officers, her amazing conversations with them, and their descriptions of their homes and family life; for years she carried on a correspondence with some of them.

When the war ended disastrously in September 1905, social life remained very much restricted, and the country was plagued by anarchistic rumblings and revolutionary rumors. In Moscow the governor general, Grand Duke Serge, whose wife, Elizabeth, was the sister of the empress, had been assassinated by a bomb thrown at his carriage. At Tsarskoe-Selo a plot was uncovered to blow up the tsar and the empress in their private chapel. Stories of workers' and students' uprisings, fragmented political parties, seemed to be heard from all sections of the country and from the rest of Europe as well. Palaces, homes, and schools were closely guarded, and every trip on the railroad was clouded by fear. It was a period of national mourning, and consequently most of the court functions were canceled.

The most important historical and ceremonial event took place on May 19, 1906, the opening of the Duma by the tsar, attended by the entire imperial family and all the court dignitaries. The Duma was to be regarded as Russia's parliament, bringing hopes for reforms and more democratic rule. After this, official social life began to be revived.

For Olga in her last year at the institute it was the time for her formal presentation at court. All the girls to be graduated were to be introduced together, dressed in their full boyar regalia, the event culminating all the training they had been so rigorously pursuing. According to custom, some were chosen to remain as ladies-in-waiting,

Family Background

or any of them could be called back during their lifetime, or requested to return and serve for short periods, as Olga's mother occasionally did.

Unlike Igor, who later fitted into St. Petersburg life and adored the capital, Olga felt more at home in Moscow. She loved the older, smaller capital and did not in the least consider it provincial. It was the intimate feeling of all the families knowing each other besides enjoying the pleasures involved with her own large circle of relatives. So Grandfather Konshin gave the special "coming out" ball in Moscow, and she was launched into the happy whirl of a young debutante, a vivacious and cultivated blonde beauty. The season was filled with parties, operas, sleighing excursions, and attentive beaus and dashing officers.

✿ The Debutante

Many a time in Englewood when our mother was dressing for the opera or preparing to go to some great party, we watched the ritual in fascination and listened to the descriptions of the same excitement as it used to be. One must recall that already far ahead there had been the many fluttering sessions at the dressmaker's and arguments with Maman as to the extent of the décolletage or perhaps a more daring color. Preparations on the great day began early in the afternoon with the arrival and ministrations of the coiffeur. To fit in a leisurely hot perfumed bath meant a battle with a bevy of babbling cousins and visitors scampering through the same necessary rituals. After a long buildup with the lacing of the waist-pinching corset and the hooking of endless layers of lacy lingerie, finally came the moment when the *gown* was lowered over the carefully coiffured head and then the tieing of the ballroom slippers. The final touches came before the dressing table mirror—dipping a large marabou pouf into a crystal bowl of white powder there was a huge cloud of scented stuff dusted all over shoulders, neck, back—and maybe even some on the face if Maman was not looking; then a little spit on a finger to smooth the eyebrows, a pinch of the cheeks to make them rosy, and a grotesque biting of upper and lower lips to make them red. At last came the final inspection before the long mirror—front view, backward look, a few steps to test that everything flowed gracefully—all to the critical look of sharp-eyed maids and the "ohs" and "ahs" of a squealing circle of admiring friends or children.

As one made one's glorious departure Nikonor, the towering foot-

Princess in Paradise

man stationed near the front door who always presided over the special heated coatroom so that the wraps would be nice and warm, would pull the fur coats around the shoulders. The final touch came as one stepped into the sleigh or carriage—the coachman would slip the dainty feet into a special fur envelope on the floor. Then at last, all bundled in fur robes and head veils, with a jingle of bells, they would be off.

The routine of the balls was hardly different in Moscow from that in St. Petersburg. The nervous young arrival had to make her way up the grand staircase gracefully manipulating her skirts. Then one heard the awesome voice of the footman announcing one's name and proceeded down the formal reception line shaking all the long, white-gloved hands, knowing that amid all the chit-chat one was being inspected from head to foot. Some of the parties were preceded by a lengthy seated dinner. Most times the ball began with dancing, each young lady having her "dance card" filled out by the young men in attendance, but always the most spectacular and most informal pleasure was the sumptuous midnight supper. A huge buffet decorated with ice sculpture holding caviar or sturgeon, fresh fruit, and flowers from the Crimea piled into gorgeous epergnes and chafing dishes with hot foods and fancifully decorated cold game, fish or eel in aspic, stood in the center of the room. The young cavaliers crowded around and kept busy bringing plates to their young ladies seated decorously at the circle of small tables. It was still the time when no unmarried daughter left home alone. Always there was an accompanying chaperone—a mademoiselle, the mother, or some old aunt. She escorted the debutante to the party, who promptly vanished into the swarm of other feminine hopefuls, to be greeted by the phalanx of young men on the other side of the room, mostly officers in an array of brilliant uniforms. The dancing would progress from the dignified opening polonaise through the cotillion or the mazurkas and polkas, at which Olga excelled and which she enjoyed with unrestrained vivacity—leading up to the sentimental strains of the closing Viennese waltzes. Then the time came to end it all—farewells, kissing of hands, and hopeful promises made in the ballroom. Finally it was back to the watchful embrace of the chaperone and the lonely ride home.

For the young men the night had scarcely begun. In their carriages, with their friends and the accompanying valets, they dashed off to the various popular restaurants, names that later became famous in their refugee havens, like Sadko, Ararat, and the Yar, the largest of all.

Family Background

There began another supper and champagne flowed again, to the accompaniment of gypsy singing and Cossack dancing in dim cavelike surrounding with deep red plush walls, oriental divans, and hanging brass lamps. The genial host and the gypsy belles knew them all as old friends and welcomed them with the happy attitude that the night should know no end. Often it was dawn when the valets and coachmen collected their charges and deposited them at home. At other times the group would adjourn to their officers' quarters or the clubs where some lived. All were familiar patrons, and there were hardly any worries about when and how the carousing would end—nor about the obligations of the next day.

The Winter Social Season

Although Moscow did not abound with as many intriguing small salons as St. Petersburg, and to which Igor as a young officer had more entrée, there were regular intellectual gatherings "at home" in the evenings. Leading attractions might be professors from the university, foreign visitors or relatives from distant provinces, artists and musicians passing through on their tours. Paderewski, the world-renowned Polish pianist, was a frequent visitor who sat down and played on Grandmama's piano. There it was that Chaliapin would come at midnight after singing at the opera and relax, clowning and acting out his comic songs.

The custom of always having all ages of the extensive family gathered together for any affair under the home roof gave youngsters, students, and budding philosophers plenty of occasions to listen, observe, and try out their own skills at dialectics. Many a friendship between an older, liberal-minded titled lady and an enthusiastic promising idealist lasted even through the war years and brought about touching reunions when unfortunate circumstances had completely changed their lives. So it was at home that Olga could listen to scholars and would-be liberals meet and converse with distinguished older businessmen and develop the charm and intelligence always so much admired when she became the hostess in her new life.

The winter social season in Moscow and St. Petersburg began in November and reached its height between Christmas and Carnival, and there was a lively exchange between the two cities. We do not realize how easily whole families would take the train and move up to St. Petersburg for a special occasion, establishing themselves with

Princess in Paradise

some special ball, at the British Embassy, for instance. The annual costume ball given by Countess Shuvaloff would bring in hundreds of guests from far-off country estates. Occasionally winter hunting parties were organized at nearby estates like Romadanova, when the "rustic" forest lodges were opened up, with fires blazing in every room, meals served on oak tables, and each one sleeping rolled up in fur robes while the wolves howled outside during the night.

Even along the snow-covered streets there would be jangling reckless sleigh races as the younger men tried to show off their horses. Much more thrilling would be the moonlight excursions with troikas streaking across the vast open fields, sometimes a bit too exciting with the wolves following uncomfortably close.

Shrovetide, called *Maslenitsa* (Butter Days)—the Sunday, Monday, and Tuesday before Ash Wednesday—became particularly gay and colorful. Different from the Mediterranean fashion of celebrating in costume and disguises, it became a season of feasting and outdoor street carnivals with the Russians' typical enjoyment of their snow. Puppet theaters sprang up; peddlers and bands took up positions at every corner; and singing groups wound through the streets. Looking forward to the strict fasting of Lent, the special treat were the *bliny,* those rich pancakes dripping with butter, rolled up with caviar and sour cream, cooked outdoors on braziers or sold from covered trays by pretty beribboned young girls. They were eaten on wooden plates in the sleigh as it jingled through the streets.

With the coming of Lent most of the big social events ceased. The only fashionable events were the weekly horse shows and the indoor parades at the Armory. They could be pleasant affairs if one went with a group of friends and knowing that in every box one was sure to recognize one's usual friends and admirers. The theaters were closed the first and last weeks of Lent, but music and the opera continued in a somewhat modified schedule.

Olga's delight at attending the opera was told as vividly to us as all her other stories. As seen in many a painting, the young ladies always appeared sitting in the tier of loges in the front seats, the illumination coming softly from below. In St. Petersburg they were a bunch of schoolgirls on their best behavior, privileged once in a while to sit in the royal box or next to it. If the idea of the opera in itself did not excite them, at least the ceremony was impressive—the hushed moment when a member of the imperial family would swish through the curtains and the whole audience would stand facing the box to sing the national anthem.

In Moscow it was more the small-town gathering of all one's friends of the same social class. The young ladies sitting amid their families or with their accompanying duenna sat there as if on display. In full view of everyone in the surrounding "golden horse shoe" sat a row of bare-shouldered, high-coiffed, beautiful, straight backed demoiselles, coyly fanning themselves and trying not to look interested in the rest of the spectators. The young officers as usual had their own section in the parquet, generally several front rows of seats. One arrived in plenty of time to enjoy the entrances of others and observe who was on hand that night. Unabashedly the men would use their opera glasses, sweeping over the boxes. One can almost imagine their muttered conversations: "Ah, there is Katerina Ivanovna, looking particularly lovely and frail tonight!" "I see the General brought along that frowzy niece of his from Minsk. Probably we'll have to go calling there for tea tomorrow." "Poor Olga Alexandrovna, she's got that old battle-ax aunt of hers on her hands!" On some special occasion a young lady might arrive at her box and find a huge bouquet of flowers awaiting her. During the intermissions the small anteroom to the box would be filled with callers making their rounds—a handsome bow, a swift kiss on the hand, a whispered compliment, then on to the next. A suitor might arrive with a box of chocolates, causing a polite flurry as it was passed around. And then of course there was invariably the surrounding older generation peering through their lorgnettes, taking note of who paid more attention to whom, the deportment of the daughters of So-and-so, and passing among themselves the gossip of the moment.

🌿 The Easter Celebration

Easter, the greatest holiday of the year in Russia, meant the end of fasting and restraint, a change from the short, gray, cold winter days, and the symbolic rebirth of man and nature in anticipation of spring. Some families moved south to their places in the Crimea, warm and fragrant with flowers, with sunshine on a bright blue sea, just as we would go to Florida or the northern Europeans swarm to the Mediterranean shores. Many preferred the celebration at home with the gathering of the families and the real feelings of uplift derived from the joyous festival of the church contrasted with the bleakness outside. The fasting was taken very seriously, much more strictly than in other countries. Besides giving up meat and resorting to fish, one was forbidden any animal products such as eggs, milk, and butter, even in the cooking.

Preparations for Easter began far in advance. First there was the ritual and upheaval of spring cleaning, taken very seriously—airing out all the bedding, carpets, changing the hangings, and polishing the floors. In peasant villages on a certain Sunday the priest with acolytes made a procession from one house to another, waving the incense and sprinkling the rooms with holy water from a fresh birch branch. Weeks of slaughtering, smoking, and the making of sausages was another principal activity. Then shortly before Easter the children were responsible for dyeing the eggs, a thousand-year-old pre-Christian symbol of eternal life. The widely known painted eggs with geometric patterns were a Ukrainian specialty, done with beeswax and fine brushes to outline the colors, often with special designs handed down within a family. The usual eggs were of solid glowing colors derived from homemade vegetable dyes and occasionally painted with very simple decorations.

It was Tsar Alexander III who in 1884 commissioned his court jeweler Carl Fabergé to fabricate some special Easter trinket for his tsarina, and the first enameled and jewel-studded egg with a "surprise" inside was created. It was such a delight that every year thereafter Alexander and his son, Nicholas II, commissioned similar gifts for his wife, Alexandra, and his mother, Maria Feodorovna, as well. They became more and more ingenious; the custom even spread to the court of Edward VII, and Fabergé objects became very popular in England. Now we are fortunate to find many of these treasures appearing in our museums, far from Russia.

For other people who wanted to give something precious and permanent, one could order from a jeweler small eggs to be hung on a chain around the neck. These too could be of precious metals and enamels, studded with diamonds and colored stones, or carved out of solitary gems. Ladies would receive these from husbands, parents, cousins, or suitors, and as they gradually accumulated more the collection would be attached to single, double, or even triple chains, thus giving even more pride and pleasure in showing them all off at once. Even so, each single one later revived personal memories.

Baking the kulich, the tall, cylindrical sweet bread, rich with butter, eggs, almonds, and candied fruits, was a hazardous duty that also was undertaken early. After the yeast mixture rose overnight and was kneaded properly, then doubling in height, it was baked in a stovepipe like pan, while the cook fiercely watched over the kitchen lest a slammed door or a passing carriage cause the greatest tragedy—"killing the kulich." These towering cakes, twelve to eighteen inches high, decorated on top with a white sugar icing, would be lined up on the Easter buffet, to be sliced crosswise and accompany the paskha.

The paskha, that treat and climax of the Easter feast, anticipated all year long, was mixed three to four days in advance, because it was made of cottage cheese that had to drain under pressure. Since it contains all the rich foods forbidden during the Lenten fast, nobody could even taste it, except for a nibble by the young children who had not yet made their first communion. It is formed in a square, pyramid-shaped wooden mold that is already carved with the three-barred cross and the letters X-B for "Christ is Risen," and served on a platter surrounded with candied fruits or colored eggs.

There is a third cake, traditional for Easter but served more often during the year, the mazurka. It is flat and pie-shaped with a very rich buttery crust, and the filling is mainly almond paste with candied fruits, the top decorated with a bright fruit glaze.

For the great Saturday midnight Resurrection service these cakes, along with baskets of eggs and breads, were brought to the churches and lined up before the altar to be blessed—the priest whisking holy water up and down the rows. After church all would be taken home to grace the already laid-out and laden Easter table. The breaking of the fast began after midnight, to be continued intermittently all through the night and the whole next day. One began simply with cracking an egg against another's egg, then started with a small *zakuska* of bread and fish, saving the really opulent feast and grand reception for Sunday, continuing it all during the afternoon and evening.

At this the central feature was usually a whole roasted suckling pig, flanked by pheasant in aspic and ham baked in pastry. Of course there were also the caviars, the sausages, the herring salad, numerous breads and pâtés, and a terrine with soup or kidneys in madeira sauce, not to mention the selection of different vodkas in decanters. Plates, napkins, service kept appearing over the hours as the callers came and went. Everywhere there was the sincere great joy of greeting each other with the traditional three kisses and "Christos Voskrece!" (Christ is Risen), to which the response is "Voistinu Voskres!" (Verily He is risen).

The general atmosphere of elation began Saturday night with the

Princess in Paradise

service in church. Everyone is dressed in his or her brightest and best,
the ladies in long evening gowns and furs (no head covering being
required), and the church becomes packed while the gospels are still
being read over the central *Plashkhanitza* (the effigy of Christ in a
symbolic tomb bedecked with flowers) as they have been continuously
since it was placed there on Good Friday afternoon. The Easter service
begins when this is removed and borne into the sacristy. Precisely at
midnight, as the bells peel out, the altar doors open, and the archbishop, now in bright robes, comes out holding the triple candlestick
and censer, announcing that "Christ is Risen." Everyone turns to his
neighbor to light his taper and pass on the flame to the next, and each
kisses the other three times on the cheeks repeating the traditional
"Christos Voskrece!" and "Voistinu Voskres!"

Then the archbishop leads the procession of priests and acolytes, all
in their most gorgeous robes, carrying large ceremonial candles, banners, and holy pictures, the congregation following, with their lighted
tapers and chanting, as they walk slowly in the snow three times around
the church. This symbolizes the women coming to the tomb with spices
early on Easter morning. Returning to the main entrance, the presiding priest faces the closed doors and raps with his staff three times,
until a voice from inside answers, at which he turns to the crowd
grouped around him and intones, "He is Risen." The doors are thrown
open, the bells are rung, the choir bursts out singing, and everyone
pours back inside. Here then begins the High Easter Mass, which
continues until about four o'clock in the morning, and during which
the congregation dwindles noticeably, as many slip out toward home
with their baskets of blessed foods.

Olga Discovers New Vistas

Leading the social life of a debutante kept Olga completely occupied for a year. Presiding in the quiet elegant home of her parents in
Kiev was different from the involved activities of the prominent industrial family at the Konshin mansion in Moscow. Besides shuttling from
Moscow to St. Petersburg, one would take off as easily to visit friends in
the Crimea—for a ball at the palace at Livadia in Yalta, to luxuriate on
the lush tropical shores of the Black Sea, or perhaps take a trip to one
of the spas in the Caucasus. Olga had already taken her educational
tours through Italy and France, and once she made a visit to Poland to
see her sister, Xenia, who by this time had borne twin daughters, Irina

Family Background

and Galina, and was leading a very modest life. Usually at some time during the summer the family took up residence at resorts like Bad Kreuznach or Bad Nauheim in Germany for the sake of General de Moravsky's health. This meant taking over a villa or small hotel and transporting in a private railroad car the family members and necessary staff; plus the wardrobe baggage, special foods, and all the paraphernalia to carry on housekeeping in the accustomed style.

The last summer at Romadanovo before it burned down was filled with the usual pleasures and entertainments that had made this in everyone's eyes a heavenly vacation spot, but somehow changes were felt. There were fewer children and governesses; the cousins and friends were now adults; the topics of discussion were more serious. One heard the adolescent worries like; "What will I do with my life?" "Could I ever tolerate a job in a government office or settle down to a domestic life with wife and children?" "How can I make some significant contribution to life?—to be remembered?" "With all the secret political activity going on, there must be a way to help bring about the much-needed reforms!"

Some of those formerly carefree young men had turned into ardent suitors. At times Olga even had to listen to her parents seriously considering the proposal made formally to them asking for their daughter's hand in marriage, although it was always understood that the final decision would be hers alone.

Suddenly it struck her that she had had enough of all the frivolities and superficial activities of the past few years. At nineteen she must have a change, and the way to do it was to go abroad, away from the family for a year. She could enter a university for a term or two and make her own choice of courses. She picked the University of Lausanne in Switzerland.

Through Mme. Jekouline, their educator and advisor, it was arranged for her to live in a young girls' finishing school. Herself too old for such a traditional *pensionnat,* she was accepted in a position somewhat as teacher and chaperone. Though she tutored in French and watched deportment at meals, she had certain privileges. She could go walking alone to attend her university classes or spend unrestricted hours in the library. She could be the respected "Mademoiselle" supervising a bevy of young charges at a concert, or she could go to a theater alone. Again surprising new vistas were opened by the acquaintance with unusual friends from strange, unfamiliar backgrounds. There was one beautiful modest girl from Egypt, several stiff and strictly

proper British young ladies, and even one intriguingly boisterous and
independent girl from America.

Attentions by men students at the university were inevitable, but she appeared not to take them very seriously. Only one incident seemed to stand out in later accounts. She and a handsome middle-aged Swiss gentleman had gone for an afternoon's toboggan ride down a mountainside. Actually it was on one of those funny little wooden sleds on high runners called *Rodel* in German, which one steers with one's feet as you rush down a prepared track. There was an accident, his right ankle or foot was obviously so painfully injured that he could not walk. Olga, solicitous as usual and never one to hesitate about taking a situation into her own hands, helped to make the three miles back home with him, sometimes dragging him on the sled, sometimes practically carrying his entire weight as he limped along or hung across her shoulders. Thus her year in Switzerland ended, apparently without romance or high adventure but something she had most wished for —independence and a degree of freedom.

In the spring of 1908 Olga's brother Mifa came to escort her home. On the way they were going to visit friends of the family in the Crimea. The Crimea, the Russian "Riviera," is the peninsula nearly surrounded by the warm waters of the Black Sea, protected at the back by a wall of snow-topped mountains and the gently sloping coast fringed with lush tropical growth. From the Crimea came the famous wines, the carloads of fragrant fresh flowers, and the exotic fruits that graced every elegant table throughout Russia on special occasions.

The Crimea was preserved as an unspoiled wilderness, except for the large coastal estates of the imperial family and the aristocracy. No railroad was allowed except for a small spur line to Simferopol near Yalta. From there the only way to reach Yalta and the other coastal villages was by *paquebot* or carriage. The slopes of the mountains were covered with pines; the valleys and the cliffs edging the sea were green with orchards, vineyards, pastures, and were dotted by small villages. In the spring it became a paradise of bright-colored wildflowers, blossoming fruit trees and brilliant with acacias, lilacs, and roses. The original settlers of the Crimea were the Tatars, so most of the natives remained Moslems and the local architecture reflected their Islamic background.

The old Imperial Palace of Livadia near Yalta was a square two-story building of red limestone set amid formal Classical style gardens. In 1911 an entirely new palace was built, dramatically set atop a cliff

Family Background

The chapel at Foross, the Ushkoff's estate in the Crimea.

jutting out into the blue sea. All in white limestone and marble, the design had been carefully supervised by Empress Alexandra herself, and it became the family's favorite retreat, especially for the Easter season. The rooms of the upper floors with columned balconies looked down into cool fountained courtyards or out on views of the sea and the mountains. The state rooms on the ground floor, all in white marble, were open and airy with French doors leading out onto the terraces and gardens. At night the fragrance of the flowers filled the rooms, and during the day breezes swept through the open expanses of rooms. Against the white building the dark green planting of the garden terraces and the shade from cypresses and pines provided the family with a soothing setting and their much-longed-for private life.

The estate of Gregoriy Ushkoffs at Foross, whom Olga and Mifa were to visit, was one of those Moorish-style rambling complexes of limestone and marble, perched on a cliff with terraces leading down to the seashore. It was hidden behind tall iron gates at the end of a long, winding private driveway. The building spread out over covered terraces, arched balconies, courtyards, and pavilions—all set off by cool green planting. Hidden farther behind the gardens were the stables and the riding ring where Mr. Ushkoff exhibited his famous horses. One of the most spectacular and romantic sites of the estate was the

Princess in Paradise

family chapel, of dazzling white, with gold onion dome and minaret, perched way out on a rock silhouetted against the blue sea.

 ## The American Tourist

Olga and Mifa, after their long train trip from Switzerland, were to take the overnight boat from Odessa to Yalta, a small coastal packet-boat with lots of deck space for the transport of natives and their wares and livestock, but a very limited space for first-class cabins and dining accommodations. They boarded early, strolled the deck, and watched the loading activity. A quite noticeable array of porters was scurrying up the first-class gangway with a large assortment of baggage, obviously foreign. A brisk little man followed and payed them off, with minor arguments and difficulties over the coins. Who could that be? Olga repaired to her cabin to change for dinner. Later, strolling on the deck, holding on to Mifa's arm, they noticed a tall, handsome, smooth-shaven man, dapperly dressed in Edwardian tweeds and talking with the shorter one they had observed boarding with that excessive amount of luggage. In the small quarters of the first-class dining salon one could not avoid glancing around at the other tables and making observations about one's fellow travelers. Olga and Mifa, a handsome young couple, spoke Russian together. Those two other men were speaking English. As they passed each other later on deck, the tall one doffed his hat politely. Mifa, dressed in his military uniform, nodded. Next morning Olga had breakfast served in her cabin. Mifa returned from the dining room and reported, "That poor man, the tall one, an American for sure, could hardly speak Russian and was having a terrible time explaining that he wanted his eggs 'scrambled' instead of boiled. I managed to help him out."

When they docked at Yalta the Moravskys were finished with their papers and customs inspection in no time and went ashore to hunt for their expected carriage. Then Olga looked back on the dock and noticed the tall American again having a dreadful time with the customs inspector. Five or six different-shaped trunks were lying about open; the two Americans were arguing; and the officer was shouting in Russian as he unmercifully pulled out handfuls of neckties and waved them in the air. Then from another trunk he dumped an assortment of shoes about on the floor, with a gesture of "what's this supposed to be, anyway?" Next he unwrapped from a leather case a handsome long hunting rifle. As they watched fascinated, the customs officials in final despair pointed to an enormous opened crate from which they lifted an elaborate leather, silver-studded saddle. In pity, mixed with a good deal of curiosity of course, Olga sent Mifa back to ask if he could be of some help.

Relieved at the sight of a friendly face and a gentleman, besides one who spoke English, the American explained that he was coming for an extended trip to Russia, that all these clothes were for his own use and not intended for sale as they were accusing him, that he was going boar hunting in the Crimea, and that he was bringing gifts for his friends. Now his valet must try to find the means of getting all this baggage transported to his destination.

"Where are the gentlemen going? There is no transportation except by private carriage."

"Well, my friends the Ushkoffs had promised to call for me here."

"You are going to the Ushkoffs? What a coincidence! That is exactly where we too are going to visit. May I present myself—Lieutenant Mifody Alexandrovitch de Moravsky; and this is my sister Olga Alexandrovna."

"Your sister?! I took you for a happy young couple on your wedding trip."

So here Emile Kluge the American businessman, six thousand miles from home and Olga de Moravsky, the promised star guest of the Ushkoffs, were brought together under circumstances quite unpremeditated. And that one might say is the beginning of a whole new story.

After an all-day carriage journey along the scenic road between the mountains and the sea they arrived at Foross and the Ushkoff estate, to be greeted by the two Ushkoff daughters, nearly of Olga's age; Olga Lopatina, Olga's maid, who had already arrived from Kiev bringing Olga's southern wardrobe and was well installed; and a houseful of other guests who had come to spend the holidays. Although it was Emile's first visit to Foross, it was not his first to Russia. He had had business dealings in Moscow, where he was acquainted with the name of the Konshin Textile Industries in Serpoukhov. In St. Petersburg, through letters of introduction from his friends the Thonet family in Vienna, he had already become acquainted with their various branches around Russia. It happened that in the United States he had met Gregoriy Ushkoff who was famous for his stable of fine racing horses. Mr. Ushkoff had come to America to negotiate the purchase of a

Princess in Paradise

special stallion, and they had met at the Richmond Hunt Club on Staten Island where Emile regularly rode to the hounds. Mr. Ushkoff insisted that on his next trip to Russia he must visit them in Moscow. After that as they rode together and admired their horses, Gregory promised that he would arrange to take Emile on a boar hunt on his estate in the Crimea if he would come for the next year's Easter season. Besides, he hinted, there was a beautiful young lady he thought he must meet.

Thinking ahead of his opulent friend and trying to find a suitably impressive gift to bring along, Emile had, on his travels in Mexico, ordered a special *Charro* saddle of hand-tooled leather, decorated magnificently in silver. So now he had arrived in Yalta bringing along the saddle, hunting rifle, and trunks of clothes appropriate for all occasions, and accompanied by young Albert Lear, his valet, who was already quite experienced in his master's way of travel and all the elaborate social routine of those days.

The Courtship

The house parties were usually spread over two or three weeks, and the many activities kept the guests busy—swimming, boating, tennis playing, horseback riding, the boar hunt, and drives in the most exciting new acquisition—a "motor car." There were other young couples in the party and plenty of attentive gentlemen to enliven the days and add romance to the moonlight waltzing on the terraces. But it was with somewhat of a personal delight that the Ushkoffs noticed the budding interest between Olga and their American friend. If they went off riding alone, excuses were made. When they disappeared on an all-day picnic in the Daimler-Benz open touring car, all bundled from head to foot in dust-defying clothes and goggles, no restrictions were put on how far they could go or when they would be expected to return. On one such expedition in the mountains the car broke down, and the chauffeur was completely absorbed for most of the day with the complicated repairs. The young couple passed the time wandering off alone. The fields were full of wildflowers, and there were the rocks to climb and they could watch the transparent blue sea breaking in hidden coves on warm sandy beaches.

Olga's reminiscences were always like those of a passionately romantic schoolgirl. Emile had a sense of humor and a captivating worldly charm as he unfolded stories of his many faraway adventures.

A snapshot is still preserved of what they called their "engagement day," showing both of them standing beside the disabled car wrapped in motoring costumes and giggling somewhat guiltily.

Though it may look as if Olga had been swept off her feet and Emile recognized immediately this precious find, theirs was, as evidenced later by many years of devotion, a really deep, affectionate relationship with respect and admiration for each other's qualities. In spite of the whirlwind courtship, Olga carefully considered the situation for the next few months, remembering her promise to her family about not marrying too soon or too hastily. However, on July 24, 1908, her twentieth birthday, the Moravsky parents and household were thrown into dismayed confusion when a special messenger delivered to Olga an enormous box of long-stemmed American Beauty roses—from her American admirer.

Before the end of his trip Emile came to pay the proper calls on the family in Kiev and to speak seriously to the General about his daughter and marriage. Conferences with the mother were much more emotional; she was appalled at the thought of her last daughter marrying and going halfway across the world to live, to that barbaric new country of America, and to a man whose family background nobody knew; but at least he was older and responsible. Emile charmed her and made many promises: they were willing to wait, though Olga was now really an independent young lady, and they would plan their wedding just as the family desired it. After that he would bring their daughter to Russia for a visit every year, and Maman must surely come to see them in New York.

In later years, and especially as I recall them now, the stories of Mami's encounters with Emile always fascinated me, not only because of what she described, but because of what was left unsaid. Attractive and socially prominent as she undoubtedly was, she most certainly must have been the object of a great deal of attention from eligible young suitors. Whether she had become attracted to any of them, whether she had been in love with someone who was considered unacceptable to the family, as in the case of her sister, Xenia, we never knew. Indeed, the possibilities were there, but if there ever had been someone whom she had loved the secret remained locked forever within that enigmatic reserve which was such a beautiful and intriguing part of her Russian temperament.

For my part, this suspicion had always persisted and would surface quietly at those times when she was under particular stress, during under the financial pressures of the depression. She had never lost her physical attractiveness nor gracious charm, and the devoted attention of her many gentlemen friends, both Russian and American, sometimes brought forth a subtle sigh or sad flutter of beautiful memories. Loving her as we did, we could only imagine and sympathize with silent understanding.

Emile returned to America via Krefeld to visit his relatives and take care of business matters, then to rearrange his New York living quarters to receive a bride. The wedding was tentatively planned for the next spring in Kiev, as near to Olga's twenty-first birthday as possible.

A busy year was ahead. All the young girls in the house and the school at Romadanovo were set to work making laces, embroidering linens, sewing fine batiste lingerie, as well as stitching monograms on sheets, tablecloths, and napkins—the "O. deM. K." still to be seen on pieces of family silver and old linens. Although Emile claimed to have a fully equipped apartment after so many years of delightful bachelor life, there were still Russian treasures to be assembled to take along. Then of course there was the wardrobe—dressmaker fittings in Moscow and furs to be made up; a trip to Paris for the latest millinery creations.

In late summer she accompanied her father on his annual stay at Bad Kreuznach in the Black Forest where the General went for treatments to his paralytic leg. Though it was a subdued visit, it was Olga's last occasion to enjoy the undivided attention to her father. Soon thereafter he became seriously ill; the leg was found to be gangrenous and had to be amputated. From then on he was a complete invalid, confined to bed or his wheelchair, with an orderly in constant attendance. Incidentally, this young man, to pass the time when not reading to the general, kept busy doing cross-stitch and drawn-work embroidery, producing some beautiful linen pieces that later became family treasures.

For Eternity

It was a family decision to hold the wedding sooner than the following summer, and in Moscow rather than in Kiev. This meant that Grandfather Konshin would preside over all the formalities—the ball at his home, the church arrangements, and the nuptial dinner—with the whole family moving to the Moscow mansion.

Family Background

The date was set for January 7, Old Style Russian Calendar (January 20, New Calendar). Emile arrived at the Moravsky home in Kiev in time for the Christmas holidays. Olga met him at the station dressed in a tight-fitting sealskin jacket with leg-of-mutton sleeves, trimmed in French blue and silver, a matching muff and perky hat, over a slim skirt of the same blue, edged with black silk fringe.

The trip of five thousand miles or more in midwinter meant endless discomforts and hardships—twelve days crossing the stormy Atlantic; the long overland train ride through the snows and mountains of central Europe; and upon arriving at the Russian border the complications of transferring all one's baggage to the Russian trains, which ran on a wider rail gauge than trains of the rest of Europe, something that actually added to their luxury and comfort.

Mifa and Igor were home for the holidays and, along with numerous curious relatives, were assigned to entertain their future brother-in-law. Many were the stories of parties, gypsy restaurants, sleigh rides till dawn to test the stamina of the groom, and the formal meetings with distinguished characters who came to call. Part of the two brothers' assignment was to show the American the cultural and architectural landmarks of Kiev, famous for some of the oldest churches in Russia.

The Pecherskaya Lavra (Monastery of the Caves), dating to the eleventh century, is situated outside the city walls on a cliff overlooking the Dnieper River; under it is a labyrinth of catacombs. It began as a refuge for hermits and large groups of the Russian early Christians fleeing from persecution. They lived and died there, sometimes carving out large chapels for worship and the enshrinement of church dignitaries. Bodies of ordinary persons were simply laid on ledges or stood up against the wall in niches.

Owing to the cold, damp, unfluctuating atmospheric conditions, the bodies were preserved in a mummified state, with the skin still stretched over the heads and hands. Often the ornate garments of the clergy and the coarse rags of the poor remained intact around the bony structure.

The two brothers claimed that they knew the place well, often having explored it like other youngsters of the town, and they even knew an old secret exit, that opened directly on the riverbank. One reaches the catacombs from the monastery church at street level by descending at least one hundred sloping rock steps, then passing through a tiny door into the passageways, which branch outward and downward in a chaotic network of paths, cells, and more cells. Of

Princess in Paradise

course it is all in utter blackness. One creeps along by candlelight (only since late in the 1960s has a meager electric system been installed), with a few bare bulbs here and there.

The adventure is exciting enough and much more interesting than the catacombs of Rome, but those two boys had to make it impressive. Disappearing with their candles ahead of their nicely dressed visitor, shouting around bends in the echoing darkness, off to find the promised way out, the safest thing Emile could do was to stand still in one place. With the icy dripping walls and the chill of the damp floor, watching his candle sputter in the drafts and burn lower and lower, this was no longer much fun. If you moved to look there was sure to be a clothed mummy lying in the shadows or a skeleton frozen into the wall. Did this ordeal last for hours or was it just a few dragged-out miserable minutes? At last, perhaps their consciences hurting or perhaps really scared, the brothers reappeared with an old monk to guide them—and to confess they had found that the secret exit had long been sealed up.

At the time for the wedding approached, the whole family assembled in Moscow. Emile was established in a hotel with his valet and his older brother, Albert, who had arrived from Germany to be his best man. For the ball the night before the wedding the Konshin house was festooned with smilax, tropical flowers from the Crimea were banked in every corner, and fountains played in the hallway adjoining the ballroom. Olga wore a daringly cut new creation of gold brocade embroidered in seed pearls and rubies (her birthstone) the décolletage and train trimmed with sable, and danced away the evening in a whirl of cousins, beaus, and other admirers. But, like Cinderella, all her fun came to an end promptly at midnight. According to the strictest traditions, stemming from old peasant customs but still maintained by most families, the bride was not allowed to see her bridegroom again until they met at the church. She was led off, surrounded by young girls and female relatives, and the party went on without her.

That is, the men took the groom in hand and rounded up all their friends, to gather downtown at the famous Yar restaurant for the bachelor party. Upstairs in the private dining rooms a sumptuous supper table was laid out; there were caviars of all kinds, smoked eel in aspic, a whole sturgeon, venison, and game birds—and of course vodka and champagne. A special gypsy orchestra was there to play the wild or soulful music on the zither and violins, and Vera Smirnova, Moscow's favorite singer, to sing the gypsy songs in her deep, passionate voice. Mifa acted as master of ceremonies, leading the speeches and

Family Background

the toasts, while Gregoriy Ushkoff kept urging on the enthusiasm to an even higher pitch. Emile sat at the head of the table and for every toast made, he had to respond by tossing down his glass of vodka.

After the rounds had been completed and as the eating progressed, there followed the same ritual with the champagne. As each person came and stood before the guest of honor to make his speech the glasses were filled again and again, then to the drumming of the orchestra and the insistent clapping of hands everyone sang. "Pey do dna! Pey do dna!" (Drink it down!), as they all emptied their glasses to the last drop and tossed them over their shoulders. As this continued over the hours the speeches became vaguer and more flowery, the gypsy girls and their songs seemed more passionate, and the Cossack dancers grew more abandoned and wilder. For the young guests to participate was part of the ritual, to show their endurance dancing between the glasses atop a table or balancing as they leaped in rhythm from chair to chair. At the end, the customary sign of a really successful party was the heap of broken glasses piled in one corner.

Adjourning to their sleighs, bundled in by their valets, the party then dashed through the streets, singing and impervious to the sub-zero cold, ending up for a breakfast of herring salad, potatoes, hot soup, and brandy-laced coffee to await the dawn from the restaurant atop Sparrow Hill above the Moskva River where Napoleon had stood as he watched Moscow burn. After that it was the responsibility of all these friends and attendants to see that they were up in time to get the bridegroom to a Turkish bath, join him for a substantial luncheon, and turn up at the church properly attired.

As for the young bride—she was taken over and completely managed by the womenfolk. There was no all-night carousing for her. She must fast and get her beauty sleep, then early in the morning, before eating anything, go to church with her mother for confession and communion. Shortly before noon the robing ceremony began, attended by a great circle of personal maids, young friends, and old aunts. The jewelry, the gown, the gold cape or train, and all the rest of the finery were laid out to be admired by the stream of visitors that now began coming in. As she sat in her lacy peignoir before her dressing table each of her attendants came and brushed her hair, a vestige of the old tradition, a reminder that she was giving up her maidenhood, and as a married woman her hair would be covered with a veil, to be the sole property of her husband. As was related earlier, the stories were that she was supposed to cry—in fact, she should have been weeping all

Princess in Paradise

night—for the loss of her freedom. Now her brothers and other male friends dropped in and were presented with a glass of vodka, as each took turns brushing the hair and teasing her, pulling it or pinching the poor bride to help make her cry. The one modern touch occurred when her worried bridegroom tried to telephone but was not even allowed to talk to her. However, his special messenger arrived at just the opportune moment to present her with a bouquet of fresh lilies of the valley.

After this levee the hairdresser came to wave and properly dress her hair for the occasion. Next she was helped into her dress. It had been made in Venice, completely of *Point de Venise* lace so skillfully designed that it was shaped from the off-the-shoulder neckline to the tight waist to the full skirt without any seams, the patterns in the lace itself making the form. This dress was worn by Thaïs for her wedding and a generation later refashioned for her daughter Ann. After that she went to her father's room where he, sitting in his wheelchair, blessed her and presented her with a special ikon for her new home. The family priest hung a small jeweled cross around her neck as she knelt before him. Then her mother gave her a tiny traveling ikon, wrapped in a handkerchief of antique Brussels lace, which had been her own mother's—and this little ikon was ever after at her bedside or accompanying her on her travels.

For the final touches her mother came to put a veil of silver cloth over her hair and adjust the diamond nuptial tiara. After that, with the gold train attached around her shoulders, she must walk along the corridors and down the grand staircase between the household servants lined up to admire her, sob their farewells, and kiss her hand, now the acknowledgment of her married status. At the front door Nikonor the footman, in full Cossack regalia, put on her new sable coat, and she stepped into the carriage with her grandfather Konshin. The rest of the family followed in a slow procession of various sleighs and carriages. It was almost three o'clock in the afternoon; the streets of Moscow were covered with several feet of snow; frost and snowflakes filled the air—and the temperature stood at forty degrees below zero!

"La bénédiction nuptiale leur sera donnée en l'Eglise Saint Nicolas à Moscou. . . ." is how the wedding invitation in both Russian and French stated it. This may sound concise, and to the poor anxious bridegroom who understood but a little Russian, any ceremony would seem long enough. However, in the Russian Orthodox Church one is not allowed

Family Background

Papi and Mami's wedding invitation.

a "rehearsal" for a wedding, so he had no conception of the ordeal ahead. As Emile always recalled, he was brought to the church by his seconds, his brother Albert and Mr. Ushkoff, like the *Opferlamm* (the sacrificial lamb) to face whatever manipulation the authorities directed, and he allowed himself, as if in a trance, to be guided through one complicated maneuver after another. Most vivid in his recollection were the temperatures. Outside it was the -40° of midwinter Moscow. He arrived at church in his formal dress nervous and perspiring. Inside, with the banks of lighted candles, the priests continually waving censers to fill the air with smoke, the packed crowd of onlookers standing around them in a close circle, and all the activities of the long ceremony, his body felt like the hottest day of July, his head was in a dangerous whirl, and his forehead absolutely dripping.

When Olga arrived at the St. Nicholas Church, they met in an anteroom to sign the papers and her eager bridegroom presented her with a huge sheaf of white roses, according to his customs the proper thing to do, but she had to hand it over to her one bridesmaid. As they stepped through the narthex, Olga, escorted by her brother Mifa in splendid white uniform (since it is not customary to have the father or

Princess in Paradise

senior relative give away the bride), the darkened church was suddenly illuminated and the choir burst forth. Just inside the door the arch-bishop, in gold chasuble and miter, greeted them and gave each a lighted taper, which they held through most of the service. Then the two pages stepped in front of them, her younger brother Igor and cousin Alexei Dobrinin, both in the uniform of the Corps des Pages, Igor holding the cushion bearing the two rings, Alexei carrying the ikon for their future home.

The service begins with the betrothal ceremony. The rings are blessed, the questions intoned, and the responses made (all in Russian, of course); the priest puts the rings on the right hands, the bride's on the groom's hand and his on hers; then, with some shifting of the candles and the customary nervousness, each slips the proper ring onto the other's left third finger.

After this they proceed to the lectern set up at the center of the church on which lie the gospels and the cross, and stand on a white satin carpet. As there are no seats in a Russian church, the congregation gathers around them in a circle. The officiating priest or bishop first crowns them symbolically with the high-jeweled crowns, one decorated with an ikon of Christ for the groom, the other with the Holy Virgin for the bride. These are not placed upon their heads but are held just above them, and must be kept there through all the steps of the following ceremony. Here the bridesmen, the men friends and relatives of the couple, step up and, standing close behind each one, hold up the crowns with outstretched arms. Since no one can be expected to endure this position for very long, two rows of reserves are lined up behind the pair to perform this honor, and they move up at intervals, passing the crown from one to another, obliged to hold them carefully in the air above the heads.

The service is punctuated by the booming bass voice of the deacon reading the instructions and the choir singing lengthy pieces from the gospels. For this special occasion Feodor Chaliapin, their old friend, had joined the choir to sing the only solo sections prescribed—the Lord's Prayer and the marriage vows. Just preceding this the priest had taken the hands of both bride and groom and, laying them together, wrapped them with a brocade stole—tying the knot—holding both their hands with his. He then leads them three times around the church, honoring the Trinity and signifying that their oath is for eternity. During this slow procession the crowns continue to be held

Family Background

above their heads; the ikon bearer and the censer-swinging acolyte precede them; and the other page helps by carrying the train of the bride.

There follows the blessing of the wine and the presentation of the "common cup," the cup of weal and woe, from which each drinks three times, meaning that they will live in concord and share with each other the cup of joy and sorrow.

After another ritual to bless the family ikon and other long passages from the gospels droned out in singsong and unintelligible Russian, one's stamina is sorely tested. If poor Emile, perspiring miserably, warmed by the wine, was suffering from not knowing how much still lay ahead, and wondering if he could hold out to the end, his attendants were likewise getting weaker in their legs and arms. The groom stood six feet four; his brother and most of his friends were considerably shorter. The final blow came when, tired of holding the crown up in the air, they rested it on his already dripping head.

The culmination of the Rite of Holy Matrimony comes when the archbishop leads the couple and the whole procession around the lectern and up to the altar where the crowns are removed. The bridegroom "is now exalted like unto Abraham and the bride like unto Sarah." They kneel on the steps in front of the ikonostasis, there to receive a brief exhortation about their duties and responsibilities from the holy father. Then follows the blessing, with reverberating Amens from the choir. At that point they may relax. They stand and kiss then turn to face the congregation as everyone comes up to kiss and congratulate them. Emile's mind could have been on one thing only—getting out into that nice cold Moscow air!

Through how many ages has the wedding day been one of shining excitement for the bride and of long-drawn-out suffering for the groom! The bride's family manages the festivities, her friends and relatives come to celebrate—and to say goodbye—while the groom stands dutifully in attendance, to be looked over and to wait patiently; even his friends play a minor role.

So the Moravskys and the huge Konshin clan carried on in traditionally proper form. The Palazzo Konshin provided a perfect setting for one of those legendary festivals of old Russia. Few survivors remain to tell of living through such experiences, and the best we can do is imagine it all from the stories that were told and the picture books and memoirs that survived.

When they returned to the house for the reception and nuptial

Wedding trip photo, probably
taken by Albert Lear, 1909.

banquet, Olga's mother welcomed them at the top of the staircase with
the traditional presentation of bread and salt. As the procession entered the flower-banked ballroom, lined with guests, the booming
voice of Feodor Chaliapin sang out "Hymeneios," the "Wedding
Hymn." Towering there over everybody else, he came forward to
envelop them in one of his characteristic huge, emotional embraces.

Sometime between midnight and dawn the entourage entered the
frostily steaming Moscow railroad station, along a red carpet, surrounded by porters with carts of baggage, enthusiastic friends and
teary-eyed family, and armfuls of flowers and gifts, to be ensconced in
their private compartment and waved off by their faithful group. As
last they were on their way.

Photographs show them on picnics in the Crimea, then with their
motor car in the Caucasus. They made the trip from Vladikavkaz to
Tiflis over the thrilling and remarkable Georgian Military Road, an
engineering feat through mountains higher than any of Europe. Then
they went from Tiflis to Sochi, another beautiful Black Sea resort like
Yalta, and a stop with the Ushkoffs at Foross. Details and logistics were
hardly ever mentioned. People then were accustomed to travel a lot but
do so leisurely; there was plenty of help, and the phenomenal amount

Family Background

of baggage that accompanied them was taken care of. As mentioned in an earlier chapter, Albert Lear, Emile's factotum, accompanied them at every step, trained to handle the complicated travel situations as well as Emile's wardrobe. Olga, whose maid did not join her until several years later, had to become used to Albert's nonchalantly taking over the duties of lady's helper besides.

Venice, the honeymooner's paradise of those days, was on their schedule. The view from the Bauer-Grünewald Hotel was romantic and the accommodations were luxurious, but February is not the season for gondola rides and moonlight strolls along the canals. We see them in a gloomy light, in full-length fur coats and Olga with her jaunty sable hat.

The next stop was Krefeld, Germany, to introduce the young bride to the Kluge family. Through a round of formal calls and trying to pair off correctly each new sister-in-law with another Kluge brother, Olga held up splendidly; and so did her girlish sense of humor. The lineup of severe upswept coiffures, tremendous imposing busts, and plump, mustached men certainly had her confused, but she was still devilish enough to respond teasingly to their ignorant and wildly fantastic questions about her homeland. One sister-in-law only, Paula, from Vienna, seemed to be near her in age and to share her lighthearted, more sophisticated attitude. Through a round of carefully staged elegant family dinners, each outdoing the others with imported delicacies and the finest wines, tables set to show off family treasures, she coyly and cheerfully played her part—the glamourous youthful bride from a mysterious fairy-tale background.

After what seemed an endless wait, they were finally aboard the *Vaterland* where Emile was well known, and they were treated as star passengers. Now in great anticipation Olga was really facing a new life, a new homeland—the fabled paradise of the New World.

Princess in Paradise

7

Xenia Zaffar Bikoff

 AITING AT THE PIER for
the docking of a hugh
transatlantic ocean liner was
always exciting enough. This time in May 1921 it was something more
emotional and even more special. Olga and Emile had come north
from Palm Beach to meet Olga's older sister, Xenia, who had managed
to escape after the Bolshevik Revolution, struggle her way from Turkey to Europe, survive in Paris, and finally be granted the miraculous
permission to enter the United States of America. For more than two
years letters and cables had been straggling back and forth, funds had
been transferred, a definite berth arranged on the *Aquitania* and the
guarantee underwritten that she would not become another indigent
immigrant.

Standing at the foot of the third-class gangway, Olga had to reflect
that she had not seen her sister in a dozen years, not since her own
wedding in Moscow. As noted before, she had had little news about
her, since, through Xenia's elopement in 1903, she was in disfavor with
the family and preferred to lead a very private and independent life.
Then as with so many other members of the elite classes, people just
vanished into the chaos of war and revolution, straggling in mobs from
western borders to the east, took up any career they could manage, and
disappeared in various forms of disguise and new personalities. It was
not only the hardship of battling the distances and overcoming the
frightful winters that took their toll; disease and starvation also were

131

132   eliminating thousands of individuals without leaving any trace of their identity.

The first news from Xenia came through the British Red Cross from a hospital in Constantinople where she was recovering from a six-month siege of that raging typhus epidemic. At least through such an agency they could keep in contact with her and send her financial help. From then on they knew vaguely that she was managing to survive, sustaining herself ingeniously, as did the pathetic crowds of others, by working at any kind of job available.

How could one expect to recognize a sister—so many years older now and disfigured by disease and starvation? No doubt her spirit was crippled by the horrors of what she had been through. As they watched the assorted, straggling, bedraggled crowd of humans limping toward them, Olga's heart must have been like lead in her stomach. Besides, Olga too might look different and even unrecognizable. Searching, peering, picking out the faces—some people sobbing, some falling to their knees, most wrapped in nondescript rags, and struggling with outlandish-sized bundles—there strode one much taller than the others. Was it a man or a woman? Then a pushing and shoving, a wild waving of arms and a bellowing "Olga!" and a six-foot-four-inch avalanche was upon them, drowning them in an enormous embrace.

There stood Xenia in a voluminous, belted man's army coat with high battered boots, and doffing a broad-brimmed soldier's hat to reveal a head almost bald except for a fuzz of tight dark chestnut curls. Never one to be abashed, she just had to reveal the state of her wardrobe. Laughing as she unbuttoned her coat, there she let flash her absolutely naked self underneath. In her hand she clutched a cheap fiber suitcase with the initials "X.Z.B." (a monogram she retained after that as her personal insignia or trademark). What was in her baggage? She later revealed a flimsy sequined creation trimmed with colored feathers, a last vestige of her Paris cabaret stint after distributing all her other worldly possessions among her impoverished compatriots.

Xenia at Englewood

Aunt Xenia immediately fitted herself into the Englewood household and won all our hearts with her exuberance, energy, good spirits, humor, and extrovert's interest in everyone. Over six feet tall as she was, she had a slim but muscular figure, topped by a restored mane of

Xenia Zaffar Bikoff in 1922.

curly, short chestnut hair, huge brown eyes, strong nose, and rather masculine chin—and to us—impressively large feet! When she told stories with her very French accent and enthusiastic voice, accompanied by the expansive gestures of her forceful arms and hands, no one in a room could resist being fascinated. In no time at all we could see that on those large feet, that big frame, and that enormous head of hair she wore the most intriguing modish shoes, elegant dresses, and dramatic hats. When she wasn't captivating men and adults, she had time for us children, spurring us on in our daily accomplishments and telling us endless stories.

As the eldest daughter of General de Moravsky, she was admitted to the Smolny Institute in St. Petersburg, the *lycée* for girls of noble birth, which, like the Corps des Pages, prepared young ladies socially for duties at the Imperial Court or for entrance into a university. When we discovered this as a source of entertainment and fantasy, we practically demanded a daily session with her. As budding young ladies of ten and eleven, Ty and I suddenly switched our interests from trapeze artists

Family Background

and swimming clubs to dreams of long trains, crowns and veils, thrones and processions, even balls and courtly gentlemen. Aunt Xenia taught us to walk as fashion models do holding one's shoulders absolutely still and gliding forward by moving the hips, balancing a book on your head—so that you could hold your crown erect! Then we had to learn to make a curtsy, not the quick "knix" taught by our German governesses, nor the English dip as you shake hands, but a slow deep descent with back straight, head up, and eyes on the throne before you. After that you must be able to rise straight and slowly without getting entangled in the hem of your long gown, and back out of the room swishing your train behind you at every step. Emile came in for this training also. He had always had to bow when shaking hands, but now it became a courtly flourish—"and don't forget to keep your eyes on the lady's eyes as you kiss her hand." There was also the etiquette of whose hand you kiss—not everyone's! All this was fun—and how we loved to play princes and princesses and drape ourselves in sheets and put feathers and veils on our heads.

But where Xenia had excelled previously at Smolny was in athletic prowess. To prepare for these straight backs and controlled deep-knee bends, we had to follow her calisthenics. Not only that, she was the one who demonstrated how to stand on your head, throw your feet up against the wall, or do cartwheels. That led to ballet exercises —learning all the positions of arms and feet, practicing at the bar, then rising beautifully from a cross-legged squatting position to standing. Of course, there were also professional exercises for reducing one's hips or strengthening the stomach muscles. All these must have benefited and entertained her as much as they amused and taught us. Imagine the space this required for all our flailing long legs, and the noise of thumping and falling, and finally the music produced by our own windup Victrola. We were assigned to a glassed-in sleeping porch and furnished with wrestling mats, a ballet bar, and mirrors. This bond between Aunt Xenia and all of us, of unabashed fun, learning, and imagination, never left us.

Xenia's Education

On the estate of Romadanovo, Xenia, Olga, and Mifa, joined later by Igor, grew up in what was to them a youthful paradise. For most of their early years they all attended the school maintained by the estate for the village children and those of the tenants and servants on the place. There Xenia was particularly interested in the local crafts which were taught the young girls—lacemaking, embroidery, crocheting, and dressmaking. She used this knowledge later when she had her own dressmaking establishment in New York where she designed dresses, blouses, and coats with the seams crocheted together in colorful Russian peasant patterns.

For a few years they were enrolled in the progressive private school of Mme. Jekouline in Kiev. Then the family took to spending the winters in Moscow. Xenia was an avid book reader; she loved the process of delving into almost anything. Mami used to describe how, if she were sent to find a certain book on a shelf, they would discover her hours later sitting on the floor in the midst of a pile of books that had completely sidetracked her. When she wasn't being the tomboy on a horse or bicycle, she would be sunk in a big chair with her books, oblivious of anything going on around her. Being the eldest child, with a practical and logical mind and this eagerness for learning, her father responded to her with particular sympathy and interest. As military judge of the district, he frequently talked about human problems and legal questions, and she was the one who would listen to him. She was able to discuss with him at length aspects of law or politics that only his male friends had time for. Unquestionably she was slated to go through the university, and no doubt he dreamed of a career in law for her. She herself was more inclined toward business. In any case, she was always fiercely independent, ambitious, and unrestrainedly enthusiastic, perhaps to a fault, interested in too many diverse things.

She went through her years of training for society—the operas, ballets, and private balls at the big townhouse in Moscow. Then came the obligatory two years of rigid finishing school atmosphere at the Smolny Institute in St. Petersburg. Between the ages of twelve and sixteen she had already made several of the cultural pilgrimages abroad or taken part in the elaborate family expeditions to the fashionable summer spas of Germany.

On one trip to Italy the magnificent world of Classical and Renaissance art was opened up to her, coupled with glimpses into the formal life of the decaying palazzos of Rome and Florence and, side by side with Pompeii, the teeming slums of Naples. Accompanying her father on a professional trip to Paris, she was the hostess to eminent intellectual gentlemen, all much older but still considered "eligible prospects"

Family Background

for her. The General introduced his daughter to the fashion salons of Paris, where he expected and received the customary special attention accorded the frequent fabulous Russian customers.

Again the world of art attracted her the most—not just the galleries and the history, but the chance to meet musicians who often visited them in Moscow, to get a glimpse of artists' studios and that mysterious realm of Montmartre, and to see the latest exhibitions of those controversial French "modernists" like Picasso and Matisse. In Russia they were the subject of much discussion as they were being collected by such advanced patrons as Schchukin and Morosov. Returning home newly enflamed by all her revelations abroad, Xenia plunged herself more passionately into her piano practicing and took up a new enthusiasm, that of watercolor painting and design.

Before her final year at Smolny and her scheduled "debut," she had already been intrigued by the writings of liberal intellectuals and had observed the attempts of the anarchists in St. Petersburg and heard much talk about the underground activity of the university students. In fact, at home she had been quite aware of the family tradition of humanitarianism and liberal thinking. Her grandfather's textile factory at Serpoukhov was a national example of progressive thinking in its treatment of the workers and the best modern industrial conditions. Their friends the Jekoulines, who had studied progressive education in Italy and Switzerland, continually discussed their interest in the Cadet Party.

General Moravsky was admired and loved, professionally and personally. And the Romadanovo estate was managed according to the most advanced agricultural practices with the best modern equipment available. As mentioned earlier, its school trained the children of all those working on the estate or in the household for vocations —domestic crafts for the girls and agriculture or forest practices for the boys. Xenia took an active part there, learning herself, then teaching, as she observed the success of her dedicated aunt Irene, who sponsored the school. In the background of all these educational activities was always the village priest who, depending on his liberal or conservative leanings, set the spiritual tone of inquiry and learning with the knowledge and guidance of the General. The private hospital with a visiting doctor from the city took care of the needs of the sick and offered a chance for nursing training to those so inclined.

Xenia had grown up in these surroundings and had heard enough about the contrasting conditions on other estates around the country.

Princess in Paradise

As she became more aware and her interests and feelings grew more intense, she plunged herself ever deeper into activities of the local village, taking part personally in cases of sickness, poverty, or injustice. Or, all afire, she would disappear on her horse to join in some political activity in a neighboring village, naturally quite a distance away, causing long and often unexplained absences. At her father's side, in the interminable and emotional conversations between his male visitors, her opinions would emerge. No doubt her inclinations pleased her father and encouraged him in his dreams for her contribution in the future. Her sister and brothers looked on respectfully and adoringly but were also rather puzzled and uncertain.

The Elopement

One day in the summer of 1903 Xenia was missing—she had really disappeared for much longer than ever before. Then the blow fell for everyone when they discovered Xenia had run off and married the chief forester of the Romadanovo estate, Zaffar Bikoff. They were already in Poland. Nobody ever quite understood it; nobody knew how the romance developed; there were no explanations demanded and no apologies.

Zaffar Bikoff was, of course, discharged. The couple was never officially received by the family. They had to provide their own means of living. Xenia never saw her father again. Even Olga was out of touch with her for years. Her mother included her several times on short trips to Europe. But the hurt to each individual of the family never healed. As has been mentioned, the result of this was that their mother extracted a solemn promise from Olga that she would not marry until she became twenty-one. Olga succeeded in Xenia's place at the Smolny and proceeded in the prescribed way toward her debut.

The older brother, Mifody, was slated to go to law school, quite against his inclinations, which were toward the military—horses, athletics, adventure—while Igor, the more intellectually inclined, was the one chosen to be entered into the Corps des Pages, presumably for a military career.

With Xenia intelligence had succumbed to passion—or was it idealism? Zaffar Bikoff, whom nobody ever knew intimately, was a university graduate in his profession and for some years had the important position of managing the large timberlands on the estate. He was also a tall, handsome, athletic man—and a liberal thinker.

Family Background

Whatever the mutual attraction was it was a complete secret. Apparently he understood Xenia and supported her beliefs and her independent ways. She wanted to go into business. She was acquainted with farm machinery, and he was technically skilled. Together they became the sole sales agents for the Belgian-made Minerva automobile in Russia, and they were successful. Moscow was the business hub of the country, and they lived there, quite apart from any of the family. Xenia had made trips to Germany and France, and her mechanical knowledge and sales ability were impressive. Very few women even thought of driving a motor car. She did, and she could repair one. She sold cars from the north to the south of Russia.

A year after they were married she produced twins—two girls, Irina and Galina. She managed to raise them according to her beliefs. She was interested in their development but not too emotionally involved. Her mother kept in touch with her, but her father never forgave her. In 1909 she appeared in Moscow at Olga's wedding and even sold Emile a Minerva at the time. After that, through the turmoil of the war and the Bolshevik Revolution, she carried on completely apart from all their lives.

In 1914, with conditions at the front desperate, every woman rushed in to do her part and to serve in some capacity. Nursing was not for Xenia, but she could drive ambulances and supply trucks and set up makeshift hospitals. She also helped to load the wounded onto the erratic and overburdened returning trains.

The "Women's Death Battalion" and Escape to America

In 1915 she heard of the "Women's Death Battalion" and joined that. It had been organized by Yasha Bachkarieva, a woman from Siberia who had fought side by side in the trenches with her husband in one of the earliest fighting units. After he fell she carried on in his place and was decorated for valor three times. When soldiers were deserting and fleeing homeward, she said, "If men refuse to fight, we will show them what women can do!" Bachkarieva went to Moscow and had great success in recruiting for the Women's Battalion, including many from aristrocratic families. They started out as a group more than two thousand strong and were engaged in active fighting in the trenches of the Austrian and Rumanian front. After two years of shifting around and fighting various revolutionary forces, the battal-

Princess in Paradise

ghastly experiences.

All defenses began to crumble by the end of 1919, whereupon the whole White Army and the civilian population began to retreat, then flee in chaos toward the Black Sea, each individual fighting for his own survival. Xenia and her family were reunited somewhere near Kiev, perhaps through the Jekoulines, who had become almost a communication center for any member of the family. Her daughters, then about fifteen, had managed to take care of themselves as nurses and clerks, and Zaffar Bikoff had been fighting in the cavalry of the Volunteer Army. They reached Odessa together on those overcrowded, shaky, harassed freight trains. There the British were doing what they could to help evacuate even a minute portion of the thousands of refugees. Every day there were different orders for the army volunteers and different rumors of help coming. Fishing boats were supposed to transport the men to the Crimea for another stand and to help the civilians get to Turkey, Bulgaria, or Rumania. But it was winter, and there was not enough fuel to power the boats; typhus was raging everywhere and only those smuggled ashore could get into the Balkan countries.

Zaffar Bikoff made every possible effort to negotiate some form of rescue for his family and himself. At last they found an owner of a Turkish fishing boat who would take money and promised to sail one night for Constantinople. When it came to the very moment of departure, right on the dock, Bikoff announced that he was not going. Just as with ever so many other Russians, desperate but fiercely patriotic, he could not desert his mother country. Furthermore, his children belonged in Russia, and come what might, they should share the fate of their native land. They were teenagers, very nationalistic, and had no vision that anything worthwhile could any longer exist beyond the land they knew and loved. They too insisted on staying. It may have been a heartrending tussle, but Xenia's strength, will to live, and independence made the decision. She was determined to survive, and she had to do it alone. She was hidden on the deck of the small fishing boat under coils of rope and on a December night in 1919, it put up sail and headed for Turkey.

In later years she never seemed to be haunted by selfincrimination or regrets. She talked about her girls but knew it was impossible ever to trace them. News of her husband's fate never came. After nearly twenty years in America, on one of her enthusiasms, she became interested in spiritualism. She claimed that after several seances, she had news of her daughters through the medium. She was willing to believe it; the situations fitted them exactly. One was happily married with a family—the one who was more the extrovert, cheerful and dedicated to others. The daughter with the more difficult temperament had been married and given it up and was a worker somewhere in Siberia. Both were dedicated Communists.

The final postcript to that part of the story: After Xenia's death in 1938 Olga received notice of a registered letter held at the Russian Consulate in New York. When she tried to claim it, explaining her sister's death, they refused to turn it over to her. After much pleading and irritation, they would do no more than hold it up in front of her, not even allowing her to handle it. She could see many crossed-out forwarding addresses, a jumble of postmarks, and could tell nothing about the original handwriting nor the sender's address. She could only decipher that it came from somewhere in Trans-Baikalia, way off in Siberia.

To return to Xenia, Constantinople—like Bucharest, Belgrade, Vienna, and Prague—was swarming with thousands of homeless, help-less, penniless Russian refugees, and each country was either refusing them entry or trying to enforce the transit visas forbidding a stay of no longer than three days unless employed. There was still a Russian Consulate and a Russian Red Cross, but it was the British and American Red Cross which were performing the most heroic jobs. Through these agencies the refugees managed to get a few free meals, but most important was the assistance in contacting relatives anywhere in the world. Even after Xenia managed to reach her sister in New York by cable, there were the complications in the transferring of money and the endless, frustrating attempts even to get into the consulates to obtain the necessary transit visas. To reach Berlin or Paris one could face the battle of eventually making it on one of the overcrowded trains. But to enter the United States one had to be sponsored by a citizen, to book definite passage through some steamship line, and then get oneself to a certain port by a certain date.

Each refugee, after a safe arrival at his final home, had his own tale to tell—of hardship, humiliation, resourcefulness, or human kindness in time of trouble. The ones who had the most difficult times were those with small children and those who tried to keep a whole family together. In each big city the Russians tended to cluster together,

making contacts and relaying news, usually gravitating to the local
Russian church, as in Paris where so many were reunited. In Constantinople women waited on tables in the big restaurants, and men did any
kind of manual labor. Some suddenly found themselves in the theater,
and we have heard many stories of how they formed singing choruses
or cabaret troupes which survived long after.

Xenia became a waitress in a night spot where she could wear a
costume, play the piano, and gradually rise to the position of hostess.
One's ambition was always to find some wealthy patron. Some arranged marrages by mail with a long-lost friend who wrote from Paris,
for example, and promised a nationality, if not security. But many just
starved and shivered, sickened, and gave up. Typhus had been raging
in Odessa; it spread here along with cholera and other Oriental diseases. Xenia, nearly penniless, landed in the hospital with typhus for
six-months. Her wearing apparel was burned and her head shaved
bare.

From there the Kluges in New York received her first message.
When she was finally discharged from the hospital, she squeezed with
hundreds of others onto a small French coastal steamer which landed
her at Marseilles. From there she had to make her way by train across
France, find temporary shelter in Paris, and get to Cherbourg for the
sailing of the *Aquitania*. This time, unlike Igor, she had a third-class
cabin, shared with five others. Thus, when they docked in New York,
she was able to disembark without being held up at Ellis Island, the
immigrant center.

This was how Aunt Xenia came into our life at Englewood in May
1921 at the age of thirty-four to begin a completely new epoch of her
own.

8

Uncle Igor's Story

WHEN Igor de Moravsky arrived in the United States in 1921 at the age of twenty-eight, a captain in the Russian army and a refugee from the Bolshevik Revolution, he had been through seven years of such ghastly experiences—physical hardship, emotional suffering, disillusionment, and disruption of his way of life—that he could not talk about them. Later, as more and more Russian refugees gathered in this country and spoke to one another in their own language with the common bond of having lived through much the same suffering, they were able to reminisce and compare experiences. However, they never felt really at ease with Americans who had no possible way of conceiving either physically or emotionally what they had been through.

Thus, it was not until 1933 that Igor wrote down the story of his war experiences. His reminiscences of prewar life are beautiful. His eyewitness accounts and comments of the very early revolutionary turmoil in St. Petersburg are unique. Then he recounts step by step his personal wanderings and nearly fatal experiences. Being a military-trained man, he had to record his observations and analyses of the tactical war in detail, the mistakes and the broad developments which had been simmering in his mind ever since he had left them behind. He also reflects on a number of personalities with whom he had direct contact, some of those commanders and their conflicting attempts at defense. Those historical parts are remarkable and valuable because they preserve at first hand aspects of military history and key personalities that are even today confused or lost.

Although Igor was not by inclination a military man, because of his education and a keen analytical mind he was often forced into a position of leadership. His judgement was relied upon when military superiors were unable to make decisions, and he was even called upon for advice by his revolutionary colleagues. In spite of himself he carried on patriotically, as did so many others, dedicated desperately to trying to save the mother country while in the back of his mind realizing that it was hopeless.

In recounting Uncle Igor's story I have relied largely on his handwritten, unpublished manuscript he entrusted to me and which he chose to call "The Salt of Life." It contains the many stories we often heard dramatically retold and elaborated, or almost muttered in cynical detachment. His descriptions and anecdotes are for the most part quoted directly and in the first person. At other times I have obviously summarized what appeared to me excessively long and complicated events. Many pages dealing with military details and historical personalities have had to be omitted, as they are too complicated and do not have a real place in this narrative. However, I hope that I have been able to convey Igor's outstanding anecdotes and a few key descriptions, as well as preserving some of his personal characteristics and attitudes.

Igor Alexandrovich, the youngest of the four de Moravsky children, was born on December 11, 1893, in Kiev, his brother Mifody being four years older. His father had decided that Igor would be the one to pursue the traditional family military career. Igor said he never could see the attraction of shiny buttons and bright uniforms nor the strict routine that went with military life. His first dreams were of being a coachman or an engineer in the cab of a locomotive.

Gen. Alexander de Moravsky had spent his whole life in the service of his tsar and his country and not only loved it passionately but believed that he had performed a significant and worthwhile function. He had begun as an artillery officer and after attending the Military Legal Academy became a military judge and often lectured at the Academy. He culminated his career as the greatly respected president of the Military Tribunal of the District of Kiev, where the family lived. He was known as a kind and just man, in spite of his imposing height and a manelike head of curly chestnut hair and the large handlebar mustache. After his retirement he spent the last five years of his life in an apartment in St. Petersburg, confined as an invalid to a bed and a wheelchair because one leg had been amputated above the knee. He was constantly attended by his long faithful military valet and was always receiving a stream of prominent military and political visitors. Igor, the young university student, thoroughly enjoyed those lengthy conversations and after his father's death in 1912 carried on the tradition of such weekly gatherings.

Le Corps Des Pages

Igor had early been enrolled in Le Corps des Pages de Sa Majesté l'Empereur, and he entered it in 1907 at the age of fourteen. Only boys from families who had a general in their direct male ancestry were eligible to attend the Academy. There was also a suggestion that if Igor joined the Corps des Pages the old family title of the Moravsky-Romandanovski line could be reclaimed, perhaps along with the recovery of some of their lands.

The Page School was primarily a military training school for future officers, which meant a thorough academic training along with a strict code of discipline. Along with that, they had to learn official court etiquette and be able to serve at court functions, from carrying the trains of grand duchesses at the balls, to attending the imperial family in public processions, to carrying torches at weddings and burials. In their last two years they saw military service, and if they remained in the school until graduation were bound to serve as officers for three years thereafter. However, those who elected to leave the school before the last two grades could enter a university as graduates of any regular lycée and do whatever they chose without further obligation. Igor was a good academic student, particularly enjoying mathematics, and thus had a natural gift for understanding artillery. But the formalities of the military life and the rigid discipline of the barracks caused him to rebel frequently, which led to his being quite well known, however questionably, among his superior officers. Also, he had a little streak of stubbornness and deviltry, which is what later developed into cynicism and an outwardly blasé attitude.

The Maltese Cross was the insignia of the Corps des Pages and a little white enamel cross was worn as a lapel pin, distinguishing ever after those who had been members. It was like a brotherhood, not only of the young men who attended the school together, but including many past generations and covered all of Russia, since prominent families from every section of the country were represented. After the

Uncle Igor in 1933.

war, with the great influx of Russian émigrés in New York City, the Corps des Pages Ball, instigated by Prince Serge Obolensky, was one of the most brilliant annual events of the winter social season. Our father, Emile Kluge, was entitled to wear the little white lapel cross which was presented to him as an honorary member of the order at the time of his marriage to Olga in Moscow.

One may wonder how the Cross of the Knights of Malta came to be the symbol of military aristocracy in Russia. Igor explains it:

The most paradoxical occurrence during the short reign of the Emperor Paul I (son of Catherine the Great) was undoubtedly the manifesto of September 22, 1798, by which the autocratic Sovereign of All the Russias and Supreme Defender of the Orthodox Church declared to have taken under his direction the sovereign order of St. John of Jerusalem, deposed the grand master of the Knights Hospitalers, Ferdinand de Hompesch, and transferred the capital of the brotherhood from Malta to St. Petersburg.

It is impossible to ascertain the idea back of this. If it was a preliminary step to take the Isle of Malta from the French for the establishment of a naval base for the Russian fleet in the Mediterranean it was an absurdity, as England would

Family Background

never have tolerated that. Was he thinking of reuniting the Greek and Latin churches? But in this case the deposition of Hompesch was a fatal mistake, for Pope Pius VI was violently opposed to it. Or was he dreaming in his insane imagination of some sort of a mystical and chivalrous revival? No one will ever be able to answer these questions. His successor, his son Alexander I, ordered the Maltic Knights out of Russia and by decree on December 12, 1802, founded the Corps des Pages de Sa Majesté l'Empereur. Its home was established in the Vorontzov Palace the former castle of the Order of St. John of Jerusalem.

In the modern Soviet regime the building still stands, its exterior design unchanged, but with a new sign identifying it as an elite military academy.

Although he objected to the regimented life, punctuated by trumpets and drums from morning till night, he did enjoy some of its luxuries. For every five boys there was a valet who made their beds, shined their shoes, pressed their clothes, and laid out their uniforms. The food was hardly that of an ordinary boarding school—grouse, wild duck, partridge, trout and venison, pastries and fruits from the Crimea—and other luxuries were abundant in the form of donations coming from the estates of the ever interested "Old Boys." Every Saturday and Sunday they were completely free unless required at the social functions of the court. December 12, the anniversary of the founding of the Corps des Pages, was their biggest celebration, with the emperor and hundreds of former pages attending a festival mass and luncheon in the great White Hall, followed in the evening by the brilliant Page Ball, one of the outstanding events of the winter season.

Igor had frequent problems with the traditional discipline and many a difficult session with his academic masters. Later on in strange situations of the war and the Revolution he would meet up with some of his former commanding officers and teachers, or perhaps their sons, who would recognize him with amazement and say, "Moravsky, how in the world did you ever get here?"—never expecting to find him serious and responsible in a military career. His mother sympathized with his rebelliousness and always feared the worst. When he arrived at the door of her apartment unexpectedly one weekday afternoon, she greeted him with: "Ha, so you've been expelled?" But it was only that the tsar had declared a special holiday.

After the prescribed three years and his graduation in 1910, he entered the University of St. Petersburg to study mathematics. It happened that at the same time his brother, Mifa, was studying at the change his course and enter the School of Law, receiving his LL.D. degree in 1915.

He enjoyed the social life of a young bachelor in the capital and in 1910 took his first independent trip abroad. His family expected him to see the beauties of Italy. But when he got there he chose to take a tramp steamer to Egypt instead. He wanted to visit Port Said, which he had heard described as "the cesspool of Europe."

An event of great importance for him was the invitation by a former page to join the Tavrichesky Lawn Tennis Club which played in the gardens of the Tauride Palace in St. Petersburg. He took up the game very seriously and soon became one of its leading and most popular stars. Women were also members of the club; they were highly regarded and played just as seriously and successfully as the men. One of Igor's partners in mixed doubles and one of the strongest players was a young lady of French descent, Ludmilla Isnard. But more about her later.

 ## St. Petersburg

Igor not only enjoyed the life of St. Petersburg but came to love its beauties and to feel deeply its special character as a symbol of power and accomplishment in achieving a position of international prestige. "St. Petersburg is not Russia" was the eternal claim of Muscovites. Even the language of society and the educated was not Russian but French. The land itself came from the Finns, and the region was always a battlefield between the Swedes and the Russians. Then there was the Germanic influence brought in by Peter the Great and Catherine II.

"Could any one city reflect the spirit of Russia?" Igor asks, then explains:

The two oldest centers of Russia were Kiev and Novgorod. The latter was a typical merchant republic at the height of its power in the tenth century, an important member of the Hanseatic Union, and its spirit much akin to that of the free German cities of Hamburg, Bremen, and Lübeck. Kiev embodied the spirit of the steppes, the wide open spaces, with its endless expansiveness and the freedom and recklessness derived from the Cossacks. But the spirit of Moscow was the dark spirit of the forest, where there is no wide horizon as on the river, the sea or the steppe, but where an enemy may lurk behind every tree. Even the heroes

Family Background

of the folklore of the three periods are different. In Novgorod it was the merchant prince who sailed his ships laden with merchandise to foreign lands over rivers, lakes, and seas, and came home bringing barrels of gold. In Kiev it was Bogatyr, the chivalrous knight, the mighty roving warrior. But in Moscow it was the 'Diak,' the shrewd, intriguing, calculating commercial government clerk.

Igor's enthusiasm for St. Petersburg, as compared with other cities of Russia, to us was always infectious and exciting. I summarize his descriptions here because it gives not only something of the character and background of the city, but it also reveals the clarity of the vision that lived on as an integral part of this family legend.

St. Petersburg grew on the site of former Finnish villages and the peasants of Tsarskoe-Selo were pure Finns. The word Neva itself is Finnish and means a swamp, and Tsarskoe-Selo used to be a Finnish village called *Saari,* meaning the Island. Saari became *Saarskle Selo* (*selo* meaning village) and after the place became an Imperial residence *Saarskle Selo* naturally became Tsarskoe-Selo. . . . In 1241 the Grand Prince Alexander Nevsky of Novgorod defeated the Swedes at the mouth of the Izora River near St. Petersburg, whence came the name Nevsky or the Neva.

The only spirit which remained unchanged throughout the whole of Russian history, as Igor saw it, was that of the conquest of the Plain, that plain which is bound on the west by the Carpathian mountains and the Baltic sea, by the Black Sea, the Caucasus, the Kopeth Dagh, the Pamirs, the Tian Shan and the Altai ranges on the south, by the Pacific on the east and the Arctic Ocean on the north. With the purely geographical conquest of the Plain came also the conquest of its secrets and the mastery of its resources. It stands to reason that during the geographical conquest of the Plain the growing Russian State had to come into conflict with various races, creeds and nationalities and had to incorporate many of them. And this spirit of expansion and incorporation is what St. Petersburg clearly reflected.

This process of incorporation was typified in St. Petersburg by the churches and temples of the various creeds and nationalities which constituted the Russian Empire. As one walked up the main street of the city, the Nevsky Prospect, one would pass the German Lutheran Church of St. Peter and Paul, representing an important element in the makeup and history of Russian Imperial power. Further on was the Roman Catholic Cathedral of St. Catherine, representing the creed and culture of Western and Southwestern Russia, and still further

Princess in Paradise

along the Armenian Church. Just off the Nevsky Prospect near the German Church were the Swedish and Finnish Lutheran churches. Thus the principal types of Christian civilization which made up the Empire were represented in the center of the city.

Across the river, opposite the Field of Mars and the palace of Prince Saltykov occupied by the British Embassy, on the site presented by the Emir of Bokhara, stood the Mohammedan Mosque, its minarets surmounted by a green cupola. And in the suburb of Novaia Derevnia the Lamaist temple had been built. These were the symbols of the extension of the Russian power into the world of Islam and into the Buddhist region.

But if the churches and temples typified the area of power the plan and architecture of the city represented the growth of that power. The conquest of the Plain was naturally a movement that grew into centralization, and centralization means abstraction, and that may be the reason why the first impression of the capital city was that of severity and coldness. But behind the bold outlines the products of the brain rather than the heart, one experienced a strong feeling of youth, not boisterous and frolicking, but youth that suddenly realizes its accomplishments and is torn between feelings of pride and fear.

The Golden Age of Russian architecture was during the reigns of Catherine the Great and Alexander the First. Foreign architects were imported and Russians were sent abroad for training. But whatever their origins or training the architects of this period were all caught in a powerful movement which was essentially Russian, and created from various elements and styles something distinctly of their own.

The most famous of the Russianized foreign architects in the reign of Catherine II was Count Bartolomeo Rastrelli (1700-71) who built the palace at Tsarskoe-Selo, the Winter Palace in part and the Smolny Convent in St. Petersburg. Under Alexander I Russian architecture rose to the highest peak it ever reached, and it was during his reign that St. Petersburg became a really beautiful city. The Kazan Cathedral with its Doric colonade and the Institute of Mines were the works of Andrei Voronikhin (1760-1814) who had been born a serf of Count Stroganov's. The St. Petersburg Stock Exchange was the work of the Swiss Thomas de Tomon (built 1804-1810). And the Admiralty with its combination of strength and grace was the work of Andrey Zakharov (built 1806-15). Under Nicholas I (1775-1849) the decadence began; but Carlo Rossi's Senate (1829-34) and Alexandra Theater (1827-32), and Ricard de Montferrant's (1786-1858) Cathedral of St. Isaak of

Family Background

Dalmatia (built 1818-58) were worthy monuments of a brilliant epoch.

It was in the portion of the city surrounding the Admiralty that St. Petersburg gave the impression of really being a Capital, more than any other city on the continent except perhaps Rome. West of the Admiralty was the Senate Square and the equestrian statue of Peter the Great with his appealing gesture toward Europe, the work of Etienne-Maurice Falconet (1716-91). Facing the Admiralty on the other side of the square stood the Senate. On the south of the Senate Square was the Cathedral of St. Isaak and beyond it another plaza, with the Mariinsky Palace, which was once the seat of the Upper Chamber of the Empire and the State Council, facing the Cathedral. Here in the center stood another equestrian statue, that of Emperor Nicholas I, which was saluted by his son Alexander II every time he passed by. But the former harmony of the whole area was entirely destroyed shortly before the war by two buildings—the Hotel Astoria of garrish Art Nouveau architecture on the east, and a very ugly example of German Jugendstil—the German Embassy on the west.

To the east of the Admiralty along the Quai stretched the long and imposing red stone facade of the Hermitage and the Winter Palace, built in 1754-64 after designs by Bartolomeo Rastrelli, with its Baroque ornamentation reflected in the changing hues of the river Neva. On the side of the Winter Palace away from the Neva was the Palace Square, kept perfectly clear except for the tall slender column topped by an angel commemorating the victory of Alexander I over Napoleon in 1812. Opposite the Winter Palace across the Palace Square was the semi-circular building known as the General Staff Building, which housed the War and Foreign Offices. A triumphal archway through this building led to the Nevsky Prospect, from the center of power to the main business thoroughfare. A short street running east, the Millionnaya, led to the Field of Mars, the parade ground of the capital. The Imperial Hermitage ran along that street followed by the imposing limestone building that housed the Preobrajensky Regiment, the first regiment of the Palace Foot Guards. In the southeast corner of the Square was the Singers' Bridge over the little river Moika, which led to the Court Choir. And next to it at No. 24 on the Moika Quai was one of the hallmarks of the town, the restaurant "Donon," a place Igor dearly loved.

Igor goes on to describe the social season in St. Petersburg which took place during the winter, starting early in November and reaching its height between Christmas and Carnival—theater, opera, ballet, all the balls and soirées, which continued even after the imperial family had moved out to Tsarskoe-Selo. "The season of 1914," he said, "brought a sudden revival of all the splendors of the life of the 'Grande Monde' of the capital city, as if it were a presentiment of the approaching cataclysm. The costume ball given by the Countess Kleinmichel, the ball at the British Embassy, the Bal Blanc et Noir at Countess Shuvalov's, and the festive ball given by the Dowager Empress Maria Fedorovna for her grand daughters at the Anitchkov Palace, the favorite residence of her husband the Emperor Alexander III—those were but some of the highlights of that season. During Lent all theaters were closed and the only social event was the horse show which took place every Sunday afternoon in the Michailovsky Armory. After Easter there were only minor social gatherings for a few weeks until everyone departed for the summer."

The Russians who for generations had been mostly landowners were in the habit of moving away from the cities to their estates, or else they would depart with their families and entourages for the Russian resorts in the south or the fashionable spas of Germany and France. Even government officials, who had only a month's vacation, would send their wives and families off to the country, and St. Petersburg would become a town of bachelors, to the great delight of restaurant owners and the demimonde. Igor stayed in town because of his father's illness and because of his increasing importance in the tournaments of the Lawn Tennis Club.

He found St. Petersburg even more attractive in summer than in winter. Even though people had to go to their offices, everyone seemed to be continually celebrating, enjoying the parks and the suburbs after the long winter, with mild weather and little rain, and especially those magic white nights which accentuated the beauty of the city. At one time he wrote:

The White Nights! I have seen them again and again in Finland and Sweden, but nowhere were they as gorgeous as in St. Petersburg. From ten o'clock in the evening on the whole sky was painted with all colors imaginable from a vivid red to a pale and delicate green. And like the Aurora Borealis these colors would move, interchange, vibrate, as if reflecting some volcanic eruption. Around eleven o'clock the sky would grow paler and then for a brief hour all color would disappear and everything would be wrapped in a ghostly silvery mist. This peculiar sickly greenish light that came at once from nowhere and from everywhere and threw no shadows would creep over the town and across the Neva,

Family Background

lying there motionless but giving the impression of some tremendous power chained within it. Walking along the quais and looking at the fortress of Peter and Paul across the water I would be reminded of the many cruel and perverse events in history that were supposed to have taken place under the influence of this hour,—and I would be seized by a craving to rush off somewhere and participate in some wicked debauchery. Then at half past twelve a faint strip of rose would announce dawn and the advent of the coming day.

The Gypsies

It was during one of those summers that Igor discovered for the first time the "field gypsies." "Gypsy music was everywhere an integral part of Russian night life. Somehow gypsy singing, passionate and voluptuous, with its quick changes from wild gaiety to melancholy sadness was peculiarly in unison with some chord in the Russian soul and made that soul vibrate and change its moods as quickly as the mood of the song. In St. Petersburg the gypsies were living in the suburb of Novaia Derevnia. In the evening their choruses would go to the big night restaurants, waiting for someone to call them to the private rooms to sing. After closing hour the party would move to the camps at Novaya Derevnia where there would be more songs and dancing and more wine until any hour. The songs they sang were either old gypsy songs transmitted from generation to generation, Russian folk songs rearranged by them to conform with their way of singing, or songs composed by Russians in the gypsy style. Those were the more usual 'Town Gypsies.' The 'Field Gypsies' were of a nomadic type, roving mostly through the southwest of Russia and toward the Balkans, migrating like birds with the seasons. It was rare that a gypsy tribe would come as far north as St. Petersburg. But if they did they would pitch their tents somewhere near the summer camps of the Guard Regiments, where their entertainment and their living sustained them quite well for the season. Then with the approach of fall they would suddenly disappear."

One August day in 1911 Igor had gone out to Krasnoe Selo, thirty-five miles away, to visit some of his former school friends now at the summer camp of the Corps des Pages, and was bicycling back to the railroad station after those in camp had to retire at eleven o'clock. Suddenly he was seized by two Hussars of the Guard, indicating forcibly that he should follow them, despite his protests, directly across the rough country fields. Puzzled and feeling somewhat guilty—not knowing exactly why except that he might have been caught in a restricted area—he stumbled along in the dark and suddenly found himself in the midst of a gypsy camp. There he was greeted by a certain colonel of the Hussars whom he recognized. When he demanded an explanation, the answer was:

I am having such a good time here by myself that I wanted to share it with some of my friends. If you are tired I shall have a blanket brought for you and you can sleep right here on the ground. But if you feel like hearing songs and seeing dances such as you have never heard or seen before, make yourself comfortable. Drink and food will be plentiful; just give the orders to one of my men. But as for going home—none of that nonsense!

It was an unforgettable night. The gypsies must have been of Hungarian origin, as they played violins, not only guitars as the town gypsies did. They sang only old gypsy songs, some of which he had never before heard. Bewitched by the dancing and by those songs with their interchange of passion, gaiety, and sadness, then the approaching dawn in the pale green sky, he felt completely transported outside himself into a state where song and dance and love were all blended in a mysterious dream world. After that there was many a time when in midmorning he checked his bicycle at the Krasnoe Selo station and rather ingloriously made his way back to town by train.

The Russian national tennis championships were being played off on the courts of the Tauride Palace. Igor and his partner, Ludmilla, had been leading in the mixed doubles. She had come out on top in the ladies' singles and he had been runner-up in the men's singles. A large group of players and visitors had gone to celebrate their victories at Luna Park on the Ofitserskaya Pristan. One of their friends unexpectedly joined them to tell them of the latest news—he had just heard that the Archduke Francis Ferdinand, heir to the throne of Austria-Hungary, had been assassinated that afternoon in Sarajevo—Sunday, June 28, 1914. The first reaction was one of horrified surprise—did such things really happen outside Russia! A very few were concerned that there might be serious consequences. Then all thoughts returned to tennis and good times.

During the next two weeks it was the international championships that were the center of attention at the St. Petersburg Club. The Austrian and German players had come up almost to the finals, but they appeared ill at ease and kept to themselves.

Family Background

❧ Declaration of War

On Thursday, July 23 came even more distressing news: Austria had served its drastic ultimatum to Serbia. The tournament committee was thrown into confusion; the German and French players were summarily called home; and a deep, depressing feeling that war was imminent pervaded the atmosphere. On July 28 mobilization orders were posted all over town, although the official statements said that these were only preventive measures. On August 1 the German ambassador, Count Pourtales, served Russia's minister of foreign affairs, Sergey Sazonov, with Germany's declaration of war on Russia.

The following day, a Sunday afternoon, Igor went to witness the historic scene when the tsar was to deliver his manifesto from the Winter Palace. An enormous crowd was packed into the Palace Square. Banners and flags were flying everywhere; ikons were being paraded; all knelt in devotion before their tsar, singing the national anthem and then breaking out into wild cheering. A day later, coming out from lunch at the Astoria Hotel, Igor stood with his friend General Lundberg, a former professor at the Page School, in the square on the steps of the Nicholas I statue and saw a crowd gathering. This time the mood was more excited. Then they heard shouts and the shattering of glass as the mob surged upon the German Embassy. Stones broke every window; the doors were forced down; and in they poured, slashing the paintings to shreds, ripping open the furniture, smashing the bronzes and Renaissance china, all the private collection of Count Pourtales, then completing the vandalism by climbing to the roof and throwing down the bronze group of two horses led by two giants.

After the pillage was over, as he and his friend walked through the streets, it was General Lundberg who said:

We shall never go through with this war. The scene we just witnessed only confirms my fears. Our masses are too susceptible to mental contagion, to mob psychology. Just as today they were pillaging the German Embassy to the accompaniment of "God Save the Tsar," two years from now having grown tired of war–and this war will last longer than that–they will be influenced by a handful of political fanatics and a dozen impracticable slogans, and they will wreck the Winter Palace to the tune of the 'Internationale' . . . In Russia the revolution will be started by the bourgeoisie, the intelligentsia, who have no real contact with the masses, and they will immediately lose control of the forces they have let loose. The bourgeois revolution will soon give place to a socialistic

Princess in Paradise

Igor was not affected by the mobilization, since he was a student and had one more year of work toward his LL.D. degree. He had carefully made up his mind what course to follow, but it was difficult to face the patriotic enthusiasm of his friends. Over luncheon at the Donon restaurant in conversation with another former page he declared, "I have worked for two years for my doctor's degree and I shan't interrupt my studies. I sincerely believe that my work is just as important for the future of my country, if not more, than enlisting in the cavalry. . . . After I receive my degree next spring, I'll be called to the colors anyway, and there will be plenty of fighting left for me. But at least I shall know precisely what I will do when this mess is over."

"But," his friend replied, "don't you think you will miss something—an opportunity to taste the Salt of Life? In a few days England will declare war on Germany. Austria is not much of a military power. Italy will probably stay neutral. Do you suppose that Germany, practically alone, can stand against the combined forces of England, France and Russia for more than three months? Come on Igor! We shall be in Berlin by Christmas!"

By September the mood of Petrograd, as the city was now officially called—St. Petersburg was considered too German—had become decidedly depressed. Newspapers were filled with casualty lists of names from the first cavalry division operating in East Prussia, names only too familiar to everyone, and the news of the disaster at Tannenberg spread gloom and somber forebodings. Germany's superiority in its munitions supply and its better transportation began to be realized.

In June 1915 after receiving his doctor of law degree Igor returned to the Corps des Pages for an eight-month officer training course during which they were supposed to pick up what had usually been taught in the final two years of the Military School. He found friends among his colleagues and the officers, and to his surprise even experienced a warm feeling of familiarity in the old buildings and a sense of pride and superiority as he watched the newcomers go through drill. Thus, in February 1916 he joined his old Guard Regiment at the front in Galicia, where they were facing the Austrians.

❧ The Medical Leave

By November 1916 Igor was sent home from the front on medical leave, with his orderly along to care for him. He had such a severe case

Family Background

of rheumatism in his right elbow and both wrists that both his arms were in slings, and he was in such pain that he could not even lift a spoon. Recovery, if the rheumatism did not spread or get worse, was expected to take about four months. He still felt rather optimistic about the front and the spirit of the troops, though everyone realized they were completely lacking in an air force, and the transportation of supplies was most often erratic.

However, Petrograd had changed noticeably. His young friends, like Ludmilla and Nina with whom he had shared so many gay dances, came home tired and gray from serving in hospitals, as did all the women of the imperial family. Houses were closed up except for a few rooms. His mother had moved back to Moscow to be with her sick ninety-one-year-old father. The transportation system of the city was breaking down, resulting in shortages of food and fuel, and that whole long winter was exceptionally cold. Lines formed at bakeries and food stores; people were grumbling and sullen; and revolutionary propaganda was everywhere in evidence. Evil rumors were being spread against the empress and Rasputin's influence on the Tsar through her.

Dr. Sergey Petrovich Fedorov, professor of surgery and president of the Royal Academy of Medicine of St. Petersburg, was Igor's uncle, married to Eugenia, his mother's eldest sister. He was admired and much beloved by all the family, and since the de Moravskys had been living in St. Petersburg, the two sisters and their husbands had become particularly close. Igor as a grown young man was a frequent visitor at his uncle Serge's apartment and could repeat many of these stories at first hand. In 1909 Professor Fedorov had been named court surgeon and personal physician to the imperial family. On many occasions the emperor showed signs of his deep personal friendship, and the little tsarevitch was known to adore him. The doctor accompanied the family on their vacations, either on the royal yacht *Standart* or to Yalta in the south of Russia. He was an early witness to the now well-known suffering of the young prince from his affliction of hemophilia, and in consultation with many others, was helpless in finding a cure. He was, however, the closest friend and constantly reminded the distraught parents that they must do everything they could to bring up their son as normally as possible. He should not be kept from playing with his adoring sisters; he wanted to play ball and learn to hunt, to march and ride and attend ceremonies in uniform like his father. The watching and control by his anxious mother and his bodyguard, Derevenko, had to be surreptitious but constant. Dr. Fedorov was personally in attendance through many an all-night crisis and witnessed the sleepless suffering of the boy's mother.

Fedorov was also a firsthand observer of the arrival and all the famous incidents involving the monk Rasputin. His opinion, as voiced to Igor, has been often quoted: "Unquestionably the man has very pronounced psychic and hypnotic powers. These hypnotic powers have without a doubt helped the Tsarevitch time after time when we, men of science, were helpless. He has made the Empress believe that without him the days of her only son are numbered. But as to his influence at court and in politics, it is not my business to discuss that."

Gregoriy Efimorovich was known as the starets, a wandering holy man, from Siberia, but his surname, Rasputin (from the word *rasputnik*, which means a rake, a seducer of girls), grew also out of the many tales about his debauchery and mad religious fervor. He was introduced in St. Petersburg in 1907 by the two "Montenegrin grand duchesses," the two rather unpopular daughters of the king of Montenegro, and he immediately made a reputation in their sensation-seeking society for his occultism, his feverish religion, and his mystic orgies. Several years later it was a sincere priest, Father Theofane, who brought him before the imperial couple, assuring them that they would benefit from listening to him, that he spoke with the "voice of the Russian Soil." Believing that, they tolerated from the first day his presumptuous familiarity and the coarse and brutal manner with which he treated them.

Uncle Serge was present at the famous incident at Spala in Poland in October 1912. Alexis bumped his hip getting out of a boat; later an internal hemorrhage appeared; the fever rose and the swelling became insufferable—yet an operation was impossible. For six days everyone watched helplessly. On the seventh day the empress came to Dr. Fedorov and said in a calm voice, "There is nothing to worry about any more Sergy Petrovich. Everything will be all right." With that she handed him a telegram. He opened it and read very clearly: "God has seen thy tears and heard thy prayers. Thy son shall live. Rasputin." It came from Tobolsk in Siberia where Rasputin had been banished. Next day, as Dr. Fedorov witnessed, the patient's temperature fell to normal, and three days later the tumor was gone. Both these tales and the accounts of his soothing and healing the Tsarevitch through numerous other crises have been thoroughly written up and documented.

After that Rasputin became the regular priest of the imperial fam-

Family Background

ily, still carrying on his infamous life of debauchery in Petrograd. As time went on, the ugly stories grew and spread about his supposed political influence and the mistakes caused by his dominance over Empress Alexandra and, through her, over the tsar. Igor was in the city when the rumor came out, followed by the actual story that Rasputin had been killed at a party in Prince Felix Yusupoff's palace in which Prince Dmitry Pavlovich and others had taken part. Dmitry was summarily banished without any consideration or chance of defense.

Uncle Serge confirms in his stories all the incidents that show Tsar Nicholas as a gentle, kind, modest, family-loving man; his sincere love of "his people"; and his belief in his responsibility as their leader. He took a personal interest in the people of his enormous household. At Christmas they and all their families were entertained at parties in the palace. At Easter, whether in Livadia or Tsarskoe-Selo, he and the empress presented two thousand souvenir eggs individually to each attendant. The tsar seldom wore showy uniforms and really wanted to mingle with his troops.

One anecdote illustrates his modest appearance and how little he was known by his people. Uncle Fedorov was with the tsar at General Headquarters at Mogilev, and they had to go to a meeting in an automobile. Noticing on a map that the highway made a large bend around a woods while a path went directly across, the tsar decided he wanted to walk with his friends and sent the cars ahead to meet him at the opposite side. In the forest they met a peasant guard and asked to whom the land belonged and if they would actually meet the main highway. "To Countess Menjunska," the forester answered; and, "Yes after going through this swamp with water no deeper than your ankles, the path will widen and lead you to the road."

A little way farther on, Dr. Fedorov turned around and observed two of their escorting guards talking animatedly to the forest warden, who took off his hat, crossed himself, then knelt down. When asked what the matter was, the guards reported that the peasant simply would not believe that the little man in uniform was the Tsar. "If he were the Tsar he would not be walking in that swamp. He would not be walking at all because he would always be on horseback. Moreover if he were the Tsar, he would be big and fat and wearing a red coat." The emperor was amused and asked him to come along. Even when he saw the automobiles and the red uniforms of the Cossacks on horseback, he

Princess in Paradise

still eyed them suspiciously. Then one of the generals, recalling the custom that anyone to whom the tsar has spoken must have his name and address recorded and a five-ruble gold coin is sent to him, asked permission to take a photograph of the tsar standing with this forest guard, for him to receive along with his reward.

Igor's last visit with Uncle Serge was in the turbulent days of March 1917 when the doctor returned to Petrograd after witnessing the abdication at Pskov and the arrest of the tsar at Tsarskoe-Selo. This is Igor's account:

While we were sitting in his study he suddenly asked me, "Do you think, Igor, that if the Emperor had abdicated in favour of his son it would have in any way changed the trend of events?" I replied, "It is a question which nobody can answer and I can only voice my personal point of view. . . . One argument is that the Tsarevitch was much beloved by the population and by the army, but I am afraid that it was a love the people would naturally have for a child and a sick one at that; and such love would not be enough to change the mood of the industrial workers and soldiers of Petrograd. . . . By the time the abdication took place, the garrison of Petrograd was in full mutiny, the Soviet was formed, and the passions of the crowds let loose. I do not believe any legal considerations would have changed the trend of events. . . . Moreover, the revolution, as I think it is clear now, was not a protest against the Emperor, but first a hunger mutiny, secondly a protest against the prolongation of the war, thirdly a protest against the political regime, and fourthly (which becomes clearer and more pronounced every day) a protest against the economic system. . . . To think that he would have abdicated without being forced to do so was foolish. He thoroughly believed that he was the leader of his country by the Will of God, and to drop that leadership at a moment when the country was undergoing the severest test in its history would be an act of cowardice. His mistakes were innumerable, but no one will ever be able to accuse him of a dastardly action. . . . We can not foretell what price he will yet have to pay for his mistakes."

"I am glad to hear that," said my uncle. "I often wonder if the decision I took was the right one. At Pskov the day before the two delegates of the Duma arrived and explained the whole situation, the Emperor called me to his study and asked 'I order you to give a sincere answer. Do you believe that Alexis can ever get well?' I knew how much depended on my answer, but my professional duty was to tell the truth to the father of a child who was my patient. . . and I gave the answer which I felt I should have given: 'No, Your Majesty, his disease is incurable.' 'That is what the Empress has thought for a long time already. I still had hopes. . . . If

Family Background

God has decided that way, I shall not be separated from my poor child.' . . . and he abdicated next day in favor of his brother."*

❧ Revolution

The year 1917 began with gloomy foreboding. The unrest in the streets and the number of bloody incidents continued to increase. Until May, through the terribly cold winter, with the hazards of rounding up food and living behind blinds in one scantily heated room, Igor continued to witness the fast-mounting Revolution and manage to get news of the war. Incredibly, he could still meet friends at the Donon, where they continued to sell the dwindling supply of imported wines. The crowds in the streets were threateningly restive; disturbances in the industrial suburbs increased; there was always firing by the police and repeated charges by the Cossack regiments upon the crowds. Beginning on February 26 when the Volynsky Guard Regiment refused to fire into a crowd, the Revolution spread with gathering intensity. Government buildings were set afire; government officials were arrested; the prisons were thrown open; stores were looted, and finally the police and Cossacks gave up their battle. "The hunger mutiny had grown into Revolution."

Out of the general anarchy three organizations were formed: The Fortress of St. Peter and Paul became the Headquarters for the Troops. The Council of Workers and Soldiers Deputies—THE SOVIET—located in the Finland Station—proclaimed a socialistic republic and demanded an immediate end to the war. The Executive Council of the Duma, with twelve members, attempted to carry on a government and inaugurate reforms. It was they who agitated for the abdication of the tsar in favor of his brother, Grand Duke Michael.

By the end of March the Revolution was spreading through the army—the cry was for *peace*! Soldiers were deserting the front lines, commandeering trains and turning them homeward. From all fronts came the reports of how, when an advance was ordered, the officers out of a sense of duty would go forward, sometimes alone, and face the enemy fire; or if they turned back to their trenches, they would be

---

* This conversation is documented in the memoirs of Count Paul Benckendorff, Pierre Gilliard, A. A. Mosolov, and others and is retold by Robert Massie in his *Nicholas and Alexandra*. Here it is quoted directly from Igor's record of Dr. Fedorov's own words.

mowed down by their own men. At Kronstadt, the great naval fortress with a garrison of 55,000, the sailors had killed over half of their officers and held the rest as hostages. In Petrograd the mobs now carried banners with inscriptions "Land and Liberty," "The Land for the Peasants," "Hail the Socialistic Republic," and a huge red banner floated over the Winter Palace.

One Sunday in March a spectacular general internment for the victims of the Revolution was planned on the Field of Mars. Two hundred red coffins were laid out in a long trench. All day processions passed by in tribute to the "Martyrs for Liberty," but no religious ceremonies were held. Finally, it was the Cossacks who started a boycott and refused to come out of their barracks. "A funeral without ikons and priests! And those coffins painted red! Sacrilege!" By next day the feeling had spread and become intense; even the passers-by and the soldiers felt remorse. And the government had to summon priests and order them to say funeral prayers over the tombs of the "Heroes of the People's Revolution."

The Russian love for pagentry manifested itself even after the fall of tsarism (which had satisfied that craving with church rituals, military uniforms, and parades) in innumerable processions. Every day some organization carrying banners, with music or chanting slogans, marched either to the Duma or to the Soviet to voice their griefs or acclaim the Revolution. Processions of Jews, Mohammedans, workers, peasants, schoolteachers, midwives, were continually parading along the crowded streets. Then one day, as a glorious epilogue to Dostoevsky's *Crime and Punishment,* Igor watched a strange procession—prostitutes, as their banners proclaimed them——marching to demonstrate their allegiance to the Revolution.

In May, Kerensky established his regime, attempting to bring some order into government. And, believing in the continuance of the war, the need for some discipline in the newly organized Red Army. Igor decided to return to his regiment at the front in Galicia for the sake of his honor and his conscience. He wandered through the streets of Petrograd for an ominous last look at his beloved sights—the statue of Peter the Great was still standing there, but the facade of the Winter Palace was pockmarked with bullet holes, and not only the German Embassy but the Supreme Court and other government buildings were now heaps of rubble.

What Igor found when he rejoined his unit in the south was quite a surprise. His former captain, Zibine, a friend from the Corps des

Family Background

Pages, was still in command. The soldiers were still saluting, going through drill, and keeping up their alternating duty in the trenches. As he analyzed it, even though there had already occurred one incident when the officers fully expected mutiny and to be shot, conditions were better because it was a Guard Regiment, not a Regular Army Corps, and the soldiers were generally the tall, strong, healthy sons of the wealthy Ukrainian peasants. There came the time when a delegation from Petrograd of the Red Army of the Revolution was scheduled to talk to the men, to explain the new organization and army regulations: of course, all ranks were to be eliminated, all officers were to be eliminated, and their leaders were to be elected. A new type of mob appeared; a surprisingly burly, unkempt bunch stood before the disciplined young men, one of them like an automaton haranguing them with bombastic language and trite propaganda slogans, while they stood fidgeting in a cold rain.

That evening, as Igor sat over his chess game, there came a knock at the door and a delegation entered.

"Please, Captain, could you explain to us what those men were saying at the meeting today." "Well yes," was Igor's reply, "It was about Comrade Lenin's instructions and his promise to end the war. And that now *you* are to elect your leaders." "But can't we elect Captain Zibine? He is better than any of us." Igor was elected second in command, and only one officer was eliminated from his post. At other posts officers were killed; and great bands of rough soldiers roamed about pillaging the estates, robbing the peasants, and then commandeering the railroads.

After this new turn of events, the men were given leaves to go home, about a hundred a day, and the officers were supposed to depart gradually, as sick or disabled, and try to join the Volunteer Army of the South. With his rheumatic wrists, Igor received his medical discharge and tried to get a train for Kiev. The freight trains were so packed that there were people and baggage on the roof. Fuel had to be rounded up, tracks were blocked, and at every station there was the uncontrollable chaos of panicking humanity. What had been an overnight trip in prewar days lasted ninety-six hours. On Christmas Day of 1917 at ten o'clock in the morning Igor appeared on the doorstep of Mme. Jekouline's house in Kiev.

Mme. Jekouline and her late husband, former well-known landowners, were old friends and neighbors of the family in Kiev. In 1900 she had become interested in pedagogy, made a very serious study of children's education in Europe, particularly in Rome where she had been a pupil of Maria Montessori (1870-1952), the famous Italian educator whose progressive theories had an international influence on preschool education. In 1902 she had founded in Kiev the first coeducational school in Russia, which Igor and his sisters had attended. Although her husband died and left her penniless with nine children and the Russian government refused to support the idea of coeducation, she reorganized the school, forming a boys' school under a prominent teacher of literature, and she herself continued to conduct the girls' school. The venture was soon so successful that she built two wings of a large modern schoolhouse in the western section of Kiev, in which she also had her own private apartment. This Christmas many members of her family had already come together there; but more were always welcomed and taken care of by one means or another.

By the middle of January, Kiev was being bombarded by the newly formed Red Army. The Bolshevik regime would not tolerate the independent Republic of the Ukraine. As the shelling came nearer to the town, the water supply was destroyed, and every window in the building was shattered. Groups of terrified townspeople, complete with belongings, children, and animals, begged to take refuge in the school basement. On January 24 as the family was gathered by candlelight over a small cake and tea to celebrate St. Xenia's day, the name day of one of Xenia's daughters, Bolshevik forces entered Kiev, planting machine guns in the snow on every street corner.

Newspapers no longer appeared, but tales were heard of the bloodbath in Petrograd. And, right now, in Kiev these bands of burly, raggedly clothed ruffians were dragging the "bourgeois" families and officers out of their homes and shooting them down in the streets. Clearly, Igor and the other men of the house no longer dared to wear their uniforms and would do better not to be seen at all. Also, it was obvious that nobody could any longer reach the Volunteer Army. After a while, order was brought to the town by the formation of the Socialistic Republic of the Ukraine and the establishment of a local soviet. Murders were fewer, but robberies and wholesale pillaging continued.

Igor had decided to go to the University of Kiev to study mathematics if possible, again with the thought that education would be useful in the reconstruction which was sure to come. The university too had been reorganized—all professors had been demoted or killed or had fled—except those in the sciences. A student had been elected to sit in

Family Background

charge—the only Communist student that could be found—a confused misfit and a cripple. He was soon succeeded by a commissar from Moscow. Not long after that, the mathematics students received a declaration: "they would be allowed to continue their studies of bourgeois mathematics only until the communists had evolved a new communistic system of mathematics, and that then they would be forced to accept that."

By March the Red Occupation Forces had gradually slipped away, and the Germans quietly occupied Kiev. A deal had been made by independent negotiators (traitors, they were considered by some) in Berlin that the Germans, who were desperately in need of foodstuffs, should move into the Ukraine to replace the Reds, and the owners of estates and the prosperous peasants would furnish them with supplies. This plan also resulted in a bloody conflict when the landowners were driven out and small bands of peasants attempted to defend their property.

Although the Germans were sociable—"especially the Bavarians"—and confident that they would be "marching on to India," the Volunteer Army of the South would have nothing to do with them, and the Germans in reprisal forbade any of the former officers to join those forces. After the Treaty of Brest-Litovsk of May 3, 1918, which established formal relations between the Germans and the Soviets, special trains, protected under international law, were run weekly from Petrograd and Moscow to bring down the skilled workers so much needed for the reconstruction, and any former Ukrainians desiring to be repatriated. Hordes of civilian refugees managed to get aboard these trains, anxious to elude what was by now a really bloody reign of terror under Trotzky as well as the newly organized Cheka (Secret Police).

Mme. Jekouline's house began to fill up—with nephews, in-laws, children, friends—fugitives from all directions. Among them Igor's mother with a friend and brother Mifa turned up. It formed quite a congenial large company, cheerful despite the daily hardships of living, most of them firmly believing that these chaotic times were only temporary and that soon everything would be better. Madame de Moravsky brought along some civilian clothes for Igor and his favorite gold cigarette case. Of her own jewelry she wore only her engagement ring.

Mifa arrived bearded, ragged, emaciated, and a nervous wreck, and he would not talk. Nobody asked questions in those days. But in their

room one night Igor, after hearing his brother's allusion to having
come from Siberia, pieced together his distraught story:

*There were twenty-five of us. We went to Tobolsk to try to arrange the escape of
the Imperial family. When we arrived the Emperor and Empress were already
transferred to Ekaterinburg. We could not follow them, so we decided to save the
Tsarevitch and the Grand Duchesses if possible. Everything was ready, but at the
last moment our plot was disclosed. I am the only one alive–by a Miracle!*

He never revealed any more. He was anxious to join the Volunteer
Army, against everyone's advice; one day he just slipped away.

Government offices and ministries began to take shape in Kiev, and
Igor was recommended and chosen for the post of secretary to the
minister of finance. This position brought in some funds and screened
his activity as undercover liaison agent with the Volunteer Army. The
newest terror was a group of extreme leftists dating back to 1905
days—the Socialist Revolutionists. They were opposed to the Germans
as well as to the Bolsheviks, caused the assassinations of government
officials right and left, and were inflaming the peasantry of the countryside. One of those peasant leaders was Simon Petlura who was an
ardent Ukranian nationalist fighting both the Red and the Volunteer
armies.

In Kiev all manpower had to be registered for duty at any moment.
By November the Germans were becoming nervous and anxious to
pull out. There were frequent skirmishes and threats of Petlura's
forces advancing. A final stand was ordered at a small suburban
railroad station, and a trench had been dug outside across the highway.
It was a bitter cold and moonlit night, and the men had to take turns
warming up in the station and manning the trench. The shelling was
coming closer and closer. At daylight everyone was ordered into the
trench, fully aware that it was a last stand. Igor heard one coming—an
eight-inch shell—and threw himself down flat, feeling dirt falling on
him as he lost consciousness when a shell exploded five feet from him.
When he opened his eyes, his friend and mathematics colleague,
Vasiliy Petrov, was helping him up. He was shaking all over, and his
head felt as if it had been split open. His colonel told him to try to get
back into town if Vasiliy would help him walk.

As they passed a schoolhouse and a group of chattering civilians,
bayonets were stuck against their chests, and two rough characters
proclaimed: "We are Petlura's men. Death to all enemies of the

Family Background

People's Government!" Petrov, who was not in uniform, was left standing in the street. A man with a wooden leg ordered four others to lead Igor into the courtyard. As they leaned him against the brick wall, the idea dawned on him that he was about to be shot. But at the same time the thought was hovering in his head: "That will mean peace and rest and the end of this horrible headache." His shaking recommenced. He heard a command shouted by the man with the wooden leg; the women were shrieking in the street; there were shots; something hit him in the left cheek; and fragments exploded around him as he collapsed into the snow. When he woke up, there was his friend, Petroff, rubbing his face with snow. Blood and sand were trickling down his side, and he could not feel the rest of his body. "You'll be all right; it was just chips of the brick wall that blew off into your face. You collapsed just as they fired! Let me get you back to the Jekoulines." The doctor's diagnosis was medium severe shellshock in the upper nape of the neck. After a week in bed with cold compresses, he was almost back to normal—except that any sudden noise would start his whole body jerking.

In January 1919 the Volunteer Army, now under General Kornilov after Alexeyev's death, numbering about twelve thousand, was still along the Don River and trying to push its way to the Black Sea. The Red Army, nearly three hundred thousand strong and now joined by many Germans, was becoming better organized, was well supplied, and was increasingly successful. Petlura's "army" had evaporated; the peasants had simply drifted back to their villages. On February 19 the Red Army easily occupied Kiev, and life became more difficult and more complicated. A new kind of Bolshevik took over—not the mob who parroted mere Karl Marx slogans, but the dreaded, vengeful Cheka with leaders sent out from Moscow. Everyone was required to register with the Soviet of Workers and Peasants, which meant that everyone had to be a worker and show identification as belonging to a union.

The Jekouline establishment was still filled with those incorrigible "bourgeois whose throats were not yet slit," as the Bolsheviks called them. That indomitable group was even celebrating a daughter's wedding on the day of the Red Army occupation—not only in a church with a priest, but with a party and singing till long after midnight. They then festively escorted the young couple to the station and sang goodbyes as they saw them off on a freight train bound for Odessa, occupied at that time by the French.

Princess in Paradise

Now the big question was how to register for a union in order to earn some money and be able to get some food. They hit upon the marvelous idea of developing a theatrical company. They would produce weekly plays on the stage of the school's assembly hall. Immediately, they all signed up and became members of the actors' union. Would anyone come to see a performance, and what kind of drama should they put on? The local political commissar, a former blacksmith, became their first enthusiastic patron, and a Red Army contingent billeted nearby regularly bought tickets and filled the hall. As for the plays, it was the standard bourgeois comedies and bedroom farces that they liked the best.

In April the Red Terror intensified as General Denikin, who had succeeded as commander of the Southern Army after Kornilov was killed, joined by General Wrangel's Caucasian Army, advanced successfully into the Don Basin. By May the Tenth Red Army was defeated. Now in Kiev huge posters blared: "Everyone up to defend the Don Basin! Fight the gold-epauletted rabble!" It became impossible to keep any contact or smuggle people over to the White Army. However, counterrevolutionary activities took place surreptitiously—now and then there was a train wreck, or a section of track would blow up—and every day there would be mass arrests; any undercover operators who were caught were publicly shot. One lived at home in constant fear—of unexpected searches by the dreaded Cheka or, if under suspicion, of being seized without questioning. One walked the streets in dread. When asked to show his identification, one young man opened his coat to reach in his pocket and revealed gold epaulettes. He was shot on the spot.

One day a woman announced herself at Mme Jekouline's and most cautiously asked to speak to Madame la Général de Moravsky. One never knew what to expect. It was Pauline, a former chambermaid from the Romadanovo estate. What would her attitude be? She had noticed a familiar face in passing on the street and secretly followed her back to the place where she lived. It turned out that this Pauline's husband, Ivan, formerly a valet of General de Moravsky's, was now a member of the Railroad Workers' Union, and living in Kiev. She insisted that Igor and his mother come to their apartment to celebrate her husband's birthday with cake and wine.

That evening they could not sing enough praises of the Moravsky household and the whole Moravsky family and "the good old days."

Then Ivan said to Igor, "As you know, the red terror is increasing

Family Background

day by day. As an officer your life is in danger every moment. Come and stay with us."

"But that would be a danger for you."

"That is the least we can do for you and your mother," was the answer.

The next day Pauline caught up with Igor on the street, told him that his room had been searched by the Cheka and his papers linking him with the Volunteer Army had been found, thus incriminating him and his other anti-Bolshevik workers. He must go into hiding immediately at their place. They would move his mother to another part of town to stay with an old friend, Mme. Stukovenko, born an Italian and probably safer. For four weeks Igor remained hidden, guarded by Ivan and Pauline. Then Ivan produced a passport made out for one Nicholas Belokonsky, a telephone repairman, who was ordered to join a Red Army contingent at a small town up the Dnieper. By morning Igor Moravsky had vanished into thin air, and Pauline escorted Nicholas Belokonsky to the docks to board a riverboat. With glasses and a four-week-old beard, a knapsack on his back, his papers were examined, and he passed the careful scrutiny of the Cheka control, leaving Pauline to take the news back to his mother.

Strange coincidences abounded during those times. On board the little river steamer heading north to Chernigov one could not help but notice a tall, distinguished man, obviously a "gentleman" unabashedly dressed in English clothes and wearing the finest English leather boots. He could only be some privileged leader of the Communist Party. Upon inquiry, Igor was told that he was the renowned singer Alexander Smirnov, the darling of the Bolsheviks, touring the republics of the south and dazzling everyone with his concerts. Igor could not resist calling on him in his luxurious cabin and introducing himself. Not only was he an old friend of the family who had sung at the father's funeral, but he had lived in New York where he was a great success at the Metropolitan Opera and a close friend of Olga and Emile Kluge. He and his wife, Thaissa Vassileyevna, were the godparents of their second daughter, Thaïs.

Back in Service

When Igor reported to the Red Army post at the small town of Kozelets on the Oster River, he joined a company of fifteen young men, all recently drafted, all students, and each one knew that each of the others was going under a false name. But in the ten days they lived together nobody asked anybody any questions.

The telephone equipment had not yet arrived. So while most of them were put to digging trenches, Igor was sent to a small monastery three miles out of town to supervise the cutting down of trees to make posts for the barbed-wire fences. When he asked to be taken to the father superior, the old monk at the door answered: "There is no Father Superior. You know very well that your government has abolished monasticism. I am the monk in charge, and we are ordered to convert this place into a home for the aged." Igor realized then that his uniform showed that he belonged to the Red Army.

He was joined in his "visitors' cell" by a Gregoriy Davidov. As the two surreptitiously eyed one another and secretly took note of the belongings they unpacked, Igor recognized him as a former acquaintaince in one of the Guard Regiments in St. Petersburg. Both of them were supposed to go out and organize the wood cutting, rounding up manpower, carts, and horses to be supplied in rotation from six villages. It was harvest time, and the peasants simply hated this idea. Igor would call together the soviet of each village, gather the peasants, and harangue them about their duty to their republic and the dire consequences should they fail, in which case he would order a whole Red Battalion down upon them. They unwillingly turned up for their labor and sluggishly cut down the easiest and smallest trees, and as supervisor he was equally casual. By the end of September only the president of one of the local soviets showed up for work. Where were the others?

"It's no use fooling any longer, your Honor. The men know the Reds are deserting and are expecting the Whites at any moment. And you are expecting them too! You and your friend fooled me at first, especially when you stamped your foot and threatened to bring the soldiers down on us."

"But how do the peasants feel about the coming of the Whites?"

"They can't wait to see the Reds go. We all have had enough of them. We believe the Whites will bring order and peace, and we shall support them. God grant they won't disappoint us."

On Sunday, Igor and Gregoriy went to Kozelets for news of his company and the happenings at the front. The town was an armed camp. Red troops were pouring in; there were guns and stacked rifles along all the streets and groups of soldiers on guard. Cannonfire could be heard to the south. Denikin's White Army was close. At the edge of town they came to the door of the house where the company command

Family Background

office was located, and one of their former work battalion colleagues gave them the news: "Kiev is in panic. The Commander-in-Chief of the Red Armies of the South, Voroshilov, and the President of the Kiev Cheka, Latzis, both came here two days ago. They have gone mad executing people. It is a nightmare. I don't know who you are or what you want to do, but I advise you to get out!"

Too late! The commissar in charge of the company, accompanied by a soldier of the special Cheka battalion, marched up to the door and noticed them. "Oh," he exclaimed, "the man in charge of the forest brigade! Come along with me." Faced by an automatic in each man's hand, Igor and Gregoriy could do nothing else. They were led to a two-story house whose back faced the swamp and the river. Cheka sentries were posted at the front door. Inside they entered a hallway with a door at the opposite end that opened onto the backyard. Then they were taken upstairs to an office, with two men seated at a table covered with papers. From pictures they recognized them as Voroshilov and Latzis. The commissar announced: "Counter-revolutionary plotting. Sending those ridiculous one-inch poles for barbed wire from our position up north. White Army saboteurs, that's what they are," thundered Voroshilov. "I cannot get rid of them even at headquarters. We have no time to waste." And turning to the sentry, he said: "Take them out in back and have them shot."

Igor's own account continues:

My chest became suddenly empty. I felt a trembling in the right knee. The scene in the schoolhouse yard of Kiev came vividly back to my memory. This time it really is all over . . . and a feeling of complete resignation filled my whole being and I became calmer. I knew there was no escape. I looked at my companion. He could hardly stand up, his face was greenish, and his eyes had turned glassy. Suddenly the door back of us flew open and a soldier rushed in, breathless. "Comrade Commander-in-Chief, the White Cavalry is entering the village two kilometers to the south!" In a second the whole scene changed as if by magic. Our Commissar was standing by his desk motionless, shaking from head to foot. Voroshilov was leaning out of the window shouting orders to the men in the street. Latzis was trying to gather together all the papers spread over the table, his hands trembling, and yelling hysterically at our sentry: "Get an automobile ready immediately you idiot!"

My fear had suddenly gone and the thought struck me that perhaps there was a chance for escape now. No drama in the world could have staged so perfectly a "coup de théâtre." Our sentry had dashed out. My companion still looked paralyzed. I grabbed him by the wrist, shook him and rushed out of the room dragging him along down the stairs. In the street there was pandemonium. I could see the soldiers rushing back and forth, shouting and gesticulating wildly. At the back door a sentry barred our way. "Where do you think you are going comrades?" "My God man you must be crazy" I shouted, pointing to the turmoil in the street. "Denikin's cavalry is within one kilometer. You'd better clear out of here with the rest." The sentry left his post and rushed to the front door. We made a dash across the backyard, leaped over the fence and after pushing our way for about a hundred yards through the thickly growing reeds, threw ourselves to the ground in the swamp.

There was shouting behind us, four shots were fired and mud spattered about us. For another ten minutes we lay quiet, then began to crawl on our knees and elbows towards the river. "I shall feel very much better when I'm over there," I said, pointing to the opposite shore. We entered the water; there were not more than twenty-five yards to swim. As my feet struck bottom I heard an explosion just to the left. What remained of the bridge burst into the air and settled on the ground in a blaze. It was hours till dark when we dared to recross the river further north. By now the town was apparently deserted. Threading our way almost blindly through the woods we made it back to the monastery by daybreak.

The next day Igor and Gregoriy decided to try to work their way back to Kiev by heading directly south for about thirty kilometers, figuring on meeting the main railroad line. At a small station crowded with women and children a train loaded with troops and ammunition stopped, and they forced themselves aboard. From other refugees they gathered the news that Denikin's calvary had never actually gotten as far north as Kozelets but had swung eastward. The panic had been caused by one small scouting party. Furthermore, it was now expected that all ablebodied men must join the White Army. They pulled into Kiev at midnight, and as the town was under martial law they had to spend the night in the railroad station. There, by a gruesome chance, Igor spotted a newspaper, September 11, 1919, listing on the front page the latest victims of the Cheka and a black-bordered funeral notice for Gleb Jekouline, the nineteen-year-old-son and last remaining male of Mme. Jekouline's family. He had been held under arrest for his anti-Red activities, and as the White Army approached Kiev, the Cheka, in panic, had shot all its prisoners.

At Mme. Jekouline's he also received the news of his brother's death. Mifa had gone to the Don area and enlisted in one of the Caucasian cavalry units and had been wounded in May near Rostov. By

June he had rejoined his regiment and participated in the successful capture of Tsaritsyn. The next advance was over open country toward a front that appeared quiet and deserted. As his company lay sleeping unprotected in the fields, a roving band of Red cavalry charged out of nowhere and shot them all where they lay wrapped in their blankets.

During September-October 1919, General Denikin's army met with its major successes. He had reconquered most of southern Russia, and his front extended in a semicircle of fifteen hundred kilometers from Odessa to Kiev and north to Chernigov and Tsaritsyn. It was this wide dispersal of troops and the inadequate supply lines that proved to be his fatal strategic mistake.

In Kiev the remnants of the Guard Regiments and a few reserves tried to form a new company of the Volunteer Army for the defense of the city. But this was difficult; the officers were either old, wounded, or crippled; and the newly enlisted men were university students and peasants who had never seen service. Igor tried to make use of his idle time by continuing to attend mathematics classes such as they were at the newly organized Workers' University. His best friend there was Vasiliy Petrov, also a former university student and considered to be one of the most promising and brilliant minds in the sciences.

The Red Army was never more than twenty miles outside Kiev, and in September, having been reinforced by two divisions from the Polish front, the army advanced for a new attack on Kiev. Igor and the small company that he still held together was billeted in the Nicholas Casern, an old fortress in the southern section of Kiev, on the side of a hill overlooking the Dnieper River. Above them was the large Alexander Park. Below, to the south, was a suspension bridge across the river. Just beyond them on the bank stood the power plant, always a primary military target. As the shelling began, more than 75,000 civilian refugees, in the chilling autumn rain, began pouring across that one bridge to camp unprotected in the opposite countryside. One shell hitting that bridge or the power plant would have meant disaster. But the crowd was more terrified by the idea of the approaching Bolsheviks than by the danger of being caught in that bottleneck or the misery of sitting cold and homeless in the open fields.

For four days Igor and his young recruits were holed up in the fortress with no communication, no supplies, and no sign of action going on. To keep up their interest and their morale, Igor managed to help them put together an old German .45-mm. cannon and found some shells nearby in the fort. Neither he nor anyone of them were trained in artillery, but they made the cannon function and could aim it in the right general direction. They occupied themselves with firing potshots at the occasional Red patrol boats on the river, causing disruption among the Reds and great enthusiasm among themselves.

Then they received the order for their company to drive the Reds out of the northeastern suburb of Podol. The Podol section is like an island hill, with narrow winding streets leading up to the mesa like top. It was an old section, inhabited by artisans, shopkeepers, and industrial workers. To reach there it took them three days and nights of street fighting, advancing from house to house. The Reds' bullets were coming at them sporadically from all sides, ricocheting against the walls of the narrow streets, often inflicting wounds much more serious than those caused by direct hits. From the fort they had been dragging along their "toy cannon," as they called it, which came into most helpful service as they blasted in the direction of the Reds' fire. As they moved on, door to door and house to house, the civilians, the bourgeois owners of shops and homes, would pour out and in gratitude offer them bread, sausages, candies and cigarettes.

As one such group stood gathered in a small square, renewed shelling suddenly began, and a big one dropped into the midst of the crowd, followed by more and more down the narrow streets. A pharmacist rushed out to try to help the wounded. Igor ran into the church for a priest, and one of his students tried to reach headquarters by telephone for ambulances. On all sides amid the confusion and the shrieking, he could see his young recruits as well as townspeople being blown to bits. There was one last big blast of shells as they tried to reach the power plant. Then the Red guerrillas poured in from the rear, savagely mowing down and massacring anyone in sight. The telephone for ambulances had brought a pitifully small contingent, but it also brought a company of cavalry reinforcements, which now fired in the opposite direction and was quickly able to annihilate the Reds.

The exhausted survivors spent the night rounding up the wounded and lining up the dead in the church. Hundreds of bodies were taken to the morgue. There the uniformed soldiers were laid out in rows, and Igor had to identify more than three hundred of his own men. The local inhabitants were strewn about in piles, practically unidentifiable. What one saw was not just the pieces of bodies torn by the shell bursts but the examples of gruesome animal cruelty—smashed jaws,

Family Background

eyes gouged out, bodies dismembered and hacked open. These were the civilian storekeepers and workers, the so-called bourgeois, upon whom the Reds took out their revenge.

After a night such as that, following more than four days of hunger and street fighting, one would think that a human could endure nothing more. But Igor felt obliged to check on his friend, Vassily Petroff, who during the fighting had gone to look after his parents in their little farmhouse in the north part of the Podol. He found the house still standing. But the doors and windows had been smashed; the house had been ransacked; and the two old people in their seats at the table had had their backs hacked by bayonets. When he went out into the garden, there lay young Petrov, his skull smashed by a rifle butt, the brains of the hopeful future scientist scattered about on the ground. At that, with an almost inhuman, animal-like howl, Igor collapsed.

By the end of October they realized that the Red Army's organization and fighting had improved. Even though the British attempted to send supplies to the Whites, the railroads were in chaos; communications along the fifteen-hundred-kilometer front were deteriorating; and the soldiers who were supposed to be fed by the population, now weary of a losing cause, had turned to pillaging and robbery. The saying was, "If Moscow is not taken by November things will be bad for us." Then at the end of October, after eight weeks of fighting in the cold and rains of approaching winter, came the massive breakthrough in the center of General Denikin's line. What was supposed to be the retreat of the White Army to the Black Sea turned into a rout, with the peasants even murdering members of the fleeing units. Igor's battalion of one thousand had been reduced to some three hundred men with a trainload of two hundred wounded. He reported to Colonel Leonov: "I am leaving. You cannot stop me. In the last eight weeks since we have been attacked I have not had my boots off. They have become so full of holes that it is like fighting barefoot in the snow. They are no protection and my feet are so swollen from frost that I can hardly walk. I have not had my clothes off in the same length of time and my shirt is crawling with little gray beasts. I have seen my company reduced to 53 men, and our machine guns are in such deplorable state that they jam easily, and my inexperienced men cannot take care of them. I have to rush constantly from one to another to fix them up. . . . Furthermore, I am afraid I must admit that we have lost the game. . . ."

"I understand," said Colonel Leonov. "I have been wondering for

Princess in Paradise

the past two weeks how much longer you would last. Tomorrow your wounded and sick will be dispatched to the reserve companies at Nikolaev on the Black Sea, and you shall go with them."

The train stood in the railroad station for a week. A locomotive had to be repaired, then tracks torn up to procure more ties for fuel. The air brakes were not working, so that on every grade the hand brakes had to be used, and they were not performing well at all. Several times cars were derailed. But fortunately because of the poor fuel the pace of the train was slow, and they simply stopped, detached, toppled over the wrecked car, and went on. Gangs of bandits would fire upon the passing train but did not manage to halt it. On December 24, 1919, they reached Nikolaev.

The reserves of the Guard Regiments were already there. The captain of Igor's company was Count de Balmain, and his wife was the company nurse. Igor recognized them both from student parties in the prewar days of St. Petersburg. A doctor immediately took Igor over, put him to bed, and watched him for the next three days through spells of high fever and debilitating chills. The diagnosis was "recurrent typhus"—less dangerous than regular typhus but annoying enough in that attacks could be expected to recur within about thirteen days and each last for three to ten days. And the condition could continue through perhaps fourteen such sieges.

In Odessa

When Igor awoke, weak and shaky from his second attack, he found himself with the Balmains and Alexey Evreinov, a Jekouline cousin, in Odessa. They had brought him there on a little crowded steamer with other seriously sick officers, while more than two hundred of his soldiers, sick with typhus, had been brought there by train. The plan was for the reserves to be shipped to the Crimea, supposedly impregnable because of the narrow isthmus, and the final hope of stopping the Bolsheviks.

Odessa was jammed with refugees streaming in from the directions of Kiev, Poltava, Kharkov. The life there was typical of a doomed town—there was drunkenness, debauchery, robbery, gambling, and speculation in foreign exchange. Moreover, the demoralization of the Whites was complete; it was impossible to organize a defense of the town. Alexey Evreinov and Igor "requisitioned" a room in the Hotel Londres—formerly the best in town, on a hill overlooking the harbor—but now filthy and without heat. Their room became a meeting place and a news center. All officers were ordered to register; then they were expected to organize the evacuation of the Crimea by sea. But ships from other Black Sea ports never came, and with the cold and lack of fuel, those in port could not operate. Their only recourse now was to join with General Bredov's army, now ten thousand men strong, and proceed by train with the sick and the wounded to the Rumanian border, reach Constanta, and from there be shipped back to the Crimea.

Returning one day to his room, Igor found a note tacked to the door. It said that his mother was in Odessa and gave her address. He rushed there to find her in a shabby little hotel, where she had been since fleeing Kiev with Madame Stukovenko, who, as an Italian subject, was leaving the next day for Trieste. An officer friend of Mme. Stukovenko's, when he was registering, had noticed the name of Moravsky with the address and had hastened to the hotel to pin the note on the door. She had lost all her baggage; her funds were low; and the only jewelry she still had was her engagement ring. She had typhus and was being cared for by a doctor, a former pupil of Dr. Fedorov, who was admitting her to a hospital the next morning.

Igor did all he could to try to persuade her to escape abroad, which he could arrange through the British Red Cross. But she said she was tired of living and that if she survived this sickness, she wished only to go back to Moscow and remain there with her family. Igor could see only too well that if she did come out of the hospital, she would be just another little old lady wandering around this hellhole of Russia or one of thousands of refugees stranded somewhere in the Balkans—and who could tell if cables or letters would ever reach America? Obviously, if he stayed with her, he would be deserting, and they both knew that. The next morning he took her to the hospital—unheated, as were all the houses in Odessa—and crowded with lines of pitiful human beings. They sat for an hour waiting for her to be registered, both silent, knowing there was nothing they could say. When her turn came, he carried her into the office and entered her name in the book. Then the nurse said, "You must go now." As an orderly lifted the tiny lady and carried her through a door, she stretched her arm toward Igor and said, "If you ever escape this hell, Igor, try to get to Olga in America. God bless you!" And with that she fainted.

That night their train was scheduled to move out of the freight station. At four-thirty in the afternoon a British boat was leaving the

Princess in Paradise

harbor, and Evreinov tried to persuade Igor to get on it, using his certificate as a typhus convalescent. "I cannot do it," was Igor's statement. "There are 250 of our men in that train, sick and convalescent, and they must be taken care of. Our two junior officers cannot do it. They are just youngsters. If I go with you, these men will be like so many lost sheep. . . . After all, they have stuck with us to the last, and I believe we owe them something. At least one of us should stand by them . . . even if it seems useless from a practical point of view." By ten o'clock the next morning, January 21, 1920, the train was able to pull out of Odessa—which was occupied by the Reds that same afternoon.

Upon arrival at Tiraspol on the Rumanian border, there was further consternation. The Rumanians had canceled the promised offer to let them pass through, being afraid of the typhus epidemic. In desperation, General Bredov decided to make a dash north along the shore of the Dniester River and try to reach Poland, which, being at war with the Soviet Russia, might treat them as allies. The chance of escaping from the Bolsheviks, who were advancing rapidly from the northeast, was very slim, and the attempt looked almost futile from the beginning.

Dniester Death March

From there on Igor tells just parts of what became known as the "Dniester Death March":

The Dniester March began the morning of January 25, 1920 and was undoubtedly one of the most pathetic episodes in the history of General Denikin's army. A train of three thousand peasant carts moved along the hilly shore of the Dniester River. The cold was unusually severe, but there was little snow so the road was covered with ice, which made the horses fall and the carts slide on each grade. Thirty thousand people had fled from Odessa in the hope of crossing to Rumania, and were now following the army. Bredov's army group, which was supposed to be 10,000 strong, was actually cut in half at the time we left Tiraspol, and dwindled down to less than 3,000 at the end of our 350 Km. march. The balance of the men either were or became sick with typhus, and amidst the refugees 60% had the same disease. All these sick people lay on top of another, seven or eight to a cart, often unable to get indoors for five or six days in succession, as the villages where we stopped for the night were overcrowded.

Igor, who had been riding in a carriage with the de Balmains, walking part of the time to keep warm, realized another typhus attack

Family Background

was coming on. The doctor ordered him to be transported along with Colonel Leonov, who was also seriously sick, in his big old open automobile, which had been commandeered from some garage. But this luxurious mode of travel did not last long. The next morning they awoke to machine-gun fire and shells bursting in the village. Sick men were thrown one over the other into the cart. The doctor and chauffeur carried Leonov to the automobile, and they joined the lines of carts heading helter-skelter out of the village. At the next hill the car slipped, rolled backward and turned over beside the road. From the hill one could see the Reds approaching.

We were now walking, supporting Leonov under his arms. Suddenly the chauffeur stopped and would go no further. Being a soldier he ran no risk if he was captured, but for us officers it meant the end. I drew my revolver: "You will help the Colonel as long as I am alive; and if I am wounded the first thing I'll do will be to blow your brains out." The argument had its effect. We resumed our march.

Ten minutes later General Shulgin caught up to them on horseback followed by a mounted machine-gun carriage with a two-passenger vehicle into which the sick men were loaded. For the next five days Igor was able to handle the machine gun, as the skirmishes with the Reds continued; then, though he became weaker with fever, he found that he could still correct the men's aim and instruct them when the gun became jammed. On the evening of the fourteenth day, the machine-gun cart pulled up in front of a house where they were to spend the night, and he heard the cheerful voice of Countess de Balmain: "Well hello, Moravsky! So you're here at last. Supper is ready. We have some hot rich goose broth for you and a bottle of fine cherry brandy." That night, as he wrapped himself in his blanket, with perspiration breaking out, he calculated that this was the fourteenth day and time for the periodic crisis to come.

When next he opened his eyes, he was on a mattress on the floor of a peasant house and aware of Colonel Leonov beside him. "Where are we?"

"In a village just across the Polish border. Your head seems to have cleared up at last. For a time the doctor thought you'd never regain your mental capacities with that typhus on top of your shell shock. He claims that you had one of the longest attacks of typhus on record."

For ten days more he could not pull boots on his swollen feet and could barely sit up in the March sunshine outside the cottage door. The

rate was now even higher than it had been through all the harrowing
conditions of the Dniester march.

They were notified that in March an agreement had been reached
between Poland, Czechoslovakia, Austria, Serbia, Rumania, and Bulgaria allowing the army units to pass through on their rolling stock,
and there was still a chance for them to reach the Crimea. One had to
declare immediately who were refugees and who were military men.
The refugees could leave or do as they wanted. The Guards Regiments
felt they had to remain a military organization. Count de Balmain,
because of his wife, was declared free.

After three more weeks of waiting they were transported to Stanis-
lawov, expecting to be sent to the Crimea. Instead, since those countries which had agreed to let them pass through again reneged on the
bargain, they were all to be transferred indefinitely to a Polish concentration camp.

In a Polish Concentration Camp

Strzalkovo, a former German prisoner-of-war camp, with long
wooden barracks completely surrounded by high barbed wire, spoke
of only one thing as they were headed through the gate: "Abandon
Hope All Ye Who Enter Here." Polish officers watched over the long
rooms fitted with two rows of wooden berths on which the mattresses
were sacks filled with straw. Rations consisted of acorn coffee, black
bread, and soup—usually made from rotten meat. Right then
everyone decided that each individual would do whatever he could do
or might choose to do—whether it meant chancing an escape, getting
in touch with relatives anywhere abroad, or whatever else seemed
possible. Igor decided to write a letter to his sister in New York, vaguely
remembering an address of six years ago and scarcely believing that
such a thing as mail service or undisrupted living existed any longer
anywhere in the world. Officers had received token payments for their
horses, so it was easy enough to bribe the guards to produce a continual
supply of vodka. Five weeks passed by in a haze of vodka and the very
real game of Russian roulette, until the pistols were confiscated, with
the menial jobs of laundry and clean up occupying their time. One day
a cable did arrive from New York. Even after his head cleared from
yesterday's vodka, there it was: "Sending money and clothing." If

Family Background

cables came through, perhaps letters and packages might come also. But how long could that take? Six weeks? Two months?

Prison routine had eased. Officers were allowed to take afternoon walks in alternating groups under the watch of a Polish guard. They would walk the one kilometer into the village and visit peasant homes where they would pay for a good meal and arrange for their next visit, then return to camp. Escape attempts were rare, since nobody knew where they would go or what they would do with themselves; fugitives would be caught and be brought back by the gendarmes. Apparently, few escape attempts were successful.

Igor decided he would try to get to Warsaw. On his next visit to the village for a meal he simply did not walk back but disappeared into a wheatfield. He lay there till dark, half asleep, half dreaming, half unbelieving, trying to recall time and dates, to figure out how long had been taken out of his life: Was it six months or six years? It was now July. Since March they had been isolated in Strzalkovo. What lay ahead? What had happened in Russia?—and the rest of the world? Suddenly a stern voice boomed: "Follow me! Back to camp!"

Igor spoke no Polish but in German he tried: "Have a cigarette." The guard immediately straightened up, asked how he happened to speak German.

"I learned it in military school, of course."

At which the guard saluted, clicked his heels, and announced: "Sargent S——, Kaiserin August Garde Grenadier Regiment!"

For an hour they smoked and indulged in war reminiscences, recalling both fronts. Then he stood up, saluted, and walked off into the dark. Igor caught the morning train for Warsaw.

In Warsaw he sold his gold cigarette case and spent the money to buy some civilian clothes and send a cable to New York. At the Russian Consulate he obtained a passport and a visa for the United States and ran into Colonel Leonov, the Balmains, and others. The days were spent at the Russian Red Cross which, through the help of the American Red Cross, provided food for the Russian refugees. It became a general meeting place. Calling at the consulate to inquire for mail was time consuming. Meanwhile, he was rediscovering the world—it had been twenty months without foreign news since the Germans entered Kiev—he learned of the Versailles treaty, a Hungarian revolution, new boundaries, new countries like Czechoslovakia and Yugoslavia, and Austria a republic!

On August 2 a cable with money did arrive. Then came the problem

only one month later. Next he paid a visit to the Greek Consulate, then
to the Italian, trying to obtain a transit visa—all were crowded; all had
long lines.

❧ Escape!

By August 10 the Polish forces were being pushed back by the
successfully advancing Bolsheviks, and the sound of cannonading was
definitely heard east of the city. Tension rose to panic; the legations
and consulates were packing up and leaving town; trains were jammed.
So, it was off again, this time to Cracow. There it was the same routine
of rushing and waiting at one consulate after another. The Czech
offices were the least crowded, and there he could obtain the visa but
not the medical certificate testifying to absence of infectious diseases.
Anyway, from Cracow it was merely an overnight ride to Teschen, a
frontier town with one half in Poland and the other in Czechoslovakia.
But at the border he was forbidden to cross without the medical
certificate. While he was sitting dejectedly in the soup kitchen at the
railroad station, an old bearded Orthodox Jew listened to his story and
offered to help.

"If the gentleman could spend 500 Marks? ..."

"I met my bearded friend at a cafe shortly before midnight," Igor
recounts. "I handed him the money; he took my suitcase and led the
way through narrow streets to a house right on the edge of the water.
There we stepped into a boat and he began to row across the river. As
we approached the other shore a voice cried out something in Czech.
My oarsman answered in the same language. In a minute we landed; a
Czech sentry stood there. Something was slipped into his hand, after
which he very politely took my suitcase out of the boat then helped me
to jump ashore. I was on Czechoslovakian territory."

However, disappointments continued to pile up. In Prague at the
Russian Legation, the only permit one could obtain was to go to Serbia
with the stipulation of enlisting in General Wrangel's army. The Czech
police would allow no one without employment to stay more than three
days. Vienna was equally crowded and equally strict. Igor knew he had
good friends in Belgrade. So the next day he enlisted in Wrangel's
army.

He arrived in Belgrade quite some time later, with pleasant stays in
Vienna and Budapest on the way. Money was jangling in his pockets;

for 75 cents one could have the best hotel room—with a bed and a bath! One could buy meals in restaurants, with wine flowing and gypsies singing. One could find sympathetic company, and one could forget. When he finally reached Belgrade, he had not a penny left. He reported at the Russian Legation and to the Russian Red Cross, where he could get free meals. He ran into Alexey Evreinov, who was now choir master for the Royal Opera. He got off another cable to his sister and located his friend, a former Guards officer, Count Vladimir Bobrinsky. To avoid being sent on to the Crimea and Wrangel's army, he had only to visit the chief doctor of the Red Cross and claim exemption from military duty because of the rheumatism in his wrist and elbow. Bobrinsky's father, now in the Ministry of Finance, had been assigned an estate formerly belonging to a Hungarian archduke, and all officers of the former Guard Regiments were welcomed there.

For eight weeks Igor passed the time there comfortably but anxiously waiting for an answer to his last cable. His sister had been off on a hunting trip in western Canada. Then came a message from Berlin, from her brother-in-law, Albert Kluge, that money had been transferred to him, with which Igor could buy passage to the United States. With the intention of going to Berlin, Igor again made the rounds of consulates, with every country denying even transit visas because of the deluge of refugees. If the American money could be released to him in Belgrade, he could try for an Italian visa and get to Trieste.

In Trieste at the Cunard Line he could obtain a cabin for May. But by going in steerage he might get on the *Aquitania* sailing from Cherbourg in January. The French Consulate, like all the others, was refusing even transit visas to Russians—the homeless, the penniless, the unwanted thousands of those days. Fortunately, after another cable and a brisk successful argument—"For what price could it be arranged?" "Well, yes, we may be able to manage something!"—his path was set. In any way possible, get to Cherbourg. On January 24, 1921, ten months after his first letter to his sister, Igor was standing on the deck of the *Aquitania* watching the lights of Cherbourg disappear behind him. What lay ahead? Faced with the prospect of an unknown country and new adventure, another thought characteristically entered Igor's mind: After all he had been through, having tasted "the salt of life," as he said, might it not also turn out to be too peaceful, uneventful—even dull?

Princess in Paradise

III

New Life in the New World

*"So they were married and began life
in the foreign land which she thought
would surely be paradise."*

Olga and her mother in New York, 1913.

9

Olga Takes Command

LGA'S ARRIVAL in New York on March 4, 1909, seemed most surprisingly auspicious. As they drove up Fifth Avenue in lovely sunshine there was little traffic, but all the lampposts were hung with red, white and blue bunting, and American flags were draped across the hotel facades. People were in holiday attire, bowing and waving familiarly—all presenting the picture of a friendly, intimate Old World city. While she did not believe in the glowing legend of "America, where the streets are paved with gold," she was delightfully pleased. Could this be to welcome her, the bride of a distinguished local personage? To discover later that it was all in honor of the inauguration day of President Taft did not spoil her warm and excited first impression.

Social Life in New York

Life of the newlyweds promptly settled down with ease—the household arrangements had already been established for her. There at the Apthorp, as described before, was Emile's bachelor apartment complete with all its gaudy Victorian decoration and elegant Viennese equipment. One special and beautiful surprise was the grand piano of Circassian walnut, the personal wedding gift to her from their friend, Charles Steinway. Like any family treasure, it accompanied them in all their later moves, stood in a featured place of honor, was admired by

185

musicians, and was faithfully practiced on by the children through many years. Beloved by all of us, both a responsibility and a white elephant, its last home was in Thaïs's Park Avenue apartment before being sold.

Marya, Emile's housekeeper of long standing, managed the kitchen and domestic problems gently guiding her new "lady boss"! There too was the ubiquitous, smiling Albert Lear—in the bedroom presiding as valet, in the living room as majordomo to handle social duties, and as business secretary with private daily reports and important documents. With the best of intentions all this should help to ease the transition for an innocent young bride from a foreign land to the new life and strange ways of the sophisticated metropolis.

Emile was forty-two, used to twenty years of bachelor freedom, a man of the world who at the same time had developed into a dedicated American. Olga was twenty-one, a foreigner, assumed to be the traditional inexperienced young bride; but characteristically, without noticeable fanfare, she soon proved herself to be an independent young lady. She was quite able to handle domestic and social affairs in her own gentle but strong way, her sense of humor seldom failing and quietly winning everyone's confidence and admiration.

Life in New York City around 1910 was lively and elegant and revolved in a number of definite social circles. Emile's office and factory were on West Fourteenth Street in a loft building belonging to Browning, King & Company, the gentlemen's outfitters on Fifth Avenue. At that time Fifth Avenue and Fourteenth Street was the hub of all business life.

Around that area were also the elegant restaurants—Luchow's and Delmonico's—the men's clubs and the first high-class department store, John Wanamaker's, on Eighth Street. Though the avenue was dusty with the traffic of horse-drawn carriages, open trams, and a few motor cars, the fashionable ladies swished along the sidewalks with their parasols, large hats, and long bustled dresses, gracefully gathering up their ruffled skirts to step off the curb and cross the streets. On Sundays everybody was out in their finery, strolling along the avenue and riding in their open carriages, bowing and greeting each other as they passed. Uptown where the residential area bordered on Central Park, those who kept their own horses were out riding along the bridle paths, passing their friends and doffing their hats to the ladies in the carriages. Everyone knew each other and expected to be seen and to see their friends.

Princess in Paradise

For lunch, which was a long, leisurely, and elaborate meal, groups dropped in at the restaurants or sat under the striped awnings at the outdoor tables, while gentlemen gathered alone in their smoke-filled kingdom upstairs, reached by their *private* entrance. Teatime in the palm-filled courts of the Plaza and Biltmore hotels, with soft string music emanating from behind the bushes, was the supreme hour of the feminine world, bubbling with gossip, showing off finery, eating dainty pastries, served by waiters who knew all their regular patrons by name and remembered each one's personal whims.

At the Metropolitan Opera it was the gathering of the most intimate of exclusive circles. In the so-called Diamond Horseshoe everyone knew which box belonged to whom and could of course note the arrival of any newcomer or perhaps the introduction of a budding young daughter. On an upper floor in Sherry's Restaurant parties gathered for midnight supper and it was genteely observed who was entertaining or paying particular attention to which opera star of the moment. Tetrazzini, Louise Homer, Geraldine Farrar, and Lucrezia Bori were among those most sought after. Caruso, Martinelli, and Walter Slezak had their own group of followers. Chaliapin, though he had first appeared in New York in 1901 and was a favorite in London and Paris, did not return to the Metropolitan as a star until 1921.

Olga and Emile welcomed a number of other "musical" friends from Europe who came to New York to perform and entertained them later in Englewood after the move there. Their closest and dearest friends were the Russian tenor Alexander Smirnoff and his wife, Thaissa Vasliliyevna, who were asked to be godparents to their second daughter, Thaïs, born at the Apthorp in October 1911.

Before she could preside in her own home, Olga was obliged to make the rounds of Emile's friends and habitués. Of those first acquaintances who became very dear to her over many years were Sam and Lillian Knopf. Sam, later famous as being the father of Alfred Knopf, was a so-called efficiency expert like Frank and Lillian Gilbreth, of *Cheaper by the Dozen* fame, whose advice helped to modernize many a well-known industry and who likewise was used by the Kluge Weaving Company to keep their production up to the latest in efficiency methods as well as ease over any labor problems. He was of course an admirer of Emile's personal achievements.

At a dinner party in her honor at their handsomely appointed home on Fifth Avenue, Olga learned one of her first lessons in American democracy.

New Life in the New World

Papi in 1910.

Princess in Paradise

Mami in 1910.

New Life in the New World

"Forget your prejudices," Emile warned her. "You may never have been entertained by a Jewish family before, but these are my special friends and you must try to play your part."

As it turned out, it took no great effort for her to respond to their warm-heartedness and to enjoy their high level of culture and the intelligence of the friends they gathered around them, and their friendship continued for many years.

But here at her first big dinner party, trying to be on her best behavior, sitting in the place of honor at the head of the table beside Sam Knopf, the object of curious attention from all eyes, she was the picture of perfect decorum. Cautiously she watched which fork one picked up first—each country does have different customs, and some things were bound to be new. First came raw oysters on the half shell, and as a good traveler she could force herself to try them. Then the sauce was passed. As she looked down into the tomato concoction over her oysters, something obviously moved; then began to crawl up from under.

Absolutely unprepared, she jumped and let out a screech— "Something moved!"

"Why, of course. Don't you know this delicacy?—live oyster crabs!"

Cute little white things about a half inch in size, with many tiny legs, that you swallowed whole along with the sauce and the oyster. The crisis passed. She was forgiven. She recovered.

The next thing on the menu was the course of fowl, a gourmet's delight, explained with much pride—whole squabs. Again a quiet sinking of the stomach, pushing the bird around a bit on the plate, looking for help. Oh, it wasn't that she didn't know how to cut them up. As she explained quite sincerely: "These are pigeons, the symbol of the Holy Ghost! I could never eat one." Her Jewish friends were mortified but sympathetic.

At the other end of the table, her good husband Emile was bragging about the sophistication of life in Russia, its luxury, its opulence, those gorgeous women with all their furs and jewels. One should see Olga's magnificent new full-length sable coat, trimmed with dark Kamchatka beaver collar and border. With "Ohs" and "Ahs" all eyes were on her again, the blushing bride, to notice what jewels she was wearing now.

Then she said, in her sweet, firm voice, with a reproachful look at her husband: "Yes! And you know I own an evening gown, too!"

Princess in Paradise

Lillian never forgot that and the Knopfs delighted in telling that story whenever they wanted to take Emile down a peg. What faithful friends they were as we children grew to know also, as they poured their affection and attention on all of us. When our parents were away on some trip, the Knopfs faithfully came to check on how we were getting along with the current governess and always invited us to their home for a luncheon or dinner visit. In 1924 it was Lillian Knopf who introduced us youngsters to Mah-Jongg, the absolute rage at the time, and saw that we had our own first Mah-Jongg set.

Earlier than that, when the move to Englewood was still a new event, the Knopfs brought along their two sons on one of their visits, both grown young men. Alfred had already long been entranced with Russian literature and things Russian and was attending Columbia University where he graduated in 1912. Olga admired the young man's knowledge and interests, and he loved to look at her Russian objets d'art and listen to her stories. But evidently the picture that remained most vivid in his eyes was the sight of our two white Russian wolfhounds (The Borzois), set free and streaking across the lawn as we sat on the porch after dinner. Sam the fatherly advisor, one of the few who could ever preach to Emile even on personal family affairs and be listened to with respect, confided how disappointed he was that his son Alfred refused to follow him in the lucrative business world. Instead, he had dreams of something more intellectual.

"However," Sam said, "Emile I believe that it is now the right way to do it; one does not force one's own career upon one's children. It is their life and one must let them make their own choices." Later we each went to Sam to plead our part for the same reasons and to ask his advice.

It was he who urged me to get secretarial training even on top of a college degree. And to my father he said, when my greatest desire was somehow to enter the publishing business: "Let her take the job on which she has her heart set. Don't pick on her about the low salary!"

Their younger son, Edwin, went to Hollywood to become a successful movie director. Alfred A. Knopf founded his own publishing firm (1915) using the trademark "Borzoi Books"—the Russian wolfhound running. His name became distinguished as a publisher of great foreign literature as well as much of the best of the American authors, and the finished books were known for their handsome design and the high quality of typography.

New Life in the New World

🌿 The Imperturbable Olga

Emile always admired what he called Olga's "Slavic temperament" and used to love to tell stories, either teasingly or in admiration, to illustrate it. She did truly demonstrate it so many times that we all remembered and learned from it—an ability to freeze at a time of crisis into a deceptively surface calm when everyone around was fluttering in panic. The degree of inner control was revealed only when the excitement subsided and nerves could be relaxed, very often followed by a migraine headache. However, as with most new husbands, he still had lots to learn about his young wife.

There was the famous incident of how Emile returned one evening to his Apthorp apartment and as they sat down to dinner he realized that something was not the same as usual.

"What has changed here? Something is different."

"Oh, nothing."

And as Maria hovered around stoically serving the dinner: "But I have the feeling that something has been changed."

"No, not really."

Finally as they left the dining room it came to him—the curtains! Where were the curtains? The windows were bare.

"Well, the firemen took them out."

"What firemen?"

"Oh, we had a little fire today! The dining room curtains caught fire, and we had to call the fire department and a few fire engines came. But they managed to put out the flames and only had to remove the burnt draperies. Everything else is fine. You see there was no other damage."

And so it always was. In Berlin in 1922 Olga, long overdue and anxiously awaited, entering the hotel room with "Now be calm, everybody! I've just been robbed. A man held me up on the street. He took my rings and my bracelet and my furpiece. But see I still have my diamond locket-watch, which I managed to hide in my bosom."

That same year they were in an auto accident in downtown Berlin. Emile arrived home obviously shaken up. But from Olga the story sounded so simple: "Our car skidded on the slippery street in the midst of all that traffic, and another car ran into us broadside. However, we were not hurt, so we could get out and walk away. Fortunately, we caught a taxi to bring us home."

Years later in Englewood in the big house where they had adjoining

Princess in Paradise

separate bedrooms on the second floor Olga exhibited the same trait of
control. When opening her eyes in bed one morning in the early light
of dawn, she saw a man standing between her and her bureau quietly
searching among the pieces of her silver dressing table set. Observing a
bit more sharply, she realized he was poking about in her long rectangular box which she called her "bead box"—and with what?—the butt
of a pistol.

"What are you doing there?" she said quietly.

As he turned around he pointed the pistol at her and said, "Come
on, lady, you know what I want—your jewelry. Where is it?" Bringing
the long box over to the bed and rummaging around in it again with his
pistol, he added: "Even I can see this is all junk!"—and dumped the
contents onto the bed.

By now she could see he was very young, very shaky, and fairly
decent looking, and she started talking, meanwhile quietly putting on
her slippers and dressing gown.

"You poor fellow, you must be very desperate or very hungry. You
know, my husband's in the next room and could come in here any
minute. And you surely must realize that any good jewelry of mine is in
a safe or in the bank. You're right—that's all only costume jewelry.
Why don't you come down to the kitchen with me? I'll give you some
food and a cup of coffee."

So down they went—she tiptoeing ahead, he behind with the pistol.

As she sat at the kitchen table after fixing him a pot of coffee and
some bread, she asked, "How did you get into this sort of thing?"

"Aw gee, lady—you know I'm poor and hungry and desperate
—and you in this big house on the hill—you've got everything!"

"But now you'll only get yourself in trouble. I'll have to call the
police."

"Oh, no, don't do that. Please, lady, you're a good sport. Will you
wait five minutes till I get beyond the driveway before you telephone?"

So there was typical Olga again. Standing calmly beside Emile's bed
at the telephone as he woke up, she declaimed: "We've just had a
burglar in the house and I ought to phone the police. But he didn't take
anything so I promised to wait a few minutes till he could get away. He
was just a poor silly boy."

Then Emile was suddenly awake and, all excited, replied: "A pistol
at your back? He could have shot you. Or he could have come after me!
How did he get in? Why did you let him go? Are you sure he really
didn't take anything from your dresser?"

New Life in the New World

"No, no, no! After all, nothing serious happened, and he was no dangerous criminal. You call the police if you want. But there's nothing much to tell. So let's just forget it!"

Return to Russia

It was during the summer of 1910 that Olga kept her promise and made her first trip back to Russia to introduce her six-month-old daughter, Alexandra, to her parents. They were living in the big house in Moscow, and by now her father was totally confined to a wheelchair. On this trip she was accompanied by Emile and Maria Coleman, who had now officially become the nanny and who could not speak a word of Russian. Consequently, a tag with her name and address in Russian and English was attached to the baby's wrist, and a similar one hung around the neck of the nurse whenever they went for their outings in the park.

Olga and Emile were free enough to travel around, visit friends, and enjoy some of the sights they had not been able to see together before. One of these was the great East-West trade fair at Nizhniy Novgorod (now called Gorki on the map). Situated on both banks of the northern Volga River, this fourteenth-century town, once the easternmost outpost of the Hanseatic League, was famous over hundreds of years for this annual meeting of the Orient and Europe. Peddlers set up their shacks and tents around the tremendous bazaar area. Tatar types from the north sat amid piles of assorted furs. The eastern tribes hung out their handwoven rugs in a variety of typical designs while their women kept busy at the looms right there. Rows of dark-skinned metal workers hammered away at their trays and pots. Fur-capped ruffians squatting in front of goatskin tents spread out in bundles of rags an assortment of sparkling precious stones gathered in the Ural Mountains. Even to a Russian it was always picturesque, exciting, and fantastic.

Emile could not resist the inevitable bargaining. Wanting to surprise his bride with a bargain of his own, he had returned to the fair to roam independently. Back in their hotel room he proudly presented her with a ragged cloth bundle. When she unfolded it, there lay in her hands about a dozen rough aquamarines of different sizes and colors. Slightly aghast, she looked at them trying to be appreciative, then studied them more closely.

"Where did you get these?"

Princess in Paradise

"From such-and-such a peddler down by the river."

"Well, you certainly have been duped. Every one of these has a flaw in it or is irregular and poorly cut. You take these right back!"

Probably feeling that she could dicker better herself or that this poor foreigner needed some backing up in handling an Oriental character, they went together. With much display of indignation and a torrent of haggling in Russian, she managed to have the peddler take back the handful of smallish stones. In exchange, she picked out one single large, rose-cut aquamarine of great depth, which she considered after careful observation to be of good quality.

As with most of those rough or unset stones discovered there, one had to take them to one's jeweler, who then designed an appropriate setting. This deep aquamarine was set into the head of an ivory handle to a white lace parasol, which later became a lady's cane and, still later, was dismounted and transformed into a drop pendant. The problem of a pair of very difficult, large deep topazes was solved by Cartier in Paris. They were set in lavender enamel and surrounded by gold leaves so that they resembled a thistle motif. Each one became the head of a large hatpin. Unfortunately in a way, this had been so skillfully done that they never could be converted into any other kind of brooch or pendant. One bunch of roughly polished Ural emeralds were simply strung together as beads, awaiting some later plan. A perfect dark blue cabuchon sapphire Olga chose for herself went into a simple platinum ring, which almost never left her finger.

The second visit back to Russia took place in May 1911. Alexandra was now about one and a half years old, and a new British nanny, Amy Westbrook, accompanied Olga and the baby on the journey, made via a German ship to Bremen, then by train overland to St. Petersburg. There the General and Madame de Moravsky occupied a large ground-floor apartment. Olga spent most of her sojourn there with her ailing father, who was considerably amused by the Russian prattle of his little American granddaughter. When Emile joined them later in July, St. Petersburg seemed very quiet in the summertime, and they had more time to visit friends and family. Igor, who had graduated from the Corps des Pages in 1910 and was now a law student at the university, had taken up lawn tennis very seriously and was playing at the Tauride Palace courts or was off on tournaments. The beloved uncle, Dr. Sergey Fedorov, had remained in town, since he was always on call as personal physician to the tsar and his family.

Through Uncle Serge they received an invitation to Tsarskoe-Selo

Ready for the Sunday morning ride, 1917.

for tea. It was a memorable trip out to the big park and to the smaller Alexander Palace where the royal family preferred to live, keeping it intimate and with the feeling of a real home. Peterhof, farther out and directly on the Gulf of Finland, was actually just a summer villa, set amid fountains and parks, from which they could make their excursions on the imperial yacht, the *Standart.*

Arriving at the Alexander Palace, the guests were escorted through halls and rooms by a modestly dressed attendant, who opened the doors into a small and cluttered library. A short, kindly faced man in simple military uniform rose from his table and came forward to greet them and shake hands. With his stature, gentle blue eyes, and carefully pointed beard, what struck Emile most was his almost twinlike resemblance to England's King George. The tsar spoke beautiful English in a low voice, asked about America and business conditions over there, and what progress Emile may have noticed in Russia. The empress was lying on a chaise longue on the balcony, dressed in lacy lavender, and greeted Dr. Fedorov warmly, immediately talking of her concern for her little son. Then they were invited through an open door onto the terrace where the tea table was set. As they sat over tea in the shade of

Princess in Paradise

the old trees looking out at the park and the gardens, other household friends joined them. The five children came up to kiss their parents and each affectionately embraced their good friend, the doctor, speaking a few words with him before they went away for tea with their governesses. Alexei, the Tsarevitch, was accompanied by his bodyguard, the tall, strong sailor, Derevenko, who never left his side and was always on the alert to shield him from any blows when playing or catch him if he should fall. The whole picture was idyllic, of a handsome, affectionate, quite unpretentious family in the midst of which the tall, slim Dr. Fedorov stood as a trusted confidant and friend.

Early in September, Olga had to return to New York and embarked on a Russian ship for the long journey home. This time she tried to take along more of the family gifts, treasures, and photographs, which she had so far not been able to do, never dreaming that this would be the last time the family would be together nor the last glimpses she would have of her mother country and the life in which she had grown up.

During the Atlantic crossing one of those frightful equinoctial storms arose which lasted almost the whole ten days, tossing about the boat and passengers so miserably that nearly everyone was confined to their beds. For Olga the suspense was dreadful; she was so sick and it was near the time for the birth of her second baby that the ship's captain and doctor were alerted to the possibility of the event. In the midst of her discomfort her greatest worry seemed to be that if it were a boy and were born on a Russian ship, he would not be the happily anticipated new citizen of the United States. However, they did make it safely to home and the Apthorp where on October 8, under the customary care of the family doctor, a red-haired baby girl was born. Though the first name registered on her birth certificate was Nadejda (Hope), it was changed to Thaïs in honor of her godmother. Tiny as she was, the little redhead promptly received the nickname "Tetrazzini" in admiration of her lung power.

✿ Englewood Discovered

With two children now, thoughts developed about a larger family and an adequate place in the country with a free and more congenial open environment. Emile's brother Adolf, with his wife Grace and their three children had already moved from their Riverside Drive apartment to a substantial home far out in Montclair, New Jersey. Adolf had already established a new and much larger weaving factory

New Life in the New World

in Pompton Lakes, and was therefore completely outside the city.

So it was that Olga and Emile, much as they loved the busy life of New York City, discovered Englewood and "Greystone," which became the legendary house on the hill of their dreams. In many ways it combined features they enjoyed in both Palazzo Konshin and Romadanovo with endless possibilities for development in the new life they saw in the future. The house had been built only a few years before by an elderly couple, was in perfect condition, decorated almost exactly to their taste, and had an expandable arrangement of rooms and porches.

Late in 1912, they moved from their New York apartment to the new home in the country. In the meantime, Emile enlarged his weaving business by establishing his own factory building in West New York, New Jersey, directly opposite Forty Second Street and handy to the Hudson River ferry service. Emile, Jr., was born on May 6, 1913, the first child in their New Jersey home, which called for a big celebration which was to combine his christening with their housewarming and the occasion for Madame de Moravsky's first visit to the New World.

10

Ludmilla and Xenia

 UDMILLA NICOLAEVNA ISNARD came from a French family which for several generations had been successful wine growers in the south of France near Grace on the Côte d'Azur. Her grandfather, Nicholas, had been invited by the Russian government in 1843 to come to Russia and try to develop the wine growing industry. They brought their French grape stock and had been given large holdings of land north of Odessa, encompassing most of a little town called La Limane, which still exists. Although her father was born in Russia (died in Paris, 1923) he kept his French citizenship, and the family—Ludmilla, a brother, Vadim, and a sister, Tatyana—were born in Russia and reared almost equally in the French tradition and the Russian.

After her early education at home and in school at Odessa, Ludmilla was sent in 1910 to Princess Obolensky's finishing school for young ladies in St. Petersburg. During the summer of 1911 when she was playing tennis at the Tavrichesky Lawn Tennis Club on the grounds of the Tauride Palace, she met Igor de Moravsky, already an outstanding player and very popular with everyone. He had graduated from the Corps des Pages in 1910 and had then entered the university of St. Petersburg to study mathematics and law. She was still a rather restricted schoolgirl, and from behind the curtained windows of their residence she used to watch for the time when Igor would march down the street heading for his classes at the university. Igor was not so bashful that he was unaware of this attention and would flash back a greeting.

For the next two years Igor and Ludmilla became known as outstanding tennis players, both of them playing in tournaments and traveling around Russia representing their club. As she said, it was a wonderful time—two girls and eleven men!—with her brother acting as chaperone. In 1912 they visited Stockholm to witness the Olympic tennis matches, though both were too young to enter themselves. In 1913 Ludmilla won the Russian women's singles championship, and with Count Michael Sumarokov took the mixed doubles. During the long visit in Moscow, Ludmilla was staying with a family friend, the mayor of Moscow, while Igor and his friends were given the liberal use of his grandfather Konshin's townhouse. During the winter social season in St. Petersburg they all moved about in the same circles of parties, became sweethearts and, through the ups and downs of conflicting love affairs, had a wonderful time with their sentimental youthful friends.

When war was declared in August 1914, all that changed; the young men playing at the tennis club were mobilized and quickly disappeared. Ludmilla, like the other women young and old, immediately joined a nursing class and by winter was serving at the front. Whatever she went through, how she escaped, and finally joined her brother in Paris, was never explicitly related, even after she appeared in Englewood in 1927.

It is sometimes difficult for me to keep the chronological sequence of these characters and events straight. We were always fascinated by the various personalities as they appeared on the scene and their individual stories that unfolded piecemeal over the years. Equally fascinating were the situations in which they found themselves as the family institution that was Englewood evolved under the Old World atmosphere maintained by Olga and Emile.

Uncle Igor and Aunt Xenia, it will be remembered, arrived in Englewood in 1921 and the Kluge establishment which had undergone a considerable degree of Americanization during the war years, now acquired a new "Russian" atmosphere.

An apartment for Igor was carved out of the billiard room on our third floor. Xenia had the "purple guestroom" on the second floor opposite Mami's, with its own fireplace and opened out onto the sleeping porch on the west side. Olga Lopatina, Mami's Russian maid since childhood, was still there, and presided in the sewing room on the third floor. These four had not been together since their younger days in the old country, and for years Mami had not had this much Russian conversation around. Here was a reunion, comfort, prospects of a new life—and there were all those memories—nostalgia as well as tales of horror, that kept them chattering for hours on end. But that all soon changed.

Uncle Igor was invited to try out a "job" in the E. H. Kluge Weaving Company as salesman. That meant departure at 8:00 A.M. in the car with Papi for the factory in West New York. If he wanted to end his day promptly at five o'clock, he had to leave by himself and take the one-hour trolley ride back to Englewood, then walk up the hill. The picture is indelible of him ambling up the driveway, his coat over his shoulder, mopping his forehead with a handkerchief, then slumping down into a chair, weary and bored. The salesman's job with Papi's company obviously did not last very long. He then moved to New York and found himself a position as an accountant which paid him enough to live on, at least for a time. With Papi's encouragement, and financial help he took night school courses at the Columbia University Business School and eventually became a certified public accountant, and was able to establish himself in positions with regular accounting firms. But, if I remember correctly, he always made more money playing bridge than he did on an official job.

After the first summer Aunt Xenia too became restless and wanted to find something to work at, which obviously had to be in New York City. She would have nothing to do with a job in the family weaving business. Somehow she landed her first position as head of the French Dress Salon at John Wanamaker's, a large downtown department store. For a while she commuted like Igor, by car and trolley, which added to the strain and inconvenience. She became an almost immediate success, moved to her own apartment in the city and was sent on various trips to Paris as a buyer of new fashions for the store. Though they both soon acquired a degree of independence they remained loyal members of the Englewood establishment and appeared regularly at Sunday dinners as well as all the parties.

Then Ludmilla Nicolaevna Isnard appeared on the scene. It was by sheer accident in New York one summer day in 1927, as she was standing on the corner of Lexington Avenue opposite Bloomingdales, that she heard two men behind her talking Russian. She turned around and there she recognized Igor! I imagine the torrents of excited Russian babble that ensued! Everyone stood around and gawked at them: the traffic was held up. Out of the years of chaos, uncertain adventures and terror—what stories to catch up on! Thus Ludmilla joined the Englewood household and very quickly became a regular part of the family.

To us she was especially intriguing because of the whispered stories about her mysterious background, her own career as a champion tennis player, then as Uncle Igor's tennis partner in the club tournaments of Russia, and finally the discovery that they had been sweethearts since their student days. As a personality she was absolutely captivating, with her vivacity and rolling accent, more French than Russian. Torrents of words would shoot out almost like a machine gun, making any story sound fierce and dramatic. She had a small round head with shiny dark hair parted in the middle and smoothed back into a knot, a delicate pointed nose and sparkling black eyes. She was short, with a lovely voluptuous Russian figure whose rounded form was quite a contrast to the current flatchested flapper style we were used to. She dressed smartly and exotically, and to us was distinguished by her prominent bosom always covered with chains and chains of jangling beads plus an armful of noisy bangles and bracelets.

The Successful Fashion Business

Needless to say it was Xenia and Ludmilla with their common interest and experience in the fashion industry—and their tremendous vitality—who became the best of friends and eventually business partners. Their first venture was a custom-design dress studio in a large apartment on Park Avenue, where Igor joined them, ostensibly as bookkeeper and business manager. In the big front room they had their "salon" with gold mirrors, a mélange of Art Nouveau and Art Deco provided largely by the Kluge's, where they could impressively receive and entertain customers. At night it became transformed into a bohemian-style Oriental den. The work went on in several back rooms, where easily found skilled ladies were employed to do the sewing and even make the hats to go with the ensembles. An elderly German lady, Frau Kluth, supervised these operations for all the years, and she also acted as housekeeper.

Xenia and Ludmilla each contributed their special French-Russian touch to their designs. Xenia revived her French-style watercolor painting to do the sketches and drew upon her practical experience of lacemaking, crocheting, and embroidery from her Romadanovo

Princess in Paradise

school days. Ludmilla, with her passion for beads, did the intricate beadwork by hand on gowns, sweaters, slippers, pocketbooks; and when she bought or knitted fancy sweaters, she would decorate them in her own style with shells, bangles and French ribbons. When we were taken there, as we frequently were, to have some of our own party dresses or traveling costumes made, we would marvel at the great array of materials piled on shelves all the way up the walls, with exotic fabrics, tassels, beads, buttons, and feathers colorfully spilling out all over the tables and other furniture.

Several times Xenia and Ludmilla were completely occupied in year-long projects, designing and sewing for the weddings of prominent families on Long Island, Fisher's Island, or at Newport. They not only made by hand the complete trousseau and outfits for the bride as well as her wedding gown and those of her attendants; they also planned the table decorations and flowers. One of those that caused the most excitement, because Ludmilla was a part of the bridal party, was the wedding of Anne Kinsolving, daughter of the Episcopal bishop of Baltimore, to John Nicholas Brown, the most distinguished bachelor of the 1930s.

Another was the marriage of Charles Crane, son of the prominent Chicago industrialist, who had long been a friend and patron of the arts in Russia before the Revolution. The father had known Ludmilla's family in St. Petersburg, and when he discovered her again as a refugee in Paris in 1920, he helped her move to the United States, as well as her sister, Mme. Tatiana Vacquier, who became a teacher of French at the University of Wisconsin. For years he continued to assist many Russian artists, scholars, and professional people in immigrating to this country at his own expense. When Ludmilla established her own dress-designing business in New York City in 1927, Charles Crane was her sponsor, as he had been for her first attempts in Paris.

In 1931 and 1932 when Ty and I both had jobs in New York City and considered ourselves rather grown-up ladies, although still much under the watchful control of home and parents; Xenia was our friend and confidante. Our young men friends, usually regarded very critically by the family, were always welcome to stay at her apartment and enjoyed sleeping on the "divan." Laurence, with his artistic interest and somewhat bizarre antics, was understood and appreciated by all of them.

We were included in the bohemiam-artistic parties that she, Ludmilla, and Igor gave. There we could relax, and we would meet some of

New Life in the New World

the most colorful professional characters—artists, writers, dancers, musicians, gypsy singers, and entertainers from the popular Russian restaurants. Constanin Alajálov of *The New Yorker;* Boris Artzybasheff and Boris Chaliapin, the illustrators; Alexander Tarzaidze, who bought jewels for Macy's; Obolensky, the singer; and Orbeliani, the young pianist, would drop in. We keenly observed a style of entertaining quite in contrast to the formality maintained by our parents, and it was our idea of rather sophisticated fun. Besides, we felt that we were respected and recognized as adult individuals with our own qualities. How flattered I was when one evening, after he had had a long talk with Laurence, Uncle Igor took me into his den and said, "Sa, I think you have found the right one; go ahead! I wish you all happiness." Then he kissed my hand for the first time—the acknowledgement of a married woman.

After we were married and returned periodically to New York with our families, we never missed a chance to visit the Xenia-Ludmilla establishment. They were always up to something new and interesting, and they took a true interest in our new lives and ideas, obviously understanding the new things we were striving for or the ideals we were trying to maintain.

As the time for our wedding in December 1932 approached, Xenia naturally was the chief consultant. Dreams of big things in bygone style had to be adapted to depression practicality, and Mami had to be gently convinced that romance and dignity could quite satisfactorily be toned down. We could make use of lots of those old Russian laces and those brocades collected from trips abroad. As to Alexandra's wedding dress—from Xenia: "Of course she must have a 'court train' falling from the shoulders!" But I could go to Bloomingdale's and buy yards of white material to match the white evening gown I had already acquired at a special sale. With the veil—"We'll cut it out and show you how you can yourself sew on the ten yards of precious antique Brussels lace, treasured since Great-Grandmother's time." And Ludmilla knew how to wire and shape a *kakoshnik*. There will be more about this part of the story later.

Xenia was not only our supporter through the customary tussles and family arguments over the wedding, but she gave us the intimate motherly advice on things never discussed at home, prodding us defiantly never to be subservient wives, to stick to your own ideas in an argument, and plunge ahead into new times, new ways.

Princess in Paradise

The Incomparable Xenia

Xenia, ever restless, always enterprising, soon worked out another idea. She, Ludmilla, and of course Igor, moved from Park Avenue to a larger and cheaper apartment on Lexington Avenue. An A & P Supermarket occupied the ground floor of a three-story building (no snobbishness at this address!). The second floor was a tremendous bare expanse that was almost a Greenwich Village type studio-loft. Xenia had become interested in politics and was an active member of the Republican Women's Club. She would rent out the back section of this space for rallies and parties. In the front she opened a pet shop —puppies were displayed in the grocery store window on the street level. She had developed a passion for tropical fish, and her favorites were the very expensive Siamese fighting fish—which had already begun to invade their living room on Park Avenue. Systems of electrically run and scientifically balanced tanks were not yet in existence. Everything had to be cleaned and maintained by hand. If a precious male fish was wounded in battle, it had to be moved to a separate infirmary tank. Then there were the guppies—who kept having more babies—and had to go into more tanks. Along the walls rows of shelves displayed the equipment, tanks, food, and plants for sale. Cages of canaries and parakeets hung all about. With the puppies and the birds and the fish to feed, one could hardly expect to get away for a weekend.

Meanwhile, on the third floor the dressmaking business went on, with Frau Kluth still the head seamstress and manager, but devoting a lot of time to caring for the animal side of the family. The studio was actually a penthouse, with a tile-covered terrace and a fountain, wicker furniture and an awning, (that is, mostly surplus equipment provided by Mami and Papi from Englewood) and banks of enormous green plants all around. To us it was all charming and artistic, and their life was as intriguing as ever.

Xenia was always attractive to men, and she collected a number of "boyfriends." The one who had us worried as the most serious was a tall, courtly Persian gentleman David Benzaria who had a truly high-quality art and jewelry business. He gave her a handsome turquoise-and-diamond ring and bought her some stunning clothes, and we began to call him our new "Uncle David." But that soon broke up—to Olga's great relief. For some strange reason it was usually the short men who gravitated to the stately stature of Xenia, and she would be packed into the front seat of some tiny sports car. The picture is unforgettable of her in the middle of a dance floor dressed in long flowing chiffon dresses, some roundish salesman type clutching around her waist, his head at the level of her bosom, her free arm waving, and from her hand a long fluttering handkerchief, a huge smile on her face, and pushing or being pushed around to the strains of "Valencia" or twisted into the French tango steps—reveling in complete enjoyment—or amusement!

When our first baby was born we brought her to New York in the summer of 1934 so that Mami could arrange a properly impressive christening in the Russian Cathedral. Afterward at the big celebration in the apartment Aunt Xenia made a toast, towering above everyone else and handsomely dressed, vivacious, and ebullient as always, wishing her new namesake, our little Xenia, all the blessings and joys she herself had experienced in life. Xenia was not the godmother; my sister Ty drew that honor. Papi was just a bit hurt that we did not name her Olga. But Mami understood and agreed—that we were sort of carrying on tradition in the name of the eldest daughter, since she regarded me as a parallel to her older sister, while Ty seemed to fall more into her own part and character.

During the summers we spent in New York, Aunt Xenia always came to look in on us, to have lunch with me, sitting and chatting for hours, inquiring about our careers, pouring out tales of her past and present. She kept busy in politics, as well as part-time work in a medical library and volunteer service at St. Luke's Hospital. She who was such an analyst, so practical, and now interested in medicine did not admit that she herself was sick. After she was admitted to St. Luke's for an exploratory operation, her cancer was too advanced to be cured. We took her in our ancient little Chevrolet—now the only car available in the family—to a West Side convalescent home, she mostly talking animatedly about her namesake, our "new" little Xenia, now four years old and of great interest to her. All through the months that she lingered, she firmly believed that she saw progress and would be out to see the spring and wear her new wardrobe. Dramatically as always, it was on September 21, 1938, the day of the worst hurricane in history, with raging winds and drenching rains, that Mami received the telephone call that Xenia had died, sitting up in her chair and eagerly looking forward to her first real meal in weeks.

Princess in Paradise

11

Le Ménage a la Vieille Russie

 HE RUSSIAN NUCLEUS reestablished in Englewood by the arrival of Xenia and Igor in 1921 was only the beginning of a long procession of characters which Papi so often called the Russian Invasion.

The Fascinating Refugees

One after another, the Russian refugees were turning up and becoming constant and fascinating visitors. There was Lidya Lipkowska, a most beautiful, vivacious, diminutive blond opera singer. Her accent and her stories had everyone in hysterics. She lived at the Plaza Hotel, and with all her charming animation she told how one day she rang for service and asked for "Zop." When they brought her the tray with hot *soup* she blew off, chattering like a bird in French and Russian, with gestures! "But I asked for Zop. You know, Zop. Everybody needs Zop!" Finally, they caught on and brought her soap.

She sang divinely, wore gorgeous clothes on her tiny slim figure, and always a string of pearls that hung down to her knees. She piled her blond curls on top of her head, held by a wide velvet band or a tiara. Her star role was the title role in *The Merry Widow* with a handsome young blond German singer, Friedrich Pasch, as Prince Danilo. Needless to say, we were taken to see a performance and were entranced. They both were often at the house and on innumerable occasions were called upon to sing the famous Lehár music and dance that heavenly waltz. We children reveled romantically in the many other popular duets which they sang in French and German. Lidya Lipkowska became Sergey's godmother and naturally was the star attraction at the big christening party in October 1921.

Russian men were welcomed if they were good bridge players. Papi needed this for his diversion. Igor was an excellent bridge player and thus not only widened his social circle in New York but was sustained himself by much-needed winnings. Oreste Demidoff and Alexander Sazonov were two of the younger men whom Igor introduced and who remained family friends through all the years that followed. Demidoff lived entirely by what he could win at bridge. Sasonov was a gentle soul who was a charming conversationalist and probably a martyr to the bridge routine. He was at times instructor in French and Russian at the Berlitz School of Languages and gave private lessons when he found the opportunity. These two were always welcome, pleasant company, and they knew they would eat heartily for their efforts in making the long trip to New Jersey and doing their gallant part in entertaining the Englewood company.

Another charming man was Prince Irbain Kaplanoff, a former cavalry officer, typically Slavic, blonde, gentle, and dignified. He, too, was more entertaining for his stories than for his skill at bridge. He made his living by driving a taxi in New York. There were others like Prince Kadir Guirey from the Caucasus who emigrated bringing along a large extended family of children and other relatives. He worked with us as riding master for a while and then, with two horses that Mami gave him from Englewood, he started a riding school and club, Boots and Saddles, in one of the old brownstone stables on East Ninetieth Street near Central Park, and developed it into quite a success.

Prince Guirey's sister, Mme. Fatima Hanum Natirboff was another of those dynamic Russian women whose elegant taste and sewing skill enabled her to become a fashionable dressmaker. By this means she was able to support her own two children, several nieces and nephews and a considerable entourage of other refugee Circassians who came to her for help and guidance. Thus, among the Russians, especially the Circassians, she became a sort of national matriarch. Her husband had been the forest manager for a large estate near the Ural Mountains, and she had stories to tell about conditions in Siberia. Thus, another whole group of Russian émigrés was introduced—Georgians, Circas-

Photo of Lidya Lipkovska inscribed
to Papi in 1921.

sians, Gruzians—from the Caucasus, of old tribal lineage, proud of
their history, yet who had been educated and received as aristocrats in
St. Petersburg.

Most of those who arrived had no particular skills or business
training but there were some remarkable exceptions. In our group the
most famous example of one who achieved outstanding success in an
unexpected career was Prince Georgi Matchabelli, a Georgian. He had
learned something about chemistry in the course of his university
education in Russia. In his loft apartment he started mixing chemical
scents in various combinations and brought in some friends to help. He
gave his fragrances new and abstract names (like Duchess of York,
Wind Song, etc.) and sold small quantities as perfumes under his
name—Prince Matchabelli—but the greatest attraction came through
the distinctive bottles he imported from Paris in the shape of a Russian
crown with a Greek cross stopper. The Matchabelli line developed into
a tremendous success.

Characteristically, those lucky enough to succeed were always will-

New Life in the New World

ing and generous in helping their compatriots. One American patron who took a special interest in the poor Russians and their families was Mrs. Thomas Lewis, head of the Elizabeth Arden cosmetics firm who in 1935 married Prince Michael Evlanoff. Helena Rubinstein (Princess Gourielli) was also a generous patroness of the Russians. Persons with former titles and positions found menial jobs to start with in their employ and were grateful. One former general was a doorman for Elizabeth Arden's Fifth Avenue cosmetic shop. Another very elegant prince rode in the back of a bank's armored car, holding a pistol. General David Yedigaroff worked in the Arden factory packing face powder into boxes; his wife, Manya, specialized in facials and false eyelashes in the beauty salon. Count Boris von Kupfer drove a delivery truck. Others developed strange new careers, like Gen. Alexander Syroboyarsky, who contentedly ran a chicken farm near Lakewood, New Jersey.

Prince and Princess Paul Chavchavadze joined the Russian colony in New York in 1927 and soon became an important and beloved part of its circle. They had been married in London in 1922, and because of their relationship with both the British and the Greek royal families, they had been able to live comfortably, and Paul had had a position in a shipping firm. Paul Chavchavadze came from a historic and respected line of Georgian rulers. The beautiful Nina Georgievna was directly of the Romanov family; her father, Grand Duke Georgiy, was one of the brothers of Tsar Nicholas. Thus, in rank she was equally important as Grand Duchess Marie Pavlovna. Nina had studied art and interior decorating in Paris, so she considered herself somewhat of a professional and kept busy with small jobs. Paul soon joined an advertising agency, and from then on writing became more and more his vocation. Everyone loved them for their unpretentiousness; their youthful, unembittered outlook; and their willing help in any charitable cause.

After frequent summer visits to Cape Cod where they felt themselves really at home, they found an eighteenth-century "Captain's house" hidden deep in the woods of Wellfleet and bought it with one of Nina's remaining pieces of jewelry, an emerald-and-diamond brooch. It took plenty of physical work, plus much imagination, to bring it into a habitable state, then even make it do, in New England style, for winter living. There were kerosene stoves, woodburning fireplaces, a large farm kitchen-living room, and even a "hurricane" room for the storage of emergency equipment.

Soon the establishment became so attractive, and the number of

Princess in Paradise

visitors so continuous, that they decided to turn it into a paying business. What did that mean? Paul became caretaker, handyman, chopper of wood, chauffeur, guide, and planner of entertainment. Nina was no longer just "housekeeper." With no help at all, she became chief cook, hostess, upstairs maid, scrubber of bathrooms, marketing errand-boy, and keeper of the garden. Summer was a strenuous time, but they carried it off with grace and good spirits. Their house was always filled with interesting people, and they seemed to enjoy entertaining their paying "guests." Most commendable of all was that they really became regular members of the community, even grew to be regarded as "natives" of Wellfleet, in spite of, as Paul said, "having inflicted such a name as Chavchavadze on a small New England town." They arranged to go off on southern trips during the winters. Paul served in the U.S. Armed Forces in Europe during World War II, and their son David entered the Foreign Service in Washington.

Although they seldom came to New York anymore, we used to see them whenever we could and even camped in their woods later on when we took our own family on summer trips to Cape Cod.

Paul concentrated on his writing and published a number of books. The first and especially interesting was his *Family Album,* with the stories of both their families. The last one was probably the translation of Svetlana Alleluyeva's (Stalin's daughter) *Only One Year.* When both of them died they were buried in Wellfleet by a Russian priest with a Russian Orthodox funeral service, something that had concerned them and that had been arranged years before.

Then there was the popularity of Russian restaurants which sprang up in all parts of New York. Some catered to exclusive American patronage like Prince Serge Obolensky's Maisonette Russe. Others, like the Kretshma on Fourteenth Street, were patterned after the all-night Parisian cabarets with gypsy music and the sensational Cossack dagger dances. The Russian Tea Room and Diadia Kostia's Moscow Inn, more in the style of the small, subdued French restaurants, became the meeting places for a regular clientele and any newly arrived Russians. Their owners were another sympathetic source of employment for destitute exiles, and many a free meal was handed out as a matter of course.

The thing that used to puzzle our father with all these émigrés—so cultivated, so highly educated, but, as he saw it, unable to fit into anything "practical"— was that they were satisfied with taking the rather menial jobs. Perhaps it was the tempo of the "boom times" of the

New Life in the New World

1920s in the United States. Everything was very fast and very big, and Americans did not have patience with foreigners; nor did the Russians quite sympathize with the American attitude. They were fascinating and socially charming, and those who settled into positions along those lines were considered by the others as cheap and mercenary. Prince Serge Obolensky was the envy of the expatriate circle because he married Alice Astor, was a society celebrity for a time, then when the marriage failed had the capital to start a business of his own with a restaurant in the St. Regis Hotel. But the Russians rather scoffed at him for selling himself, as they did at the so-called marrying Mdivanis, three Georgian brothers who bestowed their title of "Prince" upon a string of temporarily glamourous American heiresses.

When Kaplanoff arrived with the announcement that he was about to marry a wealthy American lady, the attitude of his friends was of commiseration—the poor bachelor giving up his freedom—not "Hurray, he's going to have it easy at last!" Later they took rather sardonic delight in telling how when they visited the couple in a lavish apartment, "Princess" Kaplanoff (she would never allow herself to be addressed as "Mrs.") presided in plush dignity and ordered her meek husband around.

❧ Sunday Entertainment at Englewood

Times were prosperous, and life in the house at Englewood reflected all the comforts and pleasures one would expect to go with them. We children ranged from ages eleven, nine, and seven, down to one-year-old Sergey. We still lived in our own realm on the third floor, Sergey with his nurse, we with our governess. We had acquired an English riding master, Major Stocker, and each of us went through daily horseback sessions. Our piano teacher came to the house for our lessons, and everyone was required to practice for an hour a day in a closed room.

There was plenty of help inside the house and around the grounds. A complete new landscaping scheme had included a swimming pool in a sunken garden with a little Greek temple at the far end set among cypresses. Mami and Xenia would go riding in the nearby woods, or they would sit and sew with Olga Lopatina over tea under the old apple tree—and talk, talk, talk! Sometimes Xenia would close herself in the music room and play the piano for hours on end. It could be heard throughout the house. She loved Chopin, but not for her the sweet nocturnes and waltzes. She pounded away at the polonaises, the mazurkas, or the *Appassionata* Sonata. I used to try to read her music and was somewhat inspired to go on. My taste was for Beethoven-type chords, while Ty was rather good at playing the more smoothly flowing, romantic Brahms waltzes.

Gathered at the breakfast and dinner table, the regular family included, besides us children and governess, parents, aunt and uncle, and our British adjunct Major Stocker. Sometimes Violet Orthwein would be with us for long visits. She was one year older than I and had practically grown up with us in Englewood, so that we regarded her as a third sister.

Sunday was always the biggest day of the week. The weekend exodus to the country did not begin then on Fridays, since businesses were still open until Saturday noon, and those who worked in stores could not get away until Saturday night. The group at Sunday breakfast was already enlarged by houseguests, sometimes our friends from school, everyone appearing in negligees, kimonos, and other exotic imported costumes. As one of my friends whispered, "You wouldn't dare appear in an ordinary bathrobe!" Beginning at nine-thirty, it was a big affair with traditional lamb kidneys plus the eggs and sausages and a luscious assortment of cheeses and coffee cakes. After that it was everyone out for a ride, a real family cavalcade, each of us on our own horse, from Papi on his white Irish hunter down to Sergey when he was able to master a Shetland pony.

Sunday dinner was scheduled for two-thirty, and by that time the guests had arrived. The table had been extended for any number from twelve to twenty-four and beautifully set. As time went on, Ty and I were allowed to choose the china, glassware, and linens for each occasion. Preceding dinner came the *zakuska* (hors d'oeuvres) hour in the living room, and a typically bountiful Russian table. The hors d'oeuvres were both hot and cold, fish and salads, with the central feature always a huge iced dish of caviar and the toast to go with it. Sometimes it was the luscious, grayish loose eggs of the Beluga caviar; at other times it was the special treat of the hard, "pressed caviar." Colorful decanters were grouped at either end of the long, linen-covered table, these filled with different-colored and -flavored vodka, and others with sweet or dry aperitifs.

One could count on the Russian men to know how to help themselves and take care of the ladies with a selection of goodies on small plates. They were experienced also in returning frequently to sample the various drinks and delicacies. Thus, the gathering was kept moving, standing or sitting, with an animated babble of multilingual conversations.

During these sessions we children would sit dutifully on a bench on the sidelines—and observe! We could "Oh" and "Ah" at the pretty clothes and whisper about odd-looking people and sometimes understand certain little byplays. We used to giggle unmercifully when Major Stocker, in his sporty tweeds, invariably asked in his clipped British accent the same opening question of everyone, whether it was a Russian singer or German businessman: "D'you play golf?" We knew it was coming, and we would kick each other in glee. He was our dear friend, and in private on our horseback rides we would ask him about it and laugh together. He simply said it was the easiest opener for conversation with a total stranger; either they did or they didn't; in any case, it would lead on to something else.

When dinner was announced the velvet portieres opened, and the party would move into the dining room with its heavily carved Flemish oak sideboards displaying the Russian crystal and silver, to be seated at the long rectangular table. We youngsters were scattered among the guests, dutifully silent except for perhaps whispered remarks, but wide-eyed watching and listening as the international chatter flew back and forth.

Presiding like this at a handsome table, with a remarkable variety of interesting men and women, watching the service function at its best, both Mami and Papi could really enjoy and be proud of their recreation of the familiar, elegant, cosmopolitan life of the Old World. Certainly those who came for a visit to Englewood never forgot their impression.

The only jarring note occurred at times when everyone at the table seemed to be exuberantly spouting Russian or whispering gossip to each other—and Papi, sitting at the far end of the table, and whose Russian was somewhat limited—felt completely excluded and would thunder: "*Please*! Remember, you are in America—and here we speak *English*!"

It had gotten to be what he called "the Russian invasion," and after putting up with the women's daily stream of chatter and Igor's voluminious dissertations, he was just full up with the endless *Russky Razgovor*. We sympathized with the *Russkys,* whom we loved to hear, and thought it was pretty cruel.

The one Russian whom he looked forward to with the most en-

Chaliapin as Boris Godunov. Courtesy Metropolitan Opera Archives.

thusiasm and literally welcomed with open arms was Feodor Chaliapin, the great Russian basso, who came once a year for a visit to the Metropolitan Opera. When Chaliapin came to the house a very special bottle of red wine, saved from year to year especially for him, was brought out. At the *zakuska* he already began to sing—and act —what a superb clown! When he entered the dining room and sat down at Mami's right (and I on his other side!), he was glowing with affection and enthusiasm. As the meal progressed he had more and more stories to tell—with vivid demonstrations. Finally, just bursting with joy he would stand up and sing out. As he finished, he would kiss Mami's hand, grab his glass, and stride down to Papi's end of the table. There Papi would stand up to receive him—and Chaliapin, who was even taller, a lanky, blond-tufted six foot six inches, would envelope Papi in his arms and kiss him—"my dear, wonderful old friend!"—and the two would happily drink to each other.

We children were not supposed to speak unless spoken to, but once he admired my long blonde hair, and I whispered how I hated it. Turning to me alone and stroking my hair, he said: "Oh, my dear child, you must never say that. Beautiful hair is one of woman's glories, and man dreams of the gorgeous long tresses that he can wrap himself and

New Life in the New World

warm himself in!" With this much attention I later complained to him about my big nose and got the same ecstatic tone telling me it was a wonderful Russian nose, strong and aristocratic, and that I should be proud of it. Even if I embarrassedly brushed all this off, I took it in and remembered it for a long time. Of course, I adored that man—as did we all.

After dinner in the music room he would start singing again, and his wife would play the piano. Our favorites were "Blakha," Mussorgsky's "Song of the Flea," with that great big "Ha-Ha-Ha-Ha" ending, and Mephistopheles' song from *Faust*—"Et Satan conduit le bal, conduit le bal"—with him dancing around on his tiptoes and leading with two pointed fingers on his head. Naturally when he came to New York we were always taken to one of his performances at the Metropolitan Opera. Our little group sat in the third-row center, and in *Faust* when it came to that song he pranced up to center stage and managed with a gesture of one hand to wave to us.

Another unforgettable performance was when he sang the lead in Boito's *Mefistofele*. In the Prologue, to mounting crashing music he climbs up on a mountain peak, bare to his waist—he had a strapping muscular build—balancing the world in one hand and sings to a magnificent climax. It was in this part that he made his debut at the Metropolitan in 1907; and he so thoroughly shocked New York audiences by appearing "naked to the rump," as critics reported, that he was not invited to return until 1922. Meanwhile, he had settled in Paris and was greatly fêted in London. How he loved to act and how he threw himself into it! The part of Boris Godunov, which he had developed very personally, used to wring him to complete emotional exhaustion, and he always refused invitations to go out to supper after any of those performances.

When the dinner was over the Russian men, according to custom, would go up to Mami, kiss her hand, and say "Spasibo" (Thank you). This Uncle Igor never failed to do after every ordinary meal, and Papi, waiting for her at the door, would do the same as Mami swept out.

After-dinner coffee in the music room was followed by activities according to the mood or the season. In winter it would be music on the organ or informal performances by the star guests. Bridge invariably followed. In summer coffee and bridge would be continued out in the so-called Temple d'Amour at the end of the garden, and swimming followed. The times when Papi would get the notion to show off the horses and our riding ability would be an annoyance beyond words for us, who had to change to riding clothes and canter around the front lawn while the rest all sat on the open porch watching. These were also annoying to Major Stocker and the groom who had to saddle the horses, and they were a dreadful pain for the gardeners, who watched their beautiful turf being chopped up.

Highballs and iced tea were served outside all afternoon, and maybe the help got a chance to sit down for a while and play cards in their dining room, but the scurrying in the kitchen and pantry never stopped. By seven-thirty supper would be announced and the festive table was again revealed, all set. A few people might have departed, but more likely a few more had dropped in unexpectedly.

This may have been scheduled as an "informal cold supper," but still there were candles and flowers and at least two people had to pass the platters of cold meats and salads around and around. The most irresistible part was the confusing, tempting, abundant selection of imported cheeses, often with a special feature of a tall, aged Stilton or a huge Bel Paese, served with an assortment of crackers and a marvelous array of luscious fruits. Mami presided at the head of the table, as her mother had, with samovar and poured hot tea for each person, with her beautiful cups and tea glasses on the teacart beside her.

If most Sundays exhausted one, consider the occasional Saturday nights that preceded them. A Saturday dinner party may not have been as large—about twelve guests and we children excluded—but was a much more formal occasion, often even with a printed menu. The flowers came from our greenhouse; but sometimes Maresi-Mazetti, the Italian candy store and caterer from New York, was called upon to create a special confection to distinguish a certain celebration.

After dinner over coffee there was an organ recital. That is to say, we girls put on the electric Welte-Mignon player rolls of music selected by Papi—Wagner things like *Lohengrin, Tristan und Isolde*—or for Mami, Tschaikovsky, Schubert, Puccini. If it was a planned musical evening, special guests would perform, such as Mr. Courboin a well-known organist, who brought along his boa constrictor and kept it at his feet when he played. Prince Alexis Obolensky, the Russian basso, often appeared; and Irakli Orbeliani, a young pianist, was introduced here. Later Max Panteleyev, another bass, became our special friend and favorite. Xenia in her exuberance, with very little urging, would sit down at the piano and just play away. An earnest bridge game which would surely go on for hours was confined to the quiet of the sun-porch.

New Life in the New World

But conversation never subsided. The Russians had their own special way of making any discussion seem of tremendous weight or excitement, even when one couldn't understand a thing. They carried on for hours over philosophy, art, politics, while we sat spellbound and managed to catch a famous name here and there. Uncle Igor, with cigarette holder in hand, would pace the floor, talking steadily. Ludmilla would rattle off like a firecracker if she found someone to speak French. Somebody else would be draped on the sofa in a cloud of cigarette smoke reminiscing dreamily. Then Sazonov would jump up, perhaps at the mention of Pushkin, with a "remember that?" And he and Igor would both be off reciting in swelling cadences the marvelous rhythms of *The Bronze Horseman,* in great streams of Russian, striding in opposite directions with huge sweeping gestures worthy of an opera. It was a wonderful picture. One never knew whether they were discussing politics or poetry.

When we were old enough to stay up and enjoy it, we were all too soon shaken out of the spell. It was time to serve the "midnight supper." Much as we considered this an imposition, Mami felt it was a tradition and, no matter how modest, she liked to keep it up. It may have been just sardines and cheese with beer, wheeled in on a tea cart, or simply tea and cookies, but sometimes at Papi's insistence it developed into hot meatballs or scrambled eggs and sausages. She was reliving the memories of the house in Kiev on the opera square where friends and family would drop in after the performances.

Years later, in the Ninety-sixth Street apartment, after all the family had gone away, Mami and Papi would always have tea at midnight, and any number of Russian friends on their way home from another bridge party would look up from Madison Avenue and, seeing the light on in the living room windows, come up to join them for a bit of tea and a chat.

It was this kind of schedule which was one of the things that made it hard for the Russians to work in this country. They were all used to late hours; morning deadlines meant nothing, and they had little care for time. In Russia, although the meals had been much the same, with afternoon tea and midnight supper sandwiched in, one did not get to the office before 10:00 A.M. The other concept ingrained in all of them was that the job by day was just one of those inconveniences one had to live with in order to earn the wherewithal so that one could do what he *liked* at other times, preferably at night. One pursued drama or art or dance or conversation after work was over. That was one's life, one's relaxation. Mami had a built-in timetable whereby she could not sleep

Princess in Paradise

before 2:00 A.M. So did Igor and Xenia. It was during those quiet hours which she loved that she would start her most intricate sewing or special secret projects. Igor would play bridge till daybreak, rest a bit, and get himself off to the office. And many was the ball or celebration we attended when those taxi drivers, store clerks, or factory workers would take off their evening finery in the wee hours and face the chores of the next day with resignation.

In Englewood, with Papi a dynamo of an American business executive, getting off to work every day at 8:00 A.M. and staying long after his office closed, these casual, romantic Russians were quite misunderstood: "Why don't they want to get ahead?!" and it was usually the "family," that is Xenia, Igor, and Ludmilla, who took the brunt of Papi's criticism, especially after long bridge sessions or at the end of a party. Eventually , as I have already described, they worked out their own solutions. The resulting *ménage à trois* was not exactly *à la Vieille Russie*. It was more Montparnasse or Bohemian Paris, and so were the parties they gave but they continued to be fascinating and successful just the same.

For nearly ten years this triple arrangement went on, with Xenia and Ludmilla in the fashion design business together, moving from one apartment to another, along with Igor's attempts to renew a law career, then steadier earnings as an accountant. At that time, so-called contacts were of utmost importance for business. They belonged to riding clubs on Long Island and Connecticut. Ludmilla played tennis at the Racquet Club, and she and Igor were well-known competitors at most of the suburban country clubs. In 1931 they won the mixed doubles championship of the Westchester County Tennis Club. After Igor could no longer play because of his chronic rheumatism, Ludmilla taught tennis at the Bronxville Club.

Through Ludmilla, Igor was introduced to Mrs. Calvert Cabell Osborne, a wealthy society lady from an old Virginia family, who was then living on Park Avenue. When romance seemed to be hovering in the air, Igor was invited to move out. After James Osborne's death in an auto accident and after waiting patiently for years for the estate to be settled, Calvert and Igor were married and moved to Rock Castle, her old family manor on the James River. There Igor was able to live comfortably in the style he loved, playing the role of an elegant country squire to the age of eighty-three. It seemed almost the perfect way of rounding out the circle—re-creating the atmosphere of his beloved *"Vieille Russie!"*

New Life in the New World

IV

The Fabulous Twenties

*"Here they enjoyed many years of
happiness and prosperity."*

Mami and Papi at Englewood, 1917.

12

Beginning of the Boom

OOKING BACK over the twenties the memories are of an atmosphere of exuberance, activity, prosperity, and adventure. To our generation, of course, it was significant especially in our growing up—going through the difficult changes from a restricted childhood to awareness of the world around us, growing curiosity and desire to participate, and the emergence of individual personalities and problems. In recalling those exciting youthful years, when one *Big* event seems to run right into another in ever enlarging circles, one tries now to analyze the hows and the whys of that period. How did it start? What was going on underneath? What did it all lead to?—Of all this we were childishly unaware.

The joyous awakening began with the end of World War I and the return of the troops. Armistice day, Tuesday, November 11, 1918, put the whole country into a state of hysteria. Shortly after noon we in the Englewood Public School were turned out, all carrying little American flags, with the mob rushing somewhere, whistles blowing, bells ringing. It meant little to us "foreigners" in the fifth, third, and first grades, but we walked ourselves home and found Mami in tears of joy and the servants embracing each other. Sometime later we were taken along to New York for one of the many great welcome-home parades—for the triumphal march up Fifth Avenue of the Twenty-seventh Division with our dear General O'Ryan heading it on horseback—we waving from a balcony of the Ritz Hotel and throwing streamers and confetti like everyone else, ending up with a big grown-up luncheon where we were allowed to have lobster for the first time. After that the parties resumed at the house. The generals and colonels came around in their uniforms and decorations and told seemingly endless stories of the war, describing personally the historic European leaders and imitating accents and characters. There was a noticeable increase in the household help; we could again keep enough horses for everybody; and we now had two cars, an open touring car and a limousine, both Cunninghams and both eyecatching in an unusual light beige color.

Postwar Prosperity for the Label Business

One can find the postwar boom explained in many different ways. New industries had developed, and old industries had expanded. Automobile manufacture became simplified through Henry Ford's popularization of the small cheap car for everyone and the introduction of the assembly line. Technical advances and the increased productivity of labor affected all industries, including the textile, which by 1923 claimed to rank in first place.

Closely affecting us was the growth of the garment industry—the change to the ready-to-wear clothing instead of individually designed, made-to-order items; a newly respectable status in the department store; and the popularization of fashion and the quicker changes of its dictates. There came a new forcefulness and enterprise in advertising, a switch from the disdain in which salesmanship was held. More garment businesses, more department stores, more seasonal changes in clothing, new products, new ideas—all these meant more labels! And the E. H. Kluge pioneering slogans of "Be Proud of your Product" and "If it's worth Labelling at all it's worth Labelling Well," beautifully penned in Victorian script on packages and letterhead, were now pepped up with color, and sales campaigns were inaugurated.

Every year the E. H. K. sales force—which now had representatives in the main cities all across the country—gathered in New York for a rallying kind of banquet in a big hotel; a tour of the factory to observe the improvements; a reunion photograph on the front steps; and, for the specially privileged, being personally entertained at the home in Englewood. Mami, to whom advertising and salesmanship were cheaply lower class and aggressive, had to put on a pleasant face and suffer through this aspect of things, bulwarked ahead of time by Papi's lectures to her on living in "true democracy." During the war his

Princess in Paradise

factory had been working on lucrative government contracts—the headbands for the navy caps and the arm patches or insignias for all the regiments and special services. This was an absolutely personal invention and an idea sold to the United States government by E. H. Kluge, the ever ingenious thinker and the talented, irrepressible salesman. With the proliferation of quality stores as well as work clothes, household goods such as sheets and towels, luxury items like furs or cosmetics, and then new inventions such as power-loomed rugs, he was gone regularly on extensive cross-country trips to bring in new customers with his special brand of social charm, technical competence, and imaginative enterprise.

Thus it went—Munsingwear in Minneapolis; Jantzen bathing suits in Portland, Oregon; Cannon sheets in North Carolina. At home it was the finest stores through personal contact with their owners —Bergdorf-Goodman, DePinna, Jaekel Furs, Jaeger Woolens, Elizabeth Arden, Finchley, Abercrombie & Fitch, Bruck-Weiss Millinery (don't forget hats and dresses were sold in different stores!), Gullistan Rugs, and eventually—Sears, Roebuck & Company. Always open to progressive ideas, he invested in the newest looms, packaging devices, and office management techniques. Whereas the original raw materials were only cotton and silk, when rayon threads were introduced he experimented with those, and he was ready to try out nylon and the new synthetic fibers when they came about. To almost anyone it is amazing that from the manufacture of such tiny items as woven labels, turned out by the millions, one could make (quite evidently) a considerable fortune. The factory kept humming along, day and night, expanding, with few labor troubles, managed in a very personal way—until the great collapse, with everything else, in 1929.

Real Estate, Movies and Prohibition

Another postwar development affecting us and Englewood in a slightly distant way was the expanding real estate market. Land and available money brought the beginning of accessible suburbs. With the improved railroads and the increasing number of automobiles, people could commute daily into New York or other business centers and live in smaller communities, some even leaving their families in the country. There was a building boom; housing was relatively inexpensive, and people could own their own homes rather than live in crowded, rented apartment buildings.

The Fabulous Twenties

Disconcertingly, Englewood was gradually being ringed by cheap housing developments, with hundreds of small houses lined up in rows. During those years the talk began about a "new bridge over the Hudson," and the speculation grew, subsided, and was revived, but the great George Washington Bridge did not become a reality until 1931—two years after the 1929 crash.

Papi was involved in several of these housing development schemes. One idea was a vast tract of small houses which would have been very profitable, but he rejected it because it would have been "cheap and low class." Another project was to develop his property into a group of large palatial homes, appropriately landscaped, with Greystone and the Kluge compound as its most prominent feature. Though it would have impaired Papi's expansive sense of space—and vanity—it was a good idea, but it did not crystallize because when the crash came everything was lost.

However, real estate enterprises were blooming all around the country. In 1921, while on our winter sojourn in Florida, Papi was introduced to a project by his friend T. E. Highleman, president of a Miami bank. As usual, we knew about it only from the vivid reports that Papi gave after he had seen something new and exciting. "Imagine," he would say, "being driven out on the causeway to Miami Beach and along the bay, watching dredges digging in the water and piling up the mud along the banks, being shown blueprints and plot plans on your lap in the car then a finger pointing out to the water and great diagrams in the air of all that was going to arise there.

" 'This is going to become a most exclusive residential town,' Mr. Highleman told me. 'The roads will be laid out like this; here are the lots for large houses—we are selling them now. We will call it Coral Gables.' "

And there were to be more, each larger and more fantastic than the others. Being treated as children, never to intrude in grown-up affairs, we never knew the end—Did Papi invest in Florida real estate or not?

There was another trip to California in 1922. Again there were Papi's glowing accounts upon his return, about great business success-es in San Francisco, old friends, and so on.

"But Olga, you should have seen what they showed me. [He always wanted Olga to participate in his adventures and always respected her advice.] They drove me around a new town they are laying out, muddy roads up and down hills and running way back into the valleys; and no railroads—all for automobiles. They are selling downtown business property and lots for homes stretching way out into the country. No paved streets, no trees, no water yet. They call this Los Angeles. And out in one of those valleys they are putting in another place which they call Hollywood and there those new movie companies are putting up flimsy buildings and streets with all kinds of fake scenery and false fronts. They can work outside all year around because the weather is so good."

Again, did he or did he not take the gamble? Was it a success or a flop?

At the mention of the early movie industry, I invariably recall our first awareness of it. The much-talked-of first big films, such as *Birth of a Nation,* we were too small to see. Besides, it meant going down into the village, and there was some immoral association with the "pictures." But not far away, in Fort Lee, New Jersey, there was a moving-picture company named Fox Films, and we sometimes drove by its building on the main street, which was noticeable by its number of skylights and window walls—the studios where all the indoor filming was done.

Periodically, Fox Films would request permission to come and do some filming around our place, so they could work outdoors. The arrangement Papi made was that the fee they would have paid him was to be given to the Englewood Hospital. How we looked forward to this annual excitement! Crews moved in with trucks and wires and workmen; there would be people scurrying around and men shouting through megaphones. When some setting was all prepared, the stars would arrive—a beautiful blonde lady with a tiny, very red mouth; a tall, slick-haired, snappily dressed male hero. And we sat on the grass in the background, fascinated. Sometimes it seemed boringly long and complicated: a short filming then holding up those blackboards with numbers, then doing the same scene over again. But then there were spellbinding sequences: a man chasing another over the roof and around the chimneys; somebody having to jump off into a net, then starting a new scene focusing on him picking himself up amid the bushes. When the beautiful lady had to escape out of a third-floor window and slide down the drainpipe, that was breathtaking. What made a lasting impression was that it wasn't the beautiful lady at all. We could see at close range a young man dressed in her clothes, with blonde wig and high-heeled slippers. He climbed out of the window and manipulated himself downward—cameras whirring, directors shouting, while she sat in a chair watching. Then everything stopped—"Cut! Cut!"—and she would exchange places with her dou-

The Fabulous Twenties

ble. As she turned forward, the cameras rolled again, and she would hobble toward them with an agonized expression on her face.

The discovery of the illusions and of the putting together of short sequences was a source of fun and make-believe for us for years to come, and even when we were allowed to see movies, they left us always slightly suspicious.

The effect of political events of the early 1920s was again a vital subject for animated discussion and analysis. We heard lots of talk about President Wilson and the hopes for a peaceful world through the League of Nations. The election in 1920 of a Republican president, Warren G. Harding, brought on protective tariffs, not believed in before, and these did help United States industries, certainly the textile industry, and contributed to the upward financial well-being of all.

In 1919 the passage of the Volstead Act, the enforcement of the Eighteenth Amendment—which meant Prohibition—forbidding the sale or importation of any kind of wines or other alcoholic beverages, meant a noticeable change in our social life as well as at home. Families like ours with a foreign background took wine as a matter of course. Even at a very young age we were expected to drink wine at the table and to learn the etiquette and rituals that accompanied that. The table in the servants' dining room always had its quota of wine, with extra treats for special occasions. The wine cellar was fully stocked with treasured old bottles, and was continually replenished just as the grocery shelves were. Like the linen closet and the silver closet, it was kept locked, with all the keys forming a big bunch that was controlled by Mami or the housekeeper.

When dining at hotels or restaurants it was a dreadful adjustment, for both the wine steward and the patron, not to enjoy the pride of experienced selection. The excesses of the saloons and the spending of a worker's total pay envelope on his way home were stories we heard excitedly discussed. The reason for the passage of the Volstead Act, we were told, was the pressure from abused wives and the absence of the thousands of young men at the war in Europe.

Prohibition led to events which we could not escape being aware of. There were desperate efforts to get hold of the "booze" and elaborate means developed of supplying it—by the famed "bootleggers" and rum-runners. People went to insane, illogical extremes. Terrible mistakes were made, and terrible prices were paid. One summer some work was being done on our house; there was a crew of painters; they took their lunch hour in the shade of some trees at the end of the garden. Suddenly the gardener came up shouting, "Mrs. Kluge, Mrs. Kluge, the men are dying out there in the bushes!" Always Mami came to the rescue in a time of crisis. Ambulances came and people rushed away; by evening the report to Papi was that one man had died and two had been blinded for life—from drinking wood alcohol!

At home we continued to use our wine cellar for our table. There was no more for the help. We came to recognize mysterious voices on the telephone and certain privileged callers who arrived after dark and delivered necessary supplies in boxes or suitcases. Friends returned from Canada with "gifts" of enormous size. In Florida on the boat it was easier to contact dealers from Cuba and the Bahamas, but it was more of a trick to elude watchful customs agents. Going to dine in New York City or entertaining at an after theater party at a hotel was complicated by having to bring along one's own bottles, and especially by needing to have an intimate friendship with the restaurant owner or the head waiter. The ladies swathed themselves in big fur-collared evening wraps—and carried a bottle beneath their bosoms. Ty and I grew up learning to stroll elegantly like that. Then came the "dignified" ceremony of the suave waiter with a white napkin, receiving the precious cargo and wrapping it like a baby, stowing it with aplomb under the table against the leg of a lady. Finally was the shock of drinking it. No longer did we drink from graceful, tall-stemmed crystal wine glasses; now it went into a coffee cup of thick restaurant china.

The New Freedom for Women

Another significant political event was the passage of the Nineteenth Amendment—the Woman's Suffrage Act—in 1920. Young as we were and subdued into good behavior, our ears were eager, and we could not miss the heated discussions and certain noticeable changes around us. We found ourselves taking whispered sides in the gossip.

Before the war everyone talked with admiration about those heroic women who were learning to drive trucks and ambulances, who were going to France with the troops to serve in the YMCA or to become nurses in the bloody, muddy field hospitals. Now they were coming back, not only telling of their experiences but visibly changed by the violent life in which they had taken part and which could hardly be imagined by those who remained at home in this unravaged country. Annette MacDonald and Bertha Spain had been frequent visitors

The Fabulous Twenties

before they left. They were always energetic and self-sufficient. Now they returned with their uninhibited stories and had even more independence and more energy to devote to important causes. In addition, they had cut their hair short—the French "bob"—and, still more astounding, they smoked—cigarettes in long holders, and sometimes small cigars.

The militant suffragettes parading and haranguing crowds in the New York streets had long been appearing in news pictures, shocking many and inspiring others. Naturally we all took sides with Mami, to whom all this excitement over women's independence was slightly amusing, having been brought up in Russia where women already had their own property rights, were allowed to instigate a divorce, and were highly respected in business—that is, of course, the educated ones. When her sister Xenia arrived on the scene in 1921, we all gazed at her with admiration and envy. Here was someone who argued her points loudly and intelligently; her hair was sensationally short; she smoked like a man; she had fought at the front; and she had been in business for eighteen years before coming here.

We were also admiringly aware of women driving a car. For so many years in our isolated life at the top of the hill we had a young music teacher who came once a week to give all three of us piano lessons. She lived somewhere "down in the village," but to come this distance she had to take the trolley, get off at the nearest stop, then walk half an hour up the hill. When she was finished, she took her briefcase and walked down again. Guests did the same thing, and so did the laundress and the seamstress. Suddenly, because of our broken-up school year with the winter trips to Florida we had a young, attractive lady tutor and she drove up in her own car. Also she had bobbed hair. We were wide-eyed at her daring and adored her for her casual independence.

The next change to become the subject of animated discussion and critical censure was the ladies' fashion of skirts getting so short that they exposed the knees. But it was several years before such battles as following the fashion became our own.

In retrospect, so many things followed each other and overlapped—moving children and household with every season, trips, schools, camp, personalities, and parties—that crammed each year, it is impossible to sort them out chronologically, although the diary I began keeping since my twelfth birthday has helped. It is also amazing to realize that such an overflowing period of life covered only ten years—from the upward swing after the war to the complete collapse of the stock market and of business generally in 1929.

Certainly for Papi and Mami it was the peak of their success and their ambitions, which culminated in a tremendous party in January 1929, when they celebrated their twentieth wedding anniversary. For three children, ages six, seven, and nine, it was the time of many steps in growth, physical changes, emerging personalities, and ending with a sudden plunge into adulthood. Little brother Sergey, who came along in 1921, tagged behind in many ways. He was too young to be a part of our close-linked trio; he had to fight the battles of change alone. At the time when the fun and opulence was over, he was only eight years old.

The Fabulous Twenties

13

The "Pioneer"

THE *Pioneer* was a beautiful boat. When she was acquired, in the winter of 1919-20, we were old enough to appreciate it, to look forward to the trips to Florida, to have our own fun on it, and to be curious enough to observe the other entertaining things that took place aboard. The differences from the *Joyeuse,* apart from the fact that one was a sleek oceangoing yacht and the second a large and roomy houseboat, were that we had big comfortable cabins of our own, and even a second small afterdeck of our own at the cabin level. Also, the living and dining rooms on the upper deck entirely encased by windows, opened up into each other and were furnished like a real home, and the surrounding decks and the enormous afterdeck were spacious and safe enough for us to roam and play on. She was 110 feet long and had a wide, 24-foot beam. Her special advantage was that her draft was so small that we could sail most of the way south on the Inland Waterway. There was a crew of twelve: the captain and mate, plus engineers and sailors, a chef and a galleyboy, chief steward, and messboy—and we brought along Pauline, the upstairs maid from Englewood, as stewardess. The sailors who had jobs to do around the decks were fun and managed to talk or play with us or treat us to secret visits in the crew's quarters.

Mami's and Papi's stateroom was a gorgeous affair, extending the whole width of the boat and decorated in colors instead of the usual hospital white. Ty and I had our own big stateroom with bath; Emile

had another small one; and there were additional guestrooms all
strung along a narrow corridor down below, which opened on to the
small afterdeck. The greatest thing for us was having square windows
instead of portholes. There were built-in dressers and big storage
drawers beneath the bunkbeds and the window seat. On the bridge
deck we carried two motor launches, one for service, one more elegant
for the owner and guests; and sometimes we towed along a little dinghy
or rowboat.

Approaching Florida, as it began to be warm and sunny, after what
seemed many days on the rough northern waters of Chesapeake Bay
and Pamlico Sound, the boat would wind along narrow canals banked
with green bushes and flat green fields stretching into the distance;
and like a meandering stream one could see where he had been and
where he would be going. There were bridges small and large to be
opened and hours to pass going through the locks. Sometimes an
alligator would be lying on the mudbank in the sun; or we would glide
so close to little rough wooden shacks that we could almost see inside,
and there would be small groups of little Negro children playing on the
ground and bright-colored clothes hanging on the back porch. Once in
Florida we even sailed by a Seminole Indian camp, rather hidden in the
shady jungle of the Everglades, but one could see the palmhouses built
on poles in the water and the brightly colored striped garments on the
women.

With all the fascination of leaning on the rail and watching for
hours or dashing from side to side not to miss some passing excitement, we were abliged to carry on our schedule of lessons and piano
practice! Probably our governesses had just as hard a time concentrat-
ing when we got to places like Palm Beach or Miami, as they liked to
ogle the fashionable people and the elaborate yachts that went by. We
also began to take an interest in things like that. Of course we had
always been conscious of Mami's wardrobe and how exciting it was
when she got dressed up and looked so beautiful. But Papi trained us
to use the binoculars and study the boats—as always he was very
disciplined and scientific! "Check the name on the bridge and where
she comes from," he would say, "then look it up in the yacht register
and record her owner, dimensions, and the time of day that she
passed." It did become more fun as we recognized the same boats at
various moorings from year to year, and then became aware of the
owners: J. P. Morgan's *Corsair*, or the William K. Vanderbilt's boat, and
so on, and knew which ones the family went to visit. We spent more

The "Pioneer," 1921.

than three months (from late December to March) mostly at anchor in Lake Worth, surrounded by the other wintering yachts, to enjoy the season at Palm Beach or take short cruises from there. We were taken daily for our swimming over to the ocean beach at the Breakers Hotel and often had a picnic lunch there. If we drove by the Royal Poinciana in the afternoon, we could peek through the bushes and see the outdoor tea dancing in the Coconut Grove. But most of our entertainment was simply watching the gay social life that took place on the boat.

When we tied up in Jacksonville, there was a group of special southern friends who swarmed aboard for warm and sentimental reunions. We looked forward to the stop in St. Augustine, for then we had a day to roam and play around the wonderful old fort, to see the narrow streets and Spanish houses, and to hear stories about Ponce de León and the Fountain of Youth. In Miami it was the remarkable aquarium that we looked forward to. One year a mysterious deep-sea animal of tremendous size had been washed onto the beach. It looked like a whale but was different and caused much discussion and drew crowds of sightseers. Nothing could be done to help it back to sea, so in a project that looked to us like Gulliver in Lilliput, it was hoisted onto a flatcar by means of many ropes and dragged through the streets. The next winter we visited it—stuffed and mounted—in a specially built tentlike exhibit hall to which one had to pay admission.

Princess in Paradise

We missed the cruise to Key West and Havana, which usually took place after we had been sent home by train. But that always meant a gay time, first at the naval base in Key West, then the exchange of many parties with the Upmann family in Havana. They were of German origin, from Hamburg, and were good old friends of Papi's. There was Herman, the founder and successful president of the cigar and tobacco business, with his very handsome Cuban wife, Dolores, and the younger brother, Carl with his charming blonde wife Ella, from Birmingham, Alabama. Carl and Ella were usually longtime guests on the *Pioneer* while we were anchored at Palm Beach and often stayed with us in Englewood.

Uncle Igor's Arrival

The most sensational winter of all was when Uncle Igor arrived from Europe in February 1921. Mami had received news that her brother had escaped from prison camp in Poland and had reached Belgrade in Serbia. After so much worry, then her relief, followed by the difficulties of getting into the United States, he was due to arrive on the *Aquitania,* made possible by money they had been sending to him abroad. She and Papi went north to meet him at the pier in New York.

There they stood in the February cold watching the passengers disembark, not really knowing what kind of vision to expect. But nobody even the slightest bit familiar appeared. She and Papi had the Moravsky name paged throughout first-and second-class, then through the purser checked over the passenger list. He might be under an assumed name. But they had provided him with his visa and transit passport. There was such a letdown, such frustration, such helplessness, and nothing to do but to go back home and wait.

After two days came a telephone call from the U.S. Immigration Service: "We have a man here [the Ellis Island detention center] who claims to have relatives who are U.S. citizens. If you can provide proof of his identity and post a bond for him, you may come and release him. He has no money for transportation anywhere."

Then followed the wild and exciting chase by car from Englewood over to New York, down to the Bowery, to find the boat for Ellis Island, and there to have Igor's name called out—and from amid the swarms of poor, bedraggled humanity, to watch for a brother to emerge. He was as emaciated, hollow-eyed, disheveled, and dirty as all the rest, in a threadbare full-length Russian army overcoat and a slouch hat, worn-

The Fabulous Twenties

down shoes, and baggageless. All he could ever explain, to relieve their disappointment, was that he had been playing cards in the hold of the boat and never knew where he was until they hauled everyone out at Ellis Island. Worn out, in emotional shock from all he had been through, fearful of the reaction to what he would face in a strange land, he, like so many others, just could not talk about what he had seen or what had happened to him. His brooding and his silence and his cynicism lasted for a long time.

After a week or two in Englewood for recovery, relaxation, and shopping for some clothes, they took him along on the train to join the family on the boat. One of the guests already staying with us for some time was a vivacious, young, blonde Irish lady, Ann Dowling. Extrovert as she was, affectionate and full of fun, she took it upon herself to bring Igor back into life. The first thing was an expedition to a men's outfitter for a wardrobe—consisting of white flannels, a fawn-colored doeskin jacket, a navy blazer, white buck shoes, snappy ties, and a jaunty cap—store-bought and not hand-tailored as one did in New York! Then she took Igor to the tea dance at the Coconut Grove where Palm Beach society gathered every afternoon, and introduced him to her circle as "her Prince" just arrived from Europe. When he did speak he had a fascinating foreign accent. His aloofness was most intriguing, and he was young and very good looking—and refugees of the Russian nobility were then quite a novelty.

Igor went along quite docilely, mystified but relaxed. In the mornings she paraded with him on the boardwalk of the Breakers; during the afternoons was the tea dance; and in the evenings, with no resistance at all, they joined the crowd at Bailey's Casino for gambling. We heard all the talk and the jokes about the swarms of young ladies chasing after the Russian prince, and watched with great glee the feverish comings and goings—the launch constantly going back and forth to bring guests, to deliver the family for their endless schedule of social engagements, and quite often the raucous hailing from the shore for a lift well after midnight.

❧ The Florida Social Whirl

It behooved Papi and Mami to introduce Igor properly to their friends and acquaintances in Palm Beach, so a real party was organized. It was to be a formal dinner on the big saloon deck, with a dance afterward. When I think now of the planning that must have gone into giving a properly formal party at that time, even in a home like Englewood, I wonder how everything was taken care of without our being aware of lots of frantic excitement. This was on a boat anchored in the middle of a lake. Supplies had to be bought, not ordered by telephone, at West Palm Beach (there was no car), hauled by launch, then stowed away and preserved.

For the printing of invitations and menus, one had to make a trip to the proper establishment somewhere. Flowers, decorations, and folding tables could be ordered through a caterer, but souvenirs of enough distinction had to come from New York. The dance band, once engaged, was fine. But the musicians and their instruments had to be picked up and delivered by launch, and again safely deposited ashore sometime during the night, which meant that the crew also had to be on the alert. Of course, on *the day* the boat was decked out with all the flags and bunting from mast to mast, and it would not have been a party without Japanese paper lanterns strung around the decks. The dining tables were set in a U-shape on the afterdeck and decorated with smilax and flowers; extra help bustled about; and the guests arrived, some on our launch and others on their own.

For us three children a party was great fun to watch. Properly dressed, all alike, in our white sailor uniforms, we were lined up on deck as the welcoming committee. But after enough excitement took over we could peer through the windows, or take the beautiful ladies below to the powder room, or we could slip onto the bench behind the orchestra and watch the dancing. About that time the hits were "Avalon" and "Dardenella" and the dance style was that of walking forward and backward in long strides and then occasionally doing a deep dip. All this was delightfully new to Uncle Igor, and he enjoyed his role and the attention of all the ladies, young and old. But after the champagne had been flowing for some time he must have felt really at home at last. He relaxed and grabbed the tiny Ann Dowling by the waist and flung himself into a real Viennese waltz, sweeping her off her feet, which she bubblingly enjoyed. Then every other lady demanded a turn, and the orchestra obliged with more and more vigor until Igor was red, puffing, and sailing about dizzily, swearing that the boat must be pitching from side to side. How they all got down the gangplank and into the boats to head for shore at the end of the party we were not awake to see. However, Igor's reputation was secure, and from that occasion on the "Merry Widow Waltz" was our dream of real romance, and Igor, to us as well as his many female admirers, was the picture of its dashing Prince Danielo.

The Fabulous Twenties

Papi clowns on the beach, 1921.

Princess in Paradise

It is amazing to realize that during this winter and spring of 1921 Mami was expecting our youngest brother, Sergey. She knew it since going on the Canadian hunting trip, then followed the moving of family and household to Florida on the boat, and after Christmas took more than one trip by train back to New York. Welcoming Igor from Europe was one occasion of enough emotion and strain. Another session which also took her north was when Uncle Karl, who had been living with us in Englewood—Papi's youngest brother, a bachelor and a sweet, kind, humorous man—who had been ailing for some time, was taken to Englewood hospital where he died. Sometime before Sergey's birth in May, Mami's sister Xenia also turned up in Europe as a refugee and was brought to the United States to live with us. But that was after we had all returned to Englewood.

After the end of the European war we three children were able to return to private schools, Ty and I to Dwight, Emile to the Morse Country Day School in Englewood. At that age we all accepted unquestioningly whatever decisions our parents chose to make about us. To them it must have hardly seemed anything but natural to take us out of school for the three or more months of the annual sojourn in Florida. From their own experience, one could do well enough with tutors. Evidently we did, because we advanced in our grades, and the ladies who were our constant companions must have been very well chosen. But at school it certainly added to our reputation as queer kids from that crazy family on the hill and isolated us even more.

The customary routine was to leave Englewood in early December and go south by boat, spending Christmas somewhere on the way, which became really fun if the weather was good. However, to sail the boat north in March meant too much rough weather, or too long a time, so we traveled by train, either the whole ménage together, or just governess with children. Again stops were carefully scheduled ahead, and friends came to the train at Jacksonville, Charleston, and Washington, D.C., to visit and stroll on the platform.

One memory, when we were small enough to be just little round bundles, stands out vividly. When the train started to move, Miss Field hopped aboard and Papi tossed Emile up the steps, then little Ty went flying; I was boosted aboard as the next car went by, and Mami jumped on behind—and all of us stood there howling because Papi was left behind. But he caught the observation platform of the last car and made it by himself, appearing quite calmly in a few minutes, walking through the train to soothe us all with his presence.

The Fabulous Twenties

The next winter, after Sergey was born, he joined the group on the boat with his own nurse and had his own schedule of eating, swimming, and sleeping. In subsequent years he followed the same Florida winter sojourn even after we no longer went along. But, though he was also outfitted in his white sailor suit, he could not keep up with our drills and games, so he was always regarded as the baby and the outsider.

As I mentioned before, one phase of life that was very apparent, though we did not always understand it, was Prohibition. In Florida it was just as real as it had been in Englewood and New York, only there were variations. Whereas wine or champagne with meals on board had been a most normal thing, even for us children, these now became almost impossible to obtain here, and the fashion for cocktails and mixed drinks began. There were also different rules and complications in obtaining the alcoholic supplies and the need for acquiring and drinking them in great secrecy. Yachts which could sail to Cuba or out beyond the three-mile limit were watched by the Coast Guard Patrol and were frequently boarded and searched. One lived in fear and suspense just as during the war.

We would hear long tales and there would be uproarious laughter over how one had been clever enough to thwart the authorities. The big storage drawers beneath our bunks became favorite hiding places for that beautiful Cuban Bacardi, and in the master bedroom a special closet had to be fitted out with a secret compartment for bottles behind the clothes, and kept padlocked. Once, as I remember, a Coast Guard inspector did come aboard the *Pioneer*. Papi greeted him and his uniformed attendants in his usual affable manner and managed to keep them entertained with stories in the living salon for quite some time. When our tall good-looking Negro steward, George, served coffee, he gave some sort of signal to Papi. They were then welcome to go around and search the boat and, in a very friendly and apologetic manner, acknowledged that they had found nothing illegal and departed. George and Captain Satterlee had been very busy sinking the newest supply of wooden cases with Cuban rum over the starboard side of the boat, attaching them with lines to the anchor chain so that they could be retrieved when "the coast was clear"!

🌿 The Presidential Charter

Early in the 1923 season Papi had an offer to charter the *Pioneer*. It would mean rearranging all our winter plans and require considerable effort to empty the boat of our personal belongings. The customer was Edward MacLean, a wealthy oilman, whose wife, Evelyn Walsh Mac-Lean, was famous as the owner of the Hope Diamond. They were quite willing to pay any price; they wanted to do a favor for a friend and arrange for his vacation aboard the yacht. But the charter would be in their name, and the whole arrangment must be kept absolutely secret.

The guest for three weeks was to be the president of the United States! Not knowing much personally about Mr. and Mrs. Warren G. Harding, Papi was flattered; Mami, like any housewife, got quite excited about not having enough table linens for such a party and the china and glassware were certainly not good enough. So the master cabin was redecorated and the whole boat spruced up. Papi and Mami went to Greenleaf and Crosby, the Tiffany's of Palm Beach, to pick out some new dinnerware. They ordered a set of Lenox china for twenty-four, with an ivory base and a deep blue-and-gold border, and if enough was not on hand at this store it must be shipped express from the Philadelphia branch. To go with it they picked out a set of stem glasses with a flower border, for water, wine, and champagne, as well as tall and small tumblers. From Englewood came some of Mami's best tablecloths and napkins. The steward, our stewardess, as well as the rest of the crew remained the same. One knew only that the boat would be full to capacity and would cruise offshore.

The *Pioneer* was turned over to the MacLeans. Then began the loading of the supplies for the guests and the renter's personal belongings. Wheeled up the gangplank were cases and cases of rums, whiskeys, applejack, and soft drink. Then came the crew of Secret Service men and political friends, who filled every cabin, bunk, and sofa. (Papi never greeted the president personally.)

Three weeks later, however, they were both on hand to take over the *Pioneer* again. The captain was reticent and never revealed much. But George and Pauline could not talk fast enough or sputter loud enough in their outrage. The stories they told must have been hair-raising, and the results enough to make anyone weep. The mahogany dining table had been in constant use for poker playing; there were cigarette holes burned into it, and alcohol marks were everywhere. The same went for every coffee table or sidetable that had a brocade cover on it.

Mami's greatest horror was discovering wads of chewing gum under every upholstered chair and every time she sat down to a table. The linen tablecloths had coffee stains all over and holes burned right

The Fabulous Twenties

through where cigarettes had been squashed out. Burn marks were on all the bedroom furniture and on the sheets and pillows also. Of the stemware, less than a dozen of anything remained. And the twenty-four piece Lenox china set was reduced to the greatest collection of odds and ends, not enough to set a table even for eight completely. Our crew had served faithfully, gone wherever the whims of those in charge directed them, and were on the alert through all-night parties and often quite dangerous carousing. It was one long poker-playing, gambling of other kinds, and drinking orgy, though we were led to believe it was an entirely stag affair.

In any case, the memories were pretty sour, and thereafter the risks of ever chartering again were most carefully weighed. The china and glassware were packed away to be distributed to the next generation. I can imagine what the family sentiments were in regard to the then president and later when stories were published about his political and private life.

As long as we had the *Pioneer,* which was until about 1926, she was brought north in the spring and anchored in the Hudson River near the New Jersey pier of the Dyckman Street ferry at the foot of the Palisades and very convenient to Englewood. The family took longer cruises to Fisher's Island or Newport and entertained on board quite often. But for us, being more occupied with our schools, then going away to summer camps, our visits were less frequent and not usually for overnight. We could invite our friends and they got quite a thrill out of it, but we, naughty children, were blasé and got quite bored with the customary Sunday afternoon run up the Hudson River to Nyack and back. We much preferred the island at Greenwood Lake.

Mami's Housekeeping Problems

We often heard Mami worrying about the housekeeping chores but couldn't quite sympathize with her till later when we understood such things better. For several summers she was actually running three full establishments, and they were by no means simple; there were roughly thirty-five employees to feed daily and the marketing to be done once a week in New York. The house at Englewood was always kept open as Papi's headquarters during the week, where he returned from business every night. Besides cooking for him, there were the garden staff, the chauffeur, and the stable personnel had to be fed; also there were the dogs to feed and the horses to be exercised. If we children were at

Greenwood Lake, provisions for the island had to be thought out on a weekly basis, ordered in New York, and delivered up there.

But the most demanding thing was the boat. Even before union regulations, twelve men demanded and got plenty of meat; and they consumed no small quantities of bread, fruit, vegetables, and dairy products. The shopping lists for all three places together were made every Friday—pages and pages handwritten on a pad—then the orders were telephoned to Weisbecker's Market on upper Broadway in New York City; coffee cakes, desserts, and dark bread came from Shedko, the Russian bakery; and extras like cheeses and caviar came from other regular places.

On Saturday morning or Friday afternoon a truck from Papi's factory made the rounds to collect these supplies and deliver them at home. At Englewood the cook sorted out the provisions, and everything had to be checked against the bills. There were the supplies for Greenwood Lake that Papi or the chauffeur could take along for the weekend, another load to be delivered to the *Pioneer* anchored at Dyckman Street—and the rest to be stored away in 3 iceboxes, kitchen closets and the pantry.

The requisitions were usually pretty much the same, and if Mami was off on a trip the cook or the housekeeper could carry on. It was when something really special was coming up, such as a birthday party or a weekend cruise with guests, that the planning ahead must have been terrific. Maresi-Mazetti, the caterer or the MacAlpin Hotel candy shop, would produce marvelous confections of cake and sugar decorations, or chocolate Easter eggs with individual names on each, or twenty boxes of Sherry's candy. Once I was told to stop in at the Plaza Hotel, while the chauffeur remained outside in the car, to pick up three pounds of caviar. I wondered why I was kept waiting so long as they checked with home by telephone. Later I saw the bill—$20 per pound—$60 worth of caviar handed over to a little red-faced girl. Whatever it was, Mami kept all the accounts and checked every bill.

Life on the *Pioneer* was a children's dream, whether it was during the winters in Florida or in summer cruising from yacht club to yacht club on Long Island Sound. We had our own separate afterdeck and big rooms; our activities were independently run by the governesses; and there was a continual round of exciting events and interesting visitors to observe.

During one of those early winters, Papi, always the adventurous, took his first airplane trip, with the whole family of course watching

Deep sea fishing from the "Pioneer" in 1921.

Princess in Paradise

from the shore. This was on a hydroplane, or "flying boat," anchored out in the water, approached by a bouncing little dinghy from which the pilot and the one passenger (Papi) had to climb onto the wing, and from there squeeze his big hulk into a tiny seat in the enclosed cockpit. After the propeller on the open engine began to whirr, the boat splashed across the water and finally, breathtakingly rose from the surface and disappeared into the sky. As we watched, it all seemed like a miracle. He was flying to Bimini, a tiny island in the Bahamas, on the usual mysterious business trip. A few days later we watched him reappear and climb out, followed by his customary vivid and enthusiastic descriptions of this astonishing new phenomenon: "Imagine what this could develop into in the future!"

Another season he decided to try deep-sea fishing. This required a special boat with equipment and a guide and was also the occasion for another party, with Mami and several guests along. We got the usual benefits when they returned—photographs of the people, the costumes, how the fishing was done, and eventually the stuffed fish—an enormous blue sailfish, a silvery tarpon, and a fierce barracuda. Mami also described the thrilling experience of watching the ocean floor through a glass-bottomed boat and brought us specimens of coral, fans, and beautiful conch shells. We always learned from their trips.

The Fabulous Twenties

14

The Hunting Trips

N THE FALL of 1920 and for about three years Mami and Papi began their annual expeditions to the Canadian Rockies. They went principally to Banff Springs in British Columbia for a pack trip to shoot big upland game—mostly mountain sheep and mountain goats, deer, sometimes a brown bear, and once a moose. We shared plenty of the excitement at home. First there were the clothes and the equipment, bought at Abercrombie & Fitch, tried on, showed off, and packed up for shipping ahead. Mami could handle a gun as well as anyone and looked pretty advanced in riding britches and hunting boots. Papi, amazingly for his size, kept quite fit in the saddle, and he wore his hunting clothes with dash.

However, we could never properly imagine our dignified parents sleeping on the ground and crawling into the sleepingbag contraptions, which were, of course, the newest thing—heavy waterproof canvas envelopes which one folded over oneself, then pulled together with woven straps. One slept with clothes on and lined them with woolen blankets, but the mattress was no more than a half-inch-thick woolen pad. The guns went in a special trunk, which were shipped directly to Banff with the bulky bedrolls and warm clothing.

When the family departed with their party of friends, like General O'Ryan and Kincaid and Uncle Jack Looschen, they went in the Canadian-Pacific Railway, breaking up the already gay four-or five-day trip with stops in Toronto, Winnipeg, and Calgary. Everything was

faithfully recorded in photographs, and when they returned we received our special souvenirs like bear-claw pins and were regaled with
vivid stories, graphically illustrated and described to us, so that in our
imaginations at least, we had been there too.

Later the trophies would arrive—the heads, stuffed and
mounted—which were duly hung for decoration all around the house
(not like Teddy Roosevelt, who concentrated his in a single Trophy
Room). A huge moose head with an enormous spread of horns hung
over our living room fireplace—a greatly envied showpiece—while the
heads of sheep, goats, deer, and the bear rug were scattered about.
Mami was able to tell tales of her successes as well as any of them. As
one taxidermist reflected, he was not only an artist in re-creating the
animals as they appeared in nature, but through him the reminiscences of each adventure and the mental pictures of the romantic
settings where each event took place were kept alive long after the
costly trips were over.

Mami, who shared these feelings, not only tolerated the stuffed
heads, but put up with the burden of caring for them. Every spring all
except the moose head (which got camphor balls in his ears and behind
his antlers) were taken down and moved to a mothproof storage room
next to the hayloft in the garage. Like everything else in the house,
summer meant a complete change of decor—rugs rolled up and stored
away, furniture and portieres slipcovered, rooms closed up with
shades pulled, and activities moved out to the screened porches.

On their first trip they went a bit too late in September, which took
them well into the heavy snows of October, but they were always
thrilled by the majestic Canadian Rockies, and they enjoyed the pack
trips even when spotting the white game in the winter landscape was
about as close as they came to actual hunting. All the pack arrangements were made ahead, and they took off from the Banff Springs
Hotel. For six people there were twenty-four horses in all, with about
four guides who set up the camp and did the cooking as well as guiding
them to the game and coaching the visitors on survival procedures. All
the equipment and supplies for three weeks in the wilds were loaded
on the extra horses—including pots and pans, waterproof boxes of
food, and the long tepee poles. They slept in two large Indian
tepees—the guests, men and women, in one—the guides in another. A
fire was kept going inside all night, with the smoke seeping out the
opening at the top and leaving just enough good airspace near the
ground to be comfortable lying down or sitting up. Each person had a

The Fabulous Twenties

pile of wood beside his bed and had to feed the fire periodically.

Mami and Bertha Spain were the only women to go along on these trips, and they good-naturedly put up with all aspects of the "roughing it," as well as with the camp language of the men. Breakfast was the most noteworthy meal, for the guides would have the coffee and bacon ready, then would make dozens of flapjacks, tossing them from the frying pan with a flip that would land one onto the upheld tin plate. If they shot any game the meat was cooked, but the trophies had to be hauled along. The snow did not bother them, but they had to break up the ice on many a stream for the horses to cross, or to get drinking water. It was quite believable that in September in those mountains Papi would find an unfrozen pool and plunge in for his bath; we all knew his capacity for hardihood and good circulation! He often tried to get us to do the same.

The horses they used amazed them. These were the small "Indian" ponies, stocky and strong and very smart. A special one had to be reserved to carry 350-pound Papi. The first time they were introduced to this selected one, first a gasp went up, and then a roar—his name was Midget and he looked it. But he survived his job, even though they always took a replacement along as a precaution. The second year a much more promising horse was produced. However, after the first day's workout he took off into the woods and never showed up again. Three weeks later they found out that he had gone galloping back to his stable in Banff.

For eastern riders the most difficult thing to learn was not to control one's horse by the reins; one had to give him his head and trust to the horse's good judgment in following a trail and picking his footing every step of the way. Indeed, great confidence was required, for some of these mountain trails they took were the narrowest of paths along the most precipitous drops far down into a valley. On coming down a steep incline, the best one could do was to lean way back with legs stretched forward almost to the horse's ears. At times they had to jump or climb over fallen trees, the horse almost uncannily protecting its rider if a fallen tree hung across the trail just at the level of his rider's head.

The better sense of letting the horse follow a trail was demonstrated at the beginning of their first trip. Bertha Spain, one of the guests from Toronto, could not be in Banff in time to start off with the party as scheduled. So Papi stayed behind with one guide to wait over the extra day. Without baggage, the three of them could easily catch up with the pack train in one day, and it was arranged to meet at the camp near the top of Mount Assiniboine. Bertha arrived and changed to hunting clothes, though most of her belongings had already gone ahead in the packs. They hit the trail, led by the guide, and kept riding until almost nightfall. By then, according to all calculations they should have come upon their group or at least have sighted the fires of their camp, but they found themselves miserably alone with neither campsite nor companions.

Precautions had to be taken as quickly as possible. This was the end of September, and they were high in the mountains. Between them they had a small hatchet and a waterproof box of matches. The guide built a lean-to of boughs and strewed pine branches on the ground for sleeping, but they had no extra horse carrying gear or food. The sandwich lunch had been consumed. They managed to light a fire and use the saddleblankets for cover; they were able to sleep a bit, slightly protected from the falling snow. They dared not turn the horses loose to forage as usual. They could chop through ice to get drinking water and heat it a bit in their tin cups. Then Papi remembered his ever faithful survival medicine—a pint-sized flask of rum. They rationed this and sipped it from time to time, and they were sure that this kept them alive through that night. By morning the snowfall had cleared, and they could look across a big valley at another high snow-covered peak. The guide began to have misgivings and admitted he was not really sure where they were. They decided that the only thing to do was to get down from this mountain and back to Banff; the horses would find their way home without fail.

Meanwhile, the first party had pitched camp on Mount Assiniboine and had been anxiously waiting all through the bitter cold and snow of that night. Mami had decided to keep the camp there but send two guides with extra horses back to Banff, either to get information or to send out a search party. After a half day on the trail, ringing bells and shouting, they heard an answering shot and met up with the three missing wanderers. Revived by some hot food and dry socks, they managed three more hours of riding and were brought at last into the welcome circle of friends and campfires. Amid all the excitement and rejoicing there were the questions, the most important being: What had happened? They finally figured out that the guide had taken the wrong trail and led them up toward Mount Simpson summit instead of

The Fabulous Twenties

Mount Assiniboine's. If it had been left to the horses, they would have used their noses and followed the trail left by their companions with no confusion at all.

When the three weeks of life in the woods and on horseback were over, the party returned to luxuriate in the comforts of the Banff Springs Hotel and then usually did some more sightseeing. One year it was to the roundup of the Royal Northwest Mounted Police at Calgary. We saw the pictures and heard descriptions of the remarkable riding exhibitions of the mounties in their brilliant red coats, doing drills and individual tricks of horsemanship almost as skillful as those done at the Spanish Riding School of Vienna. Some years later these troops came to the International Horse Show at Madison Square Garden in New York, and we could see for ourselves what we felt we already knew pretty well.

After another hunting trip, General O'Ryan's family—or rather Mrs. O'Ryan and their two eldest daughters, Dorothy and Janet—met the group at Banff and toured to Lake Louise and Victoria, returning together on that long scenic train ride across Canada. Dorothy was especially charming and very beautiful, and from that time on they took an affectionate and personal interest in her. Although she was not strong enough to go on the hunting trips, they did invite her to go along with them on the trip around the world in 1924.

Papi's spring sports activity was to go salmon fishing with his brother and later with his nephew in the Miramichi River in New Brunswick. As I've said before, we were not yet old enough to be included (besides, women did not go along to the Miramichi fishing camp), and our camping experiences were by ourselves either at Greenwood Lake or at the girls' camp, Mudjekeewis. It was almost impossible for us to visualize our father, who was imposingly large and very dignified, roughing it in the woods or getting into a canoe. However, we did see pictures of him in the rough river water, the canoe down to the gunwales; as further proof, we received every year a large coffinlike box, dripping with melted ice, fringed with moss, containing one or more huge and really delicious freshly caught Nova Scotia salmon.

15

Rejuvenation of Greystone

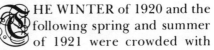HE WINTER of 1920 and the following spring and summer of 1921 were crowded with emotions and obligations, especially for Mami. While the family was settled on the boat in Florida, Uncle Igor arrived from the Revolution in Russia, which meant the trip up to New York to take care of him. Then Papi's young bachelor brother, Karl, died in Englewood, with Mami affectionately in attendance. Finally her sister, Xenia, arrived and then shortly after that Sergey was born (May 21).

Meanwhile, great plans were under way for the remodeling of the house. This soon developed into quite a little drama. First of all it meant Mami's personal supervision and decisions for every bit of the decoration: a special carved plaster ceiling for the new living room, carved wood pilasters, light fixtures, designs for each chair and sofa, and selecting the brocade for new curtains. She had her own ideas and was very definite in arguments with Mr. Wesley, head decorator from Altman's. This was going to be elegant but not ponderous, traditional but not manufacturer's standard, and the colors to be away from the Victorian, lighter and even daring.

Then Papi had his own pet dreams and was often belligerently positive about them. The former library and parlor was to be opened into one big room; it was going to be the "music room," with a tremendous pipe organ as its feature. It was not to be a "mighty Wurlitzer," but the best—so Welte-Mignon of Frieburg, Germany, was the

The refurbished music room of Greystone, 1922.

instrument chosen, and Mr. Burnham was the salesman and the supervisor. While plastering and paneling was going on above, in the basement they had to dig a twelve-foot cellar and haul out by wheelbarrow all the dirt and concrete flooring in order to build the piperoom to accommodate up to sixteen-foot bass pipes. This long and difficult job went on all summer. We did not see the carload deliveries of the different-sized pipes and the installation of the three-manual console with foot-pedal scales. But we were very impressed with the details of the finished object. At the end of the music room was the handsome walnut console and bench, surrounded by a bank of brass pipes. Down in the organ room, kept locked because of the air conditioning, were banks and banks of pipes, wood and metal, in beautiful rows, graduated in size from the tiniest tubes to enormous wooden box like ones.

As if that were not enough, Papi, who could not resist a vision (or a salesman), also wanted an "Echo Organ." So at the top of the main staircase the first bedroom in the servants' corridor was requisitioned, and into that went the pipes for the Echo Organ, with a grill for the sounds to waft down from the second floor and through the ceiling of

Princess in Paradise

the living room. It all sounded so marvelous and mystifying, except
when the tuning of the pipes began. That went on all day long, day
after day. It was a very slow procedure, because one specialist had to be
upstairs at the keyboard, and the other one had to be either in the
basement organ room or up in the echo machinery room. And that, we
soon learned, had to take place every so often, especially if some
celebrity was coming to perform for an occasion.

As usual, one thing leads to another. With this gorgeous new music
room, one could hardly tolerate the shabby-looking sunporches that
were right beside it. They were originally open, screened porches
outside the gray stone walls of the house. Now there was presented a
beautiful watercolor rendering of glassed-in arcades, green latticework covering the stone walls, tropical furniture, glass goldfish
bowls, and big lush plants—the ideal conservatory. The electric lighting was subdued, concealed amid the greenery.

But most intriguing of all, the ceiling was to be hand-painted presenting the illusion of an arched sky, complete with blue and pink
clouds and tiny lights made to look like twinkling stars (as Papi said, "If
they can have twinkling stars in the Roxy Theater, we can have them at
home"), and the cove lighting around it was controlled by a dimmer so
that one could go from bright sunshine to delicate twilight. It certainly
appealed to us youngsters much more than the music room idea did.
When it came into being, it was a favorite of young and old alike—airy
in summer, a treat in winter. Everyone wandered out onto the south
porch, especially for drinks. In no time, we were innocently repeating
everybody's witty nickname—the "Souse Porch."

By now the gardens also looked too old-fashioned. So there evolved
a complete new landscaping job. It started with balustrades to enclose
the house, which stood at the top of the hill surrounded by smooth
green lawns. And Mami always wanted a lily pond. This could be dug
next to a new teahouse or pergola with white latticework for wisteria
vines. Papi then came up with the idea: "Wouldn't it be nicer to have a
swimming pool for the children!" Soon there was another set of en-
chanting watercolor pictures of pool and terraced garden; a little
marble temple at the far end against a wall of tall cypresses; and on one
side, sure enough, a new pergola with three lily ponds.

Excavations started right away and continued all summer. The pool
was laid out in reinforced concrete; retaining walls went up; and the
garden walks were of red tile—not simple flagstones—which had to be
set on top of four-foot-deep concrete foundations. White balustrades

The Fabulous Twenties

Landscape architect's rendering for the new gardens,

were delivered in six-foot lengths. Flower vases fitted on top of those. Fortunately, none of the big old trees was disturbed. But they did have to bring in those tall cypresses for the background. There was to be a fringe of planting at the front end of the porch.

Papi got carried away again. One day there was delivered—and planted—a hedge of luscious dark green old Virginia boxwoods. How Mami missed it I do not know; she was always around. But when she came home and saw the boxwoods she fumed. She seldom "blew up" as Papi did. But she could fume and fuss and talk, talk, talk. The boxwood hedge was dug up again and removed. After that, we had tall red-and-yellow flowering cannas like those in the pictures of Romadanova.

The white-domed columned temple at the far end of the pool had a ceiling inside of blue tile with gold stars, and a small hanging oriental lamp. That promptly became the "Temple d'Amour." It *was* pretty; and it was cool there; and one had a perfect view over the garden and of

Princess in Paradise

pool, and "Temple d'Amour" at Greystone.

the activities in the pool. But it was a long way from the house; and it seemed even longer to those who had to carry trays of after-dinner coffee or cooling drinks back and forth.

All this led up to Sergey's christening on November 26, 1921, at three o'clock in the afternoon. The gigantic redecorating, relandscaping project was undertaken for this event, and the occasion was also to be the grand dedication of the new music room and the organ. The bishop and priests from the Russian Cathedral in New York were driven out to Englewood. A tub draped with lace and flower garlands was again set up in the center of the room, and the guests stood around it in a circle. The baby was being named Sergei (after Mami's distinguished uncle) Albert (after Papi's older brother), and the godparents were Lydia Lipkowska, and Gen. John O'Ryan.

The religious service went off without a hitch, with incense and the priests chanting and the baby being skillfully immersed in the font

The Fabulous Twenties

three times. After being dried, dressed in a long lace christening robe, and paraded around on exhibition, his part was over. Then came the reception and the musical entertainment. A well-known organist from New York performed, exhibiting all the great and intricate musical qualities of the organ, pedal pipes, flute and oboe stops, swelling and diminishing chords, and of course the Echo Organ. Madame Lipkowska, accompanied on the piano, sang operatic arias and trilled enchantingly in her high soprano. She was a tiny, blonde, utterly feminine vivacious creature with a manner and a Russian accent that captivated everyone.

The Russian Invasion

This was the period of parading personalities which Papi called "the Russian invasion," as I had mentioned before. Streaming into New York from the Bolshevik terror, via Paris and other parts of Europe, came the refugees; relatives and old friends were being discovered every day, and many of them at our house. Most were from the educated and aristocratic circles, but there were many ordinary and middle-class people who soon became bored and stayed away. Our house was already a babble of Russian, with Mami's brother and sister and Olga, the family maid. One day Papi brought home a Cossack coachman from a restaurant in New York. He pleaded some distant connection to the family in Moscow. His name was Nicolai Pakhom, and he was kept to help take care of the horses. On Sundays or special occasions when guests were arriving, Pakhom became the doorman. Much taller than Papi's six feet four inches and barrel-chested, he added a fourteen-inch gray fur Cossack cap and wrapped himself in his long Cossack coat, with bullets across the chest and dagger at the waist, and greeted people with a booming bass voice. If we could make him laugh, it sounded like rolling thunder.

At this same time Vera Smirnova appeared on the scene—the gypsy singer who had known the family while performing in restaurants in Moscow. With all the Russian restaurants now springing up in New York, one could go to any of them and run into these exiles. Most were penniless. Some were working in the kitchen or at other jobs; some were just sitting and being fed by the charity of the owner. But news and names and addresses soon were passed around. Vera Smirnova was dark and plumpish with that remarkably husky, almost bass, gypsy voice. She also possessed the gypsy temperament—quixotic, emotional, jumping from passionate affection to fiery indignation. She wrapped herself in a shawl when she sang, sitting with closed eyes and swaying, pouring forth unmistakable emotion. But if in conversation something was said that insulted her, she suddenly, very graphically spit forth daggers from her eyes and her throat, wrapped her shawl around herself, and walked out of the house—off to New York on foot or to sleep in the bushes. Some days one would look out at the driveway, and there would be Smirnova hiking up from the trolley, in high-heeled slippers, long full skirt, and shawl. Somebody in New York had hurt her feelings, or she was hungry, or a destitute friend had entrusted her with something precious to sell—like a big ikon, which she produced from under the shawl.

So the noisy half of Sergey's christening celebration was the Russian one. There was a big *zakuska* and a formal dinner in which we took no part. But fot the performance afterward, we were allowed to stay up and watch from the back—and this was our introduction to all the gaiety and abandon that always animated the Russian parties through the years to come. Lydia Lipowska and her handsome leading man in his white officer's coat sang songs from *The Merry Widow*. To us it was tear-jerkingly romantic. When at the end of the program they actually danced the "Merry Widow Waltz," everybody was up and shouting. Then came Vera Smirnova with her mournful gypsy songs and some gay folk songs, which she could blast out while standing and shimmying her shoulders and snapping her fingers. She had brought along five members of her balalaika orchestra dressed in their Russian blouses, carrying their triangular instruments, from the man-sized big bass to the normal, gay banjolike smaller ones. By the time they had performed themselves, and danced some of the wild Cossack dances, the spirits of the audience were well enlivened and relaxed; requests were shouted by the guests; and soon all were joining in the songs and clapping in tempo. The Russians had a way of enjoying themselves that nobody could duplicate.

Musical entertainments appeared every so often in the yearly program, though there was never as memorable a one as this. Singers and all sorts of players came as guests to the big Sunday dinners, and they loved to sit down and play and talk about their music. But it was the formally organized "musicales" that we dreaded; there was an engraved invitation, and two dozen selected guests at dinner—the "An Informal Hour of Music," as the printed program stated. We didn't know enough to make fun of them. But once Ty got hold of one of

The Fabulous Twenties

those programs and roguishly dubbed it "An Infernal Hour of Music," which we all took up hysterically—suddenly stopping dead in our tracks when we noticed Papi listening bemused just outside the door. Whether it was music we liked or not, we were curious enough to hang around in the background listening and forming our opinions. What sent us into giggles behind the portieres was when, as the guests were irrepressibly chatting over coffee and liqueurs during this informal hour, Papi would turn around and utter a long, loud "Psh-sh-ssht" or say in no delicate voice, "Won't you please be qui-et—listen to the music!"

More About School

The year of Sergy's arrival, 1921, seems to have marked the beginning of many changes in our way of life. In the preceding fall we had been taken back into our private schools. As was mentioned in an earlier chapter, we were customarily taken out of school for the three- or four-month winter trip to Florida on the yacht, and continued with a private tutor when we came back. We were still driven to school by the German and later by the Russian coachman, either in a pony carriage, the closed buggy, or an open sleigh—complete with fur robes, two horses, and jingling bells—and we invariably arrived late!

Since our school sessions were only for a half day (I began in the seventh grade, Ty in the fourth) we would be called for again at noon, pick up Emile on the way, and be home for lunch. These were the delightful sessions alone with Mami, later joined by Xenia, when stories would pour out, our own chatter was uninhibited, and we forgot the outside world. The afternoons were complicated arrangements of tutoring and homework, each of the three of us having to get in an hour's practice on the pianos—and we still had time enough for outdoor play—before dressing for Papi's arrival and dinner at seven, now with the family including Xenia and Igor, all gathered together in the dining room instead of in our third-floor nursery.

The most exciting fun we had was when there was snow and we could use our big long hill for skiing or coasting. Mami would join us in her hunting pants and boots, and with our three sleds tied together and all our joyful screaming, we were soon noticed by neighbor children. They looked on furtively, then grew curious enough to come closer, and finally we had a group of six or seven "very nice" youngsters we had never seen before. They thought Mami was wonderful, and we had a carefree time together, even to taking sides in snowball fights —but we were never allowed to go to their houses to play with them.

In school we looked and acted just as oddly as we must have appeared on the outside. Not only were we escorted in those exotic contraptions, but we each carried our books in a leather schoolbag, while others just carted them by the armful. Day in and day out, week after week, we wore exactly the same uniform—a navy blue sailor dress or middy with red tie and pleated skirt, long dark stockings, and black high-buttoned boots—and our hair in two pigtails. Strictly disciplined at home, we did not dare to speak to anyone or laugh aloud, and we were obliged to show the most humble respect to our teachers. We trembled in wide-eyed terror if spoken to by the white-haired lady principal, Miss Creighton (who, I realized later, had a twinkle in her eye whenever she said something like, "You go home and ask 'Papi' if you may do such-and-such!").

During the mornings we had gym classes when we played games like dodge-ball and farmer-in-the-dell under the supervision of the intriguingly young and attractive teacher, Miss Pryde. Once she asked me if I could manage to come back in the afternoon to try out for basketball. So I got the permission at home and made the special arrangements to take another trip to school and to be called for, and I appeared—in my dark blue wool serge uniform. Miss Pryde guided me through the first explanations and attempts to bounce and throw the ball, to be pushed around, and never winced; and though I noticed that the rest of the girls were in bloomers and white middies, and rubber-soled *sneakers,* I was too innocent or absorbed to experience any embarrassment. She managed to make a personal call at home and explained to Papi some of the facts of athletic life at school, so that we soon discovered where one could buy such equipment "for girls," and both Ty and I were properly outfitted with gym clothes and were gingerly on our way to playing with other children. The young and attractive Miss Pryde, as much a diplomat as she was an inspiring gym teacher, soon became an admired friend of the family's, and through her influence we were sent for our first summer's camp experience away from home, to Mudjekeewis in Maine. That was 1921, we at ages eleven and nine, and the second year of her new enterprise.

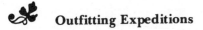 **Outfitting Expeditions**

Our clothes buying had always been somewhat of an ordeal. Not that we were aware or had much to say about choices; we put on what was assigned to us, and that was the same every day. In winter we wore the dark navy uniforms, and in the summer or in Florida, the same thing in white, with high white boots. The exciting variation was either red or bright blue collars and cuffs.

The outfitting expedition to New York City took place about twice a year, each lasting for one whole day. We all piled into the limousine with Mami and the chauffeur, were not allowed to get out on the ferryboat as we crossed the Hudson River, and disembarked somewhere downtown at a Fifth Avenue store. There all the doormen knew Mrs. Kluge, and the chauffeurs lined up around the block, waiting to be called by an electric number sign when wanted again.

Usually we accomplished everything in Altman's, which we enjoyed because of the five-story open court in the center. Sometimes we went to Wanamaker's to see the tremendous Christmas displays in their center well; once it was Jack and the Beanstalk with a vine and a life-sized puppet going up to the skylight. When Mami marched in and out of the aisles with her brood of three trailing behind her, she always wore a hat with tall egret feathers, and she would say, "Now, you watch for my hat, I cannot watch out for you!" Then we always went to Maillard's for lunch, where the head waiter would greet Mami most cordially and she rattled off French to him and all the rest. Whatever else we may have eaten, we waited breathlessly for the cart loaded with the French pastries, and each of us held up the procedure while we ogled all those familiar goodies.

Papi usually joined us for the session at DePinna's. That is where he picked out the sailor's uniforms. He sat there with his cane and big hat in hand and had all the salesladies scurrying from one department to another, putting the dresses on us and a matching suit for Emile; then came the winter coats, all alike, and appropriate hats, which he himself placed on us at a jaunty angle. And by the time we three were lined up in complete new outfits, feeling miserable enough, Mr. DePinna would arrive on the scene, and we were ordered to stand up straight, turn around, and march off to the right! "Now, Mr. DePinna, isn't that a wonderful exhibit of your goods? Am I not entitled to a discount?" We may not have exactly understood—but we were mortified. Actually, the E. H. Kluge Company made the labels for DePinna, Altman's, Best's, Franklin Simon, and Bergdorf Goodman, and Papi was personally acquainted with each of the individuals who ran those businesses, and he had his accounts with them; and it was at

Princess in Paradise

those stores that we did our shopping. Born merchant that he was, he was never reticent about asking for his discount, no matter how large or small his purchases. When the time came for sending us to camp and we had to be outfitted in quite a new way, we were taken to Abercrombie's, renewed our acquaintance with the family, and were given the usual personal treatment.

Summer Camp

When Ty and I were sent off for our first summer at Mudjekeewis, we departed with the camp group on a Fall River Line steamer for the overnight trip. As Mami waved good-bye to her two little pigtailed waifs standing by the rail alone on an upper deck, she must have felt some trepidation at our first separation from home and parental shelter. But as we turned away to be surrounded by a bunch of girls, we were surprised to find that we felt not a twinge of homesickness; in fact, we felt liberated and ready for new adventures.

The summer turned out to be a great awakening in many ways, though Ty, being the youngest in camp, did not enjoy the companion-ship and the competitiveness in athletics the way I did. Of course we knew how to swim and ride, and after our experiences at Greenwood Lake living in tents was nothing new. It was the organized activities and being part of a group that was different. For the next year at home we played counselors and campers, took turns blowing a whistle to sum-mon each other, and sang taps each night. And we did feel familiar with more people at school.

Ty formed her first close friendship at Dwight, a bright-eyed, sparkling little Betty Clapp, who told her sophisticated stories and inspired her in a series of daring escapades. Whatever she did by way of hell-raising at school or outside, she was always discreet about it and no one at home ever found out. However, when I did something that was not considered acceptable, it was soon discovered, and I got into trouble—which meant being called on the carpet at cocktail time by Papi, given a thorough tongue-lashing, and punished by restrictions. I was invited *out* to my first birthday party in the neighborhood. The little group of four made me feel that I belonged. When Papi found out that we had formed a "Secret Society" and dropped notes to each other, I was forbidden to go back to that house.

The big year of the remodeling of the house and gardens—the arrival of Igor and Xenia and the birth of Sergey in May was also when

The Fabulous Twenties

Papi took off on his first trip to Germany after the war. He had to straighten out the complications of his prewar business ties with his brothers and the family factory in Krefeld. Just what the financial arrangements were we never knew, but apparently he managed to terminate whatever obligations he had to the parent firm, so that he became completely independent. On the other hand, he did make a considerable contribution to the firm and family during that period of postwar depression and inflation.

After returning from Florida the *Pioneer* was maintained fully functioning with her crew of thirteen on the Hudson River at the Dyckman Street Ferry pier, and while Papi was away, Mami was obliged to manage the entire establishment. When he returned in September on the *George Washington,* she organized a big party including Xenia and Igor aboard the *Pioneer* and sailed down the Hudson to meet the steamer. There appeared Papi ondeck, waving happily and shouting, "I have a little surprise for you!" As it turned out, he had collected, not the single new police dog he had promised, but seven dogs (three German shepherds, two greyhounds, two dwarf deer pinschers) and a young German man to take care of them. The dogs were housed in the old wooden kennels behind the stables, where during the next winter some were continually sick from the cold, and some multiplied—so that by spring we had fifteen dogs, including our old pet house dog and Scotch collie. They were not very useful either as pets or for showing, but they had to be fed and they kept one man busy, and once in a while we played with them.

The next summer, 1922, we did not go away to camp. We moved to the island at Greenwood Lake with the usual entourage of assorted nationalities, our governess, and Sergey's nurse. Papi stayed at Englewood during the week, and the *Pioneer* was stationed on the Hudson for parties. In July, Papi went to California on a business trip; that was when he was captivated by the idea of Los Angeles real estate. He was also enchanted by the exotic tropical flora and fauna there. We never heard the details, but apparently there was a party at the home of one of his clients where he saw a beautiful solarium with tropical birds and plants—"Wonderful! where did you get them?" "Oh, we have a gorgeous petshop downtown run by a Mexican." And within a few days, Mami received by telegram the news that he was shipping east a "carload of birds" and instructions to prepare an "aviary." There would also arrive some tropical plants—so now she could have her greenhouse! Maybe he gave her some idea of how many and when to expect them. But I am sure he assumed that as always, with her intelligence and understanding, she would find out both what was needed and how to tackle the new problem. Her ideas were not restricted, and the worry never entered her head about "another thing for me to look after!" There was plenty of space for another building; maybe it meant another job on the place and probably adding another room on somewhere.

In the big original stone carriagehouse there were six box stalls for our riding horses, and the farmhorse was kept outside in a separate shelter. There was a complete two-story apartment for the head gardener and his family. Above the stables were two rooms, one for the riding master, the other for the stableboy. On the other side was a ground-floor room and bath for the chauffeur and, above that, a "trophy room" used for mothproof storage, which was converted to another bedroom. Behind this handsome big building was the service driveway. Now, for these tropical birds one needed a building that could be heated. So in this space, for the whole length of the carriagehouse and way beyond, one long concrete building was built. One end was for more stables (our growing family would need more horses). Then came garden equipment, storage, and furnace rooms; then the aviary, with a higher roof, big windows, and built-in cages with space for smaller movable cages; finally, for big dogs came the concrete-floored heated kennels with long open runways.

The Tropical Birds

Work was still going on when the phone call came from the Englewood railroad station: "Mrs. Kluge, we have a freight car here for you marked 'Tropical Birds'!" Mami, Joseph, and the factory truck managed to transfer the stacks of portable bamboo cages and liberate the surprise contents into various cages. I don't know when she learned that African goldfinches and South American parakeets or California magpies and crested cockatoos could not all get along together in the same cage, but when we children came home from the summer we saw an impressive and colorful gathering on branches in the big cage with rocks and sand and pools below. We were fascinated enough to learn the names and identify the various species.

The big parrots were the most intriguing. They were housed in separate cages by pairs—long-tailed, red-and-blue macaws, two blue-and-yellow macaws, small green Mexican parrots, a pink-and-gray cockatoo, and one big white cockatoo with a yellow crest. Of that whole collection Billy, the white cockatoo, was the single tame and friendly one. He did not have to be inside a cage; he came onto your finger when you held it out, gently climbed onto your shoulder and nuzzled close to your neck, and ate almost anything you offered in your hand. He was immediately transferred into the house and had his stand at one end of the living room. There he presided over the entrance like a watchdog and screeched for attention.

The macaws which were decidedly not friendly, remained in the birdhouse, either in their cages or flying around loose there. They were so spectacular but also very useless. In fact, the whole bird collection was meant rather for exhibition than for use as pets. After Sunday dinner, guests would stroll over to look at the birds and the monkeys and the dogs; then the horses would be brought out to pose or otherwise show off on the front lawn. Mami felt challenged to try to make friends with the macaws, so one summer she had the red-and-blue pair stationed in their cage under the big apple tree where we took afternoon tea. If she fed them from her hand, she thought they would stay close by. But when the cage was removed for them just to sit on their perch, they suddenly took off—up into the apple tree. The bright colors looked gorgeous as they dashed from branch to branch, and the household staff stood below shouting instructions and waving white cloths and brooms. Finally, Mami, always the calm one, sent everyone away, left tempting food on the perch, and had someone concealed nearby to pop the cage over each one as it cautiously came back to feed.

Most of the tropical birds survived for a winter or two; the large macaws lasted the longest. Although we had no great affection for them, Papi thought they were colorful and beautiful. Thus, as they died, one by one or in pairs, he had them stuffed and mounted in a variety of positions on perches or in groups scattered around the house—some on windowsills, some in the sunporches; and finally, the big macaws were arranged in a lifelike standing position on a perch in a corner of the dining room. They became part of the legend of Englewood and were carted along to the apartment in New York. After several years in the storage bin, the dusty and moth-eaten carcasses ended up on the rubbish heap.

The Rest of the Menagerie

Amid the shipment of birds came a character we called the "South

American Dragon"—a ferocious-looking iguana. It went into a cage of its own and lay quietly on the floor most of the time. It was about three feet long, bright green in color, with dark stripes and a lizardlike square snout—and, sure enough, a crest of spikes along its back and tail. Dumb and heavy as it was, we were quite excited about it for a while, standing and watching it for long stretches, teasing it with sticks through the cage—always waiting to see whether it would breathe fire from its nostrils. (Medieval legends and the Wagner operas were very vivid to us!)

Then there were the monkeys. In fact, we had had one monkey for a long time who became a devoted pet—named Peter—and whom we loved dearly. He was a smallish rhesus type, acquired from the Italian hurdy-gurdy man, who had him already well trained, and used to appear in our driveway every spring. His little friend would be all dressed up in a colorful suit and a jaunty hat with a feather in it, would take off the cap and bow, dance around and jump onto one's shoulders, then hold out his hat to collect coins.

Papi simply could not resist him, so Peter became the first to join the family, fancy clothes, leash, and all. He had to be kept in a cage most of the time on the sunporch. But he was so friendly and so humanlike that he would often be brought into the dining room and sit on the back of Papi's chair, being fed scraps of food, chattering and scratching, looking around with his bright beady eyes. Of course, when company came somebody had to put the fancy clothes on him—who else but Mami —and we would bring him into the parlor on his leash. Even the butler didn't mind him and thought he was cute.

But Peter's freedom ended one morning when we came down to breakfast and found him loose and chattering happily on the back of Papi's chair. The table had been set early and left in readiness for everybody while the help were busy in the kitchen. That morning everyone got prunes—a bowl at each place. Peter had beaten us all to it. He had gotten onto the dining table, sampled the prunes, and, with great relish, had hopped around from one place to the other, slurping prunes and prune juice into his mouth with his hands—forgetting about his hind feet, which also got into the bowls. With all fours he left tracks all over the beautiful white tablecloth and chair backs as he gleefully leaped from chairs to chandelier and back to the table amid the dishes. To us it was hilarious; to the rest of the household, devastating. After that, Peter was on exhibit and entertained his visitors only in his cage in back.

The Fabulous Twenties

The next monkey to join us was a fierce-looking black African colobus named Jake. He was neither as good-natured nor as interesting as Peter. He always remained in his cage in the birdhouse. But he was clever and discovered how to undo the latch on his cage. Some days the caretaker would find him out and leaping around the rafter of the birdhouse, or on the outside of the big birdcage harassing the birds. It was a job to catch him, and he got fiercer and did bite, but there he was on exhibit until one day he somehow vanished.

The third monkey was another rhesus, a tiny, delicate, affectionate, and very feminine one named Virginia—also trained by the Italian, who with great regret and for a considerable price parted with her also, and her wardrobe. She also came into the house to visit on Sundays or for parties, but I cannot remember whether she and Peter were friendly with each other or jealous. However, Mami loved her; she was so frail and was often reported not feeling well or having a cold. During her most serious illness Virginia was brought in wrapped in a white baby blanket, laid on the living room sofa in front of the fireplace under constant watchful care, and fed milk from a bottle and, at regular intervals, brandy from a dropper. Mami hovered about her and did the feeding herself, and we all waited anxiously for bulletins on her progress. The veterinarian came regularly just as seriously as he did for sick horses or dogs. Virginia survived this bout with pneumonia, but there were other times when we had to take the brandy and the dropper out to her cage and report back to Papi how much better it seemed to make her feel. Even so, she was always delicate and was the first pet we had to part with through death.

When the "Dragon" vacated his cage, he was replaced by a pair of raccoons—and they were much more fun and more interesting. They too had such human-looking faces and hands, and they were animated, climbed high up onto a branch and chattered, and could be tempted to come close for food. Their names were Patrick and Priscilla, and we always enjoyed watching them. They stayed with us for several years, mostly in their cage, until they were set free on the Island at Greenwood Lake.

They were succeeded by a red fox, brought back from a fox farm in Canada on one of Papi's trips there. He could not survive inside, and so a special outdoor cage and run had to be built. Apparently it had not occurred to anyone that foxes get desperate to be free and that they usually can manage to get free somehow. This one had a beautiful house and fence amid our pine grove. But it came as a big surprise to everyone one morning to find the red fox missing—and a carefully dug tunnel leading under the fence—and out. Now the question was how to find him. It was not long before there came a telephone call from a neighbor: "Is this your fox here in our garden snarling at our dog? Please come and get him." He was captured and brought home. A new operation was performed on the enclosure, a trench dug, and another foot of fencing put underground. It was not long before the fox dug another and deeper tunnel and was out again. This was repeated many times. But the calls from the neighbors became more frequent and more abrupt: "Hey, your fox is here again chasing our chickens. Will you get him out or I'll shoot him!"

That legend, added to the nighttime complaints from the neighbors about the pack of howling dogs, especially violent around full moon time, did not endear the Kluges to the surrounding families in the South Hills area. Since none of them ever came near the house, stories multiplied and grew extravagant about the menagerie, which supposedly included all sorts of wild animals as well as horses—and about the odd assortment of help, those queer imprisoned children, the beautiful Russian princess, and the Prussian tyrant who brutally dominated the whole establishment. So as we progressed in our schools it was not only we who felt shy and unwanted, but our classmates, who looked at us from afar with great curiosity. Only a few gradually dared to ask furtive questions, and our honest answers and descriptions must have sounded just laughable and fantastic.

The Greenhouse

Another joy, fraught with difficulties and complications, was building the greenhouse. Up till then, the flowers had been raised along with the vegetables by Karsten, the old German gardener with the Hindenburg mustache, who plowed with old Jim, the farmhorse, as slowly and methodically as he and Jim tended the lawns with a big roller lawnmower. Karsten produced amazing results, more with vegetables than with flowers. He was always asking at the back door to see Mrs. Kluge personally, to present her with the biggest head of red cabbage, or turnip, or a gorgeous display of raspberries and currants; but in the flower line it was more likely to be gigantic sunflowers and bunches of marigolds and lilies. Mami wanted roses and pretty things for the house. She also had a passionate longing for orchids. So, from that same California trip mentioned earlier came a collection of palms

The family on the South Porch, Englewood, 1923.

Princess in Paradise

and ferns and bright-leaved tropical plants, and of course hanging baskets with orchids.

The greenhouse, like everything else, started out to be a simple little project but soon developed into a huge hundred-foot-long affair with three sections and with a building for furnace and coal storage, potting shed, and root cellar. The central room was high, hot, and humid for the tropical things; one end section was for starting the seeds for the garden, the other for raising flowers during the winter. From then on the new music room was always full of gorgeous, colored azaleas and other plants; there were geranium trees in the dining room and orchids and ferns in the sunporch. And at Easter season there were wheelbarrowsful of lilies. Hyacinths, tulips, or cinerarias would be brought to the kitchen where we were enlisted to wrap them in crepe paper. Then they would be delivered by the factory truck driver as gifts to the special friends far and wide. So, by spring planting time, all the giant cannas, the geraniums, and the petunias for the flowerboxes and around the swimming pool were ready to be put out. And now the cutting garden produced snapdragons and stock and phlox of gigantic size in addition to the roses. This was something we all took pleasure in.

Our existence went along quite routinely and satisfactorily within the confines of home: homework and piano practicing, outdoor play, afternoon tea with Mami or Olga, her personal maid and companion, after-dinner playing Victrola records or the organ rolls, or would-be ballet dancing and games up in our rooms.

Then came an event which one realizes now was historic. One evening during the winter of 1922 Papi came home bringing three men who carried into the house quantities of wires, boxes of equipment, banks of batteries, and rushed around, inside and out, upstairs and down, stringing wires through the windows and down into the living room—this, we were told, was called "wireless." It had to be completed by a certain time; then we were all assembled, because Lydia Lipkowska was to sing from a station in Newark at Bamberger's Department Store—WOR, one of the earliest broadcasting stations.

When the right time came we had two sets of earphones which were passed from one to another, and if we listened very carefully and if everyone around was quiet, we could hear her singing. Then came her voice announcing, in her adorable Russian accent, her next song. Everybody was amazed, and she excitedly telephoned afterward to find out if we had heard her. From then on the batteries occupied a large sideboard cabinet in the living room, and a megaphonelike tube

The Fabulous Twenties

was installed so that several could sit before it and listen together. In the evenings we were allowed to spend a little time downstairs listening to music via the wireless.

Life at Greenwood Lake that summer followed the usual and, to us, always exciting routine, with the addition of course of little Sergey, his nurse, and our new "modern" counselor, Lucy Abercrombie. Along with everything else in the woods and on the waterfront, she now taught us to dance and play cards, and she even had young men come to visit her. The biggest event turned out to be the special cruise on the *Pioneer* to Fisher's Island with the whole O'Ryan family aboard—three most beautiful daughters, twenty, eighteen, and seventeen, and their thirteen-year-old son, Holmes. We stopped at the Larchmont Yacht Club on the way for a big dance, to which we watched them all depart, excitingly, fashionably dressed. At Fisher's Island we saw the military installations for sending by wireless across the ocean, and heard ship-to-shore telephones and underwater sound-detecting devices, and listened to General O'Ryan deliver a speech over the radio.

We all lived on board but went to the beaches to swim and watched parades during the afternoons. In the evening those beautiful girls and our counselor went off every night to dance with handsome officers at the post. Even thirteen-year-old Holmes went along and was occupied with the gossip of what went on at those parties. Although we ogled him and thought him so attractive and tried to get him to play with us, he remained aloof and ignored us. The girls fascinated us because they looked like such grown-up young ladies. They all had "permanent waves" and wore light-colored silk stockings; their bathing suits were sleeveless and form-fitting; they changed their costumes numerous times a day—and they put on "makeup"—powder and lipstick!

Princess in Paradise

16

My First Trip to Europe

F THE MANY EVENTS that year, perhaps the biggest one of my life so far began on that cruise. On July 28 the entry in my diary read: "Today Papi asked me if I would like to go to Europe with them — — — Wow!" So he said to ask Mami to get me some new clothes. Scarcely three weeks later we were ready to sail. Though it sounds so simple, there were always many complications. The other children remained at the island with the Looschens as foster parents and general supervisors. My packing seemed easy: I had a new suit and three dresses, but I also acquired my own "hatbox" and at least three hats. Mami's and Papi's packing never seemed to get done until around midnight the day before they left. The whole corps of people in the household plus friends and relatives and business associates were racing up and down the stairs, having conferences, bringing papers to sign, doing last-minute repairs, or hunting for missing equipment.

When we finally took off there were three trunks and eighteen pieces of hand luggage. Besides this, each one carried his personal coat, camera, briefcase; and Mami carried her precious little case for her jewelry. Ty and Emile came to Englewood for the good-byes, and we were joined on the *Pioneer* by the customary collection of friends and staff for a bon voyage party as we sailed down the Hudson to the Swedish-American Line pier at Fifty-sixth Street, where we were to board the liner *Drottningholm.* By the time we got there it was already so late that no visitors were allowed on board, and we had to scamper aboard as the gangway was held open for us. As the liner pulled out and went down the river, the *Pioneer* sailed alongside, with lots of waving and shouting back and forth, escorting us as far as the Statue of Liberty —only then did I feel a slight twinge of loneliness for sister and brother.

A new adventure was beginning. The family always took a *Luxus Kabine* on the upper deck, with a large bath and a sitting room, and there the sofa was to be my bed. It also meant that for the first time I was right in the midst of the adult activities instead of relegated to the children's quarters. We ate together and met new people. I could go alone to the dining room for breakfast, and I could sit on the sidelines in the salon or the smoking room and eavesdrop on interesting conversations and adult jokes.

My closest friend was a lady doctor, Dr. Louise Ball, an impressive scientist-dentist, traveling with her secretary, who had a successful practice at an expensive address on Park Avenue. I walked the deck with her and we talked, and she opened my eyes to many new things I had not thought about before, such as the problems of women in careers, especially the professions. Together we learned from one of the officers that this *Drottningholm* had formerly been the *Virginia* of the Canadian-Pacific Line and one of the ships that had come to the scene of the *Titanic* disaster, but too late to pick up any survivors. Another new experience was that most of the crew spoke only Swedish, and we promptly had to make the effort to learn a few useful words, or else gracefully accept some comical misunderstandings.

It was eleven days later, after rounding northern Scotland in quite a storm, that we maneuvered slowly up the Gota Canal and docked at Göteborg in the dark at about ten at night. There to greet us was Papi's brother Otto. He was the one who had been assigned the Scandinavian division of the Kluge Brothers' business. He spoke Swedish; he was round, jolly, and bald-headed, and always wore a bowler hat. He had a taxi waiting and hotel rooms ready. He became our most welcome guide and the next day took us on a tour of the city and to visit some of his friends at a Swedish seaside home near Malmö. We were settled for a week or more in the Palace Hotel in Stockholm.

Now, while the men went about on business, I had Mami to myself as guide, and together we went sightseeing, tried streetcars and trains, struggling with the left-handed traffic, getting around the city and into museums, then out in the country to visit palaces and old churches—to

Princess in Paradise

the eighteenth-century Drottningholm Theater and to the medieval castle, Gripsholm, for instance—and I began to collect pictures and romantic stories about kings and queens and prisoners and warriors that so vividly opened up for me history and the past.

Uncle Otto saw us off when we departed for Berlin. The usual Kluge fate of unbelievable travel adventures followed us. With all our baggage piled in and out of taxis, we barely made the train that took us to the ferry to cross over to Denmark. When we arrived in Copenhagen, we were forbidden to go ashore—our passports had no visas for Denmark! After hours of sitting on the ferry, with Papi fussing and stomping his cane, back we sailed to Malmö. It was then late when we unloaded the baggage and checked into a hotel; then another day was spent at the consulate to get the right visa. Naturally, we lost our train reservations to Berlin, so we moved in and out of another hotel and had another day of sightseeing in Copenhagen. Finally, with all twenty-three pieces of baggage loaded into compartments, we boarded the train which at midnight goes right onto a long ferry with rails, the famous Trelleborg to Sassnitz crossing, now probably a piece of ancient history, since the building of causeways and the autobahn. Next morning we woke up in the Berlin station, and there awaiting us on the platform was Uncle Albert, Papi's older brother —little, round, with a bald head and a derby hat, looking just like Uncle Otto. He had moved to Berlin after the war, and from then on we were under his management. His home was our headquarters until we moved to the Hotel Adlon.

The German Experience

It is one thing to recall the vivid parade of events experienced by a twelve-year-old for the first time in a foreign country. It is quite another to try to clarify the lessons and impressions that, upon looking back, might have had a lasting effect. We were all well-disciplined children, so I did what I was told, went where I was sent, asked no questions, and seldom received any explanations. How Papi could leave his business for nearly six months, or why he spent most of that time in a Berlin sanatorium, or how Mami could be away from home with a one-and-a-half-year-old baby and two other children and a houseful of servants, or how they decided that I could miss the whole fall of my freshman year in school—I never asked and never stopped to think about.

The Fabulous Twenties

It was a bad year for Germany. There was disastrous inflation; businesses were at a standstill. People were hungry and still bitter about the war. There were shortages of food, fuel, and clothing; beggars were in the streets and there was so much crime that houses were barricaded like fortresses behind barbed-wire fences, with endless locks on gates and every door, bars on windows, and burglar alarms everywhere. Since Emile was not only the rich American relative but had also come to help revive the family business, as always he had to stay in the best hotel, in this case the fashionable Hotel Adlon on Unter den Linden, and occupied an elaborate suite of rooms, receiving of course extravagant attention and service.

As I passed the time on the sidelines, the sitting room of the suite at the hotel was the scene of day long business conferences, with strange, shabby-looking people coming and going. There were often violently heated arguments between the brothers, with their wives retiring in tears to another room to be consoled by Olga. Then they were served the nearly extinct tea or coffee with pastries that were for them a dream out of the past. Long-forgotten distant relatives appeared to tell their woes and ask for money or favors. I never knew what he did for them, but they were usually asked to stay for dinner. It was a sight to see their eyes light up when they were brought meat and a bowlful of mashed potatoes, from which they could spoon themselves huge piles onto their plates.

After a while, my parents were settled in the sanatorium where Papi was to take the "cure." This sanatorium was a very sumptuous establishment located in the woods outside the Grünewald section, about ten minutes' walk from the end of the trolley line. Still popular today, sanatoriums like this were located in special spots all over Germany for the treatment of many ailments, from heart trouble and high blood pressure to arthritis and just losing weight. They were like elegant hotels, surrounded by beautiful parks and gardens, but with life rigidly organized under the strict supervision of a doctor. Papi was frightfully healthy, but he was always worried about his heart and high blood pressure. And he was forever concerned about losing weight.

During that time I was sent to stay at Uncle Albert's and Aunt (Tante) Erna's house with my eleven-year-old cousin, Rita. Though they were reasonably prosperous and had access to some food, they lived on a very restricted diet. That is where I learned about food rationing, especially butter and sweets. At each place at table there was a pretty little china dish, and in that dish was one's daily ration of

butter. Each individual treated his in his own way. Rita used to grab her
dish excitedly at breakfast and spread it generously and happily on her
hot rolls. If there was a little left at the midday dinner, she used that
freely too. By supper she was looking at everyone else's dish and
begging to "borrow" some against tomorrow's quota. I remember that
I spread mine cautiously and thinly at breakfast, mentally dividing it
into thirds, so there would be enough left for the evening sandwich. It
was the same with the sugar or honey or jams—the allotment usually
being a small pot of apple butter. Milk did not exist, and I heard lots of
talk about "Ersatz" coffee; we children drank a modified type of weak
tea.

When I went to the opera with Papi and Mami, we dressed up and
sat in a box, then at intermission went to a reserved table in the foyer
restaurant and had a supper with champagne. When Tante Erna took
me along on her opera subscription series, we sat on wooden seats in
the orchestra and brought along sandwiches, which we unwrapped
noisily, and cracked the hardboiled eggs into the papers; then, like
many others around us, we ate in our seats; there was nothing to drink.
As strange as this was, I followed right along and got used to doing this
on trains or anywhere, never realizing till later how embarrassed I
would be to do this at home. After the theater or opera we rushed to
the lineup of trolleys outside and rode for nearly an hour back to the
Grünewald, walking nervously through the dark residential streets till,
one by one, we unlocked the gates and doors of home.

With this return of the family from America a most confusing
assemblage of relatives turned up. Mami, who had not seen most of
them since being introduced as the young bride from Russia twelve
years ago, was the gracious and sympathetic listener to all. As for me, I
had to straighten out who were the aunts and uncles, which were the
in-laws, and which cousins belonged to which family. To me they all
looked imposingly enormous and severe. Even the cousins seemed
plump, and they stared at me, the skinny American, with great curiosity. Everyone spoke only German. So, thrown together with them for
my entertainment, I was soon amusing them with my German as I
learned it from the governesses in Englewood. In fact, I enjoyed this so
much that when I returned from a month's visit at Ingenray, Tante
Auguste's estate near the Holland border, I was talking the broadest,
coarsest Platt-Deutsch of the local peasants, to the horror of my parents and the giggles of the very proper Berlin Kluges.

Uncle Albert's home on Taunusstrasse in suburban Grünewald was a rather substantial four-story house: the ground floor was rented; their own living and dining rooms were on the second floor; bedrooms were on the third; and in the basement or [*sous-sol*] were the maid's room and a guestroom. I was continually switched around, from sharing Rita's bedroom to the downstairs guestroom, where my partners changed from one or another of the plump aunts to one or two cousins at a time (all in the same bed of course). Because of the vivid stories of break-ins, the old ones were as terrified as we were of those ground-floor windows, although they were strongly barred on the inside and had metal shutters on the outside. However, for the younger generation this was a delightfully private, unwatched lair. When the corpulent aunts were the visitors, my youthful curiosity was intrigued by the unavoidable ritual of undressing and dressing together. They looked so much slimmer in their long-sleeved heavy muslin nightgowns. In the morning I watched, surreptitiously and wide-eyed, as they strapped on their corsets. But sometimes I had to help with the laces—which pushed up all their central belly rolls of fat and pendulous breasts, which were then enclosed in large white *Büstenhalters,* thus forming the enormous, protruding tablelike chests that mystified me so—and over which hung the ruffles and laces and strings of beads.

As our stay in Berlin stretched out into the damp, cold winter months, we needed warm clothing. Although in the United States we were just getting accustomed to buying ready-made clothes in a store, this had hardly begun in Europe. Mami had to go to a tailor to be fitted for a warm suit. I went for sessions to a furrier to have a fur-lined coat made. Even shoes had to be ordered. Since wool was almost nonexistent, the warm stockings provided for me were made of wood fiber, a mustard-brown color, very coarse and extremely scratchy. Even so, I discovered what chilblain was on my feet, which made them even more miserably itchy. And, as I piled on the layers of cotton underwear, I began to be shaped like my cousins.

The money situation of that historic inflation winter was another special thing to live through. When I went downtown or to the market with Tante Erna, she carried her customary huge leather pocketbook or *Tasche,* and so did I, stuffed full of paper bills—some with quite handsome designs and colors. Or we would go to the bank to ask the currency rates for the day, and for a check or some dollar bills, or an account in Swiss francs, we would then get piles of bills pushed at us, in denominations of hundreds, to thousands and thousands of marks. To

buy food, you counted out painfully great sums of these bills in assorted sizes, and the costs kept rising every day. We carried the provisions home in the traditional string bag, hoping not to get knocked
over and robbed, and we always took along an extra mesh bag in which
to collect a few coal briquets for the living room stove—if we should
happen to find any on sale on the way.

Central heating had been rare in Germany, and all rooms were
equipped with a stove or fireplace with grate. Now, continuing the
habits learned from the war, only one room was heated, usually the
living room, and that was always kept tightly closed, even with rugs
hung over the windows. You learned to go in and out of the door
quickly and shut it behind you, no matter how many people were
coming and going, and even if you were balancing a full tray in your
hands. This meant that the bedrooms were left well chilled. One had
these enormous cozy feather quilts to jump under, but dressing and
undressing had to be managed as simply and as speedily as possible.
When the need for a bath arose, arrangements were made ahead to
turn on the hot-water heater, which might heat the room, and hang
one's towels and clothes about in the warmth; and often a line-up of
children was scheduled to share the same water.

My Visit to Ingenray

When I spent the month of November at Ingenray, the Rhine-
country estate of Tante Auguste, in its eighteenth-century castle with
stone walls two feet thick, each bedroom had a washstand with a bowl
and a water pitcher for toothbrushing and washing. On most mornings, dressed in our flannel nighties, we cracked the ice in the pitcher,
splashed ourselves, skipped the teeth, grabbed our clothes, and tore
down to the kitchen to dress around the stove. All the handsomely
furnished parlors of the house as well as the paneled dining room were
closed off and icy.

Only one room, the *Jagd Zimmer* (the master's den) was cozy and
welcoming, with fur rugs on the floor and heavy oriental hangings
over the windows. Generally one ate in the kitchen heated by the wood
cooking stove at a long board table in an alcove where the help and the
family exchanged places all day long. Only on Sundays was the long,
high-ceilinged dining room heated and the table set with the beautiful
antique Meissen china and the Bohemian wine glasses that we admired
in the cupboards. The treat for dinner would be a venison roast or a

hare or pheasants that Uncle Fritz had shot on the estate the day before.

My visit at Ingenray was without doubt my happiest memory for many years. It was not only living in a fantastically different world with strange new experiences but a new kind of family atmosphere, with freedom and laughter and open affection. Tante Auguste, Papi's youngest sister, had a twinkle in her eye and a sense of humor that showed she took any event lightheartedly. She may have looked over-weight, but in her long skirts she rode her bicycle to the village, loved to watch her daughters dance or to sing with them when they played the piano, and smoked cigarettes in a long slim holder—most daring for those days. My cousins (her daughters) Margot, eighteen, and Elsa, my twelve-and-a-half-year-old "twin," were as gay and devilish as their mother.

Though they worked hard to do their share of the household chores (and I was assigned a routine of duties as well), we always had time to fool around together or to visit, on bicycle or horseback, interesting parts of the estate. Uncle Fritz, in spite of his dignified long red beard, teased his children and joked with them, and looked like a jolly Santa Claus in his jaunty green hunter's hat, *Gemsebart* (the goat's hair brush on top of the hat), and the curved china pipe with smoke curling from it. Then there was cousin Julius, twenty-one and blond, handsome as the then popular Prince of Wales, who was very busy managing the outside affairs of the estate and who was the good fellow with the farmers, speaking that wonderfully tough-sounding peasant Platt-Deutsch.

Since Ingenray was an old and extensive tenant farm, they man-aged quite well to have their own supplies even during the difficult years of the war. Peasant families lived—and had done so for generations—in scattered houses provided for them, maintained for them by the estate, with their children going to the small local school. Each had a specialty and an obligation to provide the owner as his *Rente,* or tithe in produce, a regular stipulated amount, the rest being kept for himself or to trade with each other. This arrangement re-mained so fortunate that during and after the two world wars they managed to be self-sufficient. In fact, after the total devastation of World War II, Ingenray having been occupied by the Nazi defenders then bombed by the British, the widow Tante Auguste was one of the first to get on her feet again, and she soon became a prosperous

Princess in Paradise

businesswoman—she owned forests and a lumber mill, and wood was urgently needed for rebuilding of any kind.

Uncle Fritz had a routine system of walking or riding around to visit and inspect each of the tenant families. Either he brought most of the necessities home, or they faithfully delivered them to the main house. Thus, there were cows for those precious dairy products like butter, cattle for meat, and pigs and sheep. There was also a spinning wheel in the large kitchen, and since all the girls had to put in some time spinning the wool (even Julius, the son, did a stint), I tried my hand at that. Wood chopping and hauling was a regular chore; maintaining the fenceposts was another. Some milking was done in one of the barns attached to the house. But butter and sour cream came to the kitchen door with the dairy farmer. I loved taking part in the uproar of chasing chickens and ducks around the courtyard when one had to be caught and killed and plucked for the next meal.

What fun it was for me to go the farmer who supplied the eggs and be able to climb in the hay hunting for them! At other times we rode in an open wagon to the tiny village to deliver bags of wheat to the flour mill, or to help with the haying, riding on top of the wagon while others walked alongside and tossed up the piles. It was fall and we spent days in the orchard climbing ladders and picking apples. Potatoes were brought from the fields in carts, and we had to transfer them to root cellar along with the turnips, carrots, and beets. The avenue leading to the main gate of the house was flanked with huge old walnut trees, and we gathered bags of nuts and then spread them on the floor of the attic, where the apples were also stored.

The most exciting event of all in the fall season there was the slaughtering of the pigs. Nobody thought the *Amerikanerin* could face it, so naturally I had to accept the challenge. Most mornings it was pitch dark when we got up. This day started even earlier, and people with lanterns were scurrying across the courtyard to the special slaughtering room; it was a rather small one, with its brick floor sloping toward the central drain. Before I knew it the pig was killed; everybody rushed around to perform their duties; and someone pushed a pot into my hands and told me to catch the blood. That I stuck it out not once but three times was the subject of gossip and jokes ever after. I was too engrossed to learn the rest of the proceedings, with the two butchers cutting up sections, hanging things on hooks, and boiling and smoking for the next several days. Another pride of mine was having my own wooden shoes to wear while trooping around in the muddy yard and barns, then leaving them in the row at the door and picking up my felt *Pantoffeln* to patter around the house in.

Other Memorable Trips

The night I left Ingenray for good, the weather was like something out of *Wuthering Heights*. The wind was blowing sheets of rain, and the old tree branches were creaking and waving against the sky. Margot and I were bundled in blankets and set in the back seat of a big closed black carriage (a landau) drawn by two horses. A faint yellow lantern was lit on either side; baggage was piled around us; and all the family stood in the lighted doorway waving good-bye—then came the last glimpse of the silhouetted iron gate fading behind us. Off we were to Krefeld—small though it was, the provincial metropolis of the area —and another gathering of all the sedate members of the family. Then we went on to Berlin.

Margot and I had become close friends that fall since being through with school, and she was brought to Berlin to keep me company and do the expected sightseeing with me. Papi kept telling her mother that she was too beautiful to be stuck out on the farm, that she needed to become more sophisticated and do some traveling. So he ordered a new hairstyle and provided her with some lovely clothes—a purple velvet dress she remembers to this day, with silver kid slippers and a coat trimmed with gray squirrel. We were allowed to be quite independent, and it always amused me how she, the older one of us, got panicky about catching city trolleys or gaped in astonishment at rather ordinary traffic jams—such as we had on Fifth Avenue on any ordinary day!

One memorable trip was to Leipzig and Dresden. Papi went along for business reasons and to help out some old relatives, now nearly destitute. At the Astoria in Leipzig and the Hotel Bellevue in Dresden he took the usual suite with salon, where the bedraggled visitors came together to eat with us, but Margot and I were generally off on our own. In Dresden we marveled at the priceless examples of German Renaissance and Baroque goldsmith work in the treasury known as "Das Grüne Gewölbe" in the palace; then we went through the Zwinger Gallery where we learned how to use the guidebooks to see the many world-famous paintings there, and stood together in the hushed room before the Sistine Madonna. In Leipzig the most impressive sight was the Völkerschlacht Denkmal outside the city. This massive red stone domed tower in the middle of a field was built in 1913 to commemorate the great victory of the allies over Napoleon in 1813. It rose ninety-one meters, a solid mass with buttresses topped by twelve giant warriors, from a stone terrace; the inside (like the Invalides in Paris) was lit only by a ring of small windows at the top, with a circle of gloomy, severe chapels on the ground floor.

In Berlin, though Papi's and Mami's headquarters were in the Grünewald Sanatorium, life had been continually busy and very interesting. They had private, formal dinner parties—as for Papi's birthday in September—with flowers and fine wines and special food, and people dressed up, readily enjoying themselves. As I remember it (even after both world wars), the ritual of eating four meals a day went steadily on. The fresh rolls for breakfast never varied, though everyone mourned the lack of eggs and butter. Hot dinner was always at noon, followed by a nap.

Then came afternoon tea—really *Kaffee*. No matter where we happened to be, this pause was never missed. Sometimes we hurried back to the sanatorium to have it with Mami; when downtown, we stopped in a crowded *Konditorei* where one could guzzle the lucious-looking pastries and the inevitable whipped cream. When going to the opera or theater, tea was the meal just before it, and a cold supper was either taken during intermission or was the occasion for sociability afterward. I was included at the opera much more than at the theater. *Fidelio* was my very first and most memorable experience. Then followed *Tannhäuser, Lohengrin,* and *Tristan and Isolde.*

My parents had renewed their friendship with a beautiful blonde soprano who sang in all of these works. Eleanore Reynolds had sung in New York at the Metropolitan, but now she was married to Alfred Schlosshauer, a tall, blond, handsome Berliner, and we were frequently at their large, luxurious apartment. Again, sitting and dutifully listening, I heard so many of these wonderfully funny stories that musicians and actors tell about their profession. One that affected me most vividly was that of her singing Brangäne, the maid of Isolde. In the second act Brangäne stands guard on a balcony during the love duet, and has some long passages to sing. This was a difficult feat from the singer's point of view; behind the scenes, she, a rather statuesque woman, in her long gown, had to climb up a tall ladder and stand on the very top behind "the balcony parapet." There, she not only had to wait gracefully, then turn around and wave, but then she had to sing

The Fabulous Twenties

her part in full voice while the ladder wobbled at every breath while she clutched desperately at the flimsy scenery to keep from falling. This disillusioned me as much as the false antics in the movie productions at Englewood.

The Russians in Berlin

In 1922 Berlin was full of Russian refugees, which meant several things. Shops were full of art treasures and jewels that had been smuggled out of Russia when they escaped, and they were eager to convert these objects into money. If one had the money, as the Americans did, and generosity like Papi's, one could pick up valuable old ikons, Fabergé pieces, and quite unusual precious stones in rare settings.

In order to locate or get news of relatives and friends who had disappeared in the turmoil of the Revolution, the place to start was always the Russian Orthodox Church on a Sunday morning. Mami had only to appear in her elegant clothes, or make herself known to the clergy, and inevitably somebody would speak to her or locate her privately with a pitiful story. As the word got around, we did have some interesting surprises. A handsome young man in his twenties, Boris Mosoloff, the son of one of Mami's aunts, appeared well dressed and happy. As an engineer he had a career and was living comfortably in Berlin.

Through him she made contact with Nicholas Fedorov, a chemist who was the brother of her Uncle Serge, the Czar's personal physician, and was allowed out of Russia for a week only to attend a professional conference. He was being closely watched, and she dared to talk with him only in public places such as the hotel foyer at teatime. She would have loved to help him to stay in Germany or escape to the United States, but he feared for himself and his relatives and had to return. They did learn that Uncle Serge had been spared from the bloodbath of the intelligentsia in the Revolution; and because he was so valuable as a surgeon and a teacher, he had been kept on at the Academy of Medicine in Leningrad. He was then well on in years, but that was the last news ever heard of him.

Another man who made himself known was Vasiliy Zhenko, who had been a supervisor in the family cotton mills at Serpoukhov. Though shabby and without any means of livelihood, he, like so many of these people, characteristically presented himself with dignity and

"The White Russian Cabaret,"
1920 lithograph by George Grosz.
Collection Dartmouth College
Museum and Galleries.

deference, telling his story gently and with reticence, yet with moving
devotion to the family of his past life. He had been present when the
Bolshevik delegation came to "the old gentleman," Grandfather
Nicholas Konshin, in Moscow, to take over the factories and it is from
him that we got the story I had described earlier.

Night life in Berlin was known as notoriously gay and mysterious.
With the influx of Russians began the fashion for the Russian cabaret,
which soon became the rage in Paris and then spread to New York.
Many of these had the grimly realistic atmosphere that later became so
popular in the Expressionistic work of George Grosz and Bertold
Brecht. But I know that we went to one kind of restaurant, small, dark,
and intimate, for a dignified, quiet dinner of real Russian food. For
late-night entertainment we went to another larger boisterous kind,
like the former YAR and others in Moscow. One of the most popular,
the Chauve Souris, later came to New York, where the floor show

The Fabulous Twenties

produced the famous "March of the Wooden Soldiers" and the pathetic tableau of the "Volga Boatmen," followed by a sultry gypsy singer with accompanying violins and zithers. Then came the Cossack dancers with wild music, leaping, stamping, and throwing their daggers into dollar bills while the onlookers sat around singing, clapping, calling for more, and carrying on gaily far into the night.

But the modest little waitresses at such places, as we found out here and so often in New York, were likely to be cousins and friends, wives of nobility and generals, who had known a much better life and now had an invalid husband or a baby to support. One such made herself known to Mami as having been a housemaid on the estate near Kaluga; her husband had been trained as a valet. She would hear of nothing else but that Mami must accept her hospitality and come to tea at her tiny apartment, to see her husband and give them the honor of talking about the old times and their devotion to the family. I went along and still have a picture in my mind of climbing flights of dingy stairs, a narrow room where we sat on beds, an ikon with a little red lamp in the corner, a wobbly table between us but with an embroidered cloth and tea glasses, one precious cake being divided up, and Mami being very moved by their affection and their stories. They had helped Uncle Igor escape in disguise by boat from Kiev and were among the last to see Igor's and Olga's mother at the Jekouline house in Kiev before she fled south to Odessa, where she reportedly died.

By December there were evidently thoughts of returning home. I had hardly given this a thought. With all my trips here and there, being assigned to various relatives, visiting in all sorts of circumstances, and the great variety of things I had taken part in, I felt quite grown up and independent. Besides, I had grown taller and had been furnished with new clothes. After a series of farewell dinners in Berlin, Krefeld, and Bremen and many waving groups on station platforms, with flowers and gifts, we boarded the *George Washington* on December 11. She was one of the largest United States ships, and Papi had sailed on her numerous times, so that, as expected, we were seated at the captain's table.

There were few passengers aboard in midwinter, and it turned out to be one of the roughest crossings the ship had known. Mami kept to her stateroom, and Papi and I were almost the only people up and about. We struggled around the pitching promenade deck on our regular walks. The smoking room was generally deserted except for one table of hardy bridge players. Everywhere the furniture was stacked and lashed down. In the dining room the storm edges of the tables were put up to keep the dishes from sliding off. In the evening, with the orchestra playing in an empty ballroom, Papi insisted on dancing with me; naturally, we slid from one side of the floor to the other as the ship pitched and rolled. After more than eleven days of this fierce Atlantic storm, we landed in New York on December 23. Family, friends, and servants were lined up at home to welcome us, and the house was all festive and ready for Christmas.

It seemed a long time since we had had an old-fashioned Christmas in Englewood with snow outside and a huge tree in the living room and lots of family around. But the winter of 1923 was broken up almost as usual. Our regular school attendance seems to have been of little importance. In January, with governess and tutor, we embarked on the *Pioneer* for Florida, remaining on the yacht mostly at Palm Beach. When the *Pioneer* was chartered as of March 1, we were shipped back to Englewood by train, children and governesses under the command of Aunt Xenia, a thrilling three- or four-day adventure with the Pullmans, dining cars, and long station promenades. And so, after all these adventures, we were returned to the routine of Dwight School again, not obliged to wear quite the same odd costumes as before, but still very much the lonely outsiders.

17

The Trip Around the World

HE SUMMER of 1923 was marked by one national event—the death of President Harding (and the swearing in of Calvin Coolidge). Ty and I were again back at Camp Mudjekeewis when we heard the news. We were at the regular Sunday evening service held in a nearby cove, with all of us sitting in canoes, the rest of the congregation on the beach listening to the minister standing in front of a tiny stone chapel on a rocky wooded island. When he made the somber announcement, it seemed to affect us personally, as if Mr. Harding were a family friend, having been so involved in the excitement of the president's spending his vacation on our *Pioneer.*

Off to Boarding School

On returning to camp for our third year we felt much happier, more normal and at ease. But at home things had not changed much in the attitudes toward us "children." Surprises were still sprung on us without any preparation. So it was that when we returned at the end of August, along with Emile from his camp, we were informed that all three of us were going away to boarding school—that very September! As usual, nothing really flabbergasted us. Such decisions were never discussed. There was no use in our saying that we were a bit scared. And the rush of preparations was up to somebody else to handle. Ty and I were to live at Dwight. Emile was being sent to the Riverdale

Country School across the river in New York. We all required school
uniforms—the main worry. So with Mami we went to Best's, and were
measured for the proper things—which would naturally arrive later
than anybody else's. The Dwight uniform was a navy blue gabardine
suit and white blouse with Peter Pan collar and a pullover sweater for
variation. It was quite a relief—we were not required to wear black
stockings and high shoes—new for us.

When I was delivered to Dwight, in one of my best German dresses,
I found my roommate was to be Hallet Gubelman, a junior (I was a
sophomore), probably chosen for her quiet patience, and her own
shyness, having gone through some of the same childhood suffering
we had because of her German name. Ty was housed in the Main
Cottage so as to be under the watchful eyes of the lady principal and
drew as her roommate the sister, Marge Gubelman, who had been her
friend in second grade—now both were in the seventh grade. Still
self-conscious at never quite looking the same as everybody else, I
became acutely aware that everyone appeared with the tightly strapped,
flat-chested look stylish at the time while I, going on fourteen with a
well-developed bust, was running about obviously round and bouncy.
So I had to have a blushing conference with Mami and explain to her
about "bras," after which she escorted me to Best's and, to my great
embarrassment, openly asked for "brassieres." So that was solved.

I was still wearing my hair in two long yellow pigtails, then switched
to one big braid down the back with a large taffeta bow set at the back
on top. Ty, with her fuzzy red hair, tied into a loose curly ponytail,
looked feminine and roguish. The school life, regulated by bells and
involving bowing to the principal as we entered the dining room as well
as a long list of "do's" and "don'ts," didn't bother us a bit. In fact, it all
seemed so nice and simple, being right there to take part in activities,
hearing interesting Saturday night programs, being monitored by
students nearly our own age, and even trying to break rules such as
eating during study hours, which was forbidden. And there was the
shared companionship. We began to feel accepted.

However, there was still one thing which separated us from the rest.
When they all went together to the Presbyterian church on Sunday
mornings, we were called for and taken home early enough to join the
family at the traditional big breakfast. Then followed the family horseback outing—six or more of us trooping through the wooded trails
together—and later the preparations for the customary elaborate
Sunday dinner with the variety of curious or exciting guests, followed

The Fabulous Twenties

sometimes by a musicale or our having to show off the horses on the front lawn, again having to help prepare the table for the European idea of an extravagant "cold supper." From all this, like Cinderellas, we would have to be whisked away by five-thirty sharp and so back at school to check in for the Sunday evening ritual of supper and Bible class. Again we felt oddly noticeable—"What have *they* being doing all day?"

Preparations for the Trip

In the course of that fall we learned the reason for the sudden great decision of depositing all three of us in boarding school. Our parents had planned "a Trip Around the World." Their excitement and enthusiasm became just as much ours—the names of the strange places they were to visit, the picture books and maps gathered in preparation, Mami's gorgeous wardrobe for tropical climes being assembled, and the deck plans of the ship on which they were to sail. It was the first organized world cruise for the *Empress of Canada,* the newest, largest ship of the Canadian-Pacific. They were to sail from New York early in January and return in May, docking at Vancouver and then travel overland by train through Canada. Since they were to live for those five months on the ship, they had taken a spacious cabin suite on an upper deck. As mentioned earlier, they had invited twenty-one-year-old Dorothy O'Ryan, the general's daughter, to accompany them.

Of all the new things Mami did in preparation, such as buying many ready-made clothes and hats as well as going to her dressmakers for special fittings, the most daring was submitting to the latest "permanent wave" for her hair. We were in the city for a shopping expedition, and she spent the day at Nestlé's—the best French salon—where we stopped in to visit her from time to time. There was machinery hanging from the ceiling in a private room; Mami's head was wired to it, and she had to sit motionless for hours under almost unbearable heat while efficient, uniformed ladies bustled around in the hushed atmosphere of red plush carpets and a white-capped maid brought her lunch on a tray. By late afternoon she was released, paid the enormous price of $50 or more, and appeared satisfactorily coiffed and groomed, surprisingly elegant and relieved—not "frizzy," as the rumors had been.

The house in Englewood was to be generally closed down, except for one cook and the outside staff to care for the horses, garden, and cars. But there were little Sergey (two and a half years old) and his

French nurse; and somebody had to have the responsibility for the rest of us, even though we were in school. So they engaged Mrs. Welch, a tall, stately, white-haired dowager who had been a housemother at Emile's school, Riverdale. To make things simpler, they leased a small apartment in New York City on Morningside Drive near 116th Street, one block from Riverside Drive, across from Columbia University and just down the street from the Reverend Mr. Fosdick's new Riverside Church.

The apartment had to be furnished, and for some reason instead of bringing the things in from Englewood, they purchased entirely new but modest equipment, such as a complete set of Community Plate silverware for us to use. Sundays the chauffeur from home would call for Ty and me at Dwight and Emile in Riverdale and bring us for our usual dinner and outing all together. So, there was Sergey, his French nurse, and the elegant Mrs. Welch. But neither the nurse nor Mrs. Welch would cook. That meant there was also a cook. Mrs. Welch did oversee our clothes and did any needed mending, took us to the dentist and on Sunday museum excursions, and wrote reports to the family. One of her first shocks was that no sooner had the family departed on the ship than Emile came down with scarlet fever, and she felt her responsibility. Though he was confined to the school infirmary, she had to worry about his care and go out to visit him. But that was the only mishap—at least in the New York household.

Bon Voyage

After taking part in a tremendous bon voyage party on board in their suite, then with some emotion seeing the ship pull away from the pier tearing its tangle of colored streamers with the band playing sentimentally, in a short time that trip became as much our adventure as theirs. Mami's long, beautifully written letters, with her vivid, detailed descriptions of each place and funny or characteristic incidents, were circulated and reread. Then followed her photographs—we would recognize her glamorous outfit for Egypt, her linen suit and hat for India, Papi riding an elephant in his alpaca suit and pith helmet, the lush garden with peacocks in Ceylon, then standing beside armed guards on a Yangtze riverboat out of Canton. Between letters and photographs we would receive small packages with souvenirs—scarab bangles from Cairo, silver rings from India, batiks from Java. What we did not know was that much bigger packages, even crates, were arriv-

The Fabulous Twenties

At the Pyramids, 1924.

ing from time to time in Englewood, and even longer after they returned mysterious shipments turned up from India, the Philippines, and China. By the time they arrived home with the usual excessive amount of checked and hand baggage, there was practically a warehouseful to be unpacked in the garage. For years thereafter Mami would produce precious jewels or dainty gifts from what she called her "Treasure Chest."

Nowadays when traveling—even taking a trip around the world—is such a common experience, everyone is familiar with the historic sites in every country that have been made famous by poets and photographers, so there is no need to repeat them here. But as far as we were concerned, there were certain aspects that were very special and gradually became an integral part of the Kluge legend.

For example, Mami wrote a vivid and glowing account of the picturesque Taj Mahal and the story of the beautiful young queen whose tomb it is, the reflecting pools by moonlight, and the fragrant gardens with the white blossoms to be enjoyed in the cool of the darkness. Sometime later there arrived a package with a lovely table-sized model of the Taj Mahal building in marble and its surrounding gardens, with all the decoration of inlaid semiprecious stones, the delicate lacelike

Princess in Paradise

Papi dwarfs the transport in Egypt (left) and India (right).

perforated alabaster screens, and the four minarets. When it was unpacked at home it was all smashed to pieces, with most of the stones like gravel in the wrapping paper. So we were set at the task of gluing it all together again. It was like one of those thousand-piece puzzles, always there on a table waiting for anyone passing by to discover where another piece belonged. Following photographs, we became only too familiar with every angle of the building; and we learned the names of every one of the colored stones that made up the vines, leaves, and flower designs of the inlays. Thus we children got to know the Taj Mahal most intimately.

The same thing happened when they sent a miniature model of a Japanese house of wood, with tiny paper-paneled sliding doors, straw mats, and upturned roof corners. That arrived broken up into hundreds of bits and pieces, which took us months to reassemble and patiently glue together. When we finished, not only did we know what a Japanese wooden house looked like, but we felt as though we had lived in one ourselves.

We learned that India was not all gorgeous Mogul palaces and massive British government buildings. Mami described Delhi and Agra, big cities, and the dusty streets teeming with beggars, cripples,

The Fabulous Twenties

starving children, and wandering, cadaverous sacred cattle. They visited some of the ancient monasteries, still inhabited by yellow-clad monks, and the descriptions were sometimes frighteningly real —especially when Papi and others would later provide the gory details.

One example I shall never forget is their visit to a sacred temple compound where one is required to enter the area barefoot. Mami, Dorothy O'Ryan, and the other ladies refused, but Papi was not to be deterred. With his big bare feet and trousers rolled up to his knees, he boldly marched right ahead, through the mess of protected garbage, piles of human feces, cow flops, and assorted filth. He just wanted to see what was there.

They became involved in one way or another with a number of historic adventures that were of some significance, at least to us. At the Alpinelike village of Darjeeling they stayed at the Hotel Everest high up the side of the cliffs, supposedly to see the sunrise over the snow-covered Himalayas. Sir George Mallory and a host of Englishmen and native inhabitants were also quartered in the hotel at that time, and the place was all abustle with equipment and animals in preparation for their much-publicized assault on Mount Everest. It was only a short time afterward that Mallory and his climbing companions were last observed by telescope disappearing into the swirling clouds near the summit, never to be seen again.

In Egypt it was the excitement of the newly discovered (1922) tomb of King Tutankhamon at Luxor with Howard Carter very much on the scene and the newspapers full of pictures of the site and the excavation. Later in Tokyo they stayed at the Imperial Hotel, built (1916-22) by Frank Lloyd Wright, and famous because it had withstood the earthquakes of 1923. Mami's report, acknowledging that it was "modern" and cold (built of concrete) and Papi was constantly bumping his head on the low ceilings, was that the building survived because it was located in a section of the city which had actually been unaffected by the quakes. The greatest fame of the hotel at the time came from the garden layout with its long pools of water, which had been the only source of water in fighting the fires which swept through the area after the quake.

🍂 Papi Experiences Some Problems

Then, of course, there is an endless collection of personal adventures, obviously involving Papi in one way or another. Their arrival in

Canton was typical. The big ship anchored in the harbor, and launches brought large groups of passengers to the quai side where such an event would inevitably draw huge excited crowds of onlookers, beggars, hucksters, in addition to the shouting swarms of preordered "taxis." These were neither autos nor the rickshaws to which they had become accustomed, but bamboo sedan chairs. A single passenger sat in a wicker armchair slung between two long bamboo poles and was then lifted and carried by two coolies, one fore the other aft, who were practiced at running as a team.

Papi, with his six-foot four-inch height and very imposing 350-pound figure was an object of wonder and admiration everywhere in the Orient. Besides, he had that jolly sense of humor and spirit of adventure, coupled with a charm and quite obvious generosity. It was usually the small, scrawny natives who asked to be photographed next to him, or to touch him for good luck. Throughout the trip he had his picture taken on every imaginable conveyance and always in the appropriate costume. There was the camel and the burro in the desert (as Ty said, "Papi with a donkey between his legs!"), the elephants and the rickshaws in India, standing beside the little train for Darjeeling with his head higher than the roof of the train, and then nearly swamping their sampans in Hong Kong Harbor.

Well, alighting on the dock in Canton, ready with everyone else to be taken on a tour through the narrow noisy streets of the city, he headed for the locally provided sedan chair. Without hesitation his two coolies staggered to lift him to their shoulders; then there was splintering and crashing as the bamboo poles snapped, the unbalanced coolies were knocked over, and Papi landed on the pavement amid the wreckage of his chair. There followed much yelling from the crowd, chattering among the coolies, and plenty of laughs from other passengers. Then above it from somewhere came an authoritative shout: "Number one chair! Bring number one chair!" At last, from some hidden headquarters, the chair was produced with four husky carriers, all red plush and gold tassels, with beautifully painted wooden poles and a fringed canopy, no doubt carefully kept in reserve for one of those corpulent Mandarins or a visiting British dignitary. Papi looked just right in it and took off amid cheers. But there was always the consciousness, just as he cared for his horse, that one must give those poor carriers a chance to stop and catch their wind, or mentally adjust to the fact that the poor coolie pulling the rickshaw was one of the fortunate ones with a job and thankful to be earning a living.

The Fabulous Twenties

294

🍂 The Hawaiian Adventure

The biggest excitement of the trip was probably the volcano eruption of Kilauea that happened right in front of their eyes. When the cruise reached the Hawaiian Islands in May, they were joined by Dorothy's parents, General and Mrs. O'Ryan and her sister, Janet. Because of the personal introductions that Dorothy bore from her father to military friends throughout the trip, they had been greeted or entertained almost everywhere by local and military officials, such as by Lord Rawlinson at the British Cricket Club in Delhi and by Governor General Leonard Wood in Manila. Now again they were invited to tour Pearl Harbor and have dinner with the commandant at Schofield Barracks, the army post. The smaller islands at that time were sparsely inhabited and were not tourist attractions. The big event was the trip to the largest island, Hawaii, and the city of Hilo.

Whenever possible on the tour, the guests lived aboard the ship, making daylong trips and returning in the evening. In Hilo they debarked in the morning and were assigned to a fleet of taxis for their tour of the city sights, then the trip through the lush green tropical foliage uphill to the island center to get a view of the three volcanoes and have luncheon at the Volcano House. Mauna Kea and Mauna Loa are conical-shaped mountains several thousand feet high, known to be smoldering and periodically active. Kilauea is unusual in that its crater is far below the surface, a large round hole in the center of a barren circular lava field several miles across. Although there were paintings and tales of a fiery boiling mass one thousand feet down, Kilauea had not had a known eruption in the twentieth century. However, people talked unofficially about its floor having dropped a few hundred feet after the earthquake in Japan in 1923. In any case, geologists and climbers often went down its perpendicular rock sides.

That morning in May the fleet of cars with the tourists from the *Empress of Canada* drove across the lava plateau as usual to peer down into this unusual flat volcano. The cars were parked away a bit, and people were spread out on foot—some listening to the guides, others photographing each other in front of the hole. Suddenly the most fantastic, unbelievable explosion occurred right in front of them. With the hissing of steam and a gushing of mud and smoke, curling brown clouds went shooting up past them, swirling hundreds of feet above their heads. First there was shock, then interested surprise, then panic

Princess in Paradise

as solid stones of lava began to fall around them, first of pebble size, gradually getting larger and noticeably hotter.

Everyone started to run back to their cars and pile in desperately. Papi herded his group together and told them to head for their car. As General O'Ryan looked over his shoulder he noticed two older women left alone near the smoking edge and dashed back to help them, shouting at them to get moving quickly. They looked like the typical hardy British tourist ladies, equipped with sturdy walking shoes, mackintoshes, canes, and cameras. As he tugged and pointed and shouted, the one white-haired lady turned and yelled back at him: "Oh, please, General, let me finish recharging my camera. I must get another shot!"

The native drivers in the touring cars reacted in different ways. Some flew right into action, started up their motors, turned, and took off alone. Others just abandoned them and ran. Still others sat in their seats, paralyzed and transfixed. With the Kluge-O'Ryan group of six squeezed into the seats of their open touring car, their driver sat up front trembling and crying, moaning that he would not move. Papi, characteristically ready to act in a crisis, took his cane and brought it down in one firm whack on the man's shoulder, ordering in no uncertain tones: "You turn around and get us out of here or I'll beat you all the way back to the hotel!" That jerked him into action; they rumbled across the lava bed in a ragged swarm with all the other cars; meanwhile the rain of lava rocks grew more intense, those falling on the canvas roof of their open car being hot enough to burn through and land all around them while they tried to shovel them out with newspapers, hats, or anything else they could find. After what must have seemed like an eternity, they arrived in front of the hotel, the Volcano House, and scurried onto the roofed over porch to join the mob of other excited, amazed, jabbering tourists, watching the unforgettable sight. But this is what was almost as unforgettable: there sat a Hawaiian band, playing ukuleles and guitars, and in the middle of their semicircle was a little Hawaiian girl with grass skirt and leis, calmly singing and performing Hawaiian dances.

This famous eruption without warning has been recorded and explanations sought, the most probable being that there was a deep subterranean link with the earthquake activity of Japan. But it definitely changed the shape and status of Kilauea, vastly enlarging the diameter of the crater, and leaving the sea of mud and lava at the bottom no longer placid and solid but ominously active.

The Fabulous Twenties

🌿 The Inevitable Souvenirs

With the traditional Kluge mania for collecting, one can easily imagine what would happen once Papi got started. When visiting the hunting preserve of a prince in India, Papi was fascinated by the use and handling of trained cheetahs, the smallish, black-spotted leopard-like cats that could evidently be easily tamed and led around like pets. To him there was no question about Englewood being his own private zoo, and the ease with which he could add to it anything he wanted. Besides, it would always be interesting for "the children." So he ordered a baby cheetah to be shipped to New Jersey and continued on his trip. When he got home and all the crates were arriving and shipping invoices coming in from all over the world, there came the disappointing notice that the baby cheetah had grown to full size before it could be crated, and therefore both governments would not allow it to be shipped. Papi was much more disappointed that we were. He also told us the story that he had ordered a baby elephant for us. But it never arrived.

In India and especially in Ceylon they relived their old days in Russia, discovering precious stones, some uncut, most without settings, a few in characteristic Indian pieces, and haggling over their prices in bazaars or with native dealers, just as they had in Nizhniy Novgorod. Diamonds had never had much appeal to Mami. But here and there they collected star sapphires, star rubies, topazes, aquamarines, and pearls of many colors and odd sizes, all of which were later made into rings, pendants, cufflinks, and studs. Each one, as we received them on memorable occasions, had its own special story. From India too came a dazzling collection of saris, in many colors and all with the brilliant gold thread; these also turned up year after year, to be made into beautiful gowns for special occasions.

In Kandy, the former capital of Ceylon, which was a lush tropical paradise with brilliant flowering trees, water gardens, and wild orchids, Mami satisfied her longing to own a collection of orchids. These at least she could take along with her. So she brought potted blooms and hanging baskets of orchids back to the ship, and their suite became a showplace of tropical greenery. She tended these affectionately during the rest of the trip—past China, Japan, the Hawaiian Islands—back to Vancouver, in her way looking forward to what she would show and teach the children. Then approaching Vancouver, with all the inspections and papers to be filled out—through customs

Princess in Paradise

and immigration, and involving inspections related to diseases and agriculture—she ran into a stone wall. Neither Canadian nor American authorities would or could allow the importation of live tropical plants. Before they docked she had to drop every one of her beautiful, beloved plants overboard!

As I cannot help repeating, we learned so much about the world from what turned up at home later. That long ago it was not as common as it is now to have furniture ordered in Hong Kong or lacquered chests from Korea, all of which we knew intimately because of having to glue on the broken trimmings or dried-out decorations that had fallen off. In the Philippines the most important thing to us was Bilibid Prison. They had paid a visit there, not for any humanitarian reason, but because that was where the famous Philippine black-and-yellow rattan furniture was made. In due course the Kluge shipment arrived at home, a carload of it, causing the usual excitement among unpacking servants, children, and parents themselves. This was truly wonderful—useful furniture that was with us for years and admired by everyone. There were tables of all sizes, stools, hammocks, dining straight chairs—but, best of all, those armchairs with the huge fan-shaped backs, little and big—and of course one great big papa-bear chair for the Master!

China at that time was a collector's paradise. The objects available were not the factory-made and commercially designed junk that one sees today as "souvenirs," but the real thing—treasures that are beautiful and enduring—figurines carved in rose quartz, jade, or ivory; jewelry of gem-quality jade, turquoise, or coral; plus a variety of porcelains and textiles. In Canton they went about collecting a set of dishes for twenty-four in the traditional green-and-rose, eighteenth-century imperial pattern (known as Famille-Rose), with all the little soup bowls and lids, tea cups, serving dishes, big plates, fish plates, canapé plates, and any number of unique pieces. Fortunately, these did arrive at home well packed and safe, to be used with pride and joy through the ups and downs of many years.

They collected at least a dozen so-called Spanish shawls. We learned that these fine silk, heavily embroidered shawls, in many more colors than the customary white, had for centuries been made in China for export to Spain, and were sold by the pound, the length of the fringe also contributing to their value. In Peking it was antique textiles and Mandarin coats that they acquired. One discovered that it was no fable when told that "this came from the Empress Dowager." That famous old queen who reigned until 1901 had such a tremendous wardrobe that she could wear a costume once, then discard it, thus making it quite possible for them to disappear through various channels and turn up later in all sorts of shops and bazaars.

For all three of us that trip, in every detail, was just as vivid as if we had been there ourselves. We studied the travel albums and snapshots and read and reread the letters; and the graphically detailed stories went on for years and years, along with the careful explanations of the endless collection of objects they had acquired. In fact, once, when I handed in a composition describing the crowded, dusty streets of India and the peaceful beauty of Taj Mahal, my teacher asked me when I ever had the time for a trip to India. I hadn't—it was my mother who had been there!

There is no conclusion to this kind of story. Those "souvenirs" were divided among us children and, in turn, handed on to the next generation, becoming more cherished and admired as they became older and rarer. And the tales that held us (and everyone else) spellbound continue to be told, perhaps expanded a bit to keep them lively, but the pictures and the objects are always there to provide visible proof. Sergey, of course, was much younger than the rest of us and had to absorb most of these stories at second hand, but he has turned out to be the best storyteller of all, with much the same humor and enthusiasm as his father's. Thus, the fabulous Trip Around the World became another example of the sources from which a family's legends have grown.

Princess in Paradise

18

The Englewood Procession

HE PARADE of the 1920's rolled on for five more full years, with the continual procession of characters, interesting, odd, or charming that turned up as guests, a jumble of overlapping trips and events, and an equally unaccountable series of changes in the household help. But for each of us four children our lives and development were spinning off more independently—always, however, being brought back into the home fold and the strict family control.

 Violet Orthwein

At this time one very welcome addition into our close young clan was Violet Orthwein, who became like a sister and a daughter in the house. She brought to all of us an important new feature—a sense of humor and a detached point of view. As I mentioned before, she had been a regular summer visitor from the time when we were very small. Her widowed mother, Viola, and two aunts, Hazel and Maude, from St. Louis, were among the family's earliest and closest friends. At about the age of eight Violet showed some special talent for the piano, and Papi had insisted on contributing to her musical education. Actually she did progress and work at it until about college age, and it surely did add to her understanding and stature when later she married a handsome conductor and took her place in prominent musical circles of

299

New York. But in her youth it meant that whenever she came to Englewood she was summoned to perform at the piano, which she obediently did, and was held up to us as an example of what satisfaction good hard work could produce. It was a challenge, and we looked at Violet with awe (she was one year older than I).

However, our awe went back further than that and was a deep secret. On one of her early visits she had with her a cousin from St. Louis, Sam Priest, who must have been about eleven. He was under no obligations to our family and was quite an independent character anyway. One afternoon Violet and Sam were discovered climbing way up in the branches of the big old apple tree under which we always had tea. In fear and excitement the governesses had told them several times not to do that; then the gardener protested, and so did the maid. So they just climbed higher. Finally Papi appeared and, standing directly under the apple tree rapping his cane on the terrace, ordered in no uncertain voice: "You two come down here this minute!" With everyone standing around and we three meek angels lined up there gaping, Sam yelled back from somewhere up there: "You can't make me! You just come up here and get me!" We, who were never allowed to answer back and expected a spanking for any breach of discipline, couldn't believe it, and were quickly herded out of hearing, back into the house. We never saw Sam Priest again.

Through the years Violet took just about everything that we did. There was an exception, though. She did not line up as we were required to do when summoned to Papi's room for punishment, and each of us chose his or her cane from Papi's collection in the closet, to take our turn for the spanking, then stood passively by waiting and watching the others kick and struggle over his knee, whereupon we all marched out together choking back our howls. Violet sat through long lectures and was slapped on the back to sit up straight at table, and she had to learn to mount and ride off on a tall, jittery horse, Wildflower, that scared her nearly to death. And like us she pounded away for her scheduled hour of practicing on the piano. We could see her annoyance when suddenly amid a crowd of chattering guests Papi would call out: "Violet, play something for us." And she knew it must invariably be Papi's favorite show-off piece, Rachmaninoff's C-sharp Minor Prelude. When it came out that she always started those first three banging notes with "Oh—my—God" under her breath, that was quite a revelation to us.

We all had to carry out orders unquestioningly no matter how

irksome or ridiculous they were. I would be told to leave the Sunday 301
dinner table and go play the organ. This meant put on Papi's favorite
player roll, like the Overture from *Tannhäuser*, it having been firmly
suggested to me that when the guests came in at the far end of the
music room, I should act as if I were manipulating the keyboard and
the pedals. More than once he said to Ty: "Thaisa, go over and read in
that armchair under that lamp so we can see your beautiful red
hair"—which was really very surprising, because nobody was ever
allowed to make any complimentary remarks in front of us.

Sergey came in for his share of military training and discipline,
though by that time he had to stand up alone in his sailor suit, salute,
right turn, left turn, and so on while we watched from the sidelines in
grown-up dignity. "Yes, sir! No, sir!" Then one day in front of the
usual sympathetic audience, Papi grilling Sergey to produce those
brief snappy answers, "Well, young man, what *is* on your mind?" and
the next instant that crisp salute and "My mind is a blank, sir!" One up
for Sergey in all our minds!

It was really Violet who, without spoiling our proper submissive
outward appearance, made us see how funny some of our habits were,
or would react with hidden giggles at Papi's extravagant posturing,
and through whom we realized how Mami with her quiet dignity went
right on controlling things in her own way no matter what the bluster-
ing order was from above. Violet was also the first one to observe that
some of the goings-on in this household, which were to us chores or so
ordinary that they were boring, were to outsiders fantastically different and interesting. She loved to ride, so she undertook quite seriously
to help exercise all the horses, then learned to jump them, and she took
real pleasure in showing them off.

Those customary big Sunday dinners with the parade of strange
guests, which were to us an obligation, just fired her imagination, and
she could turn them into the most animated stories and usually see
something humorous in them. Besides, she was uninhibited enough to
converse with the guests on her own, draw them out, and be treated by
them almost as an adult.

Nationalities tended to come in groups over certain periods, the
first ones introducing more of their friends and the circle widening,
then disappearing while one or two remained as closer friends. When
we were about ten and eleven there was the Persian ambassador, Ali
Kuli Khan, a handsome, cultivated man whom Mami admired, and we
remembered because of the pretty gifts of jewelry he brought us, and

The Fabulous Twenties

who brought back from Persia on special order for them the very large, unusual ivory-background rug that fitted the whole length of the new organ room. One of his followers was quite handsome, David Ben-zaria, an antique dealer, through whom they acquired a selection of large brasses and wonderfully deep turquoise glaze ceramics, and who unsuccessfully courted and proposed marriage to Aunt Xenia.

✿ The Turkish Invasion

Then came a wave of Turks, starting with the Turkish consul, then an assortment of generals and other titles whose names we had to get used to, such as Shah Mir Effendi and Ahmed Abdul Bey. The consul's wife was a plump little dark-haired lady who spoke no English but who could charm Papi by the hour "chirping" like a bird, as he called it, and gesticulating most gracefully as he led her on. The men were happy when they could rattle on in French and be *galant* with Mami.

On the second visit the consul arrived with a retinue. He was not very tall and was followed by four even shorter swarthy men, each carrying a porcelain vase at least three feet high, certainly looking much bigger than the figures staggering beneath them. With much guttural jabbering and the consul pointing directions but offering no explanations, the vases were carried into the music room and placed two at each end, beside the fireplace and the organ. Mami watched and Papi watched. Then there were bowing and compliments in French and mutual admiration of these gorgeous things. By Oriental courtesy one never says no thank you to a gift. So Sunday dinner proceeded cordially, with toasts of friendship and polite conversation, and there was no chance for Mami to nudge Papi or even whisper a question until their departure. Then came Mami's outburst of consternation: "What in the world am I going to do with *four* of those gigantic things? They don't belong in here at all. Those people are coming back again and I can't hurt their feelings."

It was only a few days before the bill arrived—$500 for each piece! Ahmed Abdul Bey and Mrs. Bey were expected for dinner the next Sunday. Always the one to take on the tough assignments, Mami had to telephone and extricate herself. The Turks did come again to dinner; their four little men preceded them into the parlor and briskly stag-gered out again with the beautiful vases, and the afternoon was carried off with the same courtly formality as ever. But another lovely friend-ship had passed by.

Princess in Paradise

🌿 Growing Up

As we grew older we began enjoying these guests more and more, even trying out conversation in foreign languages for ourselves. Since we all came home from boarding school regularly on Sundays, we gradually began to bring along our friends. Papi would give them personal attention and be as charming to them as to any of the adults. Their eyes would nearly pop, observing this ménage—the elegant table setting, the assortment of guests and the babble of languages, the organ or singing recital that followed, or later the horse show on the front lawn for which we had to change into the proper clothes, then mount one animal after the other to make it perform. Girls our age would say to us, "My, you have an interesting family! I just love to hear your father tell all those stories! Your mother must really be a Russian princess." Goodness knows what kind of tales they passed around at school.

We, who literally trembled when we spoke to Papi, our fingers shaking so that we couldn't play the piano properly in front of him, were still being disciplined and treated like children at home. There was an undercurrent of revolt and independence brewing, aired loudly in private or turned to laughter by Violet's ridicule. Nevertheless, tall and mature looking as I was to others at fifteen, I still wore my hair pulled back with a bow and a long curling braid hanging down my back, and of course the same went for Ty. At school I twisted it into a low bun on my neck, and Ty evolved her own style with a fan-type knot at the back of her head. But Sunday morning, when we got into our car, out came the hairpins and down came the curls, and off came the lipstick so that we would look properly young and demure to Papi all during the day.

At five o'clock when we piled back into the car there was great activity in the back seat, brushing, retrieving the hairpins from our purses, pinning up, powdering, and "smearing on the rouge"—all to the great amusement of the chauffeur in front, always our friend and confidant. Also at fifteen I was allowed to wear my first pair of *silk* stockings, dyed at home to match my short evening dress.

Papi had strange ideas about bringing us up to be sophisticated and independent, yet sweet and naive, the kind of women that would appeal to nice, substantial older men. He never failed to take us in to New York for the annual Ziegfeld Follies, with seats in the front row, or European theater pieces like Ferenc Molnár's or the Lunts' comedies,

The Fabulous Twenties

that impressed him, things our friends in school would never have seen, then escorting us with great aplomb backstage to meet the stars, such as the Duncan sisters and Ina Claire, who were friends of his. One time I was invited along with them to the Metropolitan Opera, to sit in their friend's box number 1 right in front and practically overlooking the stage. Lucrezia Bori sang *Traviata*, and she waltzed directly beneath us, looked up, waved, and smiled. There I was, sitting in the front seat in a lovely décolleté evening dress, with my hair brushed out and falling around my shoulders pinned at the side with a brilliant bow, mortified beyond all description.

❧ The Endless Procession

The Sunday guests came in various groups. Papi would say, "Today we are having a Russian invasion" or "Next week the Germans are coming." Later it was "the Poles"—a dedicated group of serious bridge players, introduced through the Polish consul by Uncle Igor. They were charming and animated and not only played bridge all afternoon but appreciated good eating, so that they continued playing after supper and on past midnight when some other "snacks" like scrambled eggs or Russian *pirog* (meat pie) would be served. Eventually there was a bunch of "the Dutch!" But that story goes with my summer trip to Europe with Papi when we met them.

Chaliapin's annual visit was a treat to which we all looked forward. He was so touchingly affectionate, and so tremendous and handsome, then so happily at home and informal. With his singing at the table and his clowning at the piano afterward for those special friends of ours from school who happened to be with us that day, it was an unforgettable experience. The one time that he brought along his wife from Paris and her son by a former marriage, Arthur Paetzold, we were quite bowled over by this handsome twenty-two-year-old M.I.T. student, whose accent was as American as could be, and who gave each of us a whirl with him, as we learned the Charleston. There was also a sweet, young, unassuming, blonde daughter, Marina Chaliapin, who some years later was sent to take a room with Mami when she came to New York to study ballet.

After this visit Mami had to explain to us, delicately but with deep respect, how a great artist like Chaliapin had more than one so-called wife in several places and, naturally, the families to go with them. There was of course his earliest love in Russia, unfortunately left behind and still there. Then there was a household in Italy with several children. And the latest and largest, and apparently most permanent, was the group in Paris, who lived in a huge old-fashioned apartment in Passy, where we later visited them in 1929. In fact, it was because of these artistic liberties that the U.S. Immigration Service caused him an uncomfortable and embarrassing delay on his first return visit after World War I, and he had to call on old friends like Papi and Mami Kluge to vouch for him. In any case, Mami, combining her role of moral mentor and faithful, liberal friend, assured us that Chaliapin really loved them all and took care of all the children very generously, and although his headquarters and the largest family were in Paris, he still managed to get around to visit the others.

The "Russian invasion" really came and went for years, always anchored by the voluble trio, Xenia, Igor, and Ludmilla. They brought along the sculptor Gleb Derujinsky, already here from Paris for some time, and achieving quite a success in New York and other cities. He was young, educated, and charming in the Russian manner, and brought along or showed photographs of his very pleasing, fluid, classic Art Nouveau style figures and portraits.

Obviously many who got a glimpse inside the house at Englewood immediately put his mind to working on how he could cash in on some of this opulence. All sorts of schemers and salesmen turned up with their offerings, or else they asked for help and "connections" in the big American business world. However, with Gleb Derujinsky there was no problem—he was so modest and genuine, and already a success —except in making the choice of which piece of his to buy. When Mami had such difficulty or wavered, Papi would simply settle the matter by saying "Let me have half a dozen"—which would sort of nonplus the artist. So we had a delightful assortment of Derujinsky nudes, dancing girls, and horses scattered about the house. Some went to Xenia's apartment, and one even stood in Ty's and my bedroom.

Igor brought in the bridge players. Two who were the most faithful—meaning that they were sincere friends of all of us, right through the years of depression and old age—were Oreste Demidoff and Vladimir Sazonoff. Both absolutely as poor as church mice and living by some unmentioned menial jobs in the city, they each managed to appear in one good suit, fill in as bachelors at any party with their reliable and impeccable manners, and depended desperately on the extra money they could win at bridge—and on the good food that came with that.

The Fabulous Twenties

Their good friend, Prince Irbain Kaplanoff, making his living as a taxi driver, tried providing for himself in another way. Making the rounds, as did all these aristocratic refugees, of the prosperous homes on Long Island, New Jersey, or New York, he was taken under the wing of a wealthy dowager whom we all thought of as something like Helena Rubinstein. She decided to marry him and become "Princess" Kaplanoff, and he decided to accept the soft berth. His old friends actually mourned for him. Mami and Papi were truly fond of him and thought they could help, so they invited him and his bride out to Englewood with a group. She was really a befurred, bejeweled, busty blonde; took in all the surroundings and the entertainment with knowing, value-conscious eyes; and plagued her meek husband all evening, loudly ordering him here and there with "Oh, Prince, will you bring me my fur piece? Prince, will you get me a cigarette?" and insisted that he *stand* behind her chair while she listened to the music. Very soon poor Prince Kaplanoff dropped out of sight of his whole circle of old friends.

General Syroboyarsky was a different kind of Russian and a different kind of friend. Though he could appear with all the dignity of his old military bearing, handsome with gray sideburns and deep sad lines in his strong face, he had been beaten down by his war experiences, and he just wanted to be a hermit. So he bought a small chicken farm in New Jersey and continued to live a quiet isolated country life. However, he had a beautiful wife whom he had married in Shanghai after he escaped from Russia. She was younger and enterprising and was determined to have a career of her own. Annushka Syroboyarsky had a marvelous figure and was extremely tall, the more surprising because she was part Japanese as well as part German, and her hair was swept up into a coiffure that made her very elegant and impressive. She spoke Russian fluently as well as Japanese and German. She commuted to a job in the city and faithfully returned to the chicken farm in the country. With her charm, nobody who met her could allow her to be so isolated for long. She was flooded with invitations everywhere; besides, she was a smart businesswoman, and her days were kept full making contacts with all sorts of important executives. She took an apartment in New York and installed a real old Russian *babushka* out in the country to take care of her husband and her young son, Alexei.

Annushka did not desert the general; it was simply that, like so many Russian wives, she was able to earn the money, and he passively lived out his side of the arrangement. There was never a question

Princess in Paradise

about her being as independent as she liked. After his death when she moved about the country, she took the *babushka* and Alexei along with her and always maintained a home for them. As a buyer for the Japanese government cigarette monopoly, she had many personal friends among the largest American tobacco firms. After Pearl Harbor, when her Japanese connections might have made her suspect, she managed to remain free. To our surprise and a bit to her own astonishment, she turned up at the University of Minnesota as head of the Japanese Language School for the U.S. Air Corps Area Studies Program. Handsome as ever, she was surrounded by the highly selected, intelligent young men, with whom she spoke Japanese from breakfast through recreation time after dinner. She admitted that she was amazed how quickly they learned to speak Japanese, and once she proudly escorted a dozen or so to our house for supper and a walk in the country. She moved on to Monterrey, California, to teach at the famous Ormy Language School there, then after the war carried on a Japanese art-importing business on her own.

Among the Germans a strange guest, but very vivid in our memory, was the young Max Schmeling, who came with his promoter, Mike Jacobs. Cousin Albert, who was better acquainted with the sporting crowd in New York, and with whom Papi always attended the biggest prize fights in front-row seats, insisted on showing him off to his family in Englewood, or perhaps it was showing off his family to the New York bigshots. Much to Mami's horror, Papi used to describe in front of us the wild crowds, the contagious excitement, and the bloody brutality (seen at close range) of those spectacular fights—the Dempsey-Firpo fight, then Jack Dempsey and Jack Sharkey, and others whose training camps he visited with Albert near Pompton. Max Schmeling was the newest, most promising young star. He must have been twenty-one when I was sixteen and had been brought over from Germany under the management of Mike Jacobs. At the Sunday dinner table Mr. Jacobs, the fast-talking little baldheaded promoter with his training camp language and Brooklyn accent, was seated far down the table with Mami. I was placed next to Schmeling, because he could speak not a word of English, and it was my assignment to entertain him in German. He was quite nice looking, pleasant, polite, and so bashful it was hard to discover much of anything that interested him. After that we followed his career with vague interest—the papers reported his trips back and forth to Germany—and he actually did become the world heavyweight champion from 1930 to 1932. It was

The Fabulous Twenties

interesting to discover his name in the news as a resident of West Berlin, seventy-one years old, and instigator of a celebration to honor the memory of the U.S. Berlin Airlift of 1948.

❧ The Jantzens

Not all the passing visitors to Englewood were foreigners, although those did seem the most exotic. Actually, there was very little entertaining at homes of American business associates, at least of all those many prestigious accounts along the East Coast that the Kluge Weaving Company handled. We had annual visits from friends in Montreal and Toronto, California, Florida, and Alabama, or Chicago, Minneapolis, and Duluth. Some came to stay at the house for a week; others were the occasion for big dinner and theater parties in New York, to be reciprocated in kind when Papi made his extended business trips around the country.

About 1927 a lively new circle developed from the business with the Jantzen Knitting Mills and the Pendleton Woolens of Portland, Oregon. The rather new Jantzen Mills had been manufacturing, with their tubular knitting machines, men's undershirts and women's cotton undergarments, and some dark cotton bathing suits. Carl Jantzen and his principal executives had all been working together from the start; each was technically trained, young, and progressive. Theirs was the idea of embarking on *wool* knitted bathing suits, which would stretch yet remain firm, and they began designing suits with shoulder straps instead of short sleeves, cut out at the neckline front and back, and also with variations in color from the customary navy or black. What they needed was a distinctive new brand name and a label design.

I don't know how long it took to develop, but there must have been lots of cooperation across the country and plenty of mutual understanding. We became aware of it only when the whole thing was sprung full-blown in the public eye. Papi had come up with the original idea of the "Jantzen Diving Girl"; and they with the slogan, "the suit that changed bathing to swimming," both of which were promoted in a tremendous nationwide advertising campaign. The Kluge Weaving Company not only made the Jantzen insignia labels with a patented trademark which had to be used even on their suits sold by Sears, Roebuck, but also the curved red diving girl which was sewn as an emblem on the front of every suit, and was soon appearing as a sticker on bumpers and windows of automobiles, from east to west.

Princess in Paradise

A great bonus was that all of us had a wardrobe of Jantzen swimming suits, men's and women's, and a supply for the guests. They were indeed form-fitting. Nobody had dared appear publicly in such a thing since the high diver Annette Kellerman in her clinging tank suit of the early 1920s. And here was freedom from the customary old-fashioned suit—the "bathing suit bra"! The wool was actually more comfortable to wear, and the suits did dry faster. One style of the men's suits was made with a light-colored top and a dark bottom, or a red-and-white striped top, knitted all in one piece but to look like shirt and trunks, with the belt woven in. A year later, after serious experimenting, Jantzen produced the first color that would not fade, a women's red wool suit, and from there the company dared to go further and further—for example, experimenting to see if a yellow could be opaque enough not to be embarrassing. The whole Jantzen bunch, the executives and their wives, who came to New York or whom the family visited out west, captivated us. They were young, energetic, very healthy looking, and had a special manner of freedom and sincerity.

By the time I went to Portland to visit them in 1928 and had become friends with their daughter, Oneita, my age, their huge success had not altered but rather enhanced the fundamentals of their life-style. I toured the greatly expanded modern factory, by then making only swimming suits, where every worker was greeted by first name, and I was taken to breakfast parties in the beautiful hills of Portland or out to camps in the mountains. Carl Jantzen was of Danish extraction, a lanky outdoorsman with a long bony face, and was typically kind, placid, and humorous. He had extended his profitable enterprise in characteristic fashion—there were no extravagant houses or fancy clubs for him—he had built a Jantzen Park in the outskirts of Portland. It was invitingly laid out alongside some woods, with two swimming pools, one for children, and the recreation area equipped for picnics, with playground apparatus, tennis, and handball courts. That same summer I went with them to the Hawaiian Islands,—but more of that later.

❧ The Pendleton Woolen Mills

The president of the Pendleton Woolen Mills, Charles Wintermute, was even more of a sportsman, and the family enjoyed him equally as a guest and in his own home surroundings. His labels were never a problem; the design remained steady and conservative, and the labels were ordered regularly in profitable numbers.

Through "Uncle Charlie" the family acquired a fine supply of assorted blankets made personally significant by his fascinating tales of the West and the amount of Indian folklore that accompanied them. At the turn of the century, the Pendleton Woolen Mills had started making woolen blankets, those fleecy so-called Hudson Bay blankets, with the small stripes woven in at the side to indicate each quality, and the coats made from the same material. They were the well-known standard sportsman's outerwear all across the country.

Then followed the Indian pattern blankets. Since local hand weaving could not produce the quantity of blankets needed for robes, hangings, and floor coverings, the various Indian nations were satisfied to buy machine-produced blankets, but only if their own traditional designs were reproduced. So Charlie Wintermute paid regular visits to the Indian reservations, was very friendly with the chiefs, from those in the Southwest to those all over the Northwest, but centered principally around Pendleton in eastern Oregon.

He spoke their language, and they would give him sample designs and colors and explain to him all the symbolism and traditional uses. He would do anything to please them. The most popular was the Chief Joseph design brought out in 1922, woven on many different background colors, from turquoise, the favorite of the Zulis, to the greens, oranges, and browns of the north, and always with the robe design (like hand weaving) exactly reversible. Ty and I were each presented with the most precious and unusual version, the Princess blanket, with an all-white background and design in tan and light orange colors, especially valuable because of its long hand-tied white fringe.

The biggest event of the year was the Pendleton Roundup in the fall, not only a rodeo and carnival, but the gathering of all the western Indian tribes, which meant the families as well as the chiefs. The festivities lasted for a week, day and night, with ceremonial dances, contests, and exhibits. As their good friend, Charlie Wintermute could not refuse an invitation. He always attended, and he described the whole celebration with the greatest and sincerest enthusiasm.

When he said, "Kluge, you must come with me some time," Papi did not hesitate a moment.

"I'll be there for the next one!"—and he was.

With his enormous size and weight, Papi always managed to move himself about with agility and ease. If it happened to be camping or an outdoor picnic he could sit on the ground—and manage to get himself up again. If it meant squeezing into the cramped front seat of a model-T Ford, he would do it without hesitation, and laugh along with everyone else. If someone found a horse strong enough to hold him, he could ride with zest and confidence. There was hardly any social gathering that he could not enjoy to the fullest. They all loved him and insisted that he come back every year. He was even given an official job—one of the three judges of the Indian Maiden Beauty Contest. Could anything be better! The chiefs, the fathers, catered to him. He was one of the most honored guests, and after his task was performed he could meet the young ladies and converse with them, when he would get them to tell their stories about themselves, their careers, and their native background.

As with the Jantzen business, the Pendleton Woolen Mills became so successful that in time the company expanded into other lines beyond their original steady items, entailing new designers, fashionable styling, and yearly changes. From sturdy, serviceable men's wool shirts Pendleton Mills went to women's wear, high-style tailoring and accessories, and a wider range of material patterns. But the company's standard of quality remained the same. Everything was made of the best pure wool, and the Indian pattern blankets went right on being the mainstay of the business. In any case, all these products continued to use labels.

The Fabulous Twenties

19

Boarding School

BOARDING SCHOOL experi-
ence was generally a happy
one for each of us. Most of all,
we made *friends!* Then each began to discover his own interests and to
develop a more distinctive personality. Emile at Riverdale, with enthusiastic and understanding teachers, found new and unrestricted
pleasure in music and guidance in appreciation. He had always been
an amazing reader, and now the whole field of literature opened up to
him; he also found a new challenge in doing good writing of his own.
Probably his most lasting interest was kindled there in his active participation in the school drama—the variety of plays, the costuming,
and planning the scenery. This continued through his college years at
Dartmouth and as an avocation all during his years of business. Ty was
frequently invited to the Riverdale plays and parties, and Mami was
happy that Emile had found something he enjoyed, but to Papi this was
not the practical learning and discipline that he believed was necessary
for a young man entering the business world.

Ty made her own friends and managed to carry on with her studying, but that was not her greatest interest. She suffered as the naughty
"little sister" under the eagle eye of the Scotch lady principal, which
only made her more devilish and ingenious in outwitting the authorities. She liked to visit her friends' families in New York, where
they had "boys" at their parties; she remembered jokes, made smart,
witty conversation, and learned the latest dance steps. And she didn't

have to fight the battle, as I had to do, being the first one, to put up her hair, wear silk stockings and lipstick, and choose more sophisticated, ready-made dresses. At the time, as one said, she was "a cute girl" and she was popular.

Probably I had the reputation of being the "serious one." I had no trouble with studying because I loved it, and my teachers loved me. But my greatest joy was in athletics—baseball, javelin throwing, running broad jump, archery—and most of all basketball. What great coaching and encouragement came from Miss Pryde, who had seen us appear that first time in high-buttoned boots and blue serge dresses. As my arms and legs grew longer, and as I began to respond to her disciplined training and feel myself a responsible part of a team, my greatest thrill was to jump up for the ball that was thrown to me, rush toward the basket and either by exact timing from a distance or seeking to just reach up and tip it in—feel myself absolutely sure of making it.

We went to play against other schools around New Jersey, and someone asked once if our car couldn't be borrowed to help with the transportation. Not only the car with chauffeur arrived, but Papi also, making it quite a crowd that had to be squeezed in. Sitting in the front row on the gym floor in a South Orange School—the only man, surrounded by a bevy of mothers and schoolgirls—Papi had to ask loudly what the game was all about. He caught on that there was cheering and clapping when a basket was made, and soon sorted out that the tall beanpole with the long tail of blonde hair was doing pretty well. Always embarrassed enough at my parents, I could hear him clapping and that cane rapping on the floor, then loud and clear "Bravo! Alexandra made another basket!"

As I've said, it was always someone else who thought our parents were wonderful and so intriguing. Miss Pryde and the girls were tolerant, then enthusiastic, and finally in stitches with laughter. After that Papi became a regular and avid follower of the Dwight Basketball Team, wouldn't miss a game, and of course wanted to know all about all the girls personally; he was especially fascinated by the strange activity of that beautiful cheerleader. Even when he and Mami invited the whole team for a luncheon party at home, I was self-conscious and apologetic and acted as if I had nothing to do with it. It was as usual graciously and beautifully arranged by Mami. The table in the dining room was set with her best china. There were paper streamers (which at that time really meant a party), flowers and Easter decorations, and for each guest a personal souvenir monogram pin ordered from

The Fabulous Twenties

Papi and Mami play host to the Dwight School basketball team at Englewood in 1925.

Altman's. Afterward they wandered admiringly around the garden and the terraces, then again—Oh, horrors!—had to line up for an official picture by a photographer—which, later on, everyone was glad to have. Evidently it made us all closer friends and was to them an unforgettable experience.

During my junior year everybody was talking about the College Board exams and where they were going to college. The idea had never entered my head. If there was any such talk at home, it was that I would be sent to a young ladies' finishing school in France or Switzerland. In early spring of that year Mami's old friend from Kiev, Madame Jekouline, stayed with us in Englewood. We had heard lots about her, as I had described before, but apparently she now had an important position in the school system of the new Republic of Czechoslovakia and had been sent by President Mazaryk on an official mission to the United States. She had many errands to perform and old connections to renew. Papi and Mami drove her to visit one of her friends from prewar days, Professor Lucy Textor, who was teaching

Princess in Paradise

Russian history at a "small college" on the Hudson River in Pough-keepsie. Neither of them had ever heard of "Vassar" before.

When they returned, they were all aglow. It had been a gorgeous day and a beautiful place. Apparently they had met impressive people, including the president, Henry Noble MacCracken; had taken a thorough tour; and had been exposed to their first American college. Papi was bubbling with enthusiasm in his usual way. "Alexandra, we have just see the most wonderful place—Vaa-ss-aar College. And that's where you must go!" Now, how? I had heard about it but thought it was one of those prestigious places where one's name was entered at birth. All the girls I knew had prepared long before this, choosing their course programs, planning for those College Board exams two years ahead, enrolled by their American mothers who themselves had attended various colleges.

When Papi really decided on something, he saw to it that it was somehow accomplished. Applications could be filled out and I could take some practice exams my junior year but there was no other way to be admitted, as we understood it, except by taking the comprehensive exams in June after graduation, when a limited number of applicants were accepted according to their scholastic rating after the quota of earliest enrollees was filled. As usual the decision was made without my having any control over it, and the wheels started rolling.

As I look back at it, my senior year at Dwight does not seem to have been more special than any of the others. We were already a close group of friends and were housed together in the oldest Victorian cottage of the boarding school complex. Almost every one of us had some official title or duty in the school government. Mine was being editor in chief of the *Dwightonia,* the school annual. I acquired a brand-new girl as a roommate, Nancy Gaines, whom I had met during the summer at Mudjekeewis, and whose father was so enchanted by the discipline of the Dwight girls and their attitude that he moved her from her New Rochelle coed high school to this strict girls' boarding school for her senior year. It may have been a miserable struggle for her, but she fitted in remarkably well, even making a place for herself in the tightly knit basketball squad. She introduced to us a strange new attitude—an awareness of boys. All my friends were the serious, hearty, athletic types, actually so confined that what was really fear of the subject was expressed in contempt.

In senior year there was a tradition that one absolutely could not escape—the Senior Dance in February. A few girls had brothers or childhood friends from home whom they could invite, but for the majority, Miss Creighton, the seventy-five-year-old little white-haired Scotch principal, had a list of "eligible young men" from Englewood society, to whom she mailed engraved invitations and at random enclosed the "visiting card" of one of the young ladies. The rest of the young men, not obliged to be specific escorts, came as the stag line and stood as a phalanx along the walls looking over the girls, most of them in their first tuxedos. Probably most were too shy to cut in anyway —unless by some prearranged bargain to relieve a buddy.

We all faced the prospect with just as little joy. Again my dress was made at home by the dressmaker, although Mami tried with her usual gentleness to make it with my approval and as stylish as possible. It was very short, of turquoise blue chiffon, with handkerchief like panels hanging down all around to create the fashionable uneven hemline. My silk stockings were dyed blue to match, and I acquired my first pair of silver brocade slippers. To insure the propriety of our costumes, Miss Creighton held a full dress rehearsal where we all had to appear in her office modeling our dresses.

The night of the dance, held in the gym, decorated with paper streamers and potted palms, Miss Creighton appeared in her lavender satin finery with lace choker collar ruffle, to form a receiving line with a few teachers and Englewood mothers. The girls who expected a young man friend whom they knew were lucky enough to be greeted. The rest of us herded ourselves in a bunch to face that ghastly lineup and to wonder which boy was going to step forward to claim us. Naturally I drew a bashful young freckle-faced boy much shorter than I, the brother of one of the girls in Ty's class. Fortunately, in the light of later customs, we had dance cards on which were printed a dozen numbers with blanks, and these we had filled in ahead of time with the names of our friends with whom we had promised to exchange dances. The whole thing was an initiation that was more painful than enticing.

However, before the year was up we faced a more intriguing adventure. Gwen, one of our studious, modest, and retiring but athletic pals, had a brother at West Point, and she was quite used to going up there to visit. Imagine how she could ever undertake such a thing! She arranged for five of us to go there with her for a weekend and would provide a cadet for each one. That meant transportation, staying in the old-fashioned wooden West Point Hotel (which soon thereafter burned down), and bringing along our chaperones. My mother and Nancy's father were the chaperones. There was the same embarrassing moment when six nervous, dressed-up young girls (the term "teen-ager" had not yet been invented) waiting on the hotel porch watched a snappy lineup of six young men in those dazzling gray suits with gold buttons march up and stand at attention before us, the moment of trepidation wondering which one was for which, then the introductions, followed by eager and relaxed friendliness.

The difference was that these were slightly older college students and that their training included polishing their manners and careful instruction in handling social situations. It was a marvelous weekend for all—from the walking tour of the handsome campus and introduction to Flirtation Walk along the cliffs, to the formal dance with the open terrace overlooking the Hudson River, from which each came away with the symbolic souvenir of a precious brass button, to the moving Sunday chapel service with twelve hundred male voices singing out their sentimental Alma Mater to a tune which I recognized as an old German folk song, and the final dress parade and farewells at sundown. Our success was assured by all being invited back several more times. By graduation time, we were all a little more at ease with the idea of romance.

At home I still had trouble being treated like the young lady I considered myself. For one thing, I was just sixteen, and my friends were all seventeen and older. They had driver's licenses, and at least three received cars as graduation presents. The most fashionable thing at the time was the new tan Chrysler roadster (cars were still mostly black), a small open car with a rumble seat in back. People like Ruth Keeler and Betsy Bonbright, who came from Englewood, could toot around in theirs, and would drive up to our house with a load of friends piled in front and overflowing the back seat, and by then felt quite at ease dropping in en masse for a swim. Papi had no intention of indulging in such extravagance. He presented me with a good substantial government bond and a diamond pin and arranged for another nice all-girl party. Mami was the rebel. She took me to town and had my hair "bobbed." To me that was transformation and freedom enough.

Graduation passed, peacefully, prettily, traditionally, twenty-six of us in the class of 1926, and was followed by "Cram Week." Then came the nerve-wracking daily trips into New York to take the College Entrance exams plus the first Scholastic Aptitude tests at Columbia University. For most of us there were four or five exams—Latin, French, Spanish, math, and English, and sometimes two a day. After that it was a matter of waiting for the fatal news.

The Fabulous Twenties

20

Summer in Europe

ERY SOON I was faced with another surprise: "Alexandra, how would you like to go to Europe with your father?" I knew right away that that was not a question but an order. I had no desire to go—too many gay things had begun happening around home—least of all to be confined under the strict supervision of Papi. But arrangements were already pretty well under way. Mami was to rent a cottage at Brown's Camps on Lake Kezar next door to Mudjekeewis, where housekeeping was at a minimum and they would take their meals in the lodge. Emile would go off to Camp Riverdale. She would take along Sergey (now five) and his governess, Ty, and Violet to keep Ty company. I was jealous of all their companionship.

Meanwhile, Papi and I would sail off on the Holland-America liner *Volendam.* He was headed for his annual reducing cure at Dr. Dengler's Sanatorium in Baden-Baden. I had visions of diets, massages, walking in the woods with him alone, sitting at a table for two in a dining room surrounded by other overweight old men and women, with nothing else to do but sit in a rocking chair on the porch listening to band concerts—and then always that 10:00 P.M. curfew.

The *Volendam* was a pleasantly small and intimate ship. Papi spent most of his day in the smoking room making new acquaintances over the ever dependable game of bridge. After dinner we sat on the sidelines and watched the dancing. There was one delightfully animated young Dutch couple, both tall and slender, who danced so perfectly together that it was like watching an exhibition. Suddenly the handsome husband came across the floor toward us, bowed to Papi, introduced himself, and said: "May I dance with your daughter?" At that Papi got up, clicked his heels, introduced me, and gave his permission. I was to learn that this was a European custom, and many a time in a hotel or a restaurant I could see some gentleman starting to approach across the dance floor heading for our table and me, the lonely young thing with that old man. There was no way to refuse courteously, no matter what the looks or the size of the character might be. However, sometimes these introductions developed into very interesting and pleasant connections.

The dancing young couple were Jan and Bonnie Kleykamp who turned out to be charming and solicitous friends of us both, and introduced us to a whole circle of friends who regularly traveled back and forth on this ship. The Kleykamps were dealers in Oriental antiques. They insisted that we must come to meet their family in the Hague and see their large home, which housed both their private and business collections.

The next most interesting person was a small, dark-goateed Hollander, Kees Hermsen, who was a dealer in old Dutch paintings, also of a prominent family in the Hague, who lived in the historic house of a seventeenth-century Dutch master, Johann de Witt. By the time we docked in Rotterdam, our week was booked full with invitations.

Chinese Antiquities in Holland

The first night out was for dinner at the Hermsen establishment. Apparently, relatives of all generations had been assembled, and the program called for a properly sumptuous feast to impress this big American businessman. We sat in a room taken right out of a typical Dutch painting—with a dimly lit checkered floor, heavy furniture, and dark-framed old paintings. The long refectory table was covered with a deep-piled oriental rug, on top of which the lace tablecloth was laid, spread with an array of heavy gold-bordered dishes. The cheeses, the soup, the fish, the meats, and the vegetables kept coming; then came more cheeses with coffee; and when I thought I could not face another morsel, there was set in the middle of the table a huge, lusciously decorated cake, obviously made with personal devotion, which one simply could not refuse. Dinner was followed by a tour of the house and studios, since it was naturally expected that any wealthy American would be a sympathetic customer for very old, very dark Dutch landscape and still-life paintings.

The experience with the Kleykamp family was entirely different; the whole tone of these people and their life style was much lighter. The parents' home was really a Renaissance style palazzo, of white stone, four stories high, on the broad boulevard, Oude Scheveningje Weg No. 1, right opposite the Peace Palace. Each of the sprightly parents was a type by himself—the father a smiling, ruddy-complexioned outdoorsman whose face just belonged beneath a dark blue peaked sailor's cap, and the mother with a broad smile, high pink cheeks, and her hair in a topknot looking like the model for a Rembrandt portrait.

Their specialty being Chinese antiquities, the house was bright with Chinese rugs, brilliant brocades on sofas and portieres, jade lamps and lacquer chests, and cloisonné and porcelain vases. The small dinner party was served with quiet, restrained elegance. For coffee afterward we adjourned to a den or office on the ground floor where I luxuriated on a Tibetan lamb's wool rug. It was no effort to admire the objets d'art all about and to ask about their histories. One small thing after another came out of curio cabinets or concealed closets or was hunted up enthusiastically from some other part of the house, the conversation just bubbling along.

From Papi: "How could I get something like that to take home to Olga?"

"Oh, please, take it, take it! And how about this to go with it?"

The evening waxed friendlier by the minute, and an array of precious fragile bric-a-brac was lined up. And now something for Alexandra—just the thing! Bonnie walked in modeling an evening coat of pink silk Chinese brocade with big green jade buttons and opened it up to reveal the lining of long, curly, white Tibetan lamb. Could I resist putting it on? Could Papi resist my glowing face! Yes, yes, we must have that, too!

The entertaining continued back and forth for several days. The Kleykamps took us out in the country to their cottage right at the edge of a canal where another charming son and his Belgian wife joined us for an outdoor lunch. Then they took us on a long motorboat ride along winding and crisscrossing canals, past lush flower gardens, windmills, and other cottages, waving to friends on shore, and ending

Princess in Paradise

up for tea at their quite informal yacht club. I began to feel as if I was actually being treated as a young lady.

There was another meeting with the Hermsens—a luncheon given by the distinguished father at a somber elegant old restaurant, with the plan to take us back to their home afterward for a final tour of their galleries. I followed along as always, trying to listen, trying to learn or recognize something familiar. There was no question about it—this was their last chance to do some business, and everyone pitched in with his or her routine. Young Kees was telling about his successes in New York and the great investments in old masters, and the rotund papa with long beard and flowing artist's tie was lovingly pointing out details then standing back in glowing pride. As they walked by walls lined to the ceiling with row after row of those dark-framed pictures, from small to large size, Papi kept right on with knowing nods and intelligent compliments.

"Yes, that is a really fine one, but I think Olga would like this other one better. But the sizes! I'm not sure where that one would fit. Perhaps this one would look better in my music room. I really must wait until I get home and study the proper places for them."

Thus ended the efforts and expenses exerted with great hopes for a big business deal. Only later did we hear about the family arguments as to how these expenses, with doubtful results, were to be divided up.

The Kleykamps turned up in due time to deliver personally the collection of odds and ends that Papi had picked out, and though they were crushed that he did not make the large purchases they had hoped for, they depended on him for many years to introduce them to potential customers. In addition, they remained pleasant, attractive young friends and bridge partners and often asked if they might bring other friends along. One such couple, who fitted in immediately with the Kluge establishment, who seemed to enjoy Papi's sense of humor and to admire Mami's unobtrusive gifts, was Mr. and Mrs. Henry Keuls, also from Holland but New York residents now many years.

On to Baden-Baden

Before we left the Hague we had made numerous urgent visits to the offices of the Holland-American Line trying to arrange for return accommodations in September, which at the height of the season was virtually impossible. Even though I still did not know whether I would

Sa and Papi in Baden-Baden, 1926.

be accepted at the one college of "my choice," or if so, when I might have to appear there, it was only sensible to make every effort to get us home at a reasonable time.

So we proceeded as scheduled for our destination of Baden-Baden. Now I discovered that I was expected not only to be Papi's valet, responsible for packing and keeping track of his clothes, but that I was also going to be taught independence and assume the duties of executive secretary besides. For an eleven-day Atlantic crossing, both ways, and six weeks around Europe, one traveled then with more than a few trunks, hatboxes, shoeboxes, and an assortment of all sizes of hand baggage. Papi handed over to me all the keys, told me to get the tickets, check through the large trunks, and see that the porters delivered their loads of loose pieces to the proper compartment. He would be there waiting to count them over once more. When we came to the Holland-German border, it was left to me to go to the baggage car and open the trunks, or carry on the discussion with the customs officers about all this load being only our necessary personal equipment.

And so it continued from there. I sent the telegrams; I wrote his business letters; and I was sent down to the hotel desk before a departure to pay the bills. Of course he kept his eagle eye on me and checked over everything in his characteristic stern way. Yet one of my most

Princess in Paradise

memorable agonies was that with all this grown-up training, when I would bring the packet of incoming mail back to our room, he would look over each of my letters, asking who this was from, what did So-and-so say, and add, "Now read them to me!" Glory be, Ty was telling me about her newly acquired boy friends and her escapades with Violet, and I was getting mushy messages from West Point and a few other new ardent young admirers, enough to thrill me secretly but nearly perish if read out loud.

So I gradually worked out my system. The trick was to call for the mail by myself and bring it up just when Papi was taking his rest after the morning treatments, then sort it out on the desk at the foot of his bed, drop some of mine which could be slipped under the carpet, and in slitting open the whole pile tuck others under the blotter or into a drawer to be retrieved later. Then I would read him the office letters till he was really sleepy and mix in an innocent-looking one from one of my school friends whom he liked, trying to read the lines ahead quickly to avoid any embarrassing reference or silly joke. I never knew whether he was looking for entertainment from the young or whether he was keeping strict watch over me, because young men were just not on his program for me at that point.

Dr. Dengler's Sanatorium

We arrived in Baden-Baden after a beautiful all-day train ride along the banks of the Rhine on Saturday evening, August 5, and installed ourselves for the four-week sojourn in Dr. Dengler's Sanatorium. It was one of many similar health hostels hidden in the pine-covered hills, a rambling, old white wooden Victorian-type hotel with turrets, balconies, and porches, with views over the town below, and was surrounded by an iron fence with a formidable gate. Our large corner room, with a balcony from which one could hear the rushing river far below, had two alcoves with brass beds, one desk at the foot of Papi's bed, white wicker furniture with a round table for taking breakfast, and an enormous marble-tiled bathroom that included a wicker chaise longue for resting after the strenuous steam baths.

Our program was to be very rigid and, to be proper company, I was expected to take part in everything that Papi did—except his diet. At 6:30 A.M. we were roused by the masseur and masseuse who gave us a vigorous rubdown with Franzbranntwein (German cognac). Then, dressed in walking clothes (Papi in heavy sweatsuit and wool cap), we

The Fabulous Twenties

were off for an hour along the winding upward trails of the mountain behind us. They were beautifully laid out so that one could make a different tour almost every day, with a bench placed at every hairpin turn that was hard to resist. As we headed home Papi, in full steam, would stop periodically to take off his cap, shake the perspiration off his bald head, and mop his face. After a meager breakfast in our room, wrapped in luxurious thick terry robes, the morning was occupied by the various "treatments." Sometimes it was a Turkish steam bath; another time it was sitting for an hour in the electric cabinet, a heated box with only one's head sticking out. There were large tubs to lie in for hot medicated baths where, as in carbonated water, the bubbles collected on the skin's surface, opening up the pores and making it red and tingly.

Then there were the showers (or douches). In one big white-tiled room filled with gleaming apparatus, a white-robed barefooted attendant presided. You could have the needle spray shower, standing in a narrow circular stall where tiny jets of water peppered you from top to bottom and all around. Most suspenseful of all was the high-pressure douche where you stood holding on tight to handle bars while the attendant operated two hoses the size of those on a fire engine and played them up and down the body, back and front, then switched to alternating them, one with an ice-cold blast, the other with nearly boiling hot water. After that, one really needed a rest.

The afternoon went on in much the same way—a hike, a whirlpool bath, a massage; around four o'clock, came teatime, and freedom at last. All this was regulated by a daily visit to Dr. Dengler's office, who not only did heart and physical checkups but minutely observed the progress on the weight account. If we happened to have been out for an evening of dancing, champagne, and luscious late snacks, not only did the night watchman who unlocked the iron gate to let us in report the irregularity, but the next morning the doctor himself noted the misbehavior and the additional pounds and delivered a stern dressing down. Papi's purpose—and his accomplishment—was to take off about 50 of his 350 pounds in the course of this "cure." It was an old custom for so many prosperous Germans who delighted all winter in overindulgence to plan such a regular program each summer. Papi had already before tried sessions at Bad Kissingen and Bad Neuheim, and even Mami as a young girl had accompanied her father on one of his trips to Bad Kreuznach. I was checked in when we arrived and was weighed again only when we were about to depart. Although I did all

Princess in Paradise

the walking Papi did and occasionally took some of the shower treatments and went swimming besides, my final result was that I had not varied one pound from my original 130.

If this four-week program looked pretty bleak to me, it must also have struck Papi, who loved a good time as much as anybody, as rather dull and confining, and a poor way to introduce his young lady daughter to Europe. So he made arrangements for some of the relatives to come for short visits to keep us company, and we began to explore Baden-Baden.

Fashionable Fun

Most of these health spas were similar in that they were located in a beautiful natural setting with mountains, pine woods, gorgeous crisp fresh air, and near enough to local picturesque villages or historic sites for short excursions. Baden-Baden was especially popular as a fashionable summer resort, with the elegant villas of longtime residents, a gambling casino and night club, and in August a week of international horseracing.

The prominent center of all these resorts—"baths," "springs," "waters"—from the Crimea across Italy, Germany, and France even to Saratoga, was the *Kurhaus Trinkhalle,* or Hall of Waters, whatever else it might be called. It was usually an elaborate, airy pavilion in the midst of a park with formally laid out paths and vistas, and close around it the promenade, wide enough for crowds to stroll on and lined with benches for the onlookers, who were just as important a part of the parade. There was always music coming from the balcony of the *Kur-Saal* (the salon or general assembly room), at least at those usual gathering times, when people would emerge and fill the otherwise peaceful walks. At teatime it was probably a *stimmungsvoll* string ensemble; in the evening from eight to ten it was a full proper symphony orchestra; and around midday for the faithful who had to get down that required mug of unpleasant-tasting water which they sipped slowly as they circled the fountain, probably a bit from a rousing little brass band.

These promenades could not help but become fashion shows and animated social gatherings, with much the same atmosphere as the vivid descriptions in Henry James' novels. The same people walked by every day; one would nod, smile, tip his hat, find an excuse to strike up an acquaintance, and always of course take notice of new or sensational arrivals. One could sit in an open café over a simple cup of coffee and easily start a conversation with one's neighbor, and in a little town like that expect to find the same individuals day after day, either there or elsewhere.

The main street of town was lined with handsome shops, not the kind of open-front souvenir bazaars, but branches of the best-known silver and china manufacturers, antique and art dealers, and of course dress shops. Papi never could resist looking at elegant merchandise, and when he discovered a certain pleasure in having me try things on, with the salesladies bowing and promoting and glowing over the model, he began outfitting me in such a variety of colorful ensembles, matching dresses and hats with special handmade touches, such as I had never had before. Then he would take much pride in picking out what I should appear in for what occasion. He was irritated at first, and I was embarrassed, when an obsequious saleslady said: "Oh, but it looks so beautiful on Madame!" and he would say: "This is not Madame; this is my daughter." After a while he must have thought I was adult enough to understand and to say, "They must think you are my young mistress," and we would giggle over it together.

One of the first and most important calls one always had to make was on the bank, and naturally ask to meet the bank manager —because banking was done on a very personal basis. Your credit was obviously known by everyone behind the counter; you came in and shook hands with everybody; someone sat at a table with you while you wrote out a check; he shook hands again when he handed you the money, inquired about the health of your family, and so on. I sat by to observe and was introduced all around. Mr. Sussmann, the manager, over the final handshake, asked if he might have the opportunity to present his family, "Meine Frau and meine zwei Söhne," perhaps over afternoon coffee. Well, what was this going to be!

And a surprise it was. The gray-haired couple, in their home surroundings all smiles and good nature, produced two tall, lanky, informal, and lively university students, Hans and Wolfgang. One was blond, serious, and handsome, with saber scars on his right cheek; the other had dark curly hair and was a bubbling, humorous, clowning entertainer. Need I say more? After that I was hardly lacking for company, and each day sparkled with anticipation of what would turn up next. They introduced me to the town *Bade Anstalt* (public baths) along the river with its swimming pool, and we could meet there almost every afternoon. Papi invited them all for an evening at the Hotel

Princess in Paradise

Stephanie, the casino-night club, and I discovered that both boys could dance very well—they were very "American"! So while Papi enjoyed the company of Mr. and Mrs. Sussmann almost daily, I could look forward to a surprise greeting during the afternoon promenade or when sitting at a café, or to an invitation for an evening libation during the concert in the *Kur-Saal,* later being walked home up the hill while Papi rode in a car.

✺ Tante Auguste and Uncle Fritz Arrive

Soon Tante Auguste and Uncle Fritz Effertz from Ingenray joined us, and that was the occasion for more entertainment and showing them around. Both of them were always very dear to me, but in my diary I mention how wonderful it was to have Tante Auguste to talk to, to unburden myself, to gossip and joke about silly girlish things such as "boys," a subject that had suddenly become very important to me.

Baden-Baden is so conveniently situated in the southwestern corner of Germany that on a one-day tour one could reach any number of interesting places. As soon as Papi discovered that a good chauffeur with a comfortable Daimler touring car could be hired, we started on a regular program of exploration, partly to provide entertainment for our guests. Once or twice we made an excursion in an open horse-drawn carriage for four to the top of a nearby hill to see a ruined castle or the quaint rustic *Jagd Haus* (hunting lodge) of an old estate, where, like such tucked-away places in every part of Europe, one could be sure to find a restaurant with an open terrace for afternoon coffee. There were several trips to Freudenstadt, a famous *Luftkurort* (fresh-air cure resort) located on a plateau much higher than Baden-Baden, surrounded by the remarkably fragrant hundred-foot-high Black Forest pine trees, and maintained as an unspoiled little town with the old *Rathaus* (city hall), church, and half-timber houses—and where one simply had to indulge in the famous *Schwartwälder Kirschtorte,* a luscious cake of many layers built up with whipped cream, dark cherries, and shaved chocolate.

A bigger expedition was to the cathedral town of Freiburg, not only to enjoy the breathtaking mountain drive with the picturesque villages along the way, and of course to see the high-spired fourteenth-century Gothic cathedral and the old buildings surrounding it, but also to have lunch at the home of Mr. and Mrs. Welte, the maker of the organ which had been installed at home in Englewood five years earlier. It was an old firm, and while touring the factory we heard demonstrations of music from organs of different types and periods.

Another time we went as far as Strasbourg, just across the French border in Alsace, and made it there by lunchtime. The best restaurant was right on the square facing the cathedral in one of the oldest buildings, built with each of its timbered five stories protruding out over the lower, and with windows of the quite old bottle glass. We sat at a window table on the second floor, served by red-coated waiters who performed every little duty with a flourish that is a particular talent of the French—and all around us everybody was speaking French. Naturally we had to sample most of the elaborate food treats, accompany them with just that special French wine, and finish up with pastries.

When it was over and Uncle Fritz lit his cigar and Papi leaned back to relax, the message came across the table to me: "Now, Alexandra, you go and look at the cathedral!"

Tante Auguste liked to snooze at the table, too, so off I went by myself. Probably I enjoyed it more that way. I knew enough to pick up a guide and was already familiar with it from pictures. There was the famous Gothic facade and I found the moving earlier sculptures on the south portal of the Ecclesia and Synagoga then stood fascinated through the whole lecture and performance of the marvelous astronomical clock, towering more than a story high, with wheels and figures moving, painted with all sorts of signs, and still functioning accurately. When I returned to my elders, they had gathered energy enough by that time to wander into a store or two to pick up some crocks of the renowned Strasburg pâté de foie gras and their rich dark chocolates. By the time we started homeward it was already late, and usually on these trips the long drive through the mountains chilled everyone thoroughly. That called for a dinner stop at a recommended wayside restaurant or at a hotel in another town, which meant more food and wine—after all, Papi was trying to show his sister a good time—and turning up at Dr. Dengler's iron gate at around one in the morning. As this was repeated, more and more often Dr. Dengler was not pleased, although I find recorded that Papi lost twenty-two pounds in the first week, and after a good scolding I noted that Papi tried very hard to stick to his good behavior—for a few days.

Princess in Paradise

🍂 The Unrelenting Social Whirl

When the much-advertised racing week at Iffegheim began, Tante Auguste had departed, and another aunt, Liesel Louran from Berlin, had come to vacation at the Pension Nagel in town and act as my companion-chaperone. She, too, was jolly and sympathetic and seemed to like the company of young people. It had become quite accepted by then that the two Sussmann young men were included in all our activities; they were free on university vacation and just correct enough in their deportment to please Papi. They spent three afternoons with us at the races, with lunches at the Jockey Club, where Papi had somehow wangled a guest membership, then strolling around the stables and paddocks, placing bets, getting all excited in the stands about our wins or losses. There were tea dances at the Stephanie Hotel and evening dances there at the casino while the older generation kept busy in the gaming room. Baden-Baden was now crowded with handsome international visitors, and each hotel put on its best entertainment. We had become acquainted with more and more people, so the circle for the evening entertainment grew larger, and there seemed to be no way to turn down the variety of invitations. Papi's weight-losing program suffered again, and he was disciplined into staying over an extra week.

Meanwhile, we had to think about our schedule for getting home. Three days after we arrived in Baden-Baden a cable had come through Papi's office that I had been accepted at Vassar and was due for registration on September 15. Now the wheels had to be pushed a bit more energetically to arrange a passage back and figure more realistically what would happen if I didn't make it in time. One great relief came with the news from Holland that the only thing available was a fine cabin on the *Volendam,* the same lovely ship we had crossed over on, sailing September 15 and due to dock in New York on September 25. But I, biting my nails, knew that would be no good for me.

"Oh, Alexandra, don't be silly; something can always be arranged. I shall write to President MacCracken at Vassar College, and have General O'Ryan get after him for a special dispensation!"

Oh, dear, some more of those special requests, again asking for privileges and being treated differently from everybody else. So we waited in suspense, and there was nothing much more we could do.

The Fabulous Twenties

Embarking for Frankfort via Fokker monoplane, 1926.

✥ A Day in Heidelberg

Our last big excursion was planned for a day in Heidelberg, appropriately taking along the two boys as guides of a sort. Even with all my anticipation, it turned out to be almost as romantic as I had dreamed. In the open car we had a tour of the old town down alongside the Neckar River and collected souvenir glasses and old prints. Our guides knew every university building there and could point out, or take us into, courtyards and gardens that were the genuine favorite student gathering places. For lunch we went up the steep hillside to the Schloss Hotel terrace, almost part of the old castle; from there we had an ideal view of the town, the winding river, and the faraway open valley. After that it was the energetic young ones who climbed the towers and toured the ruins stretching along the hillside, buildings of different styles, medieval or Renaissance, some just naturally fallen into picturesque ruins, others having been blown up during the battles of all ages. For coffee—one never misses coffee time—there was a cable car which took us to the top of the mountain, the *Molkenkur* restaurant

Princess in Paradise

with its open-terrace café and another thrilling view of the old town and the surrounding valley. It was perfect weather; all the visions of *Student Prince* days danced before me; and here with me were actually two who put on their Suevi Corps caps for the occasion, who could tell jokes and relate adventures in the midst of it all.

In all this enthusiasm they said there was a place we must not miss—tourists would never see it—it was really a student secret favorite. We must go for dinner up the river ten miles or more to the little village of Neckar Gmünd, to the Greek restaurant. If Papi was intrigued, go we must. There below the slopes covered with vineyards, under an arbor of grapevines, we were welcomed by the Greek host and treated to a feast of Greek specialties, with candles lit as the sun went down, and Greek music in the background. Somebody picked out the Greek wine we should drink, but to our consternation it turned out to be almost unbearably sweet, thick, and dark. There was the bottle before us—one could not cause hurt feelings—one must make a brave try. It was the end of a long and wonderful day, but I don't think anyone was conscious of the icy drive home or our parting with our guests or of how we got through the iron gates. We tumbled into our beds at 1:30 A.M.

After that we began preparations for our departure, buying and wrapping little presents for our friends, paying the bills, making all the necessary farewell calls, seeing Tante Liesel off on the train, and arranging reservations at the Stephanie Hotel for one last evening's party. It was hard to believe that what had looked in advance like a dull, dutiful job had turned out to be an adventure full of new discoveries and new feelings. Sometime near dawn on September 5 we threw together our overnight things (I had done the complicated packing all the day before and sent off the trunks), got into our open Daimler, picked up the Sussmann family, and drove out in the country to the so-called airport.

On the Go Once More

Flying in 1926 was something quite new and adventurous and was slightly more developed in Germany than in the States. Papi had already been using every opportunity in America to try out this great new dream, flying on business trips around the country in all sorts of little planes with no end of hazards. There were hardly such things as terminal buildings, certainly not in a place like Baden-Baden. Our car stopped in a field right beside the four-seater Fokker plane to transfer our mighty big-looking pile of baggage. The boys presented me with a bunch of red roses. I was dressed in my best traveling costume with a big hat, and we stood around feeling anxious and blue.

Finally we got in, Papi always the last one to be squeezed in through the tiny door, wrapped ourselves in blankets (there was no heat or air conditioning then), and were strapped into the two rear seats, with the pilots in the two seats right in front of us—and we took off for Frankfurt. If one flew high then, it could not have been at more than one thousand feet, probably more like five hundred, so that one could see every river, road, and tiny house, and the little plane bounced along and was tossed from side to side by the wind. The explanation given then was that over every body of water there was usually an air pocket, so the plane would drop suddenly, then zoom up again, leaving one with the feeling of a quickly sinking and rising elevator, and one's stomach acting correspondingly. It was a quite different sensation from the rhythmic rolling of a ship.

Over Karlsruhe we developed engine trouble and had to land. We were invited to pass the time in the pilots' lounge, a little aluminum garage attached to the one hangar. By the time we had flown for two more hours over the hills and lakes south of Frankfurt I knew what being airsick meant, and I learned the lesson never to eat before flying, and preferably not the night before either. In Frankfurt there were no connections for Berlin, so we had to taxi into town and stop over at the Frankfurter Hof Hotel. Papi offered to take me on a tour of the city before we met friends for dinner. The next morning it was out to the airfield by 7:00 A.M. and three hours of battling winds over the Ruhr Valley to arrive in Berlin where Uncle Albert would meet us. There was a surprise. Tempelhof Aerodrome was the brand-new airfield for Berlin, developed especially for military use. It was enormous, laid out with a semicircular plan, with lots of planes and paved runways, and an imposing modern-design passenger terminal.

For three days we visited, or rather had our headquarters at Uncle Albert's house on Taunusstrasse, where I had spent so much time the fall of 1922. Rita was a bit more sophisticated and very pretty; people were prosperous again; and everything about Berlin was livelier. I loved recognizing the streets and old places and felt much happier being now formally included in the lunches, the dinner parties, and visits to night spots that were crammed into the short time we had. There was an affectionate reunion with the friends I so admired,

Princess in Paradise

Alfred and Eleanor Schlosshauer, she the opera singer, and my jolly chaperone, Tante Liesel Louran, whose husband owned an art gallery.

It was again early in the morning and dead tired that we took off from Tempelhof heading for Cologne, three or four hours later, again over the bumpy-looking woods and countless "bodies of water" of central Germany. Bedraggled but clutching another bunch of flowers presented with the farewells, we were greeted by smiling, derby-topped Uncle Otto, with a limousine to drive us to Krefeld.

Krefeld was always an obligatory stopover for Papi on any European trip. His relatives would have felt hurt and snubbed if "der junge Bruder aus Amerika"—our "young brother from America," as he was affectionately called—bypassed them. It always meant an overwhelming schedule of visits and festivities—coffees, lunches, dinners, hither and yon at one house or another, and those who were left out, or couldn't show themselves off or had time to tell their troubles, gossiped and squabbled between each other for the rest of the year.

The thing I most looked forward to was seeing Margot again and a visit out to Ingenray. It was in the plan that we were to spend all of Sunday there. That was a family gathering which did not disappoint me and renewed all the happy memories and affectionate ties I still felt so strongly from my long stay there at the age of twelve. There was the paneled dining room with the long table set full of the colorful old glassware and Dresden china, Uncle Fritz with dignity carving the roast suckling pig raised on his own estate, an abundance of rich homemade treats produced right there, and always the good-natured happy atmosphere. Margot had taken the singing lessons Papi had promised her, so she performed with a friend at the piano in the French salon. Everyone dispersed for their naptime, and after walks in the garden and a drive around, there was the table set on the terrace facing the orchard, and time for coffee—again more food, cakes, breads, and cold snacks. Before we knew it, it was time to take off once more; there were so many farewells and promises of reunions on this side of the Atlantic or the other. Uncle Otto drove us in his car to pick up our already packed luggage in Krefeld; then came the two-hour drive down to Cologne to catch the *luxus* express night train for Paris.

Our timing never seemed to come out quite right. Either we over-slept, the baggage got waylaid, or there was too much talk when someone should have been watching the clock. Halfway to Cologne one of the two brothers checked the tickets, the time, and the distance and realized that we were cutting things pretty thin. Then came the

The Fabulous Twenties

panic, and the driver took all sorts of risks pushing through the little towns, going a hazardous sixty miles an hour on the open stretches of *Landstrasse,* everyone clutching their seats and not daring to look at their watches. When we pulled up beside the station, everyone grabbed something according to plan. There was the huffing and puffing up the stairs to the platform—with no time for flowers and farewells. The train was about to leave. Everything was hurled onto a platform, and we stumbled up the steps amid the piles. Then Papi stood there with his hat off, cane on his arm, mopping his head, and calmly waved good-bye.

❧ Discovering Paris

It hardly seems possible that to all this was added my first visit to Paris—or that I can remember the place as well as if I had lived there. The sights we saw are still as vivid as if I had spent a long time studying them. We had only three and a half days there, but as usual they were packed full, and we always had the advantage of having friends who knew how to guide us around.

We moved in to the Hotel Edouard VII where we just had time to meet Mr. and Mrs. Jantzen and their party for lunch before they left on the boat train for the European tour. The friends who then took us in hand were two sisters from Costa Rica whom we had met on the *Volendam* coming over, Angelina and Elida Piza. Elida was married and had an apartment in Montparnasse where Angelina, just a few years older than I, came regularly to visit. Then appeared their brother, Sam Piza, about whom they had talked so glowingly, who managed the program of "Musical Mornings" at the Plaza Hotel in New York, a very fashionable Wednesday activity during the winters. He was unmarried and just the kind to make dowagers swoon: tall, handsome, very Spanish in appearance and accent, with polished manners, suave and solicitous to the ladies—the typical impresario being on familiar terms with all the famous artists whom he presented. Lucrezia Bori, for example, was a Costa Rican by birth, and practically a childhood playmate of theirs.

He lost no time in arranging our schedule. The first night he entertained us for dinner at the Café des Ambassadeurs, in the Bois de Boulogne, an open-terrace restaurant for dining and dancing with lanterns strung through the trees, on a much grander scale than our Central Park Casino. The next morning he had a private car with driver-guide to take us sightseeing all over Paris and stop wherever we wanted, to wait for us as long as we wanted—Notre Dame, the Ste. Chapelle, the Invalides, the Eiffel Tower. The Louvre was a separate personal expedition for just Angelina and me. But the two ladies also knew just the salons and shops to take Papi to, and he enjoyed that activity as much as any, having a bevy of salesladies scurry about and gather together a perfect ensemble for each feminine member of his family.

Nobody can visit Paris without going to the Folies-Bergère, and we were not going to miss that. Papi always had the knack of getting front-row seats anywhere, so as usual there we were, a big party strung out and very noticeable. Funnily enough, for a sixteen-year-old, I was already pretty blasé about the parade of girls, the nudity, and the costumes, which I felt were not half as spectacular as our regular Ziegfeld Follies in New York. But the setting of the huge auditorium and the gaudy decor and the eager audience around us were what was interesting to observe.

The special feature of the show was a new young American-French Negro star—Josephine Baker—who had everyone roaring and applauding the minute she appeared, and she did appear in really dramatic costumes and actually threw herself into exotic dances that were no mere poses. For one dance she was covered head to toe in shiny, slinky, skin-tight silver sequins with an enormous headdress of bright, waving feathers, making her appear much taller than she already was. Her biggest hit was her banana dance, her costume being a short, thick skirt of bouncy bananas, with a pile of the same for a headdress, done with zest and fun and athletic vigor. The finale, which had everyone screaming and standing up, was when she started picking off her bananas and tossing them, quite in rhythm, one by one into the audience—until the lights went out. After that show Papi wanted to take everyone to Maxim's, but there was a limit to our energy, and the routine of full days and late nights was catching up on us.

Luckily the Piza sisters insisted on a trip to Versailles, and with our hired car we spent one whole leisurely Sunday there. Papi was a good sport, and after he had had all the walking he could take, he would contentedly find a café to sit in and let me wander as long as I wished. The whole thing, the size and the magnificence of the palace, and the stories that went with it, enthralled me. Then I had to see as much of the gardens as possible, and the Petit Trianon and the Grand Trianon. After years of reading about these things in school and studying travel

The Fabulous Twenties

pictures, here I was actually seeing them in full color and three dimensions!

To go still further and see the Château de Malmaison on the same afternoon was to be transported to an entirely different style and a different set of tales about the lives of Napoleon and Josephine—the paintings of David, the marble copy of the Canova statue of Josephine at home, the Rostand story of "L'Aiglon." We even had time to return to Versailles to sit on the main terrace to watch the playing of the fountains, the Jeux d'Eaux, the magnificent performance put on just for Sunday afternoons when not yet done with the addition of electric light effects.

That day and our last night ended with dinner at L'Ermitage Russe, another one of the famous Russian émigré restaurants that had become fashionable all over Paris after beginning as modest little places to feed and cheer the homesick displaced Russians. This one was large, but according to Papi the atmosphere was genuine, and was still a special treat for us as they had not yet proliferated in New York. We had our Russian food and the Russian service, then the gypsy violinist playing over our table, the deep-voiced gypsy woman singer, and finally the Caucasian dagger dances which always ended the evening on a state of satisfactory excitement. The next morning we had to be up at five-thirty, to leave for Holland.

Homeward Bound At Last!

Le Bourget, the new Paris airfield, was a long drive into the country, and this time we departed by ourselves. Our Dutch plane, a Fokker, of the KLM line, was a "large" one for a change—holding eight passengers!—and it flew at ten thousand feet, even smoothly though cold, and for the first time I had the thrill of flying above the clouds. It took us three hours to fly from Paris to Rotterdam; we went from there by taxi to the Hotel des Indes at the Hague. There at last a fat package of mail from home was awaiting us. There was plenty of business to keep Papi occupied and for me a series of communications with the final letter from President MacCracken that Miss Kluge would be allowed to arrive at Vassar ten days late.

We had only that one evening in the Hague and were expected for dinner at the home of the Kleykamp parents. It was a gay reunion of old friends, and we heard the wonderful news that Bonnie and Jan Kleykamp had reservations on the *Volendam,* going on the same trip as

ours back to New York. That meant we would have the same delightful
Captain de Koning who had been so cordial to us all on the trip over,
and of course we would all sit together at the captain's table.

What a different trip this was from the crossing in July! We had a
beautiful cabin on the upper deck, though the deck appeared cluttered
with baggage. The ship was familiar and felt like home. The stewards
recognized us wherever we appeared and treated us as old friends.
Certainly my feelings had changed. I was no longer the dutiful young
daughter sitting meekly beside my father, the formidable chaperone,
speaking only when spoken to and asking permission to be dismissed
whenever I had an idea or a desire of my own. There were people who
included me in games of deck tennis or shuffleboard, even those who
asked *me* personally to dance. Besides the Kleykamps and ourselves,
our group at the captain's table included a young Spanish lady,
Claudia, whom we had met in Paris with the Pizas; a tall youngish
Hollander, Martinus Nijhoff, who owned a well-known art bookshop
in the Hague; and a plumpish, prosperous German executive from a
large dyeworks near Cologne, Mr. Willi Voos. Everyone contributed
something to the animated sessions at the dinner table, as well as the
easy friendly meetings on deck during the day or in the smoking room
over bridge or in the ballroom at the nightly dancing. Being on special
terms with the captain meant frequent parties for cocktails in his
quarters on the bridge, or late nightcaps and snacks with him either
there or in the public salons. Not that I went along on all these
occasions, but when I didn't it meant that they were busy and I was left
to myself.

When we docked in New York on Saturday, September 25, Mami
was waiting for us on the pier, but this had been preceded by a
champagne party in our cabin all the way up the river from the pilot's
immigration stop, for the purpose of entertaining his old friend,
Colonel Costigan, the chief customs officer and his assistants. When it
came time for me to assemble all our trunks, packages, and handbags
on shore, to fumble with the bunch of keys and unlock everything,
while Papi sat on the sidelines with hat and cane, perspiring and
fanning himself, it seemed that our way had been smoothed. I met with
no complications at all; nobody was interested in going through our
pile of stuff; the papers were stamped; the chalk markings were
scratched on every piece—and we were off.

At home in Englewood the whole family was assembled, and I was
excited to be with them all again. Ty and Violet couldn't talk fast

enough to tell me about all their conquests and their gay times in Maine. Emile had grown inches and wanted to show off his real mannish, big-guy language. Sergey appeared with a broken arm in a plaster cast. That really threw Papi into a fit. Why hadn't he been informed about this? When he found out that Mami had managed things in her own way, he was even more volubly furious.

Mami had installed a new riding master to replace Major Stocker, the Englishman. This was Prince Kadir Guirey, a Circassian, one of the poor displaced Russians from New York, and she had moved him into the stable apartment with his wife and little son, Chinghiz. This cute little boy with curly hair was the same age as Sergey and should be a nice playmate. But Chinghiz was a bit wild and undisciplined by temperament—a real Tatar, as Papi would say—and he was very much at home with horses. Like an acrobat or a monkey he would ride bareback, turn somersaults, or stand on the horse's back and jump off with a flip, then land on the ground on his feet. Sergey, age five, had naturally tried to imitate him. But, instead of landing on his feet, he had landed flat on his side and broke his arm. Prince Guirey was a quiet and gentle man, and after this storm blew over we all loved riding with him. Violet especially learned a lot, not only about horses, but about life in the Caucasus and about the prince's long family history. After 1929 when we moved into New York, and acquired some of our horses at a bargain, he set up his own riding school, Boots and Saddles, in an old stable building near Park Avenue and escorted the children of fashionable society families as they rode the bridle paths of Central Park. Chinghiz himself grew up to be a fine American citizen and was an officer in the tank corps during World War II.

Homecoming that Saturday was busy and exciting, and the house was buzzing with people. By five o'clock that afternoon the Kleykamps and Captain de Koning had arrived, invited by Papi for a swim and dinner. It was another big evening, and no matter what the surprises or the behind-the-scene upheavals, Mami always carried things off smoothly and appeared to enjoy the swirling, bubbling big-family activity.

The next day, Sunday, was to be my scheduled appearance at college. All the traveling equipment was unpacked, and a different trunk was brought out of the attic. The fall wardrobe was assembled, plus some books and studying necessities. One also had to think of furnishings for one's college room: bedspread, pillows, pictures, and stuffed animals. In the early afternoon Papi and Mami drove me up to

Poughkeepsie and Vassar, a place I had never seen, but I was comforted immediately in having a roommate I knew, Betsy Bonbright, and five other girls from my class at Dwight already there. Some suspense!

By then I suppose I could take any amount of excitement. The campus looked beautiful; my room was in Main Hall, the oldest and central building; and I was greeted with open arms and lots of enthusiasm, a bewildering amount of chatter, and a touch of jealous curiosity. A message was waiting. President and Mrs. MacCracken were expecting Mr. and Mrs. Kluge and Miss Kluge for tea at the president's house. So off we went. With my training of respect for one's elders, I was terrified, but here was my first lesson—the attitude that pervaded the whole college: the young ladies were addressed as "Miss" and treated as adults; personal interest in each one extended beyond the classroom to friendly, informal contacts with the faculty; and now the president himself was doing everything he could to make me feel at ease and welcome. By the next day I had met all the new girls of our corridor, had registered and attended classes, bought a bike and a desk, and was already spinning giddily into a new experience that by some good fortune turned out most happily.

The Fabulous Twenties

21

The Vassar Experience

HOSE YEARS at Vassar flew by very fast. They were years full of discoveries, busy and challenging, with a growing feeling of independence and individuality, and not the least was the enjoyment of an entirely new way of life. But perhaps the greatest revelation was in the new friendships, a deep personal interest and closer understanding of a great variety of people. I was aware at home of having to defend my choice of friends who, in appearance or background or beliefs were sometimes not quite what the family was used to. By remarkable good fortune I was thrown into a "group" composed of girls from different parts of the country, different home and school backgrounds and different outlooks—yet all were pretty consistently interested in studying and, to my great relief, not the so-called frivolous types in competitive need for "men"!

There was tiny little Skip Cole, who was interested in art and drawing courses and whose aim from the beginning was to go on to graduate study to become a landscape architect. Imogene Steeves was already an advanced pianist and used to glow when talking about her composition class or while whistling a Bach fugue or passacaglia. Cynthia Flannery, with a bewitching sense of humor and an appalling figure, endeared herself by her concern for each particular person, taking all the courses there were in creative writing. Her greatest ambition was to have a story published; and indeed she did do quite a bit of writing in later years. Anna North, the modest daughter of a

doctor and known confidentially to be a "scholarship student," was   341
dedicated to biology and the sciences, but was also involved with art,
especially painting, as well as with writing. Her wide interests as well as
practical knowledge impressed us all.

From St. Paul and the mysterious Midwest there was Roberta Gal-
loway, small, birdlike, sparkling with laughter and wit. Libby Earhart
from Ann Arbor, tall and of great dignity, and a wonderful
horsewoman, was studying music, but also practical subjects like
economics. She never revealed that her successful industrialist family
kept a large estate; later on, she was obliged to help manage the
family's financial holdings. Her major reason for studying economics,
she used to say, was to be able to hold her own in arguments with her
distinguished and dynamic father. Averell Ross from Ardmore was the
delicate, dainty one, always the choice for ingénue parts in the plays
and always reminding us of our obligations to femininity when we were
carried away by touch football games or talk of the unmarried life of
true career women. Joanna Jennings from Long Island, with an inclination to become a nurse, was the selfless, concerned, "cheer-up"
spirit, who could lead a religious or philosophical discussion into the
wee hours of the night.

Then there was my first roommate, Betsy Bonbright, who at the
time was cracked on health foods and medical remedies, a bit inhibited
and brilliant, but who gushingly softened when playing her marvelous
records of romantic music. She later became a prominent psychiatrist.
Kay Smyth was the daughter of a prominent businessman from Englewood and was interested in philosophy and religion. She later
married a clergyman and became a world traveler as a missionary.
There was only one true "social butterfly" among us, Faith Adams
from Washington, D.C., whose life, talk, obligations, and wardrobe
were all geared to her family's position in the present and preparation
for hers in the future, and she drifted in and out of our group activities
or night-long sessions.

My extracurricular time was taken up with hockey, the class basketball team, riding in the gorgeous countryside, visiting other dorms for
evening bridge games, and—besides doing the amazing amount of
library work thrust upon us—putting in hours of piano practice. And
then there were endless discussion sessions through which each of us
became acquainted with the others' backgrounds, ideas, and often
family problems. Of these I certainly contributed my share, but I also
talked about Russia, stimulated in part by Miss Textor's Russian his-

tory course, and about Papi's and Mami's travels. A big event was always at Easter time, when I would bring Russian Easter eggs along with our traditional *paskha* and *kulich*.

❦ The New Freedom

Hardly three weeks after I had entered college and scarcely settled in when Papi announced that he was coming for the weekend, "to meet my friends"! I should arrange a luncheon for all of them and send him an accurate list of each of their names so that he could bring appropriate souvenirs. Good heavens, here we go again. Couldn't I be left alone? Must we always do something embarrassingly different? They arrived in the usual chauffeur-driven limousine, even bringing little sister Ty along. Everyone turned up at the flower-bedecked, place card-decorated table in the private dining room of a quaint college restaurant—and the affair was a great success. Papi, as was his custom, delved into each one's personal story and background, meanwhile telling his own fantastic tales in his spellbinding way. Mami, in her beautiful clothes and with her gentle manner, radiated charm and entertained with her own kind of revelations. She made such a deep impression that she was thereafter welcomed as an intimate friend and urged to tell more—stories which most of them have never forgotten.

Gradually I realized that for me life was becoming almost "normal," that is, like everybody else's—buying the same clothes, wearing my hair bobbed, free to go off by train (within the college regulations), visit other girls' homes as I chose, and meet young men on dates—if any of my friends could provide such (usually their brothers). Papi too was indulging my new independence! It was nothing to phone him and say I would like to have eight tickets for Saturday night for the most popular theater in town—to see *Show Boat, Rose Marie, Desert Song*—and he would produce them and make all the arrangements for dinner and a theater party. The winter of freshman year many of my friends were making their debut in New York or had a full schedule of attending other coming-out parties, tea dances, formal dinners, assembly balls, with all the protocol of receiving flowers and gifts, choosing the precious, just-right escort, who must have full-dress white-tie-and-tails, while she is being fitted for that super white ballgown with large full skirt and long white gloves. All the engraved invitations and complicated double and return envelopes kept coming in, and I had to decide how I would ever be able to attend even the minimum of these.

Princess in Paradise

❧ My Debut

Then one day in November Papi suddenly came out with: "What's all this? How do your friends do all this? Why shouldn't you have the same thing!" How could I explain to him that their families and they had been in the Junior League for years, that there were social lists of the proper young men and women to invite, that it was a kind of ingrown elite group, but that I didn't belong in New York City society at all. But Englewood! We should have a party to introduce you to the nice upper-class families of Englewood. Now suddenly we should pay attention to the Englewood upper crust whom we had held in contempt all these years. I knew a number of girls from Dwight, but boys! Those stiff, pimply-faced little fellows who lined the walls of the gym at the Senior Dance?

Anyhow, Mami approved the idea but was as helpless as I was about how to approach the practical matters. I had to write her and telephone from college to keep filling in details. Kay Smyth's mother was the only personal friend we had in Englewood circles, and an understanding one, with three daughters of her own. So Mami had to call on her for all the guidance and pointers in this fine business, and mostly for her to provide the *List* of Englewood's social eligibles. There were no problems with the expenses, the decor, the food, the orchestra, and all those arrangements which Mami loved as much as Papi did. It was to be a tea dance in the house on December 27, my eighteenth birthday, for about one hundred, mostly strangers or those who had laughed at us funny German kids as we grew up or spread stories about our crazy household at the top of the hill.

But I had one coup that could impress them all. Through my roommate Gwen I knew ten West Point cadets, always ready to get out and attend parties, and she could help me with their transportation and overnight housing. Engraved invitations went out; Papi's favorite Negro band, Deacon Doubleday, was booked; Maresi-Mazetti, our customary fancy caterer from New York, took care of the food; and there was to be a sit-down formal dinner for twenty-four in our dining room after the dance with more music later. I had to come to town frequently for fittings of that special dress. Oh, dear—back to the old insecurity. It was not the standard white tulle hoop-skirted, décolleté affair seen in all the pictures. Aunt Xenia designed it; the material selected was a very precious Indian sari of pale blue with lots of gold thread and those gorgeous borders that must somehow be preserved.

The Fabulous Twenties

Instead of being bouffant, it was draped slinkily around me like one of Mami's brocade evening dresses.

The great affair went off very nicely; at least I had to admit it was in some ways more fun than those routine, impersonal big affairs I had witnessed in New York. The house looked beautiful. Every corner was piled with fresh azaleas from our greenhouse; the big music room was really being used; and everyone had a chance to snoop around to satisfy their curiosity. Outside the police managed the traffic and the parking, but at the door stood the good old Cossack giant, Pokhom, with tall fur hat, gleaming gold buttons, and dagger at his belt. My new friends from Vassar and old friends from Dwight were there, and then those ever dependable and impressive cadets. I had hardly any impression of those Englewood boys.

Mr. Mazetti could produce a fantastically beautiful affair, but even more so when inspired by Mami's artistic ideas. The afternoon punch was served from a huge block of ice sculpture with a light inside. The dinner table centerpiece was a big tiered layer cake decorated with festoons of cream and luscious sugar roses. In what color?—pink and gray for Vassar, of course! There were the candy baskets with pink bows at each place, which went beautifully with Mami's best Sèvres flowered china set for twenty-four. The ice cream for dessert was in individual molds of bells, wreaths, or roses served on a nest of pink spun sugar. The music played on, and one got up to dance between courses. Everything went off just as it was planned.

New Discoveries

The summer following freshman year was spent free and un-planned at the house in Englewood. Now we really began to appreciate and enjoy some adult treatment and independence and to discover that home and our family could be fascinating attractions to our friends. Cynthia Flannery came to visit, driving her father's big gray Packard touring car and bringing a jolly foursome with her. Betsy and Ruth Keeler had identical tan Chrysler roadsters and would bring other friends to ride and swim all day. Averell Ross came for a weekend and was fascinated by the exotic collection of birds, animals, oriental rugs, stained glass, palms, and massive furniture that filled the house. A new experience for her was the otherworldly formality of the dining room table—not just the Sunday dinners, but the everyday affairs—which to us was always a standard custom: Papi at one end of the table sharing a glass of wine with his sons and Mami at the other end receiving the thanks (in Russian) for the meal from each child, the boys kissing her hand formally and the girls giving her the usual embrace.

In addition to our own exotic household appendages like Xenia, Ludmilla, and Igor, they were attracted by the constant stream of outside visitors from abroad or New York, some with distinguished names, others with queer Italian or Russian accents or sensational appearances, all with an interminable stream of exciting stories and voluble conversation.

On the other hand, I got away to see how others lived and discover a whole circle of new places. There were house parties in Ann Arbor, Michigan; in Philadelphia; at Fisher's Island; in Stonington, Connecticut; or at an Adirondack "camp." The entertainment was not always elaborate; indeed, it often just grew out of the bubbling energy and enthusiasm of our group.

During sophomore year, which went along with much the same balance of study and friendly distractions as in freshman year, the family took an apartment in New York at 1111 Park Avenue. It had long been Mami's dream to enjoy an easier winter in town, and it was a spacious and beautifully furnished place. Ty and Mule came in from boarding schools for Sundays or the weekend, and I could so easily get off at the 125th Street station anytime I chose to come in, bringing guests for some special party or an opera or maybe even a class assignment.

Life at Vassar

In the light of my later experience in colleges and universities, I can look back now at my years at Vassar with a great deal of pride, love, and affection. First there was the warm and friendly atmosphere, created primarily as I have described, by the wonderful circle of friends I was fortunate enough to encounter. Then there was the cordial and enthusiastic attitude of those men and women who were responsible for the administration of the college and who by their example set the intellectual and social tone of the institution.

Most important among these was the prexy himself, Henry Noble MacCracken, a distinguished Chaucer scholar and superb speaker with a genial, outgoing personality, whose friendly presence was felt at practically every event and building on that campus. Then there were the wardens, like Jean Palmer, whose attractive appearance, good

Scene from "The Pageant of the Medici" at Vassar, 1928.

humor, and gracious hospitality made her a symbol of Vassar to many generations of students. When I arrived she was "Head Warden," which, by the way, did not refer to the chief officer of a prison guard, but was an Engligh title for the head of a division of a college. Characteristically, it was President MacCracken, along with several other prominent faculty members, who took part in a gorgeous outdoor spring pageant on the Medici, which was put on by the student dramatic society, Philaletheis. Prexy, of course, played the leading role of Lorenzo, and I was selected—I suppose because of my yellow hair—as Simonetta. It was my first (and last) experience in a dramatic performance, but it was fun.

There were distinguished teachers, well known in their respective fields, like Herbert Elmer Mills in economics, and Helen Lockwood in English, who were kindly, open personalities, always ready to talk with students. My favorite became Lucy Elizabeth Textor, a handsome white-haired lady of great personal charm who had traveled in Russia many times, both before and after the Revolution. She had therefore known both sides of the Russian political scene, the old and the new,

Princess in Paradise

had personally met Stalin, and was very cynical about the glorious "worker's paradise" of the new regime. At one time she described an interview with Stalin who, in response to a comment on inefficient railroad managers and strikers in America, suggested, "Why don't you shoot them? We do." This is what we at home knew from family experience.

I discovered that Vassar was not just a "little college somewhere in upstate New York." There were visiting artists and teachers who made a strong impression, especially in the creative writing field. One was Dorothy Canfield Fisher, a close friend of our Professor Margaret Pollard Smith, who talked about the writing of her novels and short stories; Hervey Allen taught there for a time, having just published his famous biography of Edgar Allan Poe (*Israfel*), and was already at work on his *Anthony Adverse*, which became a bestseller when it came out in 1933.

I had always admired the strong and virile character of Vachel Lindsay's poetry but had difficulty adjusting to his weak, singsong manner as he recited the poems for us. Will and Ariel Durant lectured on the problems of writing world history. And there were numerous lectures by the famous Arctic explorer Vilhjalmur Stefansson, particularly on his pioneer experiences in surviving the polar temperatures by adopting the living habits of the Eskimos, an idea that fascinated me even at that time.

For me, as for most of my friends, college in those precious years meant personal independence and freedom from parental supervision. But there were limitations. A printed code of social regulations was given to each of us so that we would know the rules. One had to be in her dormitory by 10:00 P.M. There were no long walks without a chaperone; daytime car rides longer than three hours had to have the warden's permission, as did all-day or weekend excursions to the city. Men were not allowed to be entertained in the dormitory rooms without a chaperone. Since "smoking among women is not established as a social convention acceptable to all groups," it was simply not approved.

Strict as the rules may have appeared to some, they were decidedly liberal compared with what I was used to at home, so they never bothered me. Besides, our wardens were always very understanding and cooperative, and as time went on, the rules were gradually modified. A door left slightly ajar during visiting hours was interpreted as

The Fabulous Twenties

equivalent to the presence of a chaperone, and smoking rooms were later established in each dormitory. Many of us became very adept at getting around the rules when the occasion required it.

Compared with the institutional life styles of later generations, the kind of life we lived at Vassar during those years was modest, but in an atmosphere of dignity and refinement. The mood was partly set by the architecture itself. The long wide corridors of Old Main Hall designed in 1865 by James Rudwich, provided a spacious promenade area for the Victorian ladies of Matthew Vassar's day to walk up and down in formal dress with their gentleman friends. Of course, when we entertained a group of Yale boys for one of our Saturday night "J" dances or when their glee club gave a concert, our girls were by no means stuffy Victorian "ladies," but just the same they were always very attractive and elegant.

Our meals were taken together in the beautiful, high-ceilinged dining room in Main. Tables were set with shining white tablecloths and fresh, ironed napkins. We had waitresses. Though there were always complaints about the food, the menus were varied, and I thought the food was good, with homemade bread and a general emphasis on the milk, vegetables, chicken, and other produce from the college's farm. For exotic relief we would walk out to Cider Mill, off campus, or to an ancient restaurant known as Smith Brothers for cider and doughnuts or what we called the "Vassar Devil," a concoction of devil's food cake, with thick chocolate frosting, topped with ice cream, heavy whipped cream, more chocolate sauce, and chopped nuts with a big red cherry on top of that.

Through all these varying aspects of student fun and serious living, there was plenty of evidence of the glamourous opulence characteristic of the late 1920s, but I was deeply impressed by the modest and genuine respect for what I was beginning to regard as basic values.

To the snide comments I used to hear about Vassar being a prestige institution for rich girls, I have often added the fact—which was never talked about—that at this time at least a third of the students were working at some job or other to help with their expenses.

❧ The Trip To Hawaii

The family was always acquiring new friends of various descriptions and from places far and wide. That is where the Keuls and the other Dutch bridge players came in, but the newest, most ardent friendships cultivated were the Carl Jantzens, who in the summer of 1928, invited me to join them on their trip to the Hawaiian Islands. I had to get across the continent to Portland. Although I felt perfectly capable of traveling by myself on a train, I was sent under the escort of Albert Lear, Papi's factory manager who had grown up with the family since the days of being valet and courier on their wedding trip. This was to be no simple, direct progress from one terminal to the other. No, there was a scheduled stopover in Detroit to conduct some business and to renew acquaintances by entertaining Mr. Rosenberg in our hotel. In Chicago we were met by charming friends from their world cruise who drove me on a tour of the city while Albert went about the business. For lunch we went to the Drake Hotel, the very newest, with its airy dining room overlooking the lake. When Marie Price pulled out a cigarette, and I in my new independence did the same, the head waiter very discreetly drew Mr. Price aside and told him ladies were not allowed to smoke in the dining room.

After five days of train travel across the prairies and the mountains, I entered an entirely new world of living, western style, and I was carried away by it—by the informality, the absence of pretensions, the simple but functional houses, the self-created entertainment, and the personal openness.

It was a glorious summer. I had a wonderful time in Portland as I described earlier. We sailed on one ship from Seattle to San Francisco, then on the newest Matson Line steamer, the S.S. *Malolo*, to Honolulu where we were greeted by business friends of both families with armfuls of leis. Most of the time we stayed at the new pink Royal Hawaiian Hotel right on Waikiki where the manager, Mr. Benaglia, was an old friend of the Kluges, having been manager of the Banff Springs Hotel for years. Oneita and I had our fun swimming and lounging, conscious of being ogled at as we appeared in one new, brightly colored, tight-fitting Jantzen suit after the other. The idea was not to use us as models alone but especially to give Mr. Jantzen the opportunity to watch people's reactions to his new colors and styles. Even Mr. Jantzen was modeling his new departure in men's suits—the two-piece look with flesh-colored top and dark trunks woven as one. In fact, Waikiki at that time was the only known beach where men were allowed to appear in trunks without tops.

We were taken on interesting trips to the other islands, usually an overnight sail on the little interisland ships, like the *Waialeale*, that bounced unmercifully over the waves. From Hilo we drove through

The Fabulous Twenties

the tropical rain forest with towering fern trees up to see the volcano Kilauea, now a quiet plateau with a hole in it, and stood on the same porch of the Volcano House, where my parents were in 1924. We spent the night in little cottages belonging to it, with fountains of steam coming up through the rocks, where Oneita and I leaned over to curl our hair. On Kauai we visited the family of Oneita's roommate from the University of Oregon, the Davidsons, who managed the general store. They took us in a heavy vehicle through pineapple plantations, up and down the Waimea Canyon where we saw water running uphill in the irrigation ditches, and on picnics out on the mountainous sand dunes or the lush, rocky, volcanic pools along the shore. When it was all over, I tried to remember my family training and arranged, with Mr. Benaglia's help, a special dinner party as thanks to my friends—a private dining room, our own native singer and hula dance entertainment, and gardenia corsages for the ladies.

To get home from San Francisco a different route had been planned for me. I went by train to Boulder, Colorado, where Ty, by some great coup, had managed to be sent on her own, to visit her Dwight roommate, Peggy Earle, whose father was a cattle rancher. Boulder was a charming small university town which just merged into the mountainous ranch country. Another unforgettable revelation was the handsome people, cultivated and thoroughly informed, with individual homes and life styles, and who took the greatest joy in their native surroundings and sources of entertainment. Ty and I returned together on the four-day dusty trip of the Burlington *Zephyr*, reminding each other of all the cautionary lectures we had heard about not accepting drinks from strange men, not smelling any bouquet of roses you might receive because they might be chloroformed, and always walking with your eyes straight ahead in great dignity! On our next big trip together, to Europe in 1929, we were still constantly mindful of all those things nice young ladies were supposed to do, but by then we felt ourselves secure and sophisticated enough to decide how we might dare to digress from the regime.

With this visit to Colorado and the return trip on the train, I found Ty entirely changed. Well, my little sister was really "grown-up" and quite a person. Even though she was just about to be a senior at Dwight, she seemed so much more socially at ease than I had ever been. She was bubbling with jokes and pranks and laughter; she knew what she wanted in sophisticated clothes; and she had a bush of flaming curly red hair that she piled up at the back of her head in the most bewitch-

Princess in Paradise

ing fashion. She was the one who had the nerve to speak to strangers. She was the one everybody turned to look at when we entered the diner. In a bridge or poker game she could hold her own with the most serious professional expression on her face and take in her tricks with an expert's flourish. From now on, with sort of mutual admiration or respect, we became a "team." We understood each other's tastes and desires, supplemented each other in conversation or tight situations, and knew all the tricks to get around Papi or thwart the discipline that was still comparatively strict at home.

The Year of the Great Crash

The year 1929 rolled in with as much excitement, social activity, hope, personal freedom, and feeling of opulence as ever—even a little more so. A third automobile was now added in the stable; besides the Cunningham touring car which drove Papi to work every day, and the gray Packard limousine for Mami, there was a new "modest little" black Buick four-door sedan, which I was allowed to drive, presumably for errands, but also actually for my pleasure. The day after my eighteenth birthday I had gone down to the village to get a driver's permit, and soon thereafter, with Mami's tactful prompting, I had openly produced a driver's license. Besides all my comings and goings from Poughkeepsie and much more friendly visiting around Englewood, Ty, in her senior year at Dwight, was beginning to expand into all sorts of gay activities and was having a much easier time of it with the family than I had had.

The house in Englewood was open for Christmas vacation and a month or two after that, before the family moved into the apartment on Park Avenue. On January 20 there was an enormous elaborate celebration for Mami's and Papi's twentieth wedding anniversary. It was held at the Swiss Chalet, an intimate German inn between Englewood and Paterson. Prohibition being still in effect, one had to be on very friendly terms with the innkeeper, and depend on his good relationship with the local police. Either one sent in all his own wines or trusted the quality of what the establishment could provide. For Mami perhaps there were fewer headaches than if it were held at home, but as always she had to do things with all her special touches and attention, from supervising the floral centerpieces to bringing over her silver candelabra and candy dishes, to the printed souvenir menus and place cards. The grandest personal affair, here just as at home, was the big

The Fabulous Twenties

zakuska table, with its special Russian linen cloth, carafes of vodka and aperitifs, chafing dishes with hot tidbits, a centerpiece of caviar on ice, platters of molded salads, assorted fish in sauces—and all the spreads, crackers, and relishes to go with it.

Then followed the dinner dance for fifty, with one large U-shaped smilax-bedecked central table and a lot of small tables circled around the dance floor, candles and flowers on each, with Deacon Doubleday's Negro jazz band playing once again till the wee hours. What was new and nice was that we "children," all assembled from our schools, had quite a representation of younger people. During the past summer we had met Norbert MacKenna (whose father was the mayor of Englewood) and Dave Richardson, both graduated from Princeton and working for General O'Ryan in his North Salem real estate development business. Between them they had a nice big Packard, and we considered them much more sophisticated and special than our high school and college acquaintances.

There were still a couple of cadets on the string, Ty having now discovered the charms of West Point, and there was our ever faithful family friend Andy Wineburg from Great Neck, Long Island, who also owned an open Packard. As long as any of these young men came to our home and could pass muster with the family, we were allowed to entertain them. It was when we were invited out, on "dates," in their cars, to weekend house parties, and especially to dinner or affairs in New York (which did actually involve the hazards of speakeasies and questionable roadhouses) that we went through a grueling cross-questioning before and after, were put on a time schedule, and could be sure that Papi would have the house lights burning and be awake to greet us when we arrived home.

I had another faithful follower, Dave Rowland at Harvard, who carried on a sort of mystery man correspondence ever since he had met me fleetingly at Camp Mudjekeewis with his sister. He tried to be intellectual but was polite and dull. However, he could be counted on to take me to at least one football game a season and one good theater preceded by a properly elegant dinner. Then there was Percy Jennings, Joanna's brother at Yale, who came over the horizon during sophomore year. He was just right. He came to college with a bunch of sturdy, healthy friends. We all played football, swam, and picnicked as a gang, had no problems exchanging dances as nobody was attached, and all were invited back to Yale at the same time. That's how I happened to spend the beautiful spring weekend called "Derby Day" at Yale with Percy. It was full of all the rah-rah college traditions of the time—open roadsters piled full of shouting, waving people, the young men in their blazers and "boaters" (the flat-brimmed straw hats), picnics beside the river, some groups busy with flasks and pouring drinks into paper cups, then rushing from one tea dance to dinner in town and on to another big dance, and even organized breakfast parties. There were the crew races on Saturday, the occasion for the whole thing, but of course one didn't take that too seriously.

However, during this time my romance with "Mac" MacKenna seemed much more interesting and became more complicated. He was older and seemed more experienced. He was romantic and ardent and flattering, and he was very persistent. Being independent of such college obligations and apparently prosperous in "some sort of business on Wall Street," he could come to college any time, would shower me with gifts, and even offered to leave his car there for me to drive.

So I fell seriously in love. But the family was not pleased; any young man who came to pay attention to either of us—Ty or me— individually and was not one of a gay bunch, was looked upon with defensive suspicion. Then when they realized that my new rebelliousness was no longer just adolescent grumpiness and that I might take things into my own hands, they got panicky. I was ordered not to see any more of Mac and he was made decidedly unwelcome at the house.

I was confused but I had made up my mind that I was not going to submit. Papi called him an opportunist, unrealiable, a Wall Street customer's man—which didn't sound nice—though I didn't understand it. Mami arrived at college suddenly to spend a weekend with me—specifically to persuade me not to take this affair seriously, not to build up any dreams, not to be carried away recklessly. She was always haunted by her sister Xenia's running away from home and not finishing her education. Then she said in her incomparable way: "And I don't think you would be intellectually compatible!" The natural reaction of any young person in love would be "how snobbish," and if it were so, well, people change—and I can improve him! True, he wasn't interested in the theater or music or the opera, as I noticed when I tried initiating him by taking him to *Parsival*, but he spun great plans about how successful he would be in business.

As a rebel now, I had to finagle my own arrangements. In the process I learned a great deal from Ty who, as a senior in Dwight School and president of her class, had reached a peak of independence, maturity, and success. She was popular and sensational with her flaming red hair, a big laugh, and a devilish sense of humor, continually sporting naughty jokes and bright repartee. She wore daringly short, tight, low-cut dresses and was extremely attractive to young men. If she couldn't get permission from home or school to go rumble-seat riding in sports cars or be taken to night club parties, she managed to be invited properly for weekend visits by mothers of her friends or the older sisters of nice families with an active group of younger brothers.

All my friends at college, on Long Island, or in Connecticut understood and cooperated, so that when I was invited to their weekend houseparties, Mac was automatically included. I would be able to provide his car and he contributed attractively to the general fun.

Then too, both Ty and I had a charming ally at home in our black Belgian-colonial chauffeur, Peter, who had recently been added to the staff as the successor to Jake. He was a handsome man, cooperative, and understood our problem with Papi's imperious resistance to any new idea that had to do with our social activities. We inveigled him into teaching both of us to drive the car—we never dared to ask Papi for permission—and he worked patiently with us, on odd occasions during our first grinding, jerky lessons on the big Packard limousine.

When he delivered the mail from the village post office to Mr. Kluge at breakfast at eight in the morning, he had already taken out our personal letters—all those passionate "Special Deliveries" which arrived daily for both of us—and dropped them in a box in the bushes beside the back door. If Ty was supposedly going to some innocent young girls' slumber party, he would discreetly deliver her to whatever friend's home, be it in New Jersey or Westchester, where there was a lively mixed houseparty scheduled. Sometimes instead of dropping me off at the 125th Street station to catch the train for Poughkeepsie, Peter would look the other way when we came upon Mac's Chrysler roadster parked casually on some side street waiting to drive me back to college.

So it went on through June and the early part of the summer. Ty had graduated from Dwight with great success and the usual fanfare and I was home from college, happy, excitedly in love, and quite oblivious to outside happenings. But there was something ominous going on, both at home and in the giddy way of life that was everywhere to be seen. As I look back on it now, I should have been aware that there must have been family rumblings about me personally as well as the curious parallel in the general economic situation.

Princess in Paradise

Wall Street, the name and the connotations, meant absolutely nothing to me or any of us children at that time. Many of the visitors to Englewood, we heard, were "on Wall Street." Papi used to be very interested in them and have long discussions and apparently was asking for advice or having dealings with some. As usual, the "children" were kept in the dark about such things as financial affairs or business or even such a project as selling off part of our Englewood land and starting a real estate development. Each of us would pick up what we might understand or notice in conversations, a sigh or a hint from Mami ("I don't like that man!"), or gauge the mood a certain person cast upon the two of them. Apparently everyone we knew was "playing the stock market." Cousin Albert, who owned the factory at Pompton Lakes, was putting money into all sorts of projects. His brother, Willard Kluge in Montclair, was boasting about the millions he could make in one day—and was obviously spending accordingly. As we children later were to learn, although the E. H. Kluge business was running along prosperously, there had been some supplement to provide all those extravagant pleasures on the side.

V

From Romance to Marriage

"Their two daughters in turn fell in love, each being betrothed to a royal prince."

Ty and Sa; before the double wedding, 1932.

22

To Keep Us Out Of Trouble

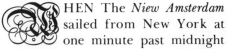 HEN The *Niew Amsterdam* sailed from New York at one minute past midnight on July 22, 1929, the Kluge sisters were aboard, feeling like two lonely waifs. No gay farewell party had preceded our departure; we knew no friendly passengers and were just introduced to the captain into whose watchful care two docile-looking young girls were entrusted. As a matter of fact, we were practically railroaded aboard. No discussions, no explanations, no plans had preceded our sudden departure. Even our trunks had been packed by somebody else. Sa and Ty were being shipped off to Europe for the summer "to keep us out of trouble"!

What happened?! It was shortly after the big July Fourth celebration that I became ill and had to have a tonsillectomy, then was sick in bed for three weeks with a high fever and general infection—and was very miserable.

One evening, Ty came into my bedroom and announced casually: "Sa, we're going to Europe!"

"How? What? Where? With whom?—and—when?" said I with a weak jump of surprise.

"Well, it's been arranged that the Schmitzes, who are going on a motor trip late in August, will take us along." The Ernst Schmitzes, a jolly, fortyish, German couple—he was then director of the German Tourist Bureau—were currently very good friends of the family, and we all enjoyed them, too.

359

"What are we supposed to do in the meantime?"

"Oh, we'll go around visiting the relatives in Krefeld."

"But how long is this Schmitz trip to last? Where do we end up? Will we get back in time for the beginning of my year at Vassar?"

"I don't know anything more. It seems Uncle Albert in Berlin is to be in charge of us and our headquarters for mail and directions from home." Finances and business arrangements never entered our heads.

"To keep us out of trouble—ha!!" We considered ourselves at nineteen and seventeen to be quite self-sufficient young ladies. After more than a month of the usual frenetic social activity, which the family apparently felt they could no longer completely control, here I was confined to bed at home with this miserable fever. I was depressed, defiant—and lonely. Every so often Ty managed to arrange for Mac to visit of an evening, bringing him through the kitchen and up the back stairs while some engrossing bridge game was going on downstairs. It was at this low point that we received the announcement of our trip to Europe. Ty had no great desire to leave all her fun, and I was too weak to do much thinking.

In this state we were deposited aboard the *Niew Amsterdam*. However, though all I wanted to do was to sleep and dream in a deck chair, Ty still managed to bump casually into the good-looking young Dutch officers as they came down from the bridge or sit attractively at the edge of the dance floor. The passenger roster was decidedly middle-aged, dignified, and dull.

This was Ty's first trip to Europe. I, of course, had already been through some of the experiences and had had a bit of training in the customs and etiquette of visiting relatives and formal older people. The first big event came on our arrival in Holland. After docking late in the day, being met by family friends, the Kees Hermsens, the art dealers, and driven to the home in the Hague of the venerable old father, head of the family, it was already dark, dinnertime, and the end of an exhausting day. Papi must have still been on their list of preferential customers, for there we found the the whole clan assembled, young and old, to offer the proper welcome to two young ladies from America. We went through much the same ceremony as I had on my first visit in 1926—the long, elaborately set table in the somber, oppressively furnished dining room, the wines, the toasts, one course following another with the solicitous urging "you must try this," without knowing what to expect next—and finally, the luscious, huge whipped-cream layer cake. Ty, sitting opposite me, was full of curiosity

Princess in Paradise

and started plunging right into it all. Then I caught some side glances of puzzlement, a hint of a sigh—and, by the time of the arrival of the final cake—a hopeless look heavenward of "Do I really have to go through with this?"

Our stop at the Hague was short, but it proved the beginning of our tourist sightseeing indoctrination. From there we went on to Krefeld by train, a short trip but the first time we crossed a border by ourselves and the handling of all our baggage. Somewhat nervously we fumbled with bunches of keys for the customs inspection and, quite unassisted, operated with gestures and jibberish in a foreign language. Fortunately, in Krefeld we stayed with our young married cousin, Margot Vetter, who steered us through all the protocol of calls on elderly relatives with endless teas and dinners and trying to sort out who was who and which belonged to whom. Through all of this Ty was picking up her German, much longer forgotten than mine had been, amusing everyone with her unabashed attempts and mixed-language wording—something like our dialect Pennsylvania Dutch—or addressing a dignified streetcar conductor with *Du*, the intimate form, the other passengers looking on wide-eyed. This mishmash English and German soon became a joke and almost a habit between us, as we tried to invent new phrases and handy bypasses of words we didn't know. "Ich hab'mein HORN ge-TOOTED" or "Dass kann ich ganz schon MANAGEN" were some that just came out easily.

The trip to Berlin gave us the chance to become more intimately acquainted with relatives and friends whom I had known before but Ty had only heard about. These included our uncle Albert (the disciplinarian and supposedly our manager) and our cousin Rita, our age and somewhat more sophisticated than the small-town Krefeld types. She had spent a year in England and also had been sent to a school in Switzerland to learn French. We heard lots about her best friend, Liesel, who had gone on the same trips with her, and her family, the Holzers, who were also the most intimate friends of the Kluge parents and close neighbors living in a large house in the same Grunewald district of Berlin. Besides, we saw photographs and heard stories about Liesel's brother Eric and his friend, Friedel Pschorr, who happened to have been at the University of London the same year the two girls were in England, and coincidentally at the University in Geneva while they were in Switzerland. However, just at the time of our Berlin visit the whole Holzer family was away traveling, so though we did not meet them, we felt we knew them quite well.

From Romance to Marriage

By the time we were to meet up with Mr. and Mrs. Schmitz in Munich, we had already become pretty adept tourists on our own and had discovered the delights of that beautiful city. The motor trip, through Salzburg, Innsbruck, Merano, and Venice, being driven in a comfortable car with interesting unscheduled stops, being registered in the nicest of the "native" hotels, having company while dining and being allowed to be on our own for after-dinner entertainment, was pleasant indeed. But somehow we began to feel uncomfortable. Mail from home—and especially allowances—reached us quite intermittently. We were not quite sure if we were guests of the Schmitzes, whether some arrangement had been made with them by the family to take care of us, or—Were we supposed to be paying our own way?

If we went to the hotel *Tanz-Bar* for the evening we could at least order our own bottle of wine. Also we discovered and had to inquire the meaning of the word "gigolo"! Two unaccompanied, obviously "American girls" could receive a lot of attention from those charming, smooth-dancing, fascinatingly mature conversationalists. We found them even turning up around the swimming pool in the daytime or popping out of the bushes at our tea table in the garden.

Summer was nearing its end, and we had no idea of plans for "what next." Hints developed into more definite orders. It would be best for both of us if we stayed in Europe over the winter and completed a little more "education," meaning by that some nice finishing school for young ladies. Ty was anxious to take up art somehow. I desperately wanted to go back to finish my last year at Vassar. There was no way at that late date that I could register in some foreign program and receive credit for it. And who was to decide where we should settle down? Strait-laced Uncle Albert thought Lausanne or perhaps Paris (!) would be best for us. We had already fallen in love with Munich, and as a matter of fact had done some research of our own.

Cables went back and forth, then pleading letters, and the Schmitzes were instructed to deposit us in Munich until Mami could come over and make the decisions. We were to meet her in Paris during the first week of October.

Meanwhile we found ourselves a most pleasant pension on Franz-Josefstrasse with a big room which included the midday meal taken with all the other guests. The matter of *Heitzung* (heating) was not mentioned. As the September air from the nearby Alps descended on the city, the temperatures grew colder and colder. Then we noticed the sign saying, "Heat will not be turned on until October 1"—and we with all our lovely summer clothes! And again it was a long time between checks from home.

By then we were getting used to solving our problems and making a very humorous affair out of each. We spent the mornings in our beds tucked warmly under the enormous *plumeaux* those lush silk-covered eiderdown quilts, until time for the already included hot dinner. Then it was an excursion, on foot, to some museum, preferably with a stone facade on the sunny side or a café where we could bask and read in the warm sunshine, ending up with hot chocolate and a sandwich before heading for a concert hall where we could take standing room for one mark (25 cents).

Thus the days passed. We weren't exactly bored, but we would have liked to have had some company. Like good little girls, we had heard all the dire warnings of talking to strangers in a restaurant or walking the downtown streets at night or avoiding the dimly lit cozy-looking bars where proper ladies were supposedly not welcome. Still it was inevitable that we would be hailed or followed—with those extremely short skirts, those prosperous-looking American clothes. Ty thought it was great kicks to have someone trailing after us muttering "Hey!—Amerikan gir-rls!" or "Hallo pretty Fraulein!" while I, in all my big sister dignity, kept whispering "Walk faster! Keep looking straight ahead." But one evening we had a little lesson, amusing in its way. Being fed up with a big burly character trailing behind us and unable to shake him, we went up to a handsome youthful policeman standing in the shadows and asked him to help us out; and he, in the broadest Bavarian drawl, came out with, "That's your own affair. I can't do anything about it!"

Every day walking along Franz-Josefstrasse from the main street, Ludwigstrasse, to our pension we noticed as we passed the same cute car, a gray Packard roadster, parked in front of the same apartment house, and knew enough to recognize it had Berlin license plates. What's more, with closer snooping we discovered a little monogram on the door: "G. H." Now, from all the pictures Rita had shown of those foreign trips we knew the Holzer son had a Packard roadster and also that Mrs. Holzer's name was Gertrude, and that sometime later that season the young man would be attending the University of Munich.

It was not a question of daring but of the proper formalities. In a wink we had out one of our very correct engraved visiting cards with Englewood, N.J., on it and wrote a little note: "If this car belongs to Eric Holzer please telephone No. 13 60 51, contact the Kluge sis-

From Romance to Marriage

ters," and deposited it on the seat of the car. Wonder of wonders, by suppertime we were summoned to the hall phone to hear a male voice with a very British accent exclaiming in amazement that indeed it was he, the Eric Holzer from Berlin, friend of Rita and the Albert Kluge family, and how decidedly clever it was of us to have deduced all this so correctly. "Now, please, can't I take you out for tea or something? When can we meet?" The answer to two maidens' prayers!

From then on it was wonderful. There was someone to take us out to tea or supper, urging us to eat all we wanted, then taking us on drives up to the mountains or to famous historical sights and obscure, picturesque villages, and most specially, someone to talk to. He steered us to contacts that would help us find better rooms or a family to live with. We discovered that the semester at the university began on November 1, and it would be practically impossible to get in. But there was one loophole worth exploring. The university accepted such a thing as *Gasthörer* (auditors) who, by paying a fee and getting special permission from each professor concerned, could attend lectures without prerequisites or without having to take exams. Then came the problem of facing endless corridors with closed doors, perhaps getting into an office with formidable females behind formidable counters and trying to make ourselves understood, just to try to get some information and perhaps finally some printed bulletin telling something about the courses being offered.

From Eric we learned who the renowned and most worthwhile professors were; those he recommended would be more important to hear rather than worrying about the subject they taught. One of these was Wilhelm Pinder, the art historian known internationally for his books and theories, who lectured to enraptured audiences in the largest auditorium available. Another popular lecturer was Professor Richard Kutscher, who gave a course on the history of the theater and arranged that his students should have special tickets to theater performances in Munich as well as out of town. A final choice was a history of the world war (World War I) given by Gustave Frauenholz. Of course, all this was speculative. The professors could not be contacted until their august official office appointments near November 1—and most important of all, we had no permission from home!

🌿 Paris and Back to Munich

So off we went to Paris, to meet Mami who was bringing along the trunks with our winter clothes. Mami was the usual youthful, funloving, understanding companion. We did the tourist routine together—monuments, museums, Versailles, the boulevards and shops, the palatial old hotels, and even the cafés. But faithful to her duty, Mami also had to lead us around to look at rooms and interview aristocratic, impoverished old ladies who would just love to take in two Americans for a season, who would pay for room and board and "private instruction." Ty and I saw everything with prejudiced eyes and regaled her with enthusiastic descriptions of the marvelous things we had already seen in Munich. Quite logically Mami could see that we would be nothing but discontented in Paris and that these vague "educational opportunities" were impossible to arrange at the last minute. So she agreed. "All right, I'll go back to Munich with you and look over the situation." And she cabled Papi accordingly.

Several days before we were to leave, we three were sitting in a café on the rue de Rivoli at lunchtime. Suddenly we noticed the newspaper boys running up and down the streets waving and selling "extras" of the Paris edition of the *Herald-Tribune*. People crowded around to buy the paper, then scurried off with excited calls to others, including patrons in the restaurants who left their tables, heads shaking, and heading off to the downtown center. The date was Wednesday, October 30, 1929, and the headlines were an assorted jumble: "Panic Hits Wall Street"; "Stocks Collapse in 16-Million Share Day"; "Greatest Stock-Market Catastrophe of All History." All banks were mobbed; so, too, were the travel bureaus, with Americans by the thousands frantically trying to get home.

Not many people, at least not we three women, quite understood all that this meant, nor the impact it would have on our future. If Mami had news from Papi, she was silent about it. We went ahead with our plans. In Munich we introduced her to the family we had found through the help of the Foreign Student Office (Auslands-Stelle), which we had already selected as practically ideal. Herr Rittmeister Kuno Cless and his young wife Franziska, with two preteen-age daughters and his refined old mother, lived in a spacious, bright, tastefully furnished apartment, complete with grand piano, on the sixth floor of a quite modern building in the near-suburb of Bogenhausen just across the Isar River, with a handy tram connection direct to the center of town. We were all invited to tea—inspection from both sides! Mami just glowed from the first minute—seeing the elegant surroundings, the charming, concerned people, the generous two-room arrangement of bedroom and den that would be ours—and the Clesses on

From Romance to Marriage

their part fell in love with Mami. We were approved! Possartstrasse 9 was to become our home for the next six months.

Now we could proceed with the endless complications and formalities of getting ourselves enrolled in our chosen activities. First came trips to the police department and the consulate for permission to stay more than three months—and hardly anything can be more forbidding than the German bureaucracy and the multiuniformed personnel engaged in it. Then came introductions at the bank—the Anhaeuser Bank in the Löwengrube where we would call every month for our bank draft, respectfully taking off our right-hand glove to shake hands with a certain upper-echelon clerk while he made polite inquiries about our family. After we had obtained all the proper papers from the university, the next stop was at the offices of the city transit company to show our student indentification, foreigner's permit, and passport, by which we could obtain a student pass on the trolley system—provided we paid a monthly call to the *Büro* to have a new colored stamp affixed. Incidentally, the nicest, easiest free pass we received was the one Mr. Cless presented to us for entrance to the UFA movie theater, since he was the local director. Before realizing that we would be kept busy enough, we dutifully looked into our customary cultural obligations. Ty was to join the Hoffmann School of Art for a life drawing class and I enrolled in the Trapp Music School for twice-a-week piano lessons.

But back to "entering the University of Munich"! For about the first ten days of November we put in daily appearances at a series of offices and managed to squeeze in calls on our various chosen professors for their permission to audit their lectures—this after finally receiving the very highest, elaborately inscribed document from the *Rektor* himself testifying to the admission of each of us as *Gasthörerin*.

Our German had already improved, but many a time we floundered with our questions and were confused by the rapid-fire answering stream from the officious secretaries. One of those days in a crowded office we noticed black-and-white saddle shoes on the feet of a personable-looking young man. We ourselves were always pretty distinguishable as Americans by our own saddle shoes.

Without a moment's hestitation Ty pushed her way up to him and said in English, "Could you help us?

"No doubt about it, I'd love to try. This is the worst runaround I've ever been in."

And Ty reported back to me: "He's from Yale!"

Princess in Paradise

And so we became acquainted with Bob Radsch, American student, not touring Europe but trying to arrange a long enough stretch of time in various countries studying and thoroughly learning the languages.

It took but a few minutes to get acquainted with a friendly character from home: Where did he live? Where did we live? What was he doing here? What were we doing? Then from him:

"Say, why don't you come to the American church this Sunday?"

"Church?! Well—"

"Oh, I mean the American library connected with it. They have a tea dance every Sunday afternoon. It's about the only place where Americans meet."

So that was arranged and we looked forward to it with great curiosity: What will happen next?

Laurence Schmeckebier Appears

On Sunday we finally found the "Anglican Church of Munich" tucked away in a dark courtyard behind a row of big stucco buildings. It was a small, rundown nineteenth-century private home just as dingy and depressing on the inside. We followed the sound of Victrola music down a dark corridor and entered a parlor-sized room lined with bookshelves where a small floor space had been cleared and library tables pushed back around the walls. But at least there were people crowded around those tables—and there were bottles of wine and glasses aplenty, and people seemed to be animated and enjoying themselves. By now it was nothing new for us, two single girls, to enter a gathering and hunt for a place and sit down among a group of strangers. Sure enough, there was dancing on the jammed little central floor. Bob greeted us and Ty was off, promptly being cut in on by one young man after another. I, with my aloof, widowlike, martyred attitude, was quite content to sit and watch.

When she came back from dancing with one particularly good-looking, dark-haired, tall boy, I asked, "Who was that?"

"Oh I don't know. He's got some crazy name like Schnucki-bear! He found out that we have a typewriter and he's coming tomorrow to see us. Has something he wants typed."

With later memories it was this "Schnucki-" person who insisted that he spotted those two sisters the minute they walked in—the one with red hair in a purple velvet dress; the other, the big one with shiny blonde hair in a bright blue velvet dress. From that time on "Schnucki"

From Romance to Marriage

became his permanent nickname with us and most of our friends. At first he tried to object: "That's what the fat German society ladies call their poodles and lapdogs," he complained. It did no good, though we did anglicize it a bit by changing the word to "Snooky."

One day a little later when we were seeing more of each other, Bob Radsch was nearly popping with the news, conveyed privately to Laurence:

"Hey, do you know who those two girls are? They come from Englewood, and I have a friend there who told me all about them. They're the Kluge sisters, and they come from that crazy family that lives way out in some fantastic old house on top of a hill. Their old man is nuts—a Prussian general or something. Their mother is a Russian princess and he keeps her imprisoned there away from any friends. The neighbors tell wild stories about all the animals they've got —monkeys, raccoons, a fox that gets out and chases kids, a dozen howling dogs and a house full of tropical birds and squawking parrots, and enough horses for a school. But nobody in the town ever sees them."

Evidently neither Laurence Schmeckebier nor Bob Radsch were scared off. They became our rather dependable escorts. The visit to our apartment at the Clesses' and the typewriter incident led from one excuse to another, especially when Laurence discovered that it was Sa who could type and edit the various articles he was trying to get published. After running into the group at the church tea dance we were introduced, courtesy of our *Gasthörer* identification, to the Internationales Studentenhaus, a sort of club and meeting place for all interested foreign students who came from many different countries and spoke any number of languages. At that time the American students in Munich were hardly more than two dozen in number, most of them doctors and scientists in the hospital and professional schools. And there were very few girls, mostly art and music students. It made for a very close and friendly bunch. We ran into each other doing most of the same things around town—at concerts or theaters, in the halls of the university, and always at the parties provided by the Studentenhaus, such as for our American Thanksgiving, and we usually congregated at the same table.

We Experience A Full Life

Our winter in Munich was not just one grand, carefree ball. There were the broadening cultural and intellectual experiences through all that the city had to offer; there were sometimes difficult disciplinary and human lessons to be learned; and there were certainly influences that changed our attitudes for life.

First of all there was the Cless family to whom we so intimately belonged. In their early forties, animated and affectionate, they were sincerely interested in what we were doing; and Mr. Cless, the mentor, was always suggesting the interesting or important events that we should not miss. Breakfast talk was not only "What did you see last night?" but "What did you think of it? What made it so impressive?" Even old Granny Cless quized her son after a party: "Now tell me everything about which you conversed." Mr. Cless (who later became "Paps" to us) was a friend and devotèe of Thomas Mann. None of us ever missed a reading by him, and had to prepare for it beforehand by studying the text and discussing other works of his. On one of these occasions we heard Mann read from the manuscript of *Joseph and His Brothers* and several parts of *The Magic Mountain*.

The films we saw at Mr. Cless's theater were unusual and superior ones. Added to the comments about the pictures were Pap's long discussions about the music he had to select and help arrange for the showings. Those were the days of the silent movies and live musicians, either a single pianist or a small orchestra, who played an appropriate accompaniment the whole way through. It was during 1929 that the first talking picture—*Ton-Film* in Germany—appeared.

Besides the doubts about their quality and whether they would endure, there was consternation at having to install new equipment; and sadder still, what would become of the musicians? Of the first, more memorable films we saw there was *Die Weisse Hölle von Pitz Palü,* a hair-raising Alpine adventure featuring Leni Riefenstahl (later to become notorious under Hitler), very athletic and performing her own dangerous stunts; and the second *Silber Condor über Feuerland,* an exploration of Tierra del Fuego from an airplane flown by Werner Plüschow, a popular World War I flier, a tiny fellow, who came to the Cless home as a most charming dinner guest. As for serious actresses, nobody in the Clesses' opinion could top Elisabeth Bergner.

Music in Munich was limitless. There were the regular symphony concerts (and once the New York Philharmonic performed as guests) at the *Tonhalle*, or single artist's recitals at the Odeon hall. One could not possibly keep up with the offerings at the three opera houses—the big National Theater, the jewel-like Rococo eighteenth-century Residenz Theater for Mozart operas, and the Prinzregenten Theater, right near us in Bogenhausen, where Wagner and Schiller were performed. Besides that, for comic, or "light opera," one could go to the Theater Am Gaertnerplatz to hear Offenbach, Lehár, and Strauss. We had a regular routine on Tuesday evenings. Our *Weltkrieg Geschichte* (World War History) lecture was from 7:30 P.M. to 8:30 P.M. We dashed out of class and while walking down Turkenstrasse to the *Tonhalle* ate our sandwiches, which we brought from home, just slipping in a few minutes late to the 25-cent standing room crowd at the back of the hall to *stand* (nobody would dare sit on the floor then) often with scores of the music through a moving symphony concert conducted by Bruno Walter or Hans Knappertsbusch. Then we went back home by tram.

The formal lectures we attended in various auditoriums of the university were properly filled, all in German naturally, and the professors very clear and well organized, though we were trying to take notes in a mixture of German and English.

The biggest event and actually the most exciting was the four-times-a-week lecture by Wilhelm Pinder on "German Art of the Four-teenth Century." The *Aula Maxima* (Great Assembly Hall) was packed to the top row. Everyone was seated and attentive. It was the custom at all German university lectures to greet the professor as he entered with a sort of general rumble, made by scraping or thumping feet on the floor. For Pinder it was thunderous. The man was charming before he uttered a word. He was bald as Mitropoulos, and about the same size. He was acknowledged with great respect as one of the most outstanding scholars of Germany; he exuded human kindliness, good nature, and humor—nothing pompous or austere. But there was respectful discipline. There was not a whisper, never a late entrance; when he raised one finger as a sign, the slide operator changed the picture like the crack of a whip. As he paced back and forth on the podium, his voice rose in enthusiasm or fell to a dramatic, hushed remark. His thoughts ranged from the specific and commonly known historical situation through biblical stories and allusions to classical times, with side references to poetry or music, and he always brought in the human conditions that brought about the creation of a great work of art. His superb photographs, and the specially selected details, held one spellbound and involved. Many a time a single slide remained on the screen for the whole hour. Then, to the minute, completing a perfect sentence at the end of the lecture, he would relax, bow to his audience, and march out—to the thunderous applause from feet under the desks.

Princess in Paradise

Pinder's popularity at the time was due to a rare combination of profound scholarship and personal enthusiasm. But it also reflected the rising tide of national pride and patriotic respect for Germany's own artistic heritage. Instead of the traditional emphasis on the great French, Gothic monuments, he stressed the parallel achievements of his own country—the great imperial cathedrals of the Rhine (Speyer, Mainz, and Worms) and the magnificent sculpture of Bamberg and Naumburg.

The same attitude was revealed in the lectures of Alfred Stange, a handsome young professor who was already one of Germany's most distinguished experts on fourteenth- and fifteenth-century German art. He stressed the significance of the great masterpieces of Stephan Lochner, Konrad Witz, and Meister Bertram as achivevements of a northern Renaissance spirit parallel to that of contemporary Italy.

Professor Frauenholz's lectures on World War I were something of a revelation to us, both because of our own experiences in Englewood at that time and because of the harrowing tales of the family in Russia during the Bolshevik Revolution. The successive stages of military success and defeat, economic collapse, revolution, and inflation, followed by a kind of national resurgence as presented from the German point of view, was something quite different from what we had learned at school.

All of this had nothing to do with the crude antics of the National-Socialist fringe which frequently made itself heard in classrooms and at the tail end of the colorful students corps processions, and was thoroughly despised. It did reflect, however—along with the experience of Thomas Mann, the superb programs of music and the opera, and the Cless family itself—the intellectural climate of the period, which profoundly changed our view of life.

The German universities, even the smaller ones like Marburg, Heidelberg, and Tübingen, provided none of the picturesque campus atmosphere or community cohesiveness I had come to love at Vassar. Social life was concentrated in the *Studenten Korps* or fraternities. There were certain traditions such as the opening ceremony for each semester with its colorful academic procession and the parade of corps students in their brilliant uniforms and gold banners. In general, the student effort was concentrated on the lectures and seminars.

At home with the Clesses the supervision of our manners and etiquette was not too painful. Granny Cless was the one to check up on us. She and I became special friends, for we played duets on the piano—arrangements of the Beethoven symphonies were the most fun, but we also enjoyed playing Schubert waltzes and romantic songs, to which she would passionately recite the words. We were asked not to entertain young men in our rooms without first introducing them to the family, and particularly not to expect to serve them food. Our own wines and beer were permissible. One of the most peculiar misunderstandings came out when Granny was delegated to ask us in private: "When we invited you to join us and our guests for Sunday night supper, how could you possibly appear in *wool dresses*?" Absolutely nonplused, we could only answer the truth: "But those were our very newest and best dresses that Mami brought from America!" Otherwise there was no overt criticism, only parental curiosity about our comings and goings, late hours, or quiet bridge parties in our den.

One of our most harrowing experiences occurred during one of these bridge parties. Granny Cless, whose room was across the hall from ours, had been sick with something approaching pneumonia for several weeks. Mr. and Mrs. Cless had been so confined they decided to go out to a movie that night. We could hear Granny's moaning and crying. There was a slow-witted Bavarian maid who attended to her now and then. When the moans turned to loud, desperate calls of "Help me! Help me! I'm dying!" (Granny's childhood language was English), I went in to ask if she didn't have a pill or something to take, offered her water, and propped her up on her pillows. I told the maid, shivering helplessly in a dark corner, that there must be a doctor's name in the family telephone book and to go and call him quickly. In the meantime, we scurried our baffled and disbelieving bridge companions out down the back stairs.

When Ty and I came back into the bedroom, Granny lay there unmistakably dead! A doctor did arrive and confirmed it—heart failure—and stayed with us to await the Clesses' return at about eleven o'clock to give them the horrible news. Everyone knows the emotional turmoil, the bafflement, and the confusion that accompanies a thing like that. It was new to us. We discreetly retired to our rooms, and the house was alive with talk, activity, and visitors for the rest of the night. The next day we offered to go out of town to the mountains till things settled down for the family.

Winter Sports in the Alps

For Christmas vacation the Clesses suggested that we go to some winter resort in the nearby Bavarian Alps, and they arranged for our

Princess in Paradise

room and meals in a small local family pension, Haus Inge in Garmisch-Partenkirchen. Like everyone else, we could easily get there by train, then a ride from the station to our abode in an open horse-drawn sleigh along the quiet, snow-covered streets past all the gaily painted peasant-style houses. We soon met up with the other American students who were doing the same thing—Bob and Laurence, a group of young doctors and their wives who called themselves "the Mayo Clinic bunch," and an old American ski instructor of local fame.

At that time the two adjoining villages, Garmisch and Partenkir-chen, were popular with the Germans but retained their quaint and modest Bavarian native atmosphere. It was not until the 1936 Olym-pics under Hitler that they expanded and attained world renown, and were further enlarged after World War II as an American armed forces recreation area.

But skiing equipment and wardrobe were not things Mami had brought along in those trunks, and we saw no need to spend our precious allowances on them. We had heavy sweaters and woolen skirts (albeit rather well above the knees) and nice galoshes for hiking through the snow. Almost everyone walked the mile or so to the cable car station at the foot of the Zugspitze, Bavaria's most famous and highest mountain. At the top there was a restaurant with a balcony gleaming in the warm sun. There one could spend all the time one wanted over sandwiches or *Brödchen* and sausages or hot chocolate and watch others showing off their tricks or stumbling through their first ski lessons. Finally, it was too intriguing to sit idly by. We found we could rent skis, but boots we would have to buy. So Ty and I, always teammates and cooperative, decided to buy one pair of boots that could fit both of us—a little tight for me, a bit too big for her—and we would alternate—one would wear the boots while the other had the saddle shoes with galoshes tied on with a string. Skis in those days were wide Norwegian-style ashboards with simple leather bindings, and the boots were of heavy but supple leather with two metal studs for the binding clamps.

Needless to say, we never got to the stage of schussing the three miles down the mountain, as some experts did in half an hour or beginners in three. However, there was another adventure we could not miss—the so-called *Rodelbahn*. All one needed to do was sit on a wooden sled and follow the track the same three miles down the mountain. The *Rodel* (now there is another and more professional name for it) was shaped like a child's sled with upturned wooden runners in front and a small square seat in the back. You leaned back,

From Romance to Marriage

stretched your legs forward, and did the steering by lowering one heel or the other into the snow and tipping your body slightly toward the side where you wanted to go, holding on to the seat behind you. It was going to be so simple and such childish fun! Our boy friends, none too good skiers yet themselves, would go down at the same time along some nearby trail and meet us at the bottom. Typically, Ty and I were all giggles and screeches.

After the first curve or two we discovered that putting down the one heel into the snow at a high rate of speed threw up a pretty big plume of spray, right into your face or onto your lap. Don't forget, our snow sport costumes were those fashionable short circular woolen skirts. And what did we have underneath? Bright pink silk knitted bloomers! The snow would pile up to an uncomfortable degree, so that we would have to stop to dump it off, brush it out of our faces and hair, then shake vigorously to clear up our undies. In addition to this, our ever present box camera was strung around one of our necks with a gold Christmas string, which would bounce as we flopped and tried to protect it from the snow. As we came to the steeper sections the speed was faster, the snow plume was much stronger, and the clothes were getting wetter. Besides, we didn't make every curve. Much too often we were tipped over into the snowbank on the side, while behind us someone screamed: "Gottverdammte Frauen—get out of the way!" Amusedly at first, then patiently, and finally in exasperation, Laurence and Bob watched this performance—and we got over our giggles. They decided to wait for us in the hut at the bottom. But that was far from the end. Exhausted, soaked, and disgruntled, there was still the one-mile hike back to the village. Only the thought of a nice cozy café at the end, with Schnapps, maybe, or hot wine and a huge piece of whipped-cream cake, kept up our spirits.

The Italian Trip

We decided that Easter vacation, when the university closed for three weeks, would be a fine opportunity to make our trip to Italy, as most of our friends and hundreds of German students were doing. We went to a pleasant young man we had met at the pension who worked at the American Express office and asked him to help plan our itinerary. Group tours then were hardly the proper thing to do. He soon produced a beautifully typed, minutely detailed program for us with hotel accommodations, train reservations, and exclusive escorted excur-

Princess in Paradise

sions. This we sent home to the family for approval and so that extra finances could be arranged. Promptly came a letter from Papi: "Your tour sounds as if you are traveling as royal princesses! Palace Hotel here, Grand Hotel there, first class *luxus* trains all over the place, private guides and what not!"

Paps Cless immediately took matters in hand. His passion as a former military captain was to spread out maps, plan routes and alternate routes, underline possible stopping places, and rummage through volumes of train schedules. He handed us *Baedekers* and local guidebooks from their own youthful trip through Italy; had us make lists of the important artworks and monuments we wanted to see; and then carefully mapped each day's walking tour of a certain city section, always with his enthusiastic: "Kinder, dass musst ihr unbedingt sehen!" (children, you absolutely must see that!). Besides, he knew small hotels patronized by the *British* tourists and respectable little pensions catering to the thrifty German travelers. When we figured out our budget, it looked more feasible. By that time we felt quite confident that we could take care of ourselves and even improvise in emergencies. A trip like this we considered as serious study business as well as a precious opportunity, and we were willing to pack into it everything we possibly could.

On April 1 we were off to Italy, hopping from one small train connection to another, then doing a mighty amount of tramping (in those tight skirts and white saddle shoes, which invariably attracted the reputed followers and pinchers!). Faithful to our schedule, we checked off on our lists the churches, palazzos, the special paintings in each museum, often wandering with trepidation down little alleyways to locate an obscure fresco. We used the third-class local transportation to reach nearby objectives, whether a crowded bus to Fiesole, the suburban train to Pompeii, or the ferry to Capri. We quite enjoyed those little family-style pensions where all guests ate together, and we observed the custom of ordering your own bottle, which appeared daily before you and on which you penciled a line to mark the level of the liquid you had left inside.

We covered the whole range of traditional "Grand Tour" pilgrimage sites, from Florence to Naples, without missing a detail or a side trip, and ended up in Rome for Easter week. One of the unforgettable memories was being in St. Peter's for the Easter service amid the solid mass of thousands squeezed into Michelangelo's vast space, the Bernini tabernacle dwarfed in the distance, the towering Baroque sculp-

From Romance to Marriage

tures lining the sides, the banks of elaborately robed church dignitaries and the glorious sounds of the Sistine Choir echoing from the vaults above us.

In Rome we met Bob Radsch with his friend John Haviland from Yale, a classics scholar. Armed with ground plans, guidebooks, reconstruction photos, and his learned comments, there wasn't a foot of the Forum Romanum we missed, not a detail of the remarkable brick arch construction and subterranean chambers of every bath or *Terme* nor finally of the tombs along the Appian Way.

Beginning to head for home, our next stop was Milan, and as we arrived exhausted in the milling crowd at the station, there, tall and smiling, appeared Laurence Schmeckebier to welcome us. Now we had the benefit of the art history student as a guide as we climbed the pinnacles of the Milan Cathedral, but especially learned the technicalities of the sad state of Leonardo's *Last Supper* and much about the northern Italian painters in the Brera Museum.

At last we had a few days to rest, lounging on the beaches of Lake Como, surrounded by mountains and quiet woods and little hillside villages—and no sightseeing but to walk and swim. Then it was off again, via a brief stopover in Lucerne, to Basel where that Schmeckebier had to do research on medieval sculpture and the fifteenth-century painter Konrad Witz, whom he was investigating because of his remarkable use of color. Finally we were aboard a train for the long stretch back to Munich. With our heads so full of images, experiences, and new knowledge, it took a long time to sort out all our copious notes and photographs—and particularly to give a thorough accounting to the eager Cless family.

❧ Back in Munich

With the change at the university to the "summer semester" at the beginning of May, there were also various changes in our life. News from home had been sparse and vague. Family events seemed to be going along as usual. We hardly noticed comments—if there were any—about business troubles. When we did read them, there didn't seem to be any sensational headlines in the international newspapers about the financial disasters and unemployment we learned about later. But there were more times when our bank transfer had been delayed, and we found ourselves carefully counting our last few marks. Also, the discussions about planning for when we were to come home were none too precise; steamer reservations usually had to be made months in advance. If we were going to stay around Europe for the rest of the summer, we were anxious to make use of our time—there was still so much we wanted to see.

Our social activities had also changed somewhat. We knew so many more people that we felt like natives and continually discovered new things to study in the city or excursions to take to obscure little villages out in the country. Almost every night we dropped in at a small *Hackerbräu* restaurant on a side street, where we knew we would find the "gang" around the same table, all eating the standard dinner for the price of *one mark*—25 cents! Ty's romantic feelings about Bob Radsch had blossomed, then cooled when he left to spend the rest of his year in France and Spain. Eric Holzer now reappeared on the horizon, back in his Franz-Josefstrasse apartment, working toward the finals for his Ph.D. in economics, but of course with time for occasional relaxation and diversions in his lovely little Packard.

A steady member of the same student group was this Laurence Schmeckebier, now in his fourth year of study in Germany and working hard to complete his doctorate in color psychology and art history. It became almost a regular joke, and he the object of much teasing, for whenever he appeared he would bring out little booklets of color samples, hold them up across the table, and ask, "What color do you see here?" Or while walking down a street, he would suddenly point to the facade of a building and say, "Do you see that *optische Täuschung* [optical illusion] up there in those columns?" To most, he was an object of pleasant fun and kidding. To some, if one listened long and seriously enough, he was intriguing. After a few sessions in a quiet *Weinstube* or café I discovered we had the same tastes and enthusiasm for the German romantic literature and was amazed at his broad understanding of music as well as at the enormous scope of knowledge and theories on art he had acquired in his very thorough study-travels to most of the European art centers.

As we saw more and more of him, his individuality and character became more intriguing. There were always new surprises. The first formal gift I received was a weighty German tome, a monograph on Peter Paul Rubens with hundreds of beautiful illustrations. "Now," said he, "you take this and study the pictures thoroughly, and then we'll meet in the Pinakothek [the art museum] and look at the Rubens paintings together." To him Rubens was one of the strongest and most colorful personalities in the history of art, a dynamic and skillful

From Romance to Marriage

painter, who combined his artistic productivity with a full, successful, international diplomatic and social life. Well, Rubens was only the first of the enthusiasms. We did spend many hours in the galleries of Munich. And as was typical of the German students, the intermissions of musical events or the theater would be taken up by animated and terribly serious discussions as they gathered in clusters or strolled around the foyer.

While my intellectual and cultural horizons had been enormously broadened, my ideas about men and my own life had undergone considerable change. I had long since given up the pose of the martyred widow. The frequent letters from Mac, first critical for not opposing Papi's dictates, then hopeful that I would eventually return to him, became less interesting, and my replies less frequent. As the ardor cooled, my enthusiasm for this new world of ideas, scholarship, and the creative life of the intellectual in which Laurence was involved was ever on the increase. With him I found life demanding but never dull. Thus began a mutual career that lasted for more than fifty years.

Frankly, it was amusing that my knowledge of art history was mainly the dilettantish information picked up at home, since I had postponed taking any art course at college till the last year. Ty, fortunately, was much better informed, since she had taken an art history course in high school—and had brought along all her notes. We depended on those and the personal opinions of her teacher as we checked off our starred objectives through one museum after another. She would give me such helpful pointers as, "Sa, you can recognize a Perugino, because someone is always running and has a foot in the air! Raphael's people are standing on the ground. You can always tell Giovanni Bellini by the way the thumbs stick out."

Since Ty and I were so compatible and so close in everything we did, our social engagements were usually foursomes. Eric Holzer apparently was developing a bit more tolerance or understanding of those "wild American girls"—and one in particular. He also found the Schmeckebier character interesting or stimulating enough to enjoy his company. The young man who shared Eric's apartment, Fritz-Georg Pschorr, was a childhood friend; they had been together on all their foreign educational stints, and it was taken for granted that he was engaged to Eric's sister Liesel.

At last some instructions came from home. We were to pack up and prepare to return at the beginning of August. In the meantime, we had left the Clesses' apartment and taken up temporary residence in a

Princess in Paradise

Pension International on Von der Tannstrasse near the big park, the
Englischer Garten. We were to spend the month of July living out on
Starnberger See, visiting Uncle Albert and Cousin Rita in the home
they had just bought, having given up their Berlin residence. It was
named the Schlössl (little castle) and was a beautiful, airy villa on a steep
bank, right at the edge of the lake where we could swim and lounge the
day away, eat all the meals on the landscaped terrace, and receive the
most luxurious treatment. To us, the sad drawback was that their
station, Possenhofen, was an hour's ride by train from Munich,
whether it meant going into town for a certain invitation or returning
late at night after an opera performance. And by now we had become
so used to being independent!

There was still at least one more trip we were determined to take
—that was to Vienna. Experienced as we now were, ever watchful for
university connections, and having learned to be thrifty, we found a
marvelous opportunity. Professor Kutscher, who had given the German drama course, was conducting a student tour to Austria over the
Whitsuntide holidays—a *Theaterwissenschaftliche Pfingsten Reise* (a theater study trip)—for the unbelievable bargain price of ten days for $80.
What matter the kind of hotels we were going to be in or the third-class
unreserved train accommodations! It included stops at Passau and
Kloster Neuburg, a boat ride down the Danube, in Vienna a special
performance of the Lipizzaner horses in the Spanish Riding School,
theater tickets to the *Burgtheater* as well as the *Volkstheater*, and a special
eighteenth-century masque in the *Redoutensaal* of the *Hofburg*—all
under the guidance, with lectures, by an unusually friendly and informal German professor.

There was even time for visits to the museum, the palaces of Schön-
brunn and Belvedere, and finally an afternoon excursion to the Vienna woods ending up with a party in Grinzing under the grape arbors to
enjoy the "new wine"—the *Heuriger*. The group of about thirty was
decidedly international with no more than a half-dozen Americans,
some French girls, a Greek, and some other European students and
one tall, handsome young Chinese who was in great demand as the best
dancer of the party. For our meals we went regularly to the university
Mensa, the general dining hall, and most of the time we were being
escorted or entertained by the local university students.

On the return trip we made an unusual stop at the old town of Graz,
again to be fêted by university students. Then at Salzburg there was an
intimate look into the behind-the-scene workings of old theaters, at-

From Romance to Marriage

tending rehearsals of dramas or music in the Rococo palaces or gardens—and finally heading for home and Munich.

To young Germans the biggest bargain in Austria was the cigarettes, compared with the sky-high cost of American Lucky Strikes or Camels in Germany. Everyone pooled their last Groschen (pennies) and stocked up, not on goodies or wine, but on Austrian cigarettes. We debarked from the train at Munich with exactly the two 25-pfennig pieces needed for the trolley to get us to our pension. There was then the walk from the main street, Ludwigstrasse, to our door, lugging along our suitcases, shopping bags, coats, and other acquired paraphernalia, this at 10:30 P.M. in the dark.

Nothing ever seemed to be a tragedy to us. We were stopping, resting on the suitcases, laughing as usual, and dragging ourselves onward. Suddenly—big surprise! "Hallo, American girls! Want a lift?" And who should it be but Eric in his Packard and Laurence with him. Knowing vaguely the time we would be returning, they had been cruising the street watching for us to check in at the pension. Of course, it was a wonderful and welcome reunion. But did they ever scold us and make us feel like dumb innocents, spending our last pennies and traveling with no reserves. It was a nice sign of true concern and more than a casual reaction.

Inevitably the time drew near when we must leave our dear old Munich. There was much more we were going to miss than the art galleries, the concerts, the beerhalls, and the nearby mountains. We had found someone who caused us to do some serious thinking about our future. One did not rush into commitments, and there really were no promises made, but there was understanding and hope. Both Laurence and Eric were deeply, seriously intent about their work—and about their determination to complete all the trials and obligations that would lead them to their doctoral degrees before the year ended. It meant buckling down to uninterrupted hard work. After that—well, plans would have to wait till later.

A real friendship had developed between Eric and Laurence, so Laurence was invited to move into the Franz-Josefstrasse apartment with Eric and Fritz Pschorr, who was also on his final semester as a doctoral candidate. The trio lived quite sedately, for students, with occasional trips and some fraternal cutting up to relieve the tensions, and each achieved his goal by the end of the winter semester of 1930.

Beyond that lay the plans for their future. Both Eric and Fritz were to enter their family's business and gain experience there. Laurence,

whose ambition was to teach, knew that he would have to do some
difficult hunting after he returned to the States. His only connections
were with academic friends at the University of Wisconsin, where his
records showed that four years before he had graduated as a top-grade
student, majoring in history and English. Fortunately, in a way, while I
was still in Munich he received a very brief letter from Oskar Hagen
chairman of the Wisconsin Department of Art History offering him a
position as assistant professor at the salary of $2,200 per year.

We looked at it together quite dubiously: "Should he make the
decision now and from here? Was that where he wanted to begin his
career? And what about the salary? It could only have been by intui-
tion, because we were so poorly informed about conditions in America,
that caused me to say, "I gather somehow that there are all sorts of job
troubles at home. Maybe you had better not wait and just accept this."
He went through with it, and so at least we had that much of an idea of
the road ahead.

After all our packing up and arrangements to leave, Eric came up
with the bright idea of driving us—the four of us—as far as Nürnberg.
There it was our last sentimental chance to wander through the narrow
old streets, linger in the Nürnberger Bratwurst Glockel and see the two
famous Gothic churches—St. Lorenz and St. Sebaldus. In the light of
later history, this was of special significance, for the churches—like all
of old Nürnberg—were reduced to rubble in the bombings of World
War II. Our next visit there would be thirty years later when they were
still partly in ruins. One could also see, in some cases, the remarkable
restorations that had been done using both the original old materials
and the newly fashioned pieces specially carved to fit into the original
structures.

From Nürnberg there was a long, subdued, meditative train ride to
Holland and our embarkation, with no fanfare at all, on the small
steamer, the S. S. *Rotterdam,* headed for home. There was no way of
guessing or imagining what we would face, our own next steps, what
had been going on in the family, or how we would be treated when we
got home. Certain it was that here were two quite new and different
personalities from those two carefree girls who had been sent abroad a
year ago "to keep them out of trouble"!

From Romance to Marriage

23

The Return to Reality

T WAS A HOT and humid August afternoon when the *Rotterdam* edged its way toward the dock of the Holland-American Line in Manhattan. The trip had been dull and uneventful, and the sparse crowd waiting on the dock against the hazy silhouette of New York's skyscrapers did not seem to make the welcome any better.

But there stood Mami trim and elegant as ever, with a big smile as she waved to us, and Peter, the handsome black chauffeur. There was no trouble with customs, since we had nothing to declare, but it was interesting to see some of the customs agents hurl confiscated bottles of liquor at the side of the ship—"Oh, all that good Scotch whiskey and those beautiful bottles of Gordon gin!" We had forgotten about Prohibition in the Land of the Free!

There was an ever increasing excitement as we chattered, and Mami listened while the baggage was being trundled to the car outside the gate. The car! There stood a huge black shiny new Packard!

"But Mami, I thought everyone was broke! What about the depression?"

"Oh," was the calm reply, "that was Papi's surprise for my birthday last week. We had a big dinner party, and as a grand climax to the event he led me out the front door to this new car all decorated with red-and-white ribbons. That was about the last thing I needed at this time."

Well, that was only the beginning. New York was still wonderful, but as we drove up Broadway we could see many changes from what we had remembered a year ago: there were groups of shabby-looking men standing behind boxes of apples on the street corners; long lines of depressed-looking people shuffling toward an improvised soup kitchen; and, whenever there was a vacant lot, there was one of those miniature golf courses, the latest craze in popular recreation. Down the side streets there seemed to be larger groups of people standing in front of dark brownstone houses at cocktail time. We knew about speakeasies, of course, but never realized how many there were. Someone said that by that summer there were more than 32,000 speakeasies operating in New York alone. Then we noticed a crowd standing around an open space in front of a hotel on Madison Avenue. "Probably another stockbroker," suggested Peter with a smile through the intercom. "The other day two of them jumped hand in hand because they had a joint account!"

As we drove up the long driveway toward Greystone, the place was still gorgeous, but we could see the changes. The lawns had not been mowed for some time; the bushes were untrimmed; and the beautiful flower gardens around the pool were overgrown with weeds.

Papi came home early for the festive dinner to welcome his wayward daughters. Cocktails were served on the veranda, but Mami brought out the tray of glasses and the big silver cocktail shaker. The cook was there, but there was only one maid to help her, and Peter now doubled as both chauffeur and butler to serve at the table.

While we managed to carry on an excited chatter about our adventures, there was an ever increasing pall of shocked silence as the evening wore on. Not a word was said about conditions by either parent. It was not until later that evening in the kitchen and the next day that the story gradually unfolded—as told by the servants and the chauffeur. Sergey was too young to know what was going on and Mule had no clear idea of what was what either, being too busy with camp and school, after having just graduated from Riverdale and now enrolled as a freshman at Dartmouth, but he was well aware that *something* was wrong.

❧ Goodbye to Greystone

So what was it? To support the increasingly lavish way of life of the past ten years—and he was confident that it could not end—Papi had invested heavily in the stock market. Not only the house and property but the factory as well were mortgaged to the hilt. When the collapse came, he—like everyone else—could get no credit and found himself unable even to meet his payroll. Orders for labels were slow in coming and then practically ceased. All the horses and animals were sold; the servants were discharged except Peter, the cook, and one maid; the house and property were being sold to pay taxes; and the mortgage holders were taking over whatever they could get their hands on. We were obliged to move out by the end of the year. There was talk about a fortune to be made through the sale of the property in the coming real estate boom promised by the new George Washington Bridge, but that was soon forgotten. We had lost everything but the household furniture.

The E. H. Kluge Weaving Company was declared bankrupt, and while Papi continued to go to the office for a time, he soon became the target of subpoenas and lawsuits, and the management of the company was turned over to his supposedly longtime loyal friends and assistants, Albert Lear and Mr. Stalter, with the active encouragement of Cousin Albert, whose rival firm was ready to take over the lucrative label market which Papi had dominated for so many years. In the end, he was obliged to remain a virtual recluse to avoid the process servers, first in his study in Greystone and then in the Eighty-fifth Street apartment. With his boundless energy and booming resentment at the turn of events, he was almost impossible to manage.

We had to make quick decisions, each in her own way. I say "we," because at this point Papi remained mysteriously silent and apparently helpless, while we had to make up our minds as to what to do. Mami continued with her household chores, and then would disappear to the city to look for apartments. It never dawned on us to even ask her where or why or how. Ty registered for a secretarial course in the School of Business at Columbia University. Any thought of my return to Vassar to finish college seemed out of the question, so I enrolled in the one-year secretarial course at Katharine Gibbs on Park Avenue.

That all sounded logical and easy, but it soon proved to be a long and exhausting grind. From our house we had a fifteen-minute walk down the hill to the trolley car stop. From there to Fort Lee the trip was about forty minutes. Then we had to take the ferry across the Hudson River, walk to the 125th Street station (at that point elevated), and then take the subway downtown. Ty went only to 116th Street, but I had to go to 42d Street. We had to leave at seven in the morning and were lucky if we returned by six that evening. Then we trudged up the hill

Princess in Paradise

again and, if it was hot and the pool still functioning, took a quick
dip—and then went to work packing.

Packing! It took months—the entire fall—for the three of us to sort
out the assorted debris of twenty years in that big house—furniture,
china, crystal, linens, bric-a-brac, trunks, and enough sports clothes
and equipment to outfit a safari. Cousin Albert had volunteered to
provide storage space in his factory in Pompton Lakes for some of the
furniture, trunks, and boxes. Each box was numbered and the contents recorded in Mami's notebook. Mami finally found a suitable
apartment that would take our massive furniture; in another notebook
she had sketched each room with its dimensions and all the measure-
ments of the furniture she hoped to place. We were each to have our
own room and were permitted to choose our color schemes.

🌿 A New Life

My memory is blurred, but by Christmas 1930 somehow we had
moved. The apartment was beautiful, and everything fitted just as
Mami had planned. However, now the big problem was the cooking.
There was no cook, and there were no servants. None of us had ever so
much as cleaned a potato. Mami had ordered and supervised many
gorgeous banquets—but cook?! However, we were game, and of
course we all had to eat. Papi maintained his regular routine, as though
nothing had ever happened, and would sit in his big chair in the library
and wait for his drinks and hors d' oeuvres to be brought to him while
we floundered around in the kitchen. Mami had an old Russian cook-
book, which naturally did us no good, so she would stand at the stove,
the book beside her, as she translated the recipes, while we tried to
figure out the directions.

But we managed—in fact, we managed so well that in a short time
we were providing lovely dinners for ourselves and the poor hungry
Russians who were always available; most of Papi's old social and
business friends had disappeared, and we needed company to keep
him entertained. It did not help to leave the large silver platter or the
silver vegetable dishes in the oven and find them melted, or use the
elegant Sêvres china for everyday dinners. We soon learned. The silver
was put away, and we descended to our antique Chinese dinner service.

Still no word was said about the family's financial situation. Having
engineered the bankruptcy and taken over most of Papi's customers,

we learned that Cousin Albert had agreed to provide the rent for the apartment but no more. This family relationship with Cousin Albert was always difficult for us to comprehend. He was a shrewd, calculating and determined business operator and had no regrets or conscience about taking over Papi's business—"Papi got himself into this mess," he would say, "and he can jolly well work his own way out of it"—which of course Papi never did. But on the other hand, Albert was sentimentally attached to the family. He adored Mami and, like his father before him, maintained the deepest respect for her as a person and for the way she was able to manage her household and of life with dignity and self-respect through so many difficulties. Like all the Kluges he loved parties and had quite a following of drinking companions but one never knew just what mood would prevail, especially when discussing financial matters at this time.

Mami was not the one to be subdued. She solved the problem by taking in a collection of roomers which according to the lease was not allowed. She called them household guests. Not only did they pay a substantial rent, but they had to be carefully screened for "social acceptance," which meant their ability to play bridge and entertain Papi. By this means she was able to provide food and the necessities of daily living.

In the meantime, the letters from Laurence in Munich faithfully reported his progress. He was still very much in love with me, but was working desperately on his thesis and was terrified at the prospect of the oral exams, which he had hoped to complete before Christmas. In the end, the dissertation was finally completed and accepted with the high sounding title of "Die Erscheinungsweisen Klein-Flächiger Farben" (The Modes of Appearance of Small Patches of Color). It was a psychological study, using modern and scientifically controlled laboratory techniques for the same problems of color perception which had concerned the Neo-Impressionists during the late nineteenth century and which were to fascinate Joseph Albers and the Op-artists among the moderns. It was written and presented entirely in German, and one of the professors had remarked that one could not have detected the fact that it was done by a foreigner. He became something of a curiosity among the examining professors, so that when the time for the orals arrived, he was obliged to take, not only the one in art history with Wilhelm Pinder and psychology by Gustav Pauli, but also philosophy (since psychology was not considered at that time as a major field and was included in philosophy) and, for good measure, aesthetics and English literature. He had been a major in history and English as an undergraduate at Wisconsin, and they were curious about how much he knew! On December 22 I received the cablegram: "Doktor mit Eins!" He had survived the entire ordeal with a summa cum laude.

Laurence Arrives

It was a cold and blustery January afternoon when Ty and I, with Henry Nordhausen, Laurence's artist friend, watched a tall, slim young man, looking very elegant in his dark English suit, black hat, and chesterfield coat walk down the gangplank from the third-class deck of the *Europa*. He had a trunkful of books and one battered suitcase—the English suit and coat were the only new clothes he had bought during the entire four years—but he still looked good to me. What Papi and Mami would say I had no idea, and at that moment I did not really care very much. I had him home.

The dinner at the apartment that night proceeded with regal splendor. Laurence was to be duly impressed; in turn, he seemed to make a favorable impression with his slightly German accent, his European manners and conversation, and his characteristic enthusiasm. Mami did the cooking while Papi entertained at cocktails. The atmosphere was appropriately festive, with our massive furniture, soft candlelight, white linen tablecloth, embroidered Russian napkins, our best Sèvres china, and sparkling crystal. The several courses were served on the big silver platters in continental fashion, with the wine in tall-stemmed glasses and Ty and I alternating as maid and butler. When it was over and we retired to the kitchen to do the dishes, Laurence promptly jumped up to help and keep us company, but he was just as quickly shushed back into his chair for liqueurs and demitasse—"No, we don't do that here—the servants [that is, our daughters] will take care of the dishes."

Well, Laurence was never one to hide his affections, and it soon became apparent to Papi that ours was not just a casual relationship. He did manage to keep a lively conversation going with Papi at the table and afterward in the library, but soon found an excuse to get back to us in the kitchen, then left for his room at the Hotel Manger.

And so my problems started all over again. Gentlemen friends and suitors were all right, but before anything serious might develop, their backgrounds should be properly reviewed for elegibility. With the present financial situation, this could be very clearly defined. Ty's interest in Eric Holzer with his wealthy family background in Berlin was perfectly fine, but Sa should find herself someone equally substantial (to get *us* out of our troubles—financial, that is!). Papi had frequently dropped pointed remarks about what a nice man and substantial family Andy Wineburg represented (one of our old friends, perfectly nice, but at least four inches shorter than I was) and even suggested, to my horror, what a marvelous catch Cousin Albert might be.

"But this here Snooky—or whatever his name is—where does he come from—the Midwest? And the University of Wisconsin, where is that? That is out there in Indian territory. On top of all this, he is going to be a professor—a teacher at a university! There is certainly no financial future in that profession."

So Papi's red-faced ranting went on—long after Laurence had departed—while we sat and listened in embarrassed and resentful silence.

I must confess that Snooky was not very helpful in this matter, and as time went on the situation became more difficult. He, too, came from a German background, his father having been born in Pomerania (in northern Germany), and with few resources had worked his way through dental school at the University of Chicago. Eventually he established a successful practice on the South Side, in Chicago Heights. As an undergraduate, Laurence was something of a rebel, again in keeping with what he called the Wisconsin tradition. From his stories, I got the impression that, while he was no crusader for established causes, he was at times outrageously independent. He had always been a devoted follower of Henry L. Mencken and shared that self-styled moral theologian's disdain for the American "booboisie." Remembering the spectacle of the political convention which Mencken characterized in "The Clowns March In," Laurence took delight in pointing out the annual academic processions at commencement time, and indeed, when Orozco later painted the pompous professorial specters supervising "Modern Education" in his murals at Dartmouth College, he just beamed. He loved people and certainly had nothing against society as such but simply maintained the conviction that if he were faced with a phony he had the right—even the obligation—to tell him so.

With Papi, he did not say so exactly, but kept an amused and detached distance. Such a martinet—as he bluntly characterized

Princess in Paradise

him—had been a common phenomenon he had learned to live with in Germany. "But what a perfect Georg Grosz character!" he exclaimed to me—"bald head, round neck and rubber-tired torso, a glass in one hand and a wurst in the other, and always with a bevy of ladies about him. Rubens would have loved him for a Bacchus model!"

The next day we arranged a cocktail party so that my Vassar and Dwight friends could have a look at Snooky. I was all dressed up for the occasion with a new flaming red dress. As Ty described it, he practically melted when he saw me in the living room, and I thought he looked pretty good, too. So did the girls. They were all there: Anna North, Betsy Bonbright, Ruth Keeler, Libby Earhart, Joanna Hadden, and the rest. Everyone was bubbling with excitement as the party progressed, and an air of expectancy seemed to dominate the room. Papi sat in his big chair. Mami busied herself among the guests making animated conversation. People looked at one another.

"Isn't some one going to say something? Is the engagement going to be announced?"

They looked at me, then Laurence, then Mami. Silence.

So the big moment had come and gone. I had had great expectations and felt crushed. We went out to dinner by ourselves that night and had a long discussion. I was convinced that he loved me as deeply as I was devoted to him, but he felt too unsure, even doubtful about his future to make any commitment, and I had to console myself with hopeful patience.

Our time together was short but blissful in spite of the situation. I had to attend classes, but we managed a visit to the Metropolitan Museum, where it was I who took him on a guided tour for a change, rather than he taking me, and then went to the newly founded Museum of Modern Art, at that time in the Hecksher Building on Fifth Avenue. New York, with all its zooming taxicabs, crowded subways, and shuffling mobs of people at rush hour, was a new experience for him. Its artistic resources were a genuine revelation. Henry Nordhausen, native New York chauvinist that he was, insisted that I take Laurence to the New School for Social Research to see the new Orozco frescos in the refectory on the third floor.

The impact of the Orozco murals on him was overwhelming: "My God, look at that!" he exclaimed—"A square modern space, strong color, equally strong expressive forms—all designed and intergrated into an impressive and comprehensible social statement." Enthused as he was with contemporary art—not so much the great artists of Paris,

From Romance to Marriage

but rather the strong and creative personalities of the Expressionists groups he had followed in Germany (especially Georg Grosz, Max Beckmann, and Emil Nolde), he felt that these murals revealed an artist with larger ideas of political and social significance. Rather than the European modernist's concern for the abstract problems of pictorial form and personal expression, here was a new concept involving broader human values and purposes. The recognizable portraits of Lenin, Gandhi, and the revolutionary Mexican Carillo Puerto added a new dimension, an ominous warning of developments to come. He was convinced that here indeed was the first sign of a cultural wave of the future.

I must confess that with my personal and the family's financial problems at the time, I was not particularly interested in any artistic "social statements" or cultural waves of the future. But it is curious to me, as I look back, how I had unconsciously led him into a situation which not only was vitally expressive of the time (1931), but caught the eye and fired the imagination of a young scholar at the moment of transition from one phase of life to another. Indeed, I was responsible, watched it happen, and became involved myself. My friends have often wondered how it was that the two of us had worked together on so many projects. I cannot "explain" it, but I can point out situations where it happens and the mutual identity of interests, enthusiasms, and a vague but positive vision of the future takes hold. This was one of those situations.

The remainder of the afternoon was spent rushing around to find out more about Orozco and his background. Thus began a commitment to the study of modern Mexican art and its social as well as aesthetic problems that was to involve both of us for many years.

❧ Laurence Returns Home

While I certainly had my problems, those which Laurence had to face had only begun. The letters he wrote faithfully from Chicago and Madison during the next six months read like Goethe's *Die Leiden des jungen Werthers* (*The Sorrows of Young Werther*), in which the difficulties he found at home, with the new job and his own feelings of inadequacy, as well as his loneliness combined to make him a very desperate young man for a time.

As he stepped off the train in Chicago, he was shocked to find his parents had aged terribly during the four years he had been away. His

Princess in Paradise

father had given up his successful practice in Chicago Heights in order to specialize in oral surgery and prosthodontics, and had established a new office, first in downtown Chicago and then in Evanston. The depression had hit him as it had everyone else: there was no business; whatever assets he possessed were frozen; even the bank with his savings account had closed. While Laurence had an International Student Exchange Fellowship the previous year, his parents had had to borrow money in order to keep him going during the past year. On top of that, his father had been ill with pneumonia, which had left him with a serious heart condition. All this was news to him. In many ways he was as naive about the economic situation as we were.

In an especially long letter, Laurence reported that Madison and the university were as beautiful and impressive as ever, but that the situation had changed. For Laurence life was no longer that of the freewheeling fraternity undergraduate, but involved new responsibilities of a young faculty member. Wisconsin's reputation for beautiful coeds was still very much in evidence and right there in his classes, but he soon realized—or was reminded by his academic superiors —that engaging in social activities with students was not a good idea, especially for a young and eligible bachelor.

The future looked rosy—at first. He was welcomed with open arms by the department chairman and introduced to many of his prominent academic colleagues. Oskar Hagen was well known as a musician as well as an art historian in Göttingen, Germany, and had been a pioneer in the study and revival of the Händel operas in the famous Händel festivals held in Göttingen during the early 1920s. He served as a Carl Schurz Memorial Professor at Wisconsin in 1924 and was invited to stay and organize an art history department, which soon became a popular and highly successful major academic discipline in the university program. He had added a number of instructors and junior staff members to the department, some Americans, but mostly young German Ph.D.'s with European training and experience who had difficulties with both the language and American customs and did not last long. The prospect of Laurence, a midwesterner and Wisconsin graduate with German training and the Ph.D., was ideal for the full art history program he was trying to develop.

And so, in German fashion, Laurence practically became one of the family, in much the same way that he had been taken into the intimate family life of his professors during his first year at the University of Marburg, and as Ty and I had been included by the Clesses in Munich.

From Romance to Marriage

Mrs. Hagen, a gracious hostess and mother, was also a musician well known for her performances as a leading soprano in the Händel operas at Göttingen, and there were two highly talented teenagers, Holger and Uta (the latter was to become one of America's most distinguished actresses). There were many musical evenings, which Laurence loved, and a great deal of animated conversation—all in German of course.

But the mores remained German—and very much on the petit-bourgeois level—and that's where Laurence got into trouble. Professor Hagen, like Papi, was outwardly the generous and humanitarian man of the world, but at home he was the imperial head of the family, and while he spoke to Laurence with the familiar nickname of "Schmeck," he let it be known that he was to be addressed with proper respect as "Professor" or "Doktor" Hagen. At the office it was assumed that the "assistant" would hold the coat for the professor. When going out the door, he would hesitate for a moment so that it would be opened for him. That kind of treatment Laurence had been used to as a student in Germany, but his letters bristled with resentment as he discovered that this was to be a way of life in an American university.

Trial and Error

A major blow fell just a few weeks later. Laurence had plunged immediately into his research and writing; he was particularly working on an article on color psychology based on his dissertation and on the new ideas he had developed about modern Mexican art. Perhaps he had not spent as much time on the preparation of his lectures as he should have. Though he was an enthusiastic and articulate scholar—at least, I thought he was—his studies and most of his thinking during the past four years had been in German. Somehow he had the mistaken idea that the English would come automatically when he was discussing the sometimes complicated problems of art and history.

Without warning one day, the professor suddenly appeared in his class to hear his lecture. It was a fairly large auditorium; the class was small; the subject was rather dull (on the fifteenth-century Venetian painters of the Vivarini family), and the lecturer was obviously not properly well prepared. The result was an absolute disaster. The more flustered and embarrassed the speaker became, the more agitated and red-faced the professor appeared until, when the fifty-minute ordeal was over, he followed the crestfallen performer back to the office and exploded into a tirade that could be heard through the entire west wing of Bascon Hall.

"That was terrible! Who do you think you are? You don't know any art history! You can't even speak English properly! From now on I want you to attend my classes so that you can learn how to organize a lecture and how to speak English. . . ." And so it went. Laurence returned to his next class—the students knew what had happened and waited sympathetically—and he apologized for his tardiness: "I'm sorry to be late. I had to see a man about a dog."

For the next four months he was obliged to attend the professor's lectures, which he came to properly dislike as pompous and superficial, but he did manage to concoct the required proper pleasantries and polite compliments. He had learned his lesson, and from that time on every single lecture was written out beforehand and the notes thoroughly memorized, so that he did not have to refer to them while speaking; eventually, he developed the habit of delivering the full lecture without the use of notes or manuscript.

Indeed, the professor did appear in his class a short time later, again without warning. But on this occasion Laurence was ready for him. The subject was the stylistic development of Titian's painting, and instead of discussing the usual principles of Renaissance style, he switched to a description of Titian's studio procedure and an analysis of the artist's painting techniques, which he was sure the professor knew nothing about. The performance was a complete success, and the professor was surprised and even beamed. "Now, that was very interesting!" And it was the last time he ever appeared in class.

Another episode was even worse. It seems that the Wisconsin Historical Society had just installed an exhibition of newly acquired old master drawings from the Gregory Collection in its rather dingy gallery on the top floor of the library building. These included works by Rembrandt, Michelangelo, Titian, Tintoretto, Rubens, and other great masters. One of the students in Laurence's class commented on the exhibition with the remark that those were wonderful drawings, but "The artistic quality you are describing in class here does not seem to apply to the originals there in the museum!"

That was a challenge Laurence could not resist. He promptly marched himself down to the museum, checked the related books and catalogues in the library, and then reported to the class that these were not original drawings but were in all probability nineteenth-century forgeries—and not very good ones, at that. Using slides and reproduc-

From Romance to Marriage

tions, he explained why and gave the references for further study.

As it happened, one of the students was a part-time reporter for the local *Wisconsin State Journal*. The story appeared on the front page the next day with the lead—"Old Masters at U.W. Counterfeits,—Says Young University Professor." The director of the museum responded with a huffy denial—"There is no one in Madison capable of such a judgment"—and promised to submit the drawings to competent and recognized outside experts for appraisal.

The storm made good local news, since Charles Noble Gregory came from a prominent local family and had been a former dean of the university law school. The Historical Society had long been known for its stuffy aloofness. Laurence's friends were delighted and proud of him. But the next morning at the office, Professor Hagen stalked in, gave him one glaring look, and after a moment of stony silence, slammed the door in his face. It was not until several months later that another lead article appeared with the headline, "Schmeckebier Sustained; Old Masters Declared Counterfeit." The drawings had been submitted to the curatorial staff to the Metropolitan Museum in New York and to W. R. Valentiner at the Detroit Museum of Art. The opinion was unanimous and obvious: the drawings were indeed not the original old masters' works they were supposed to be.

I could have cried when I read the first letter and the newspaper clippings. How could he be so stupid? As usual he was right, but he certainly did not endear himself to his academic superiors. Mr. Hagen knew very well they were not authentic and said so privately, but not in public. The idea of backing up his embattled young colleague never occurred to him.

Meanwhile, word about the original ruckus got back to Mami and Papi. "Aha! What did I tell you? He's no good!" Of course, nothing was said about his remarkable success and recognition during the remainder of that semester and the following year. His lectures improved to the point where he became something of a celebrity, and enrollment in his classes increased dramatically, even rivaling the large introductory class which was taught by the professor. He gave public lectures and radio talks. He was active as advisor and promotor of the student-run exhibition gallery in the new Memorial Union. He helped reorganize and rejuvenate the venerable Madison Art Association, which soon became a vital force in the artistic consciousness of the university and town community. With all this activity he was accepted by the various social groups and became close friends with the leading intellectual personalities on campus, including many of those who were associated with the young Governor La Follette and his progressive policies.

His first articles were published that year, one on "The Orozco Murals in the New School for Social Research" and another on "Color Psychology," which curiously enough was accepted by H. L. Mencken for his *American Mercury*. Of course, what even I could not understand, especially in a university that took such pride in its tradition of liberal education, were the pointed remarks made by his department chairman about "those Mexican artists—they are all communists!" and "If you want to do research in color psychology, you should go down to the Department of Psychology." Laurence was hurt and still resistant, but he managed to swallow his pride, hold his peace, and do what he was told. As long as he did so, his job was secure and the future looked promising.

From Romance to Marriage

24

The New Way of Life

T HOME, a new way of life developed in the Kluge establishment on Eighty-fifth Street. Mami had arranged the best of the massive furniture, the gold hangings and brocades, the giant oil paintings and oriental rugs from Greystone so that the apartment looked very impressive indeed.

Englewood's once exotic animal menagerie was now reduced to two characters: one was Blitz, the beautiful German shepherd, which Papi had acquired from a woman who had trained the police dogs of Switzerland. He was an energetic, powerful animal with a tremendously long tail, which swished the liquor glasses and coffee cups off the cocktail table and waved like a banner when he tore up and down the long waxed hallway back to the bedrooms.

He adored Sergey. Sergey, now an exuberant ten-year-old, was enrolled in Public School No. 6 on Madison Avenue at Eighty-third Street. About three o'clock, Blitz would run to the windows yowling and then barking madly when he saw Sergey come skipping down Eighty-fifth Street. Later one could see Sergey on roller skates hanging on to Blitz's tail tearing down Madison Avenue, one barking and the other yelling wildly as they slithered their way along the crowded sidewalk through the parked cars and moving traffic on the street.

The other character was Billy, our beloved cockatoo parrot. He was all white, with a beautiful yellow crest which would stand up whenever he shook his head and screeched. The screech was shrill and penetrating, something you could never forget. He stood on his tall perch by the window and greeted everyone on Fifth Avenue. In later spring and summer when the windows were open, friends riding on the upper decks of the buses could hear him all the way down the avenue. That's Billy, the Kluges' parrot, all right. The neighbors complained, and Mami apologized—but Billy remained a fixed member of the establishment.

After settling in to the new apartment, Mami went back to her church activities. She would take the subway to the Russian cathedral down on Houston Street and spend long hours working with the sisterhood where she was always the patrician and the lady in charge. Whenever the archbishop came from California, it was Olga Alexandrovna who made his bed and did the cooking for him; and when he had guests or entertained at official gatherings, she and the ladies of the sisterhood did the work. She would mend his vestments or make new ones. She would have gorgeous golden damasks and brocades, which she had collected in an old Russian trunk, spread out all over her bedroom and spend hours figuring out how to make them.

Billy got lonely sitting on his perch in the living room. When he heard the sewing machine or Mami mumbling at the desk as she worked on her accounts with her abacus, he would climb off his perch and waddle the entire length of the hall to the bedroom, leaving (as birds do) evidence that Billy passed here. Once there, Mami put him on the back of her chair, and so he remained, in regal contentment. At dinner parties, too, Billy often ended up on the back of Mami's beautiful mahogany Queen Ann chair, sipping her liqueurs—port wine was his favorite—or coffee from her demitasse. When he had too much, he would doze and almost fall off his perch, then he would wake himself with a jerk and sit upright again.

The Hungary Russians and Their Friends

We had many wonderful friends. The business and parvenu celebrities we used to collect at Englewood disappeared, but the hungry Russians remained and brought their friends. They were of all types, but mostly Georgians and Caucasians, and when we had parties there were never fewer than thirty or forty. And there were many new personalities, such as Professor Tchterkin, who was a botanist with the New York Botanical Gardens and had been an underwater diver with Jacques Cousteau. He was also a fabulous cook, and when Papi would

From Romance to Marriage

return with salmon from a Canadian fishing expedition, he would dress them up on a huge platter with green peas for eyes and all sorts of beautiful embellishments to dramatize the party.

Another was one of Laurence's friends from the University of Wisconsin, Professor Alexander Vasilieff, a distinguished scholar in Byzantine history, who became a regular visitor and was often the life of the party. He was rather short and rotund, with a long handlebar mustache, a short cropped military haircut, and thick prismlike glasses; but he was both a brilliant conversationalist and a pianist, usually involving Tchaikovsky and the other great Russian composers of the nineteenth century.

They loved parties. No matter what the daytime activity, when these gentlefolk went out in the evening, they wore their one good suit or fancy handmade dress, their best pearl studs and beads, and looked positively regal. They all had a good time and would dance and sing and do plenty of toasting with vodka.

Plenty of vodka! The vodka situation was always Papi's specialty. With Prohibition and the high cost of bootleg liquor—and everybody broke—Papi had learned from the Russians how to make his own vodka, and from practically the first day after his arrival, Snooky became one of his most ardent pupils—an activity which eventually, after so many difficulties, brought the two of them together as very close friends.

The idea was to buy the regular grain alcohol in a gallon tin from the bootlegger, which was usually the cheapest and the safest one could get, mix it with distilled water on a 50-50 basis, add two or three drops of pure glycerin, soak the thinly pealed skin of one lemon in the combined mixture overnight, and then add two or three strands of *zubrovka* to the bottle or container being used. This *zubrovka* is a Polish marsh grass (also called buffalo grass) which at that time was available—practically in bales—at the Russian and Polish delicatessen. It is slightly aromatic and lends a kind of anise flavor to the vodka which, with the glycerin, gives it a very smooth and attractive flavor. Of course there are all kinds of vodka flavors, peppercorn, caraway, mountain ash berry, cherry, currant, and other fruits—but we all liked the *zubrovka* best. And with the endless variety of fish, cheeses, and usually highly seasoned tidbits that were spread out on the big table for *zakuska,* there was nothing more enjoyable and animating.

Through one of their society friends, a member of Prince Eristoff's wife's family, the Russians wangled the loan of a beautiful old house and estate on the Hudson River near West Point, where they could go on picnics and vacations, at no cost, during the late spring and summer. There they would flock, especially on weekends, by train or in their old cars, loaded with food, wine, and vodka. Always too, there were a couple of musicians with at least one accordian and several balalaikas to provide the entertainment, along with roaring fires; plenty of fish, rice, and *shashlyk* (grilled skewered lamb); and much singing of the old Russian folks songs and dancing the wild Caucasian dances. Papi always loved it, and because he usually brought the most bottles of vodka and loved to eat, he usually got the most attention.

They called the place Alaverdy and even organized themselves into an "Alaverdy Society." Once a year they held a grand ball in the Plaza Hotel to honor the former members of the Imperial Corps des Pages. Everything was aglitter with gold braid, colorful epaulettes, and shiny medals. Several of the generals had managed to escape with their old uniforms; if they had none, they managed to concoct some sort of a fancy military costume. The ladies wore their traditional Caucasian gowns with long flowing split sleeves, a little pillbox type hat, and the white lace handkerchief. *De rigueur*–that lace handkerchief. The native dances—wild dagger dances, group circles, and toe dances—were performed mostly by the men. Then there was a succession of the traditional mazurka, the polonaise, the quadrille, and of course the old-fashioned waltz.

Undoubtedly the most beautiful of these was the Caucasian *lizginka*, which calls for the gentleman to invite his partner to dance; then the couple glides around the floor in a large circle, face to face but about four feet apart. The lady is reserved and coy; the man is gently aggressive as he woos her. The ever present handkerchief is alternately held before the eyes, then dangled from the fingertips with outstretched arms, first one side, then the other. Mami dearly loved this dance, which she performed so gracefully, and it was usually the handsome and elegant Prince Matchabelli who selected her as his partner.

Mami, I thought, was so elegant and blissfully romantic in some of these dances, but she was capable of dramatic surprises. At one of these Corps des Pages balls, I remember a group of Caucasians was wildly swirling about in the center of the dance floor doing the trepack—and there was Mami in the midst of them, performing this most demanding and difficult feat with the enthusiasm and athletic skill of a profes-

From Romance to Marriage

sional. "Where did you learn that?" we asked. "Oh," she said, "we were always obliged to dance in the festivals at Romadanovo."

🥀 The Ménage on Eighty-fifth Street

There were other personalities who added color to this parade. Some of them were attractive young business ladies, like Henriette Herz, who was an editor with me at Knopf's, and Fran Conger, who was head dietitian for the White Turkey restaurant chains. And there were several Russians like Baron Wrangel and Vladimir Sazanoff; the latter was always hungry and broke but made his living largely by playing bridge for high stakes (as did Uncle Igor).

This posed another problem, because while Papi loved to play bridge and was quite good at it, he was not as good as he thought he was. He was constantly on the phone—"keeping in touch," as he called it—to organize a game, and with these semiprofessionals he was usually on the losing side. And who paid? Mami, of course.

As I have said, dear Sazanoff was always hungry and often would come early to have dinner with us before the bridge game. To repay us in some way he offered to teach us Russian. Coming back from school and later the office, Ty and I had to plunge into dinner preparations, bring Papi his drinks and *zakuska* in the library, serve the dinner, and then clean up. It was usually about ten o'clock when we were finished, and then we had our Russian lesson. We were both exhausted and fell fast asleep. I learned something, I suppose, but Ty always said that the only thing she ever learned was the word for dog—*sobaka*. That was almost symbolic.

Papi's daily routine usually consisted of sitting in his pajamas in the big chair in the library, listening to the news on the radio, and reading the newspapers. Then he would bellow forth, "Mami, come sit with me. I want to talk to you!" So, to keep peace, she had to stop doing her kitchen and cleaning chores (she did it all now) and sit with him, to listen to his discussion on the news, the political situation, and the state of the economy.

Occasionally he appeared, all dressed up in his best suit, and announced that he was taking a group of friends to lunch at the Plaza or to an expensive restaurant. Later several cases of good liquor would be delivered to the back door for Mr. Kluge. Where did he get the money? Did Cousin Albert give him a special check? Only later did Mami discover that another piece of her precious jewelry (which included some of the finest by Fabergé) had disappeared from its hiding place in her dresser and had been sold in a pawnshop on Third Avenue.

At this time, the role of Cousin Albert took on considerable importance in the new life of the Kluge establishment. In the earlier days, we had not seen much of him in Englewood, but now, for obvious reasons of financial survival, Papi felt obliged to cater to his whims and curious foibles. He too was big, though not quite Papi's size, an able businessman whose Artistic Weaving Company now had the monopoly of the label field. In spite of the depression, the business was very successful, with the profits further enhanced by his activity in the stock market, and, as I have said, though he was an able businessman and a freewheeling bachelor, he was sentimentally attached to the family. Not only did he help with the support of Papi and Mami, but he was responsible for his brother Willard and his family, whose entire fortune was lost in the crash, and Willard ended up a hopeless alcoholic.

Papi and his financial dealings were continually frustrating problems. Periodically Cousin Albert would send Papi off on sales trips across the country to Chicago, Minneapolis, St. Louis, and the West Coast and we all hoped the commissions would provide some help for the household. But the expense accounts were limited and came no where near what Papi was used to spending in the old days, so he simply blew whatever he made on commissions on his customary lavish entertainment. The result was that when he returned, he had had a good time and many new stories to tell but was just as flat broke as he was when he started.

Cousin Albert was also a great sports enthusiast and outdoorsman. Every spring and fall he would take Papi to New Brunswick for salmon fishing on the Miramichi River, and they would ship back huge boxes of fish which had to be kept on ice in the bathtubs and were the excuse for another Russian-Georgian-Caucasian party.

On Lake Sunapee in New Hampshire he maintained an elaborate summer camp with a staff of cooks and caretakers. There he entertained in his way, which usually involved factory and labor leaders, his political friends from New Jersey, and his somewhat questionable lady friends. Mami learned from experience not to accept his invitations, but Papi would go at the drop of a hat, partly because he was obligated to Albert, and partly because he simply loved drinking parties too.

Papi usually managed to control his drinking; if he had too much, he—like Billy, the cockatoo—just fell asleep. But after a few drinks, Cousin Albert would go wild, and sometimes would go on a rampage

From Romance to Marriage

for days. After such a Lake Sunapee "vacation," Papi would come home with some of the most harrowing tales. One was an all-night bout in which Max, the little German caretaker (who was always invited to participate in the celebrations) complained about an ache in his stomach. "Maybe its appendicitis," cried Albert, "let's operate!" And gleefully he tore after the little fellow with a giant butcher knife. All over the house, around the yard, over the pier and the boats they ran, little Max just out of reach and big Albert right after him, while everyone laughed hysterically. Maybe it was all a joke, but poor Max did not think so.

Albert owned the biggest and fastest Chris-Craft speedboat on the lake. It was his pride and joy. During one of these parties on a beautiful moonlight night, he invited everyone to go for a ride in his new boat. He was already having difficulty standing on his feet, so most of the guests declined his invitation and suggested that he go alone. So off he went at full speed, cutting big circles and figure eights, the hull making resounding splashes as it crossed the waves and Albert waving as he stood up to acknowledge the crowd's cheers—until he landed on a pile of rocks just off the nearby point and smashed the new boat to smithereens. As usual he was not hurt, but it was sheer luck that Papi was not in the boat with him.

Meanwhile, Ty's romance with Eric Holzer seemed to be progressing very successfully. He had worked hard during the spring semester of 1931, finished his dissertation on Atlantic shipping, and passed his Ph.D. exams with flying colors. As a reward, his father gave him a trip around the United States.

When he arrived to be introduced to the family, Ty had to go through the same routine that I had several months before. But this situation was quite different. Eric was not a struggling professor but a smart young businessman from a wealthy family, well-bred, and quite a gentleman. He would do.

❧ The Aborted Trip to Wisconsin

Eric took off on his trip around the country and suggested that we meet with Laurence in Madison in May. As we were just finishing our secretarial courses and each had saved a little money, we thought it was a great idea. So off we went.

With great excitement and expectations we arrived at the Northwestern station in Madison. There again were our two boys, Snooky and Eric, with a handsome Packard car which Eric had rented for the trip, and we toured about that fantastic campus and the state's capital.

The next day we drove around the beautiful Wisconsin countryside with its rolling hills and sparkling blue lakes, its prosperous dairy farms and wholesome-looking people. There were many French names like the towns of Fond du Lac and Prairie du Chien, which we naturally pronounced as in French. This made Snooky laugh, because he said here you call it "Prairie d'Sheen," or no one would know what you were trying to say.

Ty and Eric took off by themselves, and very successfully. As Ty tells the story, they drove around Lake Mendota and parked under the trees in front of the famous state insane asylum directly opposite the city with the distant panoramic view of Madison. A terrific rainstorm hit, which did not bother them, since they were much more concerned with making love than with the weather. After a while, the storm subsided, and they could see the shining dome of the State Capitol and the towering buildings of the university on the opposite hill hovering in the distance over the glistening waters of the sunlit lake. "Eric was hemming and hawing about something or other until I finally said, 'if you are asking me to marry you, the answer is yes.' " And that was that.

My problems were not resolved so easily. As far as his future was concerned, Snooky was more confused than ever. Owing to the new university budget restrictions, his original salary of $2,200 was cut to $1,200 beginning that following September, but he could teach summer school to help tide himself over until then. That same day (Saturday) a telegram arrived from Papi: "KNOPFS PHONED TWICE OFFERING POSITION IMMEDIATE START. REQUESTED DELAY UNTIL TUESDAY BUT SUGGEST YOU LEAVE MADISON IMMEDIATELY. THEY PROMISE HOLDING POSITION UNTIL TUESDAY. OPENING CAME SUDDENLY. URGE ACCEPTANCE."

My Publishing Career

Again, I asked no questions but did what I was told, and so, helpless and with a heavy heart, we boarded the Sunday train back to New York. Ty did not mind too much; in fact, she was delighted. She was anxious for new worlds to conquer. Tuesday I started my job with Alfred A. Knopf, first in the publicity office (I didn't even know what the word meant), and then as foreign reader at $15 per week. Within a few days Ty landed a position as secretary at $35 per week with Pan American Petroleum through Papi's connection with Bill Green, who

From Romance to Marriage

had rented our Park Avenue apartment several years before. Her boss was a tall lanky Texan who was an electrical engineer directing the electrification of oil wells at Lake Maracaibo, Venezuela. The atmosphere of the office was relaxed and informal. The man would dictate with his big feet up on the desk in front of her face. He was always smoking a pipe loaded with Players Cut, which she had to roast under the desk lamp for him.

But it was a different world in the offices of the A. A. Knopf Publishing Company. First there was the inspired leadership of Blanche and Alfred, whose intellectual brilliance was matched only by their personal devotion to creative artists, their sense of cultural responsibility, and their uncanny ability to work together. Their enthusiasm and dedication infected the entire office. Strange people —clerks, secretaries, editors, copy writers, accountants—all were dedicated, hardworking (and mostly young) men and women, firm in their belief that Knopf's was the greatest publishing enterprise in the world.

Within a short time my desk was stacked with books of all kinds, mostly French and German, but many in Italian and Spanish as well. What I didn't know by way of grammar, vocabulary, or background, I had to learn—and quickly. It was a constant challenge, and I loved it. The report on each book had to be brief and to the point, provide a résumé of the content, an opinion about its significance, and present the reasons for that opinion.

The biggest thrill, especially later when I became Mr. Knopf's personal secretary and had to entertain them, was the constant stream of celebrities who paraded through the office. Henry L. Mencken and George Jean Nathan were always in and out, both of them genial, outgoing, understanding, and colorful. Then there were the great women authors like Sigrid Undset and Willa Cather, and internationally distinguished personalities like Thomas Mann, Knut Hamsun, Ivan Bunin, John Hersey, and one of my favorite authors, Conrad Richter. When I left just before the wedding in December 1932, Mr. Knopf gave a little office party and presented me with a precious first edition set of Ivan Turgeniev's complete works.

Meanwhile, our two romances progressed, each in its curious and unique way. When Eric returned to New York after his tour of the country, he presented himself properly in formal costume—gray spats, white boutonnière, and all—to Papi with the request for Thaisa's hand in marriage. Papi, who several months before was most enthusiastic about Eric as a well-established prospect for his daughter's hand, seemed to have cooled off a bit and *hrumpped* his way through the interview with a weak, "Let's wait and see how the economic situation develops." That didn't faze Ty and Eric, for they went right ahead with their engagement and wedding plans, with a come-what-may attitude. Before he sailed on the *Europa,* he left an order with a nearby florist for a beautiful box of roses to be delivered to Ty at the apartment every Sunday morning. What an excitement that caused for the entire family for the next six months!

We were both very *sparsam* (frugal) with our salaries, always bringing our own sandwiches to work for lunch and sharing expenses with Mami. By February 1932 Ty had saved enough money to go to Berlin as guest of the Holzers in their elegant house in Grünewald. She wrote wonderful letters about the pampered life; the continuous round of concerts, theater, and opera performances she enjoyed; and Eric's remarkable progress as a junior member of his father's shipping firm—all this in spite of the growing economic and political tensions that threatened the family and their friends. She stayed until October 1932, when she returned home to prepare for the wedding.

Snooky Returns

After completion of his summer school classes in Madison, Snooky arrived in New York, ostensibly to work in the libraries and galleries on his Mexican art project. His attitude had become somewhat chastened and much more modest, but his ardor and enthusiasm were still unrestrained. He stayed with us in one of the little guestrooms at the Eighty-fifth Street apartment, managed quietly to get along with Papi, largely because he could drink as much as Papi without being visibly affected and because he would listen to Papi's stories. He loved Mami and spent long hours with her in the kitchen, listening sympathetically to her stories and occasionally her problems.

There was never a complaint from her to us, but every so often, while she was preparing dinner or in the quiet hours of the morning after breakfast (Papi seldom got up before eleven), she would talk to Snooky. Once he watched her standing at the hot stove preparing a big dinner with three or four pots of vegetables bubbling and a big pot of messy-looking stew which she was pushing around with a heavy spoon. Her long eyelashes were wet, the tears rolled down her cheeks as she slowly shook her head. "In Russia and the Old World we had such a beautiful life. Why do I have to suffer this endless misery? . . ." Then

From Romance to Marriage

she stopped, wiped her eyes with her apron, and regained her composure.

Snooky took to the Russian parties like a native Russki, but our most thrilling memories were the weekends we spent alone with my friends, Cynthia Flannery in Philadelphia, Anna North in Connecticut, Ruth Keeler on her big farm in North Salem, New York, and Henrietta Herz at the artist colony in Woodstock, New York. They were full of fun, and they all loved him. And, though our future was hazy, we loved each other and were blissfully happy.

It was in Woodstock that Snooky picked up a 1924-vintage four-seater Chevrolet for $25. It made more noise than Jack Benny's Maxwell and had a whistle from a leak in the engine block that could be heard half a mile away. But it ran. There was a big hole in the middle of the roof, which we patched with bright red oilcloth and adhesive tape, and we made beautiful seatcovers out of some cretonne with big red roses which we bought from a dime store.

Since our fancy Packard had been surrendered to the creditors long ago, this old jalopy became our mode of transportation. We parked it in front of the apartment, which was still possible during those early depression years, and though Papi looked down at it with disgust and would never ride in "that noisy thing," he always did when picnic time came. He could barely get himself through the narrow door, and, when he sat down in the back seat, the whole car would sink to the level of the rear axle. Then Sergey and Mami, the vodka bottles and the picnic basket, and Papi's cane would be sandwiched in around him. The whistling Chevy was later given to Mule to use to drive his gear to college at Dartmouth. It continued active service as an informal taxi which Mule conducted for his friends as a means of earning a little extra money. It came to a peaceful end two years later in a ditch outside Hanover.

The summer of 1932 provided a new rash of excitement and a new outlook on life for me. Through the year Snooky had managed his vacations with us in New York at Christmas, between semesters, and during the spring vacation. My parents were still not happy about his presence—he was "really not good enough for our Alexandra"—but under the circumstances they could do nothing about it, and they tolerated him. He was reasonably discreet, was busy with his research projects, and was always attentive to Mami.

His major project was now the book on modern Mexican art. He had been very careful about saving money; had received a substantial raise in salary, which put it just $200 above what it had been when he was hired; and was awarded a three-year contract at Wisconsin, so that he knew he had a job for that period of time. Thus, instead of teaching summer school again, he arranged to go to Mexico to study the murals and personally meet the artists who had become so prominent internationally during the past two years.

He arrived in New York in the middle of June, and we had two precious weeks before he was to sail on the S.S. *Oriente* for Vera Cruz and Mexico City. He talked to a number of publishers who were interested in the book and had already collected a variety of letters of introduction from his friend José Clemente Orozco to the leading critics, fellow artists, and officials in the Ministry of Education; thus, he was assured of an effective entrée into the important art circles. His plans and passage reservations were all made.

On the train back home, after a wonderful weekend at Ruth Keeler's farm in North Salem, Snooky gently took my hand and whispered, "Sasha, how about going to Mexico with me? I have enough money for both of us, we still have time to get married at the city hall before the ship sails, and I know I can change my reservation to a cabin for two on the *Oriente*."

I was dumbfounded. What had struck *him*? The worst part of the situation was that I was sorely tempted. There was no question about our being in love, but I also liked my job, even though the frustrating life and routine at home was continuous and exhausting. With Ty away in Europe and Mule at college most of the time (he had just come home to take a job at the German Tourist Office with Mr. Schmitz), I was the one who was obliged to perform the endless chores—along with Mami, of course—of the kitchen, serving at the table, cleaning up afterward, and serving the drinks and midnight sandwiches for Papi and his bridge companions. I had reached a state of fierce resistance to Papi's selfish domination and was constantly on the verge of rebellion.

But again, I did not rebel. With the vivid memory of Aunt Xenia's and Mami's stories of their youthful hopes and frustrations, and considering Mami's present state of mind, I did not feel justified in doing anything that would make her life any more miserable than it was. And Snooky understood. So we made plans for the Christmas vacation.

Snooky's letters from Mexico during his two-month stay there were vivid and exciting, though in many ways lonely and frustrating. Through his letters of introduction he was graciously received and entertained by a number of distinguished personalities, particularly

From Romance to Marriage

408   the art historians and critics—Jorge Juan Crespo and Justino Fernandez, Frances Toor and Howard Phillips, the enterprising editor of *Mexican Life*. Through them he was able to meet most of the working artists, visit their studios, and study their work. From his little room on the top floor of the Hotel Geneve he quickly established a regular routine of interviews, trips to the libraries and various public buildings to study the murals, and hours at the desk to write up his notes. He even managed a first handwritten draft of the proposed book, which he sent on, chapter by chapter, for me to edit and type up in a presentable form.

It was indeed a very tired but confident young man whom I met when the S.S. *Orizaba* docked at the Ward Line pier in New York. He had worked hard and accomplished a great deal, but the project became much larger and more important than he had originally planned, and there was much more work to be done. Actually, it was seven years later, 1939, that the book was finally published, and it then became one of the pioneer studies in this important area of contemporary art.

At this point, however, we had no time for elaborate discussions about contemporary art and history. We had plans to make and problems to solve before he took off again for the midwest. We talked fast and furiously during those three precious days, and I was finally able to convince him that some kind of compromise and adjustment on his part was necessary to clear the atmosphere for me at home. As far as I was concerned, I was determined, and as I kissed him good-bye, I reminded him, "This is the last time you leave without me!"

Princess in Paradise

25

The Double Wedding

HAT FATEFUL YEAR 1932 ended with our double wedding in the Russian Cathedral. But before it was finally accomplished there was a stream of episodes, sometimes painful, sometimes funny (as I look back on it now) through which we had to struggle.

Ty returned from Berlin in October, after six months of living a beautiful, sheltered life with the Holzers in suburban Grünewald. She and Mami immediately set about preparations for her wedding. Out of one of the old trunks came the gorgeous *Point de Venise* lace dress which Mami had worn for her wedding in 1909. The long and elaborate train with its many rosettes and insets had been taken off to make it a formal evening gown, which Mami now proceeded to piece together and reconstruct into a modern wedding dress.

There was obviously no money for a proper wedding and reception, but Mami figured that she could collect enough cash for expenses by selling some of the furniture. Ty and Eric had planned to have the wedding in the little brick Presbyterian church nearby on Park Avenue. When Papi heard of that, he blew up and shouted at her, "Whose wedding is this, anyhow? You do what your mother says!" She didn't know that Mami had already gone ahead with plans for the Russian church wedding or that it had even been discussed. So again, one did not ask questions but was expected to do whatever one was told.

At this point I was left out of the discussions. I knew Snooky and I were going to be married—but how or where I did not know. There were no comments from anyone, least of all from Papi. And Mami's silence was equally ominous. I had convinced Snooky before he came back from Mexico that he had to talk to Papi about our plans, and specifically to ask his permission. An appointment was formally arranged (by Mami!), and Papi received him in the library. Snooky proceeded to describe, in his best professional manner, how he and Alexandra had been in love for a long time and knew what we were doing. Though there had been difficulties, the economic situation had now improved: his appointment as assistant professor had been renewed for a six-year term; he had received a raise in salary; and we planned to be married. Mami was listening behind the portieres of one door; I was hidden behind the other, tearful and practically wringing my hands. "Why can't he humbly ask for permission?" No—not a word. The discussion went on, with Papi muttering something about responsibilities to the family and ending with a lame, "Well, let's see how the election comes out." As though the survival of Herbert Hoover had anything to do with it!

Here was another disaster, and more tearful discussions with my difficult Snooky. I finally convinced him that when he got back home he should write to Mami asking for her help, which he did. She responded with a long, gracious, and motherly letter, reminding him that "you have never been very friendly with Mr. Kluge and have not taken into consideration his age, character or psychology. There are certain principles and ideas that a man of his nature cannot possibly change . . . So be a man now, Laurence," she continued, "and write us a very nice, official, solicitous letter requesting permission from us as parents to have Alexandra become your wife . . ."

So he wrote the required letter. I can hear him mutter "Oh, what the hell!" as he did it. I never saw or heard what he wrote, but apparently it was effective, because it brought the following response from Papi, written in his best, somewhat florid Victorian script:

Dear Professor,
I quite appreciate the contents of your letter, to which I acquiesce in principle, while it still seems hard to reconcile ourselves to the "crude" way in which matters were handled so far. This is from the parents' point of view as frankly explained to you when you approached this subject at your last visit here.

Princess in Paradise

However, knowing your attitude now better, we believe and feel that you willingly accept and endeavor to comply more readily with the simplest form of consideration commonly shown and due to parents under normal circumstances. Many thanks for the invitation to visit your parents, which I quite appreciate and which I am sure would help "break the ice," so to speak. However, I am sorry to state I am not ready for a Chicago business trip as yet.

My nephew, Mr. Albert Kluge, will be at the Hotel Stevens in Chicago for several days from this Thursday on. I outlined conditions to him in general. He would like to meet your parents.

Could you prepare for this and ask them to get in touch with him at the hotel? Maybe then it can be arranged for Alexandra to visit your family around Thanksgiving or Christmas time. Meanwhile, Mrs. Kluge or I may find an opportunity to do the same, and then—and only then—should definite decisions and plans be formulated—all, we think, for the best and most harmonious good of everyone concerned.

Please bear this in mind and let me see to what extent we can depend on your own cooperation.

Sincerely your,
E. H. Kluge

There was not much Snooky could do after receiving that one, except to send it on to me with the question, "With everyone flat broke, who is going to finance all these official visitations back and forth?" I felt more miserable than ever. But I did receive a lovely letter from Snooky's father in response to one I had written him a short time before, expressing confidence that "you are everything that Laurence has described so devotedly. Your frankness makes us feel that you are closer to us than we realized. Mrs. Schmeckebier is delighted with the thought of a daughter which she has so long wanted and waited for and your letter makes her feel the nearness of a happy future. . . . "

Snooky, of course, did not arrange for his parents "to get in touch with" Albert at the hotel as ordered, but Cousin Albert appeared one evening unannounced at the Schmeckebiers' Evanston apartment for the official "inspection." They were delighted to see him, and Dr. Schmeckebier brought out a bottle of his best prescription whiskey, which Albert finished in due course. He told them all about the Kluge family and its problems and especially about his favorite cousin, Alexandra. The visit lasted over three hours. Everyone was animated and visibly pleased, according to later reports, except that Snooky's mother was upset that the taxi driver was sitting outside on the street with the motor running the entire time. She considered that an unnecessary extravagance.

A telegram was immediately dispatched: "EXTREMELY IMPRESSED WITH MR. AND MRS. SCHMECKEBIER NOT MILLIONAIRES BUT WONDERFUL AMERICAN PEOPLE ALL SIGNS OF REFINEMENT AND HAPPY HOME. MR. SCHMECKEBIER WRITING EMILE—ALBERT."

Preparations For the Big Day

So we got over that hurdle. At home, nothing more was said, as far as I was concerned. Papi apparently assumed that he had effectively avoided the confrontation, so Mami, Ty, and I simply went ahead with our plans. A double wedding could be done just as cheaply as a single one, and we would have it in the Russian Cathedral with the reception at home afterward.

Given the silent treatment from my parents, Snooky too moved right ahead on his own with our plans. He was able to rent a modest furnished apartment in Kennedy Manor at half price, since most of the building was empty because of the depression. He arranged for the announcement of the wedding on the day he left Madison, and he arrived in New York to stay at Aunt Xenia's apartment two days before Christmas. With all our confusion and talk (or lack of it), he did not know whether there was to be a double wedding or not—or any wedding, for that matter—and with the reception he expected from Papi he had every intention of taking me down to city hall to be married there. His father had bought him a new dark suit; he had the wedding license; he had a room reserved for December 26th at the Barbizon Plaza; and he had the two gold rings, which he had designed and his father had cast for him in his dental laboratory—so he was prepared for any eventuality.

Meanwhile, the apartment was in a constant whirl of activity. Papi was completely ignored and really didn't know what was going on. Ty and I, as always, worked as a team in coordinating our thoughts and plans. Mami, now full of hope and enthusiasm, had taken complete command of the situation. She managed to get some money together—how or from what source I never knew exactly; but it must have come from the sale of some of the furniture stored in Albert's factory. She and her skilled Russian ladies, especially Lara Kupfer, Ludmilla Isnard, and Fatima Natirboff, fitted the wedding dresses and made the veils. Ty's Venetian lace dress was just perfect, since they were both the same size, and there was plenty of extra lace for both veil and train. I bought a white satin evening dress for $10 from a sale at Gimbels with some extra material for long sleeves; and Ludmilla made the veil out of a long roll of Brussels lace, which Mami had used for her wedding veil with a *kokochnik*-type wire frame for the headpiece.

Mami made all the arrangements for the wedding at the cathedral with Bishop Leonti, who would perform the service. The reception at home was to be appropriately modest with the caterer providing the tables, tablecloths, some flowers, along with chicken á la king with rolls. Our Russian ladies were to bring the *zakuska*, and there were gallons of vodka in the closet.

Eric arrived from Germany and took a room at the Waldorf-Astoria. Then Snooky appeared, full of enthusiasm and ready for action, but he soon discovered that all the plans were established, and there was nothing for him to do but submit—like the traditional *Opferlamm* (sacrificial lamb)—as he said, to the existing authority. He did not even object to my insistence that he go with me to visit Mami's devoted Metropolitan Platon. The blessing of our marriage by that venerable and saintly clergyman was a touching experience that neither of us would ever forget. One felt exalted, as the scripture says, by the prayers and presence of holy men.

First, the new blue suit that Snooky had bought would not do. From Violet's friend, Arthur O'Neal, I borrowed a formal cutaway with stripped pants and wing collar. The coat and length of the pants fitted perfectly, but the waist was considerably larger than Snooky's trim thirty-two inches. So we had to pull several pleats together and fasten them in the back with safety pins. Thereupon he looked perfectly respectable. Eric appeared with his beautifully tailored cutaway, wing collar, bow tie, and patent-leather shoes, and looked very impressive indeed.

But we had not counted on Papi; and in fact, since he seemed very much preoccupied with outside business matters of some sort, we had almost forgotten him.

Early that morning came the avalanche. From a Fifth Avenue florist came two huge bunches of red roses, supposedly for our wedding bouquets. From the bootleggers came a dozen cases of champagne, whiskey, and gin. A squad of waiters appeared from Diadia Kostia's Moscow Inn—Papi's special friend, and also his favorite Russian restaurant—with cartons and cartons of food and supplies which they proceeded to unpack and arrange on the big table in the living room.

From Romance to Marriage

Somehow Papi had wangled a substantial check out of Cousin Albert so that he could provide an appropriate reception "in honor of his beautiful daughters." To us that was a laugh, and we were furious. We had already bought our small bouquets of white lilies and felt that the red roses were both gaudy and inappropriate. The champagne and liquor we knew everyone would love, especially the Russians, and the food was already there—a beautiful spread of endless *zakuska* with a gigantic salmon in aspic as its special feature. So there was nothing to do about it.

Meanwhile, Ty and I had been busy in our respective bedrooms getting ourselves dressed, with much talk and lots of help from Violet and Bobbie Robertson, our maids of honor, as well as from Aunt Xenia, Ludmilla, Lara Kupfer, Fatima Natirboff, and several other Russian ladies. There was a quiet, solemn moment when Mami came in, gave us each a gentle kiss, and presented both of us with an old family ikon, a "Christ Blessing" for me and a "Virgin and Child" for Ty, which were to be carried into the church for the ceremony and become one of our most treasured possessions ever afterward. Then Mami disappeared. With the sudden influx of Diadia Kostia and his food and waiters, though at first nonplused and furious, she immediately took charge and set about organizing the tables and food for the reception after the wedding.

As the hour approached, we had the photographers in for a picture-taking session in the living room. Then Papi called Snooky into the library for "inspection." Looking him over, he discovered Snooky was wearing regular black street shoes, and roared: "That will never do! You should have patent-leather shoes!" At this late moment there was no time to go out and buy new shoes. "That's all right," said he. "You can wear a pair of mine." This was no time to argue, so the proper patent-leather shoes were provided, several sizes too large and floppy, but they would do.

"Now, Laurence," said Papi with a kind and, for the first time, fatherly smile, "please sit down here with me. The time is short and I want to talk to you!"—Now what's he up to? we all wondered.

"You are faced with a very serious situation," he went on, "and you are going to need all the courage and reenforcement you can get . . ."

So he poured out a water glass full to the brim with bourbon whiskey—Golden Wedding, no less—and of course poured one for himself. Snooky was not going to argue about this either, so he drank it down and was excused.

Princess in Paradise

Then came Eric's turn for inspection. The first thing Papi spotted was the bow tie: "That won't do," he stated in his very positive tone. "You'll have to change that to a four-in-hand." "Oh, no," retorted Eric. "In Berlin we wear a bow tie with a formal cutaway." Papi's face grew red. "But you're not in Germany!" he thundered. "You are in Amerr-r-ica, and you do as the Amerr-r-icans do!" But Eric was just as "German" as Papi and would not change.

Papi was furious. From then on the state of imperial grace for the two young men was reversed. Eric, who up to that time had been considered the wealthy and cultured European "man of distinction," was now in the doghouse, while Snooky, the crude barbarian from the Middle West, became Papi's fairhaired boy. From then on, wherever we were, whether it was Wisconsin, Minnesota, or New York, Papi and Snooky were the best of friends, each contributing his odd but characteristic share of stories, ideas, and entertainment whenever they were together.

We were already late, so Eric and his best man, Mr. Weigelt, who was head of the New York office of Eric's shipping firm, and Snooky with his best man, Charley Caddock, a French professor from Wisconsin, set off for the church in Mr. Weigelt's car. According to Charley's story, Snooky provided lively entertainment for the hour's trip downtown by singing his old fraternity songs and ballads for the benefit of his shocked European colleagues. In due course we, too, were loaded into Albert's big limosine with all our veils and finery, Mami, and our maids of honor, Bobbie Robertson and Violet Orthwein.

The Russian Cathedral was a rather sizable structure of limestone and brick in Victorian Gothic Revival style designed by William A. Potter and Robert H. Robertson in 1876. It had originally been a fashionable Episcopal Chapel, dedicated to St. Augustine as a part of Trinity Parish, but when the area deteriorated, and the Russian congregation was desperately in need of a home after its old Ninety-seventh Street church had been taken over by the Soviets, Bishop Manning arranged for its transfer as the archbishop's seat as head of the Russian Orthodox Church of America. There were various buildings attached to provide living quarters for the clergy, and there were rooms for school and social activities.

The church itself was a large, auditorium-type room with benches and pews removed and a tall ikonostasis built across one end to separate the sanctuary from the congregation area. This screen, or partition, is richly decorated with Byzantine-type overlife-sized saints and

From Romance to Marriage

The Russian Orthodox Cathedral on Houston Street, scene of the double wedding in 1932 was formerly the Episcopal Chapel of St. Augustine. Photo courtesy of Trinity Church Parish Archives.

Princess in Paradise

martyrs, in three tiers, separated by carved wooden frames in glittering gold. The doorway in the center leads from the sanctuary to the wide nave; before it is the free-standing altar. The light in the entire space is rather subdued by the heavy stained-glass windows and the soft flickering of candles, which the gold of the altar and ikonostasis reflects in a steadily moving glow.

❧ The Double Wedding

On arrival we were met by our sponsors, Cousin Albert for Ty and Uncle Igor for me, and were led to the little anteroom where the various marriage documents were signed. At that point, Uncle Igor presented each of us with a ten-dollar gold piece, which he inserted into our slippers so that we would forever walk in wealth and comfort. The comfort idea was something less than obvious, and the wealth I never experienced thereafter, but it was a lovely symbol.

Then began the procession, led by little Sergey and his friend David Chavchavadze, dressed in blue with shining white collars and carrying our respective ikons. There followed a double phalanx of robed priests and acolytes bearing the processional crosses, lighted tapers, swinging censers, and the gospel books. The room was crowded, the men on one side, the women on the other, the air heavy and fragrant with incense, and the rich voices of a full chorus resounded through the dimmed atmosphere with a mighty hymn of praise.

Before the altar we were welcomed by the priest—the venerable and ascetic Bishop Leontiy—with the sign of the cross. An opening prayer was read, and we were given lighted tapers, which we held throughout the service. There were two pieces of pure white silk stretched on the floor before the altar as the two couples were led forward. Everyone watched with bated breath to see which of the two, bride or groom, would step on the cloth first, which would seem to indicate which would have the upper hand in the marriage. Wouldn't you know, it was Ty who made it first with a very positive step; whereas with us, by sheer accident, Snooky and I each put our right foot on the cloth at exactly the same time.

As the priests moved in procession to each side of the altar, our ushers moved into position beside each of us to hold the crowns over our heads. These glittering, jeweled crowns were heavy, and the service was long, and so there were six of these faithful characters for each

From Romance to Marriage

of us, a total of twenty-four whom we had to recruit from among our friends, a formidable array of princes, generals, and solid Americans.

The service began—three hours of it—in Russian, which included the traditional recitations of the marriage vows and the exchange of rings as in the Episcopal church, but embellished by the rich and sonorous readings from the Gospel, the Psalms, other portions of the Old Testament, and the Exhortations of the Saints, together with the melodious responses from the choir.

There were repeated prayers, chanted by the priest, calling for the blessing of eternal God, as He did bless Adam and Eve, Abraham and Sarah, Isaac and Rebecca, Joachim and Anna, and the vast repertory of biblical betrothals. There were the exhortations to mutual love, reverence, and faith as proclaimed by the Holy Martyrs and Prophets, the God-crowned Kings and Saints. These were reinforced and dramatized by the booming voice of the deacon and the sonorous replies by the choir with their "Amens," "Lord, have mercy," "Glory to Thee O God—and with Thy spirit."

With the glow of the lighted candle in my hand, Snooky beside me, the deep bass of the chanting deacon, the rich, resounding tones of the choir and the awesome space of the cathedral about us, I stood almost transfixed. After these many years of struggle, a kind of continuous trial by ordeal—which I did not see as the punishment of the Inferno but as the purification of Purgatory—we had reached the fulfillment, or perhaps the beginning, of that long love.

I caught a fleeting glimpse of Mami over on one side standing in her luminous lavender dress and quiet, regal manner, watching with misty eyes her two daughters in the candlelight. On the other side sat Papi —the only one sitting—like Old King Cole, wiping his bald perspiring head and fanning himself. What was Mami seeing? Was it her two daughters and their partners here before her, or was it the vision of another era, the brilliant altar and colorful assemblage in the ancient church of St. Nicholas in Moscow twenty-five years before? These questions raced through my head. I knew I would never have any answers.

Then the priest delivered his exhortations about the Sacrament of Marriage, the necessity for living godly and uprightly in the wedded state. The administering of the vows, and the exchange of rings followed, and to the question, "Hast thou not promised thyself to another man?" spoken in his melodious Russian, I answered, quite clearly, "Yes!" The poor priest became flustered, shook his head and wavy beard, and repeated in his husky voice, "No, no, no," he said, pointing to the word *No* in the book. So the record was properly corrected.

More prayers followed: "Bless this Marriage, O Lord our God," and then came John's account of the marriage in Cana at Galilee. Then the common cup was brought, and after the priest had blessed it, he extended it three times to each of us. The first time Snooky missed the rim of the cup and almost had the wine spilled down his front. The second time he made it all right, but in a moment of dead silence while he swallowed came the voice of Papi loud and clear from out of the crowd: "Atta boy, Laurence, take a good drink!" Thus we shared the cup of joy and sorrow and quietly vowed to live our life in peace and concord.

This completed, the priest took the joined hands of each couple in his; wrapped his gold-embroidered stole—the symbol of purity and humility—around them; and walked us, each with his and her respective retinue of crown bearers in a circle, three times around the golden altar. This took a bit of negotiating and some fancy footwork on their part, with our long veils trailing behind; and not only were the men tired from stretching up with those crowns, but some, like Andy Wineburg, were short and none too agile. But they managed to keep the crowns up there even though they had to jump back and forth over the veils.

On completion, the priest took the crown from each bride and groom, and as the chorus sang its hymn of rejoicing and exaltation, he prayed to the Holy Martyrs, "who fought the good fight and have received your crowns: Entreat ye the Lord that he will have mercy on your souls!"

Finally came the Benediction, with the presence of Christ our true God, the prayers of His all-holy Mother, the glorious Apostles, the Holy Martyrs, and the God-crowned Kings and Saints. "Glory now and forever, . . . the Lord have mercy upon you, for He is good and loveth mankind." And with the thunderous alleluias of the full chorus we kissed and turned to face our friends—and the world!

As much from relief after the long ordeal as from the joy of the event, the crowd became alive with chatter and excitement. We quickly arranged an informal receiving line and embraced each one as they came by—the beaming Russians, my lovely Dwight and Vassar friends, and our faithful family. And who should appear in the line but Norbert MacKenna, very proper and Princetonian in his formal cutaway, striped trousers, white spats, windsor tie, and white boutonniere. (Odd that I should have made that almost Freudian slip during the service!) Though I had received several letters and telephone calls from him during the previous three years, I had not seen him and certainly felt no regrets. Snooky was very friendly and pleased to have met him.

🌿 The Reception

When we returned home, the apartment was ablaze with glittering lights, colorful food, and animated people. From across the long living room came the deep bass voice of Max Panteleiev, at that time a popular star at the Russian Opera in New York, singing the beautiful Hymenaeus, the traditional Hymn of Welcome. Then Mami received us, presenting the traditional bread and salt on a richly embroidered linen towel over one of her treasured Russian painted plates.

And the *zakuska*! In the traditional Russian household—at least as Mami maintained it—the *zakuska* was always a standard feature, and the ritual of the food table was almost as important as that of the church service itself. At one end of the huge oval table was a giant salmon in aspic shimmering in pink and silver. On the other end were the bowls of caviar: the gray *Beluga*, the most highly prized with the largest eggs and the darker *Sevruga* and *Osetrova*, with a platter of dry toasted white bread beside them. Then there was a platter of red caviar spread on buttered Russian dark bread and pumpernickel with thin slices of hardboiled eggs and sprinkled with chopped onion greens.

For color contrast and taste there was a selection of other fish: the dark and delicious smoked eel, golden sprats in oil, pickled herring in sour cream, silver pilchards, a plate of anchovies pounded with butter into a paste, and a variety of sardines. There was a wide assortment of cheeses and thinly sliced hard sausages. Then there were several hot casseroles, flaming chafing dishes: veal kidneys in Madeira; chicken livers in sour cream; and *Bitki*, tiny meat balls in a rich, highly seasoned sauce. And of course there were plates of *pirozhki*, the delicious small pastries filled with chopped meat, and *pashtet,* the pâté of chicken or calves liver. Each dish was lavishly decorated with bright and colorful designs: wreaths of carved turnip rosebuds for the pâté, carrot daisies for the aspic, chains of onion rings for the herring and scallions made into white peacocks with spreading green fantails.

Scattered over the tables were the shapely vodka bottles with little glasses, like those of the Protestant communion service—one doesn't sip vodka, one swallows it in one gulp—and they were in their various colors: the clear (Krasnaia Golovka), the orange (Riabinovaia) made from the berries of the mountain ash, the yellow (made with lemon peel) the ruby colored (Smarodinovka, from the black currant leaves) and the clouded gray (Pertsovka, with black pepper)—plus lots of Papi's favorite, the Zubrovka vodka.

How this was all managed we never knew. Of course, once Papi had plenty of money from Cousin Albert's last-minute contribution, it was easy to get the full service of Diadia Kostia and his caterers as well as the champagne and other liquors, but the varieties of vodka he had to concoct somehow, and that was probably why he was so busy and out of everyone's sight in the days before the wedding. But then, how Mami managed with all her difficulties and not knowing what Papi was up to and that he had any money—and then when it all descended on them the final day, to have the total operation brought under control as she did—was nothing short of a miracle. The reception was a brilliant success.

There were other ceremonies that were part of the ritual. There was the big silver *Römers*, the beautifully embossed goblets which had been collected on Papi's and Mami's various travels and were given to each of us filled with champagne with the cheers of the whole crowd to "drink-it-down"—in Russian, *Peydodna*–and the cheers would not stop until the goblet was empty. And then someone would fill it again.

After a while Eric got impatient, so he and Ty left for their Waldorf-Astoria suite without even having a piece of the wedding cake. Snooky and I stayed on to enjoy the miracle to the fullest. There was nothing more amazing to me, after all these months, even years of struggle, than to see Papi and Snooky toasting one another as the best of friends and Papi boasting about his professor son-in-law and the great work he was doing out there in "Veesconsin." We finally left to go to our little room in the Barbizon Plaza, but the party went on until almost daylight, with Papi fast asleep in his big chair at the head of the living room.

The next morning was my birthday—I have never gotten over the idea of waking up to find a husband in my bed as a birthday present. A miracle had indeed been achieved. But of course, with the Kluges a birthday calls for another celebration. We got back to the apartment to find a very sorry-looking sight. Ty and Mami were already busy cleaning up the debris, and there in the kitchen we discovered the huge tub of chicken a la king which Mami had originally ordered and had been completely forgotten. Then Papi appeared in his pajamas and got his

From Romance to Marriage

422 vodkas and liquors organized. We all set to work, and before long we had the Russians assembled and a new celebration under way.

Ty and Eric were scheduled to sail on the *Europa* at midnight that night. What all happened until that time I really don't remember except that the party went on and the entire crowd arrived at the pier singing and cheering the happy couple as the huge ship slowly pulled away amid the great floodlights and the blast of sirens.

The next morning it was our turn. We had gone back to the hotel, alone with each other and blissfully free, until as we strode down the long red carpet on the platform of Grand Central Station to the waiting *Twentieth Century*, there appeared the entire crowd of Russians singing and cheering us on our way. With tears of gratitude and joy, we waved to the past and turned to a new life and what would surely be a glorious future.

Princess in Paradise

Epilogue

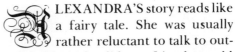

LEXANDRA'S story reads like a fairy tale. She was usually rather reluctant to talk to outsiders about her family history, but when she did our friends would shake their heads in disbelief: "It's incredible!" But it is not a fairy tale. The characters she describes were and are all real. I have seen most of them, watched them perform, argue, sing and laugh, and I've listened to their stories. I have watched the joyful abandon and sad nostalgia of the Russian émigré friends at Alaverdy and the parties at the Kluges'. Aunt Xenia was just as flamboyant as Sa had described her, only more so, and Uncle Igor, with his taciturn reserve, sharp legal mind, and military bearing, had a quiet nobility about him that seemed strengthened by his years of war and misery during the Russian Revolution.

I have seen the baleful monuments of a paradise that once was: the burned-out hulk of Greystone on the hill overlooking Englewood, the black-topped parking lot where once stood the flourishing Kluge textile mills in Krefeld, and the bombed-out graveyard where the scattered bones of the Kluge ancestors were reassembled into a common grave.

And Papi! In spite of my early prejudice, the years of our friendship provide a treasury of memories that fairly bubble with good humor and a zest for life that seemed to be the product of an inner discipline rather than the contrary. Once you had known him, he could never be forgotten.

423

Lastly, it was the Princess Olga Alexandrovna, whom General O'Ryan used to call "Lady Olga," who was the noble heroine of this remarkable pageant, as she moved through those opulent years in Englewood, the miseries that followed in the depression, to an eventual and lonely triumph of religious faith and moral integrity. In many ways, her career forms a curious parallel to that of lovely St. Elizabeth of Marburg—the thirteenth-century Northern counterpart of Italy's St. Francis of Assisi—the fabled lady of noble birth who devoted her wealth and life to the love and service of others less fortunate.

What happened to the various personalities in this pageant in the years that followed the wedding would fill another book, but the reader might be interested in a few of the main events.

Ty and Eric were established in a newly decorated apartment on the third floor of the Holzer home in Grünewald as Eric resumed his duties with his father's shipping firm. However, with the fast-moving political events of 1933 and the drastic takeover of the German government by the Nazis, the Holzers quickly became the target of persecution. The newlyweds were then moved to London where Eric became part of the Holzer branch office, specializing in transatlantic shipping. The father, Marcell, was imprisoned on trumped-up charges and then began the long struggle to salvage as much of the property and their resources as possible and to get the family out.

During this process it was Ty, with her American passport and personal charm, who was able to travel back and forth to Berlin and do most of the negotiating. Eventually the Holzers were freed and, with their good American connections, established a new shipping company in New York. This company, through sheer hard work and brilliant management, first under Marcell and then Eric as president, developed through the depression and World War II years into one of the major shipping operations of the country. They lived happily in Scarsdale, New York, until Eric was killed in a tragic automobile accident in 1968, when the firm was taken over by their son, Peter. Some years later Ty married Henry Keuls, whose wife had died, and who had long been among Papi's and Mami's most loyal friends in the early days at Englewood and Eighty-fifth Street. Remembering Papi's various problems with his daughter's suitors, Henry would often say with a wry smile, "If Papi only knew!"

Mule—Emile, Jr.—graduated from Dartmouth as an economics major in 1934, but remained an ardent student of literature and music as well as an active participant in amateur theater. He took three years of graduate work in the Philadelphia Textile School, and then became part of Cousin Albert's Artistic Weaving Company until World War II. After five years of distinguished service as captain in the U.S. Air Corps and again during the Korean War, he returned to Artistic Weaving as a plant manager and executive. Mule never married but, like a true Morovsky-Kluge, he was always devoted to the family and became the beloved "Uncle Mule" to the host of his nieces and nephews—our four, Ty's two, and Sergey's three. He died in 1971, a victim of cancer.

Sergey, the youngest of the four children, had perhaps the most difficult time. After the wedding and the departure of the girls, he became the sole target of Papi's fierce attention, but his was a strong as well as resilient character, and he managed somehow to survive. After graduating from grade school, P.S. 6, he was sent to the Lincoln School, which at that time was considered one of New York's most modern and progressive schools. Its freewheeling policy of relaxed learning based on personal initiative rather than imposed discipline threw Papi into fits until he met someone whose son was attending Admiral Farragut Academy in Lakewood, New Jersey, and raved about it.

"That's where my son must go!" He never asked Sergey what he thought about it or whether he had the scholastic standing to get in, but he maneuvered the acceptance and Cousin Albert's financial support. As it happened, Sergey did well and loved it. On graduation he was sent—again, not because he wanted to go there, but because he liked to work with tools and was supposed to have a flair for engineering—to Stevens Institute of Technology in Hoboken.

That did not turn out so well, but the war intervened and Sergey left school to work in a war industry in St. Paul, where we were living. There he met and married a lovely girl—we were the hosts and sponsors this time, not in the old tradition but on a very modest and limited wartime scale—before he entered the armed forces as a U.S. Navy Seabee. After several years' service in the Pacific theater, he returned to New York to work with Eric's company specializing in ship-loading and eventually became one of the experts in the new container ship system which Eric was developing. He is still active in this field.

Through all this, Papi continued his colorful and inimitable career. After the wedding, the family moved to a less expensive apartment on Ninety-sixth Street—smaller but still large enough to accommodate the ménage of paying guests to keep the household afloat—the chief

Epilogue

problem was always that of keeping Papi occupied. For that purpose the routine remained the same, with the changing houseguests, the continuing bridge games, and the faithful but hungry Russians dropping in at all hours, and all under Mami's selfless management.

At fairly regular intervals Papi arranged his special sales trips to the West to see his old friends and customers on behalf of Cousin Albert's label business. On these occasions he was, of course, provided with a substantial expense account and at the end would stay with us as long as his finances held out. In Madison during the Great Depression, he was always considerate of our limited circumstances and on arrival would immediately take off in a taxi to make the rounds of the gourmet food and delicatessen shops to collect a load of provisions and, of course, plenty of liquor. "Now, Alexandra," he would say, "we must have a party!"

It was no trouble to assemble a group of young, attractive, and enthusiastic friends for a party; and Sa, like her mother, was almost a genius at arranging things—usually in the Russian manner with *zakuska,* vodka, and the traditional Russian specialties—so that it was a social and artistic success without anyone knowing how it happened.

And they loved Papi! His huge and imposing figure, jovial manner, endless collection of stories, and sharp eye for the attractive young ladies made an impression that was unique and unforgettable. As one of the Vassar girls said, "I had never seen anyone like that outside of the circus!" She was so fascinated, she could not keep her eyes off him and remained an ardent listener through the entire evening.

Papi and I remained the very best of friends. His major concern, however, was why a supposedly intelligent young man in this academic profession could not make money the way they do in other fields. "Laurence," he would say, "we've got to figure out some kind of a ra-a-cket, so that you could make some money on the side." I would try to explain that that was precisely what I was trying to do, but somehow I could not convince him that research and writing on modern Mexican art and Italian Renaissance painting was the way to do it.

During the difficult war years at the University of Minnesota, those visits continued; and, with the wider circle of friends we had in St. Paul and Minneapolis, the parties were extended into a series. We would have a big party for him shortly after his arrival, and then the various friends would insist on entertaining him in their way. Papi just loved that, too.

At this time, not only were our limitations financial, but food and supplies were rationed as well. That made no difference to Papi. He would arrive in town from the airport, find himself a taxi and the proper connections, and appear at our house with a load of liquor and rationed food supplies such as we had not seen in months. Where or how he got them we never knew, and he was never the one to tell us.

With new and changing audiences the old stories were still good, but each time Papi went on one of those trips there were new and harrowing adventures. On one such occasion his plane developed engine trouble on the way back from Los Angeles and had to make an emergency landing in a desolate Nebraska cornfield. The rescue plane dispatched to the area was a small, six-passenger single-engine biplane of questionable vintage. In the process of loading the passengers, Papi, with his wide girth, got stuck in the narrow doorway, so tightly in fact that the desperate attendants could not move him one way or the other until finally they managed to twist him around—corkscrew fashion —before he fell inside, to the cheers and laughter of the other passengers both inside and outside the plane. He enjoyed telling that story fully as much as the passengers did watching it happen.

The last we saw of Papi was in the summer of 1947, the year after we had moved to Cleveland, when we spent a happy two-week vacation at the Looschen cottage on Greenwood Lake in New Jersey. It was like the halcyon days of old but under vastly different circumstances: there was no longer the big entourage of servants and nurses, and the group attention was directed at our family of four lively youngsters rather than at the original three Kluges. But Papi was as active as ever, the first one on the pier in the early morning to plunge into the cold water with a resounding *ka-boom,* fanning himself in the shade at midday, and calling for someone to sit with him while he had his highball and *zakuska.*

He knew that he was not well, and in spite of the doctor's stern warnings that he must cut down on his cocktails, there was no way to change him. On the other hand—though he was born a Lutheran and had seldom expressed any interest in the church himself—he had always maintained the deepest respect for Olga's religious convictions. And so it was that he quietly asked Olga—he was not giving orders this time—if she would arrange for the bishop to come to see him. After the proper instructions and ceremony, he received absolution and was accepted as a member of the Russian Orthodox Church. Shortly afterward, just a few weeks before his eightieth birthday, he died in his sleep of acute heart failure.

Epilogue

Portrait of Papi painted in 1948 by John Teyral from life sketches made the previous year.

Princess in Paradise

The solemn requiem and burial service in the Russian Cathedral provided an impressive and touching climax to this long and colorful career. We had not seen the church since our wedding day and stood in awe before the huge bier on the tall catafalque in front of the altar and shining gold ikonostasis. The great space was brilliantly illuminated, packed with a dark, moving crowd of people—mostly the Russian friends—in a semicircle around the catafalque.

Olga stood slightly forward and isolated to one side, a slim, dark, quietly elegant figure with head bowed and hands gracefully folded. The full tone of the Russian male chorus filled the room with its penetrating, all-enveloping sound—swelling, deliberate, positive, and unrelenting.

The service itself is based on the writings of the great poet and ascetic, St. John of Damascus. Its emphasis is not on the sorrow and tragedy of death but on the celebration of life. "God is God of the living, not of the dead." The specter of the grave is identified with the Holy Sepulcher, which is not only the grave of Christ but the eternal Spring of Life for all men. The vision is that of Heavenly Peace—"Blessed is the journey. . . ." That testimony of faith and hope is carried by the chorus as it echos back and forth with the chanting of the priests, the booming bass voices of the deacons, alternating with the soft cry of the tenors in frequent "Lord, have Mercy" and "Peace be with you." All these then combined in a tremendous and powerful final crescendo of alleluias. Papi, the great lover of parties and pageants, would certainly have enjoyed this beautiful celebration.

Olga's story, on the other hand, is much more complicated, mysterious, and difficult to characterize. In many ways, Papi's burial service was as climactic an experience in her career as much as it was in his. Through nearly forty years of marriage, full of adventure, excitement, and great personal achievement, life had not been easy for her. She loved her family and her children, but through the years of prosperity and depression, success and adversity, the pain and suffering caused by endless difficulties remained her responsibility. First it was her family, her children, then her grandchildren as they came along. Then it was the many unfortunate and helpless Russian refugees, both in the early 1920s and after World War II. Beneath it all was her unswerving love and commitment to the church. Perhaps it was her Russian temperament or the distinctive character of the Eastern Orthodox faith, but it was in any case a mystery that remained forever hers. It was not accidental that so many of her closest friends in later years regarded

Epilogue

her as a saint. Her own road to release was one of continuous love and devotion to others.

Igor and Xenia had often said to her, after an hour-long torrent of abuse by Papi over some insignificant comment at bridge or in company, "Why don't you give up this mess and get out?" (They would speak in Russian, of course, which would infuriate him still more.) But Olga would only shake her head and look down in silence.

For eight years after Papi's death Olga maintained the apartment on Ninety-sixth Street as the "Kluge establishment," and thus provided a home to which her children and their families could come on their periodic visits. Most of her time and energies, however, were devoted to the work of the sisterhood at the Russian Orthodox Church; the activities of the Tolstoy Foundation in its program of assistance to the new flood of Russian refugees after World War II, and regular visits to a long list of elderly Russians, many of them still the generals, princes, and duchesses of old times, now left alone, sometimes bedridden, tired, and forgotten. When she died of a stroke in 1953, it was one of these, her old friend Vera Smirnova, the gypsy singer, who discovered her alone in the apartment.

Knowing Alexandra's background as she told it here, one could almost predict what would happen when she arrived in Madison and took over as a newlywed faculty wife. But there were many beautiful and incredible surprises. When her photograph was published in the *Wisconsin State Journal* just before her arrival, the question was raised: "Where in the world did Schmeck ever pick up *her?*" The answer was: "In the little American church in Munich," and I had often described the storybook vision of these two gorgeous Kluge girls as they entered the modest vestry, one a tall blonde in a velvet dress of royal blue, and the other a flaming redhead in Tyrian purple.

Perhaps through awe or the usual social reticence of an academic community, Alexandra's formal introduction to Madison's society was a bit slow in coming. There was some question as to whether the art history department chairman or the dean of the liberal arts college or who should sponsor such an event. With characteristic flair and competence, the young bride did not wait for the officials (or their wives) to make up their minds. She proceeded to organize her own reception in our sparsely furnished three-room depression apartment. The Athenian elite were all there: the full professors, academic deans, state officials, and our working colleagues. Her gracious charm, wit, and stunning appearance carried the day, and from then on Madison was always aware of her distinguished presence.

So it was through the nearly five decades of our academic career that had more than its share of trials and tribulations but was always exciting, productive, and the result of unswerving collaboration. First it was Madison, which at that time boasted itself as the "Athens of the West"; then it was urbane Minneapolis and St. Paul, where I was chairman of the Department of Fine Arts at the University of Minnesota; then culturally fantastic Cleveland, where I was director of the Art Institute; and finally as dean of the professional art school of Syracuse University before our retirement to the green hills of New Hampshire in 1971.

The social and political requirements of academic life, whether it be teaching, research, administration, or just plain sociability—to say nothing of the standard demands of family, home, and the community—she carried with consistent dedication, love, and distinction. In her own particular way this attitude seemed to carry over into the various circles of friends whom she cherished throughout her lifetime.

Thus there were the diverse groups from Dwight School, Vassar College, the faculty and town groups in Madison, Minneapolis, St. Paul, Cleveland, Syracuse, and finally Hanover and our little community of Lyme. In a sense, they are an extension of the family—not mechanical Christmas card listees—but devoted friends whose common experiences and ideas were a constant source for new thoughts and exchanges as expressed in variously timed but consistent correspondence.

She was not what one would usually call a clubwoman. However, she believed in community participation and was a loyal participant in those organizations which were doing something she felt was worth doing and where active, creative people were involved in the business of either helping others or engaged in a significant cultural enterprise. The various Vassar clubs were always her first loves. As a loyal faculty wife she participated in each university's faculty women's organizations. Where one did not exist, as at the Cleveland Institute of Art, she initiated its organization as a Women's Committee and gently nurtured it into a major instrument in that great institution's social and financial support. She worked with the Cleveland Museum of Art Junior Council, the Social Arts Club of Syracuse, and the Utility Club

Epilogue

of Lyme. In the last years, one of the most rewarding activities was her work with the Friends of Hopkins Center at Dartmouth College.

Like most academic professionals, we had assembled a considerable number of books, which usually became a major problem whenever we were obliged to move. "What a mess!" she exclaimed one day after we had just moved into a new house in Syracuse. So, determined character that she was, she enrolled in the graduate course in library science at the university, and finished the program within two years with top honors and a thesis that was considered significant as a scholarly contribution, so that it was published by the university—and this at the ripe age of fifty-four, when many of us are content to settle into a comfortable routine of mature living.

This idea of graduate study, I hasten to add, was entirely her own. I had long ago learned that if I exercised my so-called academic prerogative of giving advice in these matters I was doomed to failure, if not outright resistance. What impressed me, however, was her uncanny ability to master the rigid discipline of the art of librarianship in such a way that it became an integral part of her own creative process. It was not a newly acquired skill but simply an extension of what she already had, which helps in part to explain the incredible versatility of her later work.

Part of my activities at Syracuse University involved not only the management of an exhibitions program but also the acquisition of a substantial permanent collection of artworks. From 1963 to our retirement in 1971, Alexandra served as both registrar and curator of the collection. She was responsible not only for the cataloguing system that was set up but also for many of the special exhibitions from the collection sources which were developed.

Ours was always a team operation in which somehow we maintained a working balance. As I became involved in various writing and research projects, she was always the sharpest critic as well as the most faithful supporter. From typing scribbled manuscripts through the final editing process, she was involved in all my books and articles. Indeed, she had systematically edited the scores of pamphlets and catalogues produced by the Syracuse University Art School as part of its exhibition program and was herself the author, not only of the Wampler Collection catalogue, but a superb centennial catalogue of the entire university collection and a number of guidebooks to special collections such as the *Folk Art of India* and a *Background for the Study of Indian Art*.

Princess in Paradise

Sa with Rudolf Serkin in 1976 at a reception in his honor sponsored by the Friends of Hopkins Center at Dartmouth College.

The threat of cancer hovered constantly in the background. It struck her aunt Xenia in 1938; Sergey's wife, Virginia, in 1960; and her brother Emile in 1971. Whether it was on her mind or not, we never knew. That again is part of the beautiful mystery of the Russian temperament. With the discovery of the disease and the successive decisions that were made on surgery and therapy, it was she who reacted with characteristic courage and clarity: "Let's get on with it. I want to see what's on the other side of the bridge." By this she meant, not the mystic view into life hereafter, but this world with its inexhaustible human resources, its rich beauty and endless promise. Even in the worst of her difficulties, she had the will and clear intention of winning. There was no fear of reality, but we believed in miracles. And the biggest miracle was life itself, which was revealed in everything she did, whether it was in the home, the family, the company of friends, or the religious service. She often quoted Uncle Igor's dream of ancient Romadanova as "Paradise on Earth." Indeed, she was firm in her belief that life was not Purgatory but Paradise itself.

We stood in awe and admiration as we watched that struggle. In December she rallied and was home for Christmas, always our biggest and most beautiful celebration of the year. This time there were no parties, no family or friends, just we two with a small festive tree, flickering candles, a bottle of champagne, the soft melodies of Christ-

Epilogue

434   mas carols on stereo, the distant memories of the cathedral choir at the wedding service, and the glowing promise of a new birthday—this time her seventieth.

Early in March I was obliged to give a lecture for the opening of a retrospective exhibition of the work of John Steuart Curry in Davenport, Iowa. At the same time she had developed new symptoms, and the doctors suggested she remain in the hospital for a few days for her greater comfort. She insisted, however, that I make the trip. After the lecture and the reception, I called her at the hospital to give my report. She seemed short of breath. "I can't talk much," she said, "you talk." And so I described the exhibition as it appeared in this new and modern museum, the crowd at the reception, and of course how I got along in the lecture. "That's fine, you come home now . . ." I could hear her breathing became shorter and more labored—". . . I love you so," she said softly as the phone dropped from her hand, and she slipped into a coma.

She died just thirty minutes before I arrived the next day.

Princess in Paradise

Princess in Paradise
has been published in a first edition
of fifteen hundred copies.
Designed and illustrated by A. L. Morris,
the text was composed in Baskerville
and printed by Courier Printing Company
in Littleton, New Hampshire, on Finch Opaque Cream White.
Jacket and endleaves were printed on
Curtis Tweedweave Text, and the binding
in Joanna Western Mills' Arrestox
was executed by New Hampshire Bindery
in Concord, New Hampshire.